COLERIDGE,
PHILOSOPHY AND RELIGION

Coleridge's relation to his German contemporaries constitutes the toughest problem in assessing his standing as a thinker. For the last half-century this relationship has been described, ultimately, as parasitic. As a result, Coleridge's contribution to religious thought has been seen primarily in terms of his *poetic* genius. This book revives and deepens the evaluation of Coleridge as a philosophical theologian in his own right. Coleridge had a critical and creative relation to, and kinship with, German thought. Moreover, the principal impulse behind his engagement with that philosophy is traced to the more immediate context of the English Unitarian–Trinitarian controversy of the eighteenth and nineteenth centuries. This book re-establishes Coleridge as a philosopher of religion and as a vital source for contemporary theological reflection.

DOUGLAS HEDLEY was educated at the universities of Oxford and Munich. He is a fellow of Clare College and lecturer in the Philosophy of Religion at the University of Cambridge in the Faculty of Divinity.

COLERIDGE, PHILOSOPHY AND RELIGION

Aids to Reflection and the Mirror of the Spirit

DOUGLAS HEDLEY

University of Cambridge

CAMBRIDGE
UNIVERSITY PRESS

PUBLISHED BY THE PRESS SYNDICATE OF THE UNIVERSITY OF CAMBRIDGE
The Pitt Building, Trumpington Street, Cambridge, United Kingdom

CAMBRIDGE UNIVERSITY PRESS
The Edinburgh Building, Cambridge CB2 2RU, UK   www.cup.cam.ac.uk
40 West 20th Street, New York, NY 10011–4211, USA   www.cup.org
10 Stamford Road, Oakleigh, Melbourne 3166, Australia
Ruiz de Alarcón 13, 28014 Madrid, Spain

First published 2000

Printed in the United Kingdom at the University Press, Cambridge

Typeface 11/12.5pt Baskerville   [CE]

A catalogue record for this book is available from the British Library

ISBN 0 521 77035 1 Hardback

Mind and understanding is, as it were, a diaphanous and crystaline globe, or a kind of notional world, which hath some reflex image, and correspondent ray, or representation in it, to whatsoever is in the true and real world of being.

(Ralph Cudworth, *The True Intellectual System of the Universe*, vol. ii. p. 517)

Contents

Acknowledgements

The origins of this book lie in a doctoral dissertation submitted to the Ludwig-Maximilians University, Munich, in 1992 under the supervision of Werner Beierwaltes, a judicious teacher and an inspiring Platonist. I also owe an enormous debt to my friend Jan Rohls of the same university who guided me through my post-doctoral work funded by the Deutsche Forschungsgemeinde, and my fellow 'Rechtsrohlsianer' in the Schellingsalon. I am grateful to Siegbert Peetz, Christoph Horn and Philip Clayton, Ralph Häfner, and Martin Mulsow for the help and instruction they gave me in Munich. I was privileged to be able to profit from the teaching of Wolfhart Pannenberg, Dieter Henrich, Rolf-Peter Horstmann, Friedo Ricken and Gerd Haeffner.

In Oxford Geoffrey Rowell introduced me to Coleridge and has been supportive ever since. I am grateful to Maurice Wiles, Bob Morgan, and Mark Edwards for their assistance and encouragement. Kenneth Stevenson, Barry Nisbet and Ian Stewart have provided useful aids of late.

I have learnt much from Wayne Hankey, Stephen Clark, Leszek Kolakowski, Michael Allen and the late A. H. Armstrong; from Wilhelm Schmidt-Biggemann, Michael Vater, Christoph Riedweg, Alfred Denker, Edward Booth and John Heywood Thomas.

My references cannot reflect my debt and gratitude to many Coleridge scholars, but I am especially indebted to John Beer. Friedrich Uehlein was also a great source of insight and instruction, and I have learnt much from Graham Davidson, James Engell, Dan Hardy, Colin Gunton, Ann Loades, Heather Jackson, Mary Anne Perkins, Reggie Watters, Dorothy Emmett, and especially George Watson.

I am very grateful to the Cambridge Divinity Faculty, and the enormous stimulus and support which they have provided, especially my alter ego in the 'philosophy of religion', James Carleton Paget, Jeremy Morris and George Pattison, Petà Dunstan's aid in the library and Rosalind Paul's generous and critical eye. Brian Hebblethwaite, but also Janet Soskice, Nicholas Lash, David Ford, William Horbury, Markus Bockmuehl, Graham Davies, Winrich Löhr, Tim Jenkins, Julius Lipner, Nicholas de Lange, Richard Rex, Philip Dixon, and Toby Jackman. Friends and students have helped me at various stages, and David Grumett, Lewis Owens and Holger Zaborowski deserve a special mention. I am indebted to the Master and Fellows of Clare College for providing such an exciting collegiate environment, and Terry Moore, Dominic Scott and Nicholas Sagovski for aids to reflection.

Sections of the book were read to various conferences and seminars. I am particularly grateful to members of the British Society for the History of Philosophy, especially Sarah Hutton, John Rogers, Stuart Brown, Martin Stone. Victor Nuovo and Neil Hitchin have been both critical and instructive. Basil Mitchell, David Pailin, Roger Trigg, Paul Helm, Richard Swinburne and the members of the British Society for the Philosophy of Religion have all reminded me that 'natural theology' is not a museum piece. I am very thankful for the splendid efforts of Kevin Taylor and Jane Wheare at Cambridge University Press.

The Romantics saw the child as the father of the man: Robert Murray SJ has helped me more than I can estimate and Julian Roberts encouraged me to study in Germany. I owe an enormous intellectual debt to Margaret Barker for her inspiration and guidance, and her love of the divine drudgery of scholarship. My aunt Patricia Margaret Wardrop (1941–77) has been an abiding presence.

My boys Clemens and Justin were painfully absent during the final preparation of the manuscript, but they have nevertheless accompanied me. My debt to my parents is inexpressible, and this book is dedicated to them.

Abbreviations

Aids	*Aids to Reflection*, edited by John Beer, London: Routledge and Kegan Paul, 1994.
BL	*Biographia Literaria*, edited by James Engell and W. Jackson Bate, London: Routledge and Kegan Paul, 1983.
Brinkley	*Coleridge on the Seventeenth Century*, edited by Roberta Florence Brinkley, Durham, NC: Duke University Press, 1955.
CCS	*On the Constitution of the Church and State*, edited by John Colmer, London: Routledge and Kegan Paul, 1976.
CL	*Collected Letters*, edited by Earl Leslie Grigg, Oxford: Clarendon Press, 1956–71.
Coburn	*Inquiring Spirit: A New Presentation of Coleridge from His Published and Unpublished Prose Writings*, edited by Kathleen Coburn, London: Routledge and Kegan Paul, 1951.
F	*The Friend*, two vols., edited by Barbara E. Rooke, London: Routledge and Kegan Paul, 1969.
Lectures	*Lectures 1795 On Politics and Religion*, edited by Lewis Patton and Peter Mann, London: Routledge and Kegan Paul, 1971.
Lit. Rem	*The Literary Remains of Samuel Taylor Coleridge*, edited by Henry Nelson Coleridge, 4 vols., London: William Pickering, 1836; New York, 1967.
Logic	*Logic*, edited by James Robert de Jager Jackson, London: Routledge and Kegan Paul, 1981.
LS	*Lay Sermons, being 'The Statesman's Manual' and 'A Lay Sermon'*, edited by Reginald James White, Princeton University Press, 1972.
Marg	*Marginalia*, edited by George Whalley, London: Routledge and Kegan Paul, 1980.
NED	*Notes on English Divines*, edited by Derwent Coleridge, 2 vols., London: Edward Moxon, 1853.

Notebooks *The Notebooks of Samuel Taylor Coleridge*, edited by Kathleen
           Coburn, London: Routledge and Kegan Paul, 1955– .
PL   *Philosophical Lectures, 1818–19*, edited by Kathleen Coburn,
           London: Pilot Press, 1949.
SW   *Shorter Works and Fragments*, edited by H. J. and J. R. de J.
           Jackson, 2 vols., Princeton University Press, 1995.
TT   *Table Talk, recorded by Henry Nelson Coleridge and John Taylor
           Coleridge*, edited by Carl Woodring, London: Routledge
           and Kegan Paul, 1990.

Notes on the text

The textual basis of this work is the new excellent critical edition of Coleridge's *Aids to Reflection* edited by John Beer. This is based upon the corrected edition of 1831 rather than the original 1825 edition. John Beer's critical edition of *Aids to Reflection* is cited as *Aids*. I have excluded all textual history and much of Coleridge's biography in this work because it is dealt with precisely and thoroughly in the extremely rich and informative new edition. References to other Coleridge texts are as far as possible to the Princeton critical edition. I have tried to avoid manuscript references, and if I mention hitherto unpublished material, I refer to journals or books where these materials are quoted and discussed.

For reasons given, this interpretation of *Aids to Reflection* is not meant to be an exhaustive account of Coleridge's thought. In particular I omit considerations about the development of Coleridge's mind. It also seems appropriate to leave to one side discussions of Coleridge's plagiarisms and citations of Schelling in the *Biographia Literaria* and developments in the *Opus Maximum*. I refer the reader to the seminal work by John Beer, Robert Barth S.J. and James Engell on Coleridge's intellectual milieu. John Muirhead's book *Coleridge as Philosopher* (London, 1930) is still excellent on Coleridge's general philosophy. Graham Davidson's *Coleridge's Career* (Basingstoke, 1990) is a powerfully argued vision of Coleridge's intellectual development. Mary Anne Perkins' *Coleridge's Philosophy* (Oxford, 1994) is a full and useful account of the sources and development of the logos concept in Coleridge's projected *Opus Maximum*. Friedrich Uehlein's *Die Manifestation des Selbstbewußtseins* (Hamburg, 1982) is a complex and rigorously argued account of Coleridge's notion of Subjectivity, especially in relation to Schelling.

I do wish to explain something of my reference to, and quotation of, Plotinus and the German Idealists. I use a capital with the term

'Neoplatonist' in order to emphasise the particular structure of this tradition of thought, including those elements in the philosophy that are not strictly 'Platonic'. Plotinus' writings are usually referred to as the 'Enneads' or 'Nines' because his pupil Porphyry arranged his master's work into six sets of *nine* treatises. It is hence strictly inaccurate to write of 'Ennead VI 8' when one wishes to refer to the individual *Treatise* vi. 8 since this is precisely the eighth treatise in the sixth Ennead. Further, we write Plotinus' *Treatise* vi. 8 (39) and then chapter and verse because this was the *thirty-ninth* treatise which Plotinus composed. Quotations are always taken from A. H. Armstrong's authoritative translation (which fortunately preserves Porphyry's division into nines and sixes). Coleridge's 'Platonism' is roughly Plotinus mediated by the great Renaissance Christian philosopher-theologian Marsilio Ficino. Coleridge's direct interest in Ficino is limited, but Ficino provided the lens through which Plato was perceived by Coleridge: both Christian and Nepolatonic.

The situation with respect to German Idealism is, unfortunately, much less satisfactory than with Plotinus. He is a very difficult and surprisingly technical philosopher, but there are few serious scholarly controversies in Plotinus studies. The German Idealist philosophers, on the contrary, have been subject to very controversial interpretation. Many leading scholars of German Idealism minimise the potent religious component in this philosophy. Coleridge on the contrary, saw the movement as profoundly religious, and I shall explain why this was entirely justified. Schelling, in particular, was largely ignored until after the Second World War when he began to be seen as more than a stage on the way to Hegel. There is a revival of Schelling studies at present but interpretations differ strongly. The critical Schelling edition is in its infancy, and only a small section of Schelling's opus has been translated into English. References to Schelling are to the edition of his son K. F. A. Schelling in fourteen volumes (Stuttgart/Augsburg, 1856–61).

Prologue: explaining Coleridge's explanation

> And Coleridge, too, has lately taken wing,
> But like a hawk, encumber'd with his hood,
> Explaining metaphysics to the nation,
> I wish he would explain his Explanation.   (Byron *Don Juan*)

The Anglo-Saxons, namely, are naturally no more pure Empiricists than other people, and they have shown this clearly in their Renaissance poetry and their theological Platonism.   (Ernst Troeltsch)[1]

Coleridge, like some great river, the Orellana, or the St Lawrence, that had been checked and fretted by the rocks or thwarting islands, and suddenly recovers its volume of waters and mighty music, swept at once, as if returning to its natural business, into a continuous strain of eloquent dissertation, certainly the most novel, the most finely illustrated, and traversing the most spacious fields of thought, by transitions the most just and logical, that it was possible to conceive.   (Thomas de Quincey)[2]

S. T. Coleridge's seminal work *Aids to Reflection* was in part composed with the idea of countering the Cambridge 'Atheism' and 'infidelity' which seemed to have influenced his son Derwent, a student at St John's College (*Aids*, p. lxxiii). Coleridge visited Cambridge at the end of his life in 1833 to attend a conference of the British Association for the Advancement of Science, and he showed his friends Joseph Henry Green and Dr James Gillman his old under-graduate haunts. We shall argue that the Cambridge connection was of particular significance for Coleridge's thought. It was at Cambridge that the tradition of Locke was pre-eminent in the eighteenth century, especially through the figure of William Paley. The Lockean tradition, represented by Paley, was a formative influence upon the young undergraduate Coleridge at Jesus College,

---

[1] *Die Bedeutung des Protestantismus für die Enstehung der Modernen Welt* (Munich: Oldenbourg, 1928), p. 81.

[2] *Recollections of the Lake Poets* (Harmondsworth: Penguin, 1985), p. 45.

and it forms a major and recurring target in Coleridge's mature thought. Coleridge was the first of the nineteenth century British Idealists and the founding spirit of the liberal Broad Church movement in Victorian English theology. In both roles, he was reviving the values and temper of the 'latitudinarians' or the Cambridge Platonists of the seventeenth century. His revival of this thought owed much to a powerful infusion of contemporary German thought, in particular Schelling. Cambridge is important for our study both in the sense of producing the immediate backdrop of Coleridge's thought and also as the home of the seventeenth-century Cambridge Platonists – a liberal and rational tradition of theology which Coleridge was consciously trying to reinvoke.

There is a another town which will play a role in our narrative; one, however, which Coleridge never visited: Munich. Most commentators on Coleridge associate Schelling exclusively with his heyday in Jena as the young author of the *Transcendental System of Idealism* of 1800. Yet in the vital period of Coleridge's own intellectual development, the first decade of the nineteenth century, Schelling had moved south to the capital city of Bavaria, and had started to develop a powerful alternative form of Idealism which found expression in 1809 in his essay *On Human Freedom*. It is this phase of Schelling's thought which is instructive for any consideration of Coleridge and his German sources.

The present work will concentrate on *Aids to Reflection* (1825; 1832[2]), Coleridge's major published work on the philosophy of religion. This book was highly influential in England and America in the nineteenth century and ran into twelve editions (*Aids*, cxlv, p. 547), but fell into neglect at the turn of the century. Setting aside a few reprints, John Beer's critical edition of 1993 is the only new edition to have been produced in the twentieth century. *Aids to Reflection* is a seminal work in the philosophy of religion and the history of ideas that has been barely considered by modern scholarship, despite the resurgence of interest that coincides with the modern critical *Collected Coleridge*.

There has been much superb scholarly work, both in editions and expositions, on the thought of Samuel Taylor Coleridge in the second half of the twentieth century. Yet, despite the increase in information and reliable texts, he remains a much disputed figure in Anglo-American intellectual history, and one whom many critics feel happiest to treat as primarily a poet. Richard Holmes' vigorous and exciting biography, *Coleridge: Darker Reflections*, is a good example of this tendency. To use an image from Locke, the ambition of this work is to be an 'Under-Labourer'; to clear the ground for others. Coleridge's œuvre has not yet been published in its entirety in the critical edition, and when his projected *Opus Maximum* and the *Notebooks* appear our view of him will become much more accurate and complete.

The eminent Victorian Cambridge divine F. J. A. Hort observed that 'It is a common delusion that Coleridge is well known'.[3] The delusion persists. It was just as the Anglo-American idealist professoriate which had its roots in Coleridge (philosophers like John Muirhead or A. E. Taylor) was dying out between the two World Wars that Coleridge was rescued from relative oblivion as a literary critic. It is an indication of a rich and decisive mind that Coleridge could inspire and tease minds who no longer shared the aims and ideals of the Victorians, and who no longer explicitly sought the foundations of a manly character in godliness. Coleridge's thought belongs to grand-theory philosophy and yet he is a master of the aphorism and fragment. He was, as Walter Pater suggested, striving for the absolute – possessed with a hunger for eternity – and yet he was intensely interested in the details and darkness of human existence. But the institutional parameters of twentieth-century English Literature have tended to marginalise the religious and philosophical core of Coleridge's thought.

The widespread reluctance to treat Coleridge as a thinker in his own right is, in part at least, due to the persisting influence of certain misapprehensions about the parameters and temper of his thought, and the intepretation of his sources. Whitehead famously called western philosophy a series of footnotes to Plato; but there have been many Platos, and if we approach Coleridge with inappropriate presuppositions it is easy to discover what an incoherent thinker he was – what a bad Platonist or Kantian he was. Some of the misapprehensions which figure in the work of such influential Coleridge scholars as Wellek, Orsini, and McFarland are perfectly reasonable, but they nevertheless distort our perception of Coleridge's thought.

The primary reason for Coleridge's enigmatic position in recent

---

[3] Hort, 'Coleridge', in *Cambridge Essays contributed by Members of the University*, (Cambridge University Press, 1856), pp. 292–351, p. 293.

English thought is the continuing influence of the anti-Hellenism of the Ritschl–Harnack tradition of the nineteenth century and the intransigent hostility to philosophical theology of the most influential twentieth-century theologian, Karl Barth. This has been compounded by the official Roman Catholic Neo-Thomist opposition to Platonism and idealism as sources of various dangerous heresies: 'pantheism', 'ontologism', 'emanationism', etc. This is to say that the backlash against nineteenth-century religious thought in the twentieth has done much to block our access to Coleridge's mind. In philosophy, continental thought has been dominated by Nietzsche's and Heidegger's polemic against Platonism, and analytic empiricist philosophers are often engaged in disentangling 'Plato's beard'. For contemporary thought, the Platonic legacy of mind–body dualism, foundationalism, and contemplative rationalism provides a chain of exploded tenets; a series of momentous errors. I cannot hope to defend Coleridge's views exhaustively on such fundamental issues in an exposition of his philosophy of religion; however, it is important to be aware of the considerable distance between contemporary and early nineteenth-century horizons. Some commentators, troubled by the relation of German 'idealism' to Coleridge's 'theism' or the topic of 'pantheism', in fact import twentieth-century perspectives which do not represent an increase in wisdom, but a fundamental rejection of Coleridge's assumptions. Coleridge belongs to a Christian Platonic tradition which stretches from John Scot Eriugena to Hegel, which sees Jerusalem and Athens in harmony, and is inclined to identify philosophy with theology. This is an odd position for contemporary minds, but it is not a symptom of Coleridge's intellectual aberrations.

The first reasonable misapprehension is that Platonism and Idealism are opposites. This is reasonable because Platonism is apparently a doctrine about objectively existing ideas and Idealism is prima facie a doctrine that reality is determined or constructed by a priori subjectivity. Hence Platonism seems ultra-realist: knowledge is discovery; whereas idealism seems anti-realist: reality is constructed by the subject, by the knower. Despite the initial plausibility of such a contrast, it often collapses under scrutiny. Platonism has a strong doctrine of the a priori in the doctrine of recollection, and the dialogue 'Alcibiades I' was chosen as the introduction to philosophy in the Platonic Academy because it introduced the central idealistic topic of 'self-knowledge'. Furthermore, the great revival of Platonism in Germany in the eighteenth century was ushered in by Kant. Like

Augustine and Descartes, Kant found Platonic notions a welcome tool against the spectre of sceptical empiricism.

Another reasonable misapprehension lies in the domain of ethics. Platonism is a theory about the good and happiness, whereas Kantian ethics is determined by duty and the right. Coleridge must be mistaken if he conflates these two radically different ways of construing the 'good life'. Yet once we look at the arguments and the temper of both thinkers in detail, this apparent dichotomy becomes a striking affinity. The Athenian aristocrat and the Prussian professor share a strident belief in unconditional moral obligations, and a rather pessimistic anthropology. How can this 'crooked timber of humanity' attain genuine goodness, not out of deference to custom, society, or instinct, but out of sheer respect for the good, the moral law; this otherworldliness endows both thinkers for Coleridge with an almost pentecostal power, and distinguishes them from the breezy optimism of Hume and the prudent worldly moral scrupulousness of Aristotle.

Coleridge's appeal to Kant may seem as quixotic as his use of Bacon as the British Plato. Yet Kant inaugurated a Platonic renaissance in German thought. This may seem counter-intuitive; after all, Kant attacked Mendelssohn's Platonic proof of the soul's immortality in his famous *Phaedo* 1767.[4] But this would be a hasty interpretation. The revival of Platonism in the late eighteenth century rests upon the refutation of scepticism: Plato against the Sophists, or Augustine and Descartes against the sceptics, in maintaining that reason is objective, and that it is not just the expression of the contingent finite point of view. Kant's criticism of Hume's scepticism parallels Augustine's or Descartes' critique of scepticism through its appeal to the 'transcendental unity of apperception'. One of the standard moves is to employ sceptical arguments as part of a larger strategy to show the ineluctability of reason itself. This argument has the rough form that even when one is challenging the rational credentials of a particular judgement or domain of arguments one has to rely at some point on thoughts which themselves are not subject to intelligible doubt.

In chapter one of Treatise v. 5 (32), Plotinus attacks Epicurean confidence in sense perception. He argues that sense perception is

---

[4] Kant, *Critique of Pure Reason* translated by N. Kemp-Smith (London: Macmillan, 1982), B414ff.

open to sceptical objections because the known object of sensory awareness is *exterior* to the knower and knowledge of the senses is *mediated* by images; i.e. representational. The inadequacy of such sensory awareness, however, inspires the mind to seek truth at the level of the (divine) intellect, where knower and object known are unified and unmediated by images. Plotinus' deployment of sceptical arguments to establish truth as interior, immediate, and divine bequeathed a clear legacy to Augustine and Descartes: scepticism about the external world leads to interiority, immediacy of genuine knowledge, and divine guarantee of truth. Strikingly, the German Idealists were philosophers in this tradition: whereby truth is conceived primarily not as the correspondence of propositions and facts, but as the self-disclosure of the divine intellect.

Another interpretative problem arises from the assumption that the Enlightenment was essentially a revival of classical paganism in conscious and cultured opposition to the medieval barbarism of Christianity. Some writers, such as Gibbon and Voltaire, could present their age in such terms, but the period preceding Coleridge was still dominated by Christian concerns about heresies, especially concerning the Trinity and the Incarnation: Arianism and Socinianism. Atheism remained clandestine, and strict deism was the viewpoint of a radical, but nevertheless marginal, group. Proponents of non-orthodox forms of Christianity are more typical for the eighteenth century than adherents of outright atheism or agnosticism: in this sense (Socinian?) Locke and Arian Newton formed a powerful precedent for the following century. The intellectual parameters of Coleridge's thought are more theological than is sometimes assumed, because the actual Enlightenment backdrop was dominated as much by Christian theologians such as Priestley and Paley as by the cultured despisers of religion – Hume and Gibbon.

When we consider such issues as Coleridge's 'Platonism', it is necessary to put his thinking into the context where the English universities still demanded subscription to the Thirty-nine Articles, the first being the doctrine of the Trinity, and where thinkers such as Priestley were arguing that the doctrine constitutes a non-biblical 'corruption' smuggled into Christianity by Platonizing Church Fathers. Hence the 'Platonism' at stake is *not* that of Plato's dialogues, or the 'unwritten doctrines' of the Academy, but the allegorising metaphysics of Middle and Neoplatonism which, indeed, formed such a crucial component of Christian theology, and the stream of 'Christian Platonism' which was so potent in the early modern period in Florence and Cambridge.

We shall argue that this distinctively Christian context of the debate about Platonism is a vital clue to Coleridge's thought. The doctrine of the Trinity, which seemed both the archetype of a scholastic trifling and yet a pillar of priestcraft to the radicals of the Enlightenment, was revived by the German Idealists in the early nineteenth century, and these German philosophers were drawing upon a Neoplatonic tradition of speculation about the Trinity which has its roots in Plato's *Parmenides* and *Timaeus*. Neoplatonism is characterised by a hierarchy of three 'divine' principles, and in particular a division between two principles – the divine intellect and the supreme source: the One. Christian theologians identified the divine intellect with the Logos or Son, but insisted upon its 'consubstantiality' with its source, the Father. This was a process of effectively 'telescoping' the attributes of two carefully distinguished principles into one absolute but internally differentiated principle. Hence Christianity developed a metaphysics of 'divine subjectivity' in both opposition to and dependence upon late antique metaphysics. The attempt of the German Idealists to replace Spinoza's substance monism, where reality is presented in terms of the modes and attributes of one infinite substance, with subject monism, whereby reality is conceived of as the explication of an absolute 'I AM', does not merely have structural affinities with Christian Platonic speculations, but was in part the product of Enlightenment debates about the 'origins' and 'corruptions' of Christianity which put such Neoplatonic and Christian Platonic topics and ideas into particular – if usually negative – prominence.

For the contemporary mind many of Coleridge's concerns constitute an astonishing confusion and jumble of 'theology' and 'philosophy' and antiquated cultural and political debates about the privileges of the Church of England. Yet we have to attempt to unravel these, by now somewhat alien, concerns. The aim of this work is to set out Coleridge's 'philosophy of religion' as presented in his major published work *Aids to Reflection*, and in particular to try to put Coleridge's book into some context. It is particularly suited for our purposes because it demonstrates *ad oculos* how theological Coleridge's Platonism is. Now Plato's work is usually defined by his use of the dialogue form and the doctrine of the 'ideas' or 'forms'. Such a modern perspective is the product of the Enlightenment critique of Christianised-Neoplatonic Plato, the 'Attic Moses', and German nineteenth century philology which drew attention to the precise concerns and form of Plato's œuvre. But within the *living* Platonic tradition, as it were, neither the dialogues nor the ideas play a central role. Since the ideas were placed within the divine mind in the second century AD, Platonists identified the ideas with God's creative intellect, and saw philosophy as the journey or ascent of the finite mind towards the absolute intellect; part of a struggle to become 'like God'. Within this meditative context, a common medium of philosophical writing was a treatise form like that of Plotinus' 'Enneads', a spiralling ascent of the mind; a spiritual exercise aimed at divesting the reader of materialistic assumptions and errors, and providing aids to a bending back or 'reflection' of the soul to its divine source. Hence I wish to consider Coleridge's *Aids to Reflection* as a text akin to Bonaventura's *Journey of the Mind to God* or Nicholas of Cusa's The *Vision of God*: a tradition which pursues the Platonic vision up the divided line and out of the cave[5] into the divine light.

Aids to Reflection began as a collection of 'beauties' from a Scottish mystic and Platonist, Archbishop Robert Leighton. It became a complex and rich philosophy of religion, and the nearest Coleridge came to his projected *Assertion of Religion* or *Opus Maximum*.[6] *Aids* was the product of his maturity, and unlike the *Biographia Literaria*, Coleridge was quite satisfied with the book as an expression of his spiritual philosophy. The thesis of this book is that the speculative or philosophical doctrine of the Trinity is the central idea, or better the hidden agenda, in *Aids to Reflection*. Coleridge claims that he has not 'entered on the Doctrine of the Trinity' (*Aids*, p. 156). By this he means that he does not discuss exhaustively and systematically ideas such as 'unity', 'person', 'generation', and 'creation', which are necessary for a thorough treatment of the doctrine. However, his aim is to give an account of the spiritual nature of man, and for Coleridge the spiritual nature of man cannot be separated from the topic of the Christian idea of God as tri-une. *Aids to Reflection for the formation of a manly character on the several grounds of Prudence, Morality and Religion* attempts to show that a man-ly, that is a *virtuous*, character, is only possible on the condition of participation in the divine: the life of virtue presupposes and passes over into godliness, that is, god-likeness.

---

[5] *Republic* 509d (Harmondsworth: Penguin, 1987), pp. 249ff.
[6] This is the view of his pupil F. D. Maurice. See his *Moral and Metaphysical Philosophy* (London: Macmillan, 1882), vol. ii, p. 670.

Aids to Reflection is about the bending back of the soul to God. Yet this bending back or re-flection is only intelligible as the work of the indwelling Logos, the second person of the Trinity. The spiritual nature of man is defined in terms of reflection to God. This reflection to God, Coleridge insists, requires divine aid. The good life can only be understood on this basis: the deepest and richest resources of the moral life coincide with the aids of the divine spirit. The attempt to imitate the good is rooted in the renewing activity of the indwelling Logos. This is why Coleridge repeatedly appeals to the Delphic Oracle 'Know Thyself!': the task of philosophy is to reflect and turn within oneself and thus to transcend oneself and to 'find' God. Philosophy and theology corroborate each other: finite freedom must be thought of as re-flecting into and participating in divine freedom.

The central idea is Platonist, or, to employ a dangerous but pertinent term, 'mystical'. Coleridge is concerned to distinguish his mysticism from the excesses of religious enthusiasm and irrationalism, but feels that eighteenth-century rationalism had almost extinguished the flame of genuine Christian thought and spirituality. The concept of spirit is directed against a shallow *humanism* that sees the good life as attainable through prudence and self-sufficiency. Coleridge believed that 'To feel the full force of Christian Religion it is necessary, for many tempers that they should be made to feel, experientially, the hollowness of human friendship, the presumptuous emptiness of human hopes' (*CL* iv. 893). Coleridge discovered Leighton during the spiritual crisis of 1813: the culmination of his agonies following the collapse of his friendships with William Wordsworth and Sara Hutchinson. It was a period of experience of the impossibility of 'any real *good will* not born anew from the Word and the Spirit!' (*CL* iii. 463). The work was composed at a time of great sadness and anxiety. His son Hartley Coleridge had lost his fellowship at Oriel College, Oxford, in 1820 through a recklessness and 'intemperance' which seemed to mirror his father's agonising problems, and left Coleridge with a profound sense of failure as a father.[7]

Yet this idea of a spiritual philosophy and theology is also directed against a forensic and postivistic scheme that envisages the God of Christianity as a *deus ex machina*, a strictly supernatural suzerain, who intervenes merely to reward and punish his subjects. Coleridge presents a theological humanism which concentrates not upon God

[7] R. Holmes, *Coleridge, Darker Reflections* (London: HarperCollins, 1988), pp. 510–18.

as a transcendent object, but upon the meeting of the human and divine spirit. For all his emphasis upon the 'will', Coleridge is not a voluntarist. He does not affirm the will over against reason. In fact, his criticisms of both Paley and Schelling (otherwise unlikely bedfellows!) rest upon their construal of God as in some sense *primarily* 'will'. In response to both, Coleridge upholds the characteristically Platonic insistence that the divine will is identical with his nature as good and rational, and cannot be prior to these.

The Christian philosophers of late antiquity saw a genial and providential coincidence between the God of Platonism as the creative *prius* of all being and the Christian vision of God as both:

1. transcendent: rapt in self contemplation
and
2. immanent: the creative activity of the Word and communion with the Spirit.

This re-flection as the work of the Logos is 'evidence' of the Trinity; that is God as self-conscious unity and the effective and sustaining power of moral aspiration. Since goodness is unattainable with purely human resources and since God should be thought of as not just the goal of moral aspiration but its very source and sustenance, Coleridge finds in the *philosophical* doctrine of the Trinity an inalienable element of any rigorous theory of ethics. Coleridge felt that the English theology of the eighteenth century was largely insufficient because it denied the Logos as the creative link between the divine transcendence and the world and the Spirit as the principle of the return of creation to its source. In short, the eighteenth century forgot its Trinitarian heritage and its Platonic metaphysical backdrop. What Gibbon and Priestley isolated as the point of the pestilential infection of western civilisation through Neoplatonism, the Christian patristic infatuation with divine triads, and consequent supersition, darkness, and priestcraft, becomes for Coleridge the point at which he seizes upon Lessing and the post-Kantians: their revival of the metaphysical doctrine of the Trinity in Germany. In order to renew the idea of the immanence of the divine, Coleridge turned to the German Idealists: albeit with a critical and independent mind.

The metaphysical doctrine of the Trinity is the key to both Coleridge's 'Platonism' and his 'Idealism'. Some scholars have questioned the coherence of the very term 'Christian Platonism'. I follow my own teacher Werner Beierwaltes on this point – Christian

Platonism was a philosophically genuine form of 'Platonism'. In particular the doctrinal formulation of the Trinity represents the use and transformation of Platonic ideas for Christian purposes. The Christian affirmation of the absolute as a self-related mind means that for Christian Platonism the true system of the universe is intellectual or intelligible, whereas the strictly Hellenic Neoplatonism rejected the idea of intellection in the supreme source of being as incompatible with its unity. This difference between a metaphysics of an inclusive-relational unity of the Christian Godhead and the exclusive unity of the Neoplatonic good constitutes a profound characteristic of Christian Platonism which has very little explicit basis in the biblical tradition. Hence it is anachronistic to dismiss the theological tenet of the Trinity as unphilosophical or irrelevant to the estimation of Coleridge as a philosopher.

Because of the deep influence of Plotinus upon Christian theology and mysticism, it is hard to know, and often irrelevant, whether Plotinus is the direct or indirect source of a particular idea. Plotinus is nevertheless a model of philosophical mysticism for Coleridge, whose philosophical mysticism is idealist *and yet* deeply suspicious of abstract conceptuality; a system of thought that is contemplative and yet very much a philosophy of *life* and *experience*. This seemingly paradoxical mixture of the noetic and the affective has its roots in Plato's *Symposium*, but its most striking philosophical expression is in Plotinus. I shall refer to Coleridge as a philosophical mystic throughout the text, and I mean exactly this temper of mind in Plotinus that veers between a strongly contemplative rationalism and an emphasis upon that which resists conceptual analysis: will; life; experience; God. Some make the mistake of seeing 'Platonism' as purely contemplative or rationalist and then argue that Coleridge is thus 'not entirely' a Platonist. In a sense the 'Platonism' of Coleridge lies precisely in the tension between 'reflection' and 'experience'. The appeal to 'experience' is characteristic of the Platonic approach in the philosophy of religion.

It is anachronistic to assume that 'German Idealism' is a modern secular philosophy that is hostile to 'religion', or that the 'absolute' cannot be conflated with the religious idea of God. Hegel and Schelling were trained as theologians, and German Idealism was deeply imbued with Christian theology. Secondly, German Idealism generally drew upon the intellectualist strand of the Platonic-Neoplatonic tradition of 'natural theology' which (via Plotinus and

Augustine) emphasised the possibility of direct knowledge of God. Schelling is a good example of this; however, in his Munich period he draws upon that other, apophatic, aspect of the Neoplatonic tradition which is most evident in later Neoplatonism (Iamblichus, Proclus, and Pseudo-Dionysius) which envisages the absolute as 'unprethinkable'. Untangling the web of idealistic and Neoplatonic tenets and concepts is very important in understanding Coleridge's philosophy of religion. Gibbon ironically wrote of Plato words which apply beautifully and strictly to Coleridge: 'His poetical imagination sometimes fixed and animated these metaphysical abstractions.'[8]

Absolute idealism may seem like a secular substitute for theism because so much *Religionskritik* has sprung from Hegelianism: Feuerbach, Strauss, Marx. Much depends on one's intepretation, but we can at least establish that Coleridge was not confused here. In particular the idea of the 'Platonic Trinity', we shall argue is a point of genuine contact between Coleridge and the Idealists. The dogmas of Trinity, Incarnation, and Atonement, the Pauline idea of dying and rising with Christ, were not just interpreted philosophically but deeply influenced their idea of philosophy. Philosophy for Hegel or Schelling is not the maid of theology, supplying apologetic arguments, but the conceptual expression of a specifically Christian vision of the relationship of world and its source: philosophy is itself a form of Christian theology.[9] Schelling rejected a chair at Tübingen because he was refused permission to teach both theology and philosophy, and Hegel's scathing contempt for Schleiermacher in Berlin was in part based on Hegel's sense of his own superiority as a theologian. The specifically Christian element in the German Idealists is something of an embarrassment to modern critics but it should be emphasised in relation to Coleridge's project of a philosophical assertion of the Christian religion. Coleridge was not trying to force Christian ideas on to the Procrustean bed of German pantheism. We shall argue that Coleridge's attempt to employ ideas from German Idealism in order to revive an anthropology and theology of the Cambridge Platonists and other philosophical mystics is entirely intelligible and even compelling.

It is necessary to consider the resources of Coleridge's thought in

[8] E. Gibbon, *The History of the Decline and Fall of the Roman Empire*, 3 vols., edited by David Womersley (Harmondsworth: Penguin, 1994), vol. i. p. 771
[9] The most eminent living German theologian is a product of this tradition. See W. Pannenberg, *Theologie und Philosophie* (Göttingen: Vandenhoeck, 1996), pp. 257ff.

depth – *resources not sources.* Coleridge was an innovator. There was no Platonic tradition in nineteenth-century England which Coleridge could simply perpetuate: Norris, Collier, and Berkeley belonged to the previous century, and writers such as Cudworth and Henry More seemed positively antiquated in their methods and interests in the 1820s. Furthermore, it was far from clear to an Englishman between 1810 and 1825 that German Idealism was a defined school of thought: the Idealists disagreed as much as they agreed. Coleridge was writing at a time when Schelling had changed radically the direction of his own thought and almost entirely stopped publishing. Coleridge could not simply *describe* the Platonist or mystical tradition that he loved, nor *expound* the German Idealism which he found so invigorating. These were rather the resources from which he could develop his 'spiritual' or 'dynamic' philosophy. The parameters of his religious thought are Idealistic: the primacy of subjectivity and spontaneity, the question of the absolute, inter-twining of philosophy and theology, the philosophical interpretation of Christian dogma, Higher Criticism, and all-embracing 'system'. The real nerve of Coleridge's thought, however, lies – as he himself always claimed – in a Christian religious philosophy *Platonico more.* In his recent work Wilhelm Schmidt-Biggemann presents a fascinating depiction of the Christian-Platonic speculative tradition of phil-osophy stretching from Origen via Ficino to Schelling.[10] This *perennial philosophy* is the broad context of Coleridge's metaphysics. Yet this truth can be gravely misunderstood. Once we consider Coleridge's detailed proposals, we can see that, despite certain affinities with the hermetic and esoteric tradition, Coleridge is within the mainstream of western thought and, in many respects, temperamentally averse to the more fantastical fringe of Platonism. Coleridge is a visionary philosopher, but a philosopher nonetheless.

A book about *Aids to Reflection* is faced with a serious structural problem. Coleridge changed his conception of the book during its printing and much of the subsequent reorganising of the text means that it is impossible to pursue exactly a continuous argument. Coleridge discusses some topics such as 'language', 'nature', or 'spirit' repeatedly with minor variations throughout the text. Coleridge does, however, specify his wish:

---

[10] W. Schmidt-Biggemann, *Philosophia perennis. Historische Umrisse abendländischer Spiritualität in Antike, Mittelalter und Früher Neuzeit* (Frankfurt: Suhrkamp, 1998).

1. To direct the Reader's attention to the value of the Science of Words, their use and abuse . . .
2. To establish the *distinct* characters of Prudence, Morality and Religion . . .
3. To substantiate and set forth at large the momentous distinction between REASON and Understanding. . .
4. To exhibit a full and consistent Scheme of the Christian dispensation . . .
(*Aids*, pp. 6–9)

Correspondingly we shall discuss the general project of a spiritual philosophy in *Aids to Reflection* and then turn to the four specific issues above. We consider the idea of a spiritual philosophy and its intimate relation to the doctrine of the Trinity in the first chapter: 'The true philosopher is the lover of God.' Coleridge's spiritual philosophy is based upon a rejection of empiricism. Coleridge has a mystical conception of philosophy as reflection and experience, i.e. the bending of the soul back to God as its source. The context is to the Trinitarian–Unitarian controversy. This theological debate, we argue, is the key to understanding Coleridge's philosophical development and thought. Here we are confronted with the speculative or philosophical idea of the Trinity as the dynamic reflexive life of the absolute divine subject: as absolute *reflection* of the Father in the Son, and linked by the Spirit. If we combine the images implicit in the word 'reflection' of mirroring, bending back, and thought, we can see why the term is used in the Christian-Platonic tradition for the self-contemplation of the tri-une Godhead: the Son as the *image* of the Father, the Spirit bending back to the Father, and the relation of the persons as one of *self-contemplation*. With this conception of God as the hidden agenda of *Aids to Reflection*, we consider the four aims of the book:

1. The inner word: considers the first of Coleridge's aims: 'To direct the Reader's attention to the value of the Science of Words, their use and abuse'. This is the question of reflection in the sense of *meditation* or introspection and the chapter explores Coleridge's use of aphorism and theory of language in relation to his logos metaphysics. Rigorous reflection upon *meaning* leads to the communicative aspect of the Godhead, the Word that is the *ineffable* source of all meaning.
2. The image of God: considers the relationship of ethics to religion: 'To establish the *distinct* characters of Prudence, Morality and Religion', and here the primary sense of reflection is the *optical* insofar as the genuine ethical agent *reflects* the divine in the *life* of the

spirit. True ethics, for Coleridge, is transformed into religion: the life of godliness is literally god-likeness.

3. God is truth: considers Coleridge's ontological theology: 'To substantiate and set forth at large the momentous distinction between REASON and Understanding'. Coleridge uses the Augustinian idea of God as *veritas*, and distinguishes divine reason from the *reflective*, i.e. understanding of the finite mind. This is a speculative theology that emphasises the limits of the unaided intellect. The renewal of the will is seen as the heart of genuine wisdom.

4. The great instauration: considers the essence of Christianity: 'To exhibit a full and consistent Scheme of the Christian dispensation'. There is a vision of the spiritual meaning of the dogmatic content of Christianity and especially the idea of the Trinity which envisages the essence of Christianity as consisting in the *conversion*, i.e. reflection of the soul through the indwelling Logos.

The final chapter of the vision of God elaborates upon Coleridge's view of freedom, education, and the clerisy, a 'permanent learned class'. It is appropriate because the book is directed at those who have 'dedicated their future lives to the cultivation of their Race, as Pastors, Preachers, Missionaries, or Instructors of Youth' (*Aids*, p. 6). The mystical vision which permeates Coleridge's thought is not primarily a punctual, individual ecstasy, but the source of principles of the humane social fabric. Coleridge is fond of the Biblical Proverb, 'WHERE NO VISION IS, THE PEOPLE PERISHETH' (Proverbs 29: 18) and relates this to his central distinction between reason and understanding (cf. *CCS*, p. 58).

In this manner we can see how Coleridge drew upon Platonic and Idealistic themes and ideas and produced a philosophy that came to influence the Victorians so powerfully and remains a source of inspiration for contemporary thought. The broad structure of the argument is as follows.

Coleridge is attacking what he perceives as the dominant forensic model of religion and ethics as presented by William Paley. Here Christianity consists of external evidences of the divine will, but Paley is quite sceptical about knowledge of the divine essence or nature. The Platonist and Idealist Coleridge is adamant that Christianity offers insight into the divine nature as goodness. In order to perceive this divine essence, the Christian must turn within, and not depend upon external facts such as miracles. By reflection upon the conditions of thought and language, Coleridge argues for a spiritual transcendent ground: the divine logos as the basis of words, the intelligibility of being as the presupposition of communication. This constitutes a meditative component in Coleridge's thinking. The awakening of the mind leads to the issue of the good life. This is the imitation of the transcendent spiritual principle, and the ethical life is seen as an ascent to this principle. The possibility of science rests upon an essentially ethical and religious frame of mind, a discipline of the spirit and reverence for truth. Religion is the awareness of man's natural estrangement from the ground of being: his sinfulness. The Christian religion is the historical and symbolic expression of the return of finite beings to God. Christianity is the spiritual religion because it incarnates and enunciates an eternal intelligible principle: the dying and rising of the divine word.

We argue that Coleridge's rejection of voluntarism, and his Platonic insistence upon God as defined – even constrained – by the law of his goodness, help to explain his rejection of Schelling's philosophical theology, as well as his objection to Paley. It also helps explain, we shall argue, Coleridge's admiration for Kant – despite the latter's rather desiccated theology and rather attenuated vision of metaphysics. Schopenhauer remarked that Kant was like a man dancing at a ball with a masked lady, who takes off her mask to reveal his wife – and his wife is theology.[11] It is this aspect of Kant which illuminates Coleridge's fascination for his work. Kant's concept of autonomy is clearly incompatible with a God who is an arbitrary external force, as brute power; however, it is not clear that it is incompatible with the Christian Platonic view of ethics as participation in the archetypal goodness of the divine; a mirroring of the spirit.

This book is an attempt to revive the discredited thesis that Coleridge's close relationship to German Idealism was not merely derivative, but grounded upon the genuine affinity of Coleridge's Cambridge Platonism with the reflections of Schelling in his Munich period. Coleridge had a critical and creative relation to, and kinship with, German thought. Moreover, the principal impulse behind his engagement with that thought was the more immediate context of the English Unitarian–Trinitarian controversy of the eighteenth and nineteenth centuries.

---

[11] Arthur Schopenhauer, 'Über die Grundlage der Moral', Zürcher Ausgabe, *Werke in zehn Bänden* (Zürich: Diogenes, 1977), vol. vi. p. 209.

It might be assumed that *Aids* is merely a preparation for students, a set of exercises which should prepare the ground for Coleridge's genuine and substantial works. If this were true the *real* Coleridge is to be found in the manuscripts, and the *opus maximum*, and should reawaken those familiar complaints about why Coleridge was unable to fulfil his promises!

I wish to offer three arguments for the paramount importance of *Aids to Reflection* in the appreciation of Coleridge *as* a thinker. Firstly, Coleridge was a natural commentator, a scribbler of inspired marginalia. This suggests a crabbed and scholastic mind to many; but the apparent deference to the text masks an originality rarely to be found in English systematic statements of philosophico-theological principles. We should not believe that since *Aids* is about Robert Leighton or Jeremy Taylor it follows that here we cannot find in it the *authentic* Coleridge. Secondly, Coleridge's philosophical writings are not incidentally 'applied' philosophy. Like Plato, he believes fervently in the identity of knowledge and virtue, and it is quite appropriate that in his greatest work we should find 'exercises' rather than a store house or, worse, museum full of elaborate and unverifiable doctrines about the supersensible empyrean. Thirdly, *Aids to Reflection* marks Coleridge as a spiritual writer: 'Reason is preeminently spiritual, and a Spirit, even our Spirit, even *our* Spirit, through an effluence of the same grace by which we are privileged to say Our Father!' (*Aids*, p. 218). He wishes to speak to the heart, and it is clearly the product of his own experience as tormented by guilt and failure – a veritable wreck by worldly standards – and yet not losing his trust in providence, his Christian hope. The Pauline tenet of 'gain through loss', paradoxical to the materialist, is his own bitter and liberating insight. And this explains the repeated polemic against any merely juridical theology; towards systems delineating what Christ has done *for* mankind. For Coleridge the essence of Christianity lies in the Christ *in* mankind, and the spiritual meaning of salvation is the realisation of the divine image and purpose, a Pauline 'living through dying' which necessarily clashes with crude conceptions of a cosmic *suum cuique*.

Once we see *Aids to Reflection* as a collection of spiritual exercises, a Christian-Platonic ascent of the mind to God, we can see that here we find not a late theological aberration, full of absent-minded philosophical forays, tedious sentimental piety, and abstruse arguments with deceased divines, but the most trenchant and characteristic expression of Coleridge's mind.

CHAPTER I

The true philosopher is the lover of God: Coleridge's spiritual philosophy of religion[1]

God said to Moses, 'I AM WHO I AM' (Exodus 3: 14)

The Trinity means the divine mystery: the content is mystical, i.e. speculative.   (Hegel)[2]

It is the doctrine of the tri-unity that connects Xty with Philosophy . . .
(Coleridge, *Notebooks* iv. 4860)

Coleridge repeatedly asserts that the essential ideas that interested him in Schelling were known to him through the English Platonic tradition. This claim has led scholars to scrutinise Coleridge's contact with Neoplatonic philosophy before his visit to Germany in 1798–99. Generally scholars have concluded that Coleridge is lying or they are forced to claim a depth of study and insight that is barely supported by the evidence of his notebooks and letters. Wellek argued that Coleridge has no sense of the incompatibility of his seventeenth-century English sources and German Idealism:

a storey from Kant, there a part of a room from Schelling, there a roof from Anglican theology and so on. The architect did not feel the clash of styles, the subtle and irreconcilable differences between the Kantian first floor and the Anglican roof. Coleridge's 'untenable architectonic', and his inability 'to construct a philosophy of his own . . . drove him into a fatal dualism of a philosophy of faith, which amounted to an intellectual justification of this bankruptcy of thought.[3]

Norman Fruman attacks the claim that Coleridge felt a genial affinity with Schelling by remarking that the 'specific influence from

---

[1] Augustine, *City of God*, translated by H. Bettenson (Harmondsworth: Penguin, 1984), §8, 10: '*verus philosophus est amator Dei*'; cf. *Aids*, p. 41.

[2] 'Die Dreieinigkeit heißt das Mysterium Gottes; der Inhalt ist mystisch, d.h. spekulative.' *Vorlesung über die Philosophie der Religion* iii., edited by G. Lasson (Hamburg: Meiner, 1966), p. 69. cf. *Lectures on the Philosophy of Religion*, edited by P. C. Hodgson (Berkeley: University of California Press, 1984), vol. iii. pp. 280–3.

[3] R. Wellek, Immannel *Kant in England 1793–1838* (Princeton University Press, 1931) pp. 67–9.

18

antiquity or the Neoplatonists consists of scraps and tatters'.[4] Our counter thesis is that Wellek and Frumann are mistaken. Coleridge's claim is ingenuous and his achievement ingenious. The post-Kantians revived the doctrine of the Trinity in a philosophical manner. The sources of this revival rest ultimately in Neoplatonism and especially via the Cambridge and Florentine forms of Christian Neoplatonism. If we take seriously Coleridge's early and entirely earnest involvement in Unitarianism and his particular admiration for Priestley, together with his early interest in Ralph Cudworth, we may construe Coleridge's remarks about his sense of déjà vu in German metaphysics quite intelligibly without recourse to the view that Coleridge is dissimulating. He is, of course, notoriously inaccurate about a number of issues concerning his biography.[5] Nonetheless, it is possible to reconstruct his meaning without being either unduly sceptical or fanciful.

Coleridge's assertion in the *Biographia Literaria* that he was Trinitarian 'ad normam Platonis' before he became a Trinitarian in religion is enigmatic. It is hard to explain why Coleridge himself should come to see his own biography as the move from a Platonic Trinity to the Christian Trinity. This is mysterious because even the most allegorical interpreter of Plato's *Timaeus* or *Parmenides* is hard pressed to find direct analogies. Even if one takes the 'ad normam Platonis' to be a reference to the three hypostases of Neoplatonism, the tag remains opaque. The Neoplatonic triad of τὸ ἕν--ὁ νοῦς--ἡ ψυχή is not, in the manner of the Christian Trinity, consubstantial, and there has been no explanation of what Coleridge meant by his move from being a *philosophical* Trinitarian to being a *religious* Trinitarian. Some scholars have evaded the issue entirely: most notably McFarland who claims: 'The Trinity . . . [is] suspended in its mystery both One and Many.'[6]

Significantly, we have an important clue as to Coleridge's meaning. He claims that, as in Augustine's case, the 'libri ... Platonicorum' helped him towards his reconversion to Trinitarian Christianity. In an age when philosophy has become self-consciously secular, it is hard to appreciate the theological parameters of much

[4] N. Frumann, *Coleridge: The Damaged Archangel* (London: George Allen and Unwin, 1972), p. 174.
[5] cf. E. K. Chambers, *Samuel Taylor Coleridge: a Biographical Study* (Oxford: Clarendon, 1938), p. 1.
[6] T. McFarland, *Coleridge and the Pantheist Tradition* (Oxford: Clarendon, 1969), p. 229.

philosophical work in the seventeenth and eighteenth centuries. Cudworth's discussion of 'Platonism' was saturated by theological tenets and debates. The attack on the Church dogmas of the Trinity and the immortality of the soul by the Socinians/Antitrinitarians motivated the uncovering of the Platonic corruptions of Christianity. Coleridge believed he was able to extricate himself from bad theology (Unitarianism) after extricating himself from bad philosophy (necessitarianism). Indeed, he is quite explicit that – as in the case of Augustine – it was Platonic thought which helped him reconvert to the 'whole truth in Christ':

Nevertheless, I cannot doubt, that the difference of my metaphysical notions from those of the Unitarians in general contributed to my final reconversion to the whole truth in Christ; even as according to his own confession the books of certain Platonic philosophers (libri quorundam Platonicorum) commenced the rescue of St Augustine's faith from the same error aggravated by the far darker accompaniment of the Manichaean heresy. (*BL* i. 205)

We might compare this with Gibbon's irony: the doctrine of the Logos was taught in the school of Alexandria in 200 BC and then *revealed* by the Apostle St John in AD 97![7] Yet Coleridge is being utterly serious. Coleridge himself was for a time a Unitarian but came to believe that the doctrine of the Trinity is at the very heart of Christian belief and that the defence of the dogma demanded an explication of the doctrine of the Logos rather akin to that undertaken by the Alexandrine Fathers: he believed that Christian theology worthy of the name cannot be divorced from idealistic thought. He felt an attraction to Unitarianism as a young man and a revulsion towards the 'toad of priesthood', and it was through German Trinitarian metaphysics that he came to develop his own specific vision of a Christian philosophy.

   Coleridge claims that his Trinitarianism has its sources in Scripture, in Bishop Bull, and the 'best parts' of Plotinus (*Lit. Rem.* iv. 307) and he was not alone in linking the concept of spirit or intellect to the Trinity. George Berkeley, perhaps one of the greatest British philosophers, was concerned to insist that 'how unphilosophical soever that doctrine may seem to many of the present age, yet it is certain, the men of greatest fame and learning among the ancient

[7] In the table of contents to E. Gibbon, *The History of the Decline and Fall of the Roman Empire*, 3 vols, edited by David Womersley (Harmondsworth: Penguin, 1994), vol. i. pp. 23, 776.

philosophers held a Trinity in the Godhead' (*Siris*, §364).[8] Berkeley consciously drew upon 'Doctor Cudworth' and the locus classicus of Christian Platonic Trinitarian speculation: Augustine's claim in the *Confessions* vi §9 that the doctrine of the Logos in John's Gospel 'was also found in the writings of philosophers, who taught that God had an only begotten Son by whom are all things' (*Siris*, §359). Coleridge's Platonism is primarily an exercise in philosophical theology.

A SPIRITUAL PHILOSOPHY

The most important concept in *Aids to Reflection* is 'spirit', and the employment of this term is not the bland expression of Romantic religious piety, but blatantly metaphysical; Coleridge asserts that those materialists who judge spiritual things with the mind of the flesh are like those who would try to judge Titian or Raphael by 'Canons of Criticism deduced from the Sense of Smell' (*Aids*, p. 270). He asks: 'how is it possible that a work not *physical*, that is, employed on Objects known or believed on the evidence of the senses, should be other than *meta*physical, that is, treating on Subjects, the evidence of which is not derived from the Senses, is a problem which Critics of this order find it convenient to leave unsolved' (*Aids*, p. 81). This emphatic appeal to metaphysics is a clear rejection of John Locke's *Essay Concerning Human Understanding* where 'metaphysics' is used disparagingly, and dismissed from the definition of philosophy, which is reduced to natural philosophy, ethics, and logic. Kant, by way of contrast, is fond of the term and uses it often in *titles* of his works: *Metaphysics of Morals* or *Prolegomena to any future Metaphysics* are examples. The use of the word 'metaphysics' immediately signals an anti-Lockean and Germanic-Kantian temper in Coleridge's thought.

A number of those philosophers and theologians who loom large in Coleridge's early thought, such as Hartley (1705–57), Priestley (1733–1804), and William Paley (1743–1805) were largely influenced

---

[8] Beierwaltes, *Denken des Einen* (Frankfurt am Main: Klostermann, 1985) pp. 368–84 and esp. p. 379: 'Nicht minder wichtig als geschichtliche und sachliche Vorgabe und als ständiger authoritativer Bezugspunkt für den Platonismus von Chartres, aber auch für Cusanus ist *Boethius*: a) sein Gedanke der gegenseitige Bedingung von Eins-Sein und Sein . . . b) sein strenges Festhalten an der Nicht-Zahlhaftigkeit der Trinität und von daher sein Vorgriff auf "Wiederholung" der Einheit in ihrer eigenen oder als ihre eigene Gleicheit.' The roots of the association of 'being-one' and 'being' are to be found in Plato's *Parmenides*.

by John Locke (1632–1704). Coleridge believed that the basic tenets of Lockean empiricism had been refuted by the German philosophers, Kant and the Idealists, and that with German tools he could renew something of the vigour of 'spiritual platonic old England' (*Aids*, p. 182).

Locke's *Essay Concerning Human Understanding* was an attempt to apply the fruits of experimental philosophy (natural science) to philosophy itself. This leads to a combination of scepticism and realism in Locke; he is sceptical about the mode of philosophical reason in the scholastic tradition, such as the concept of substance, and employs central ideas in his philosophy that are derived from empirical science. The best example of this reverence for science is the distinction between primary and secondary qualities.[9] This was certainly not a reductionist programme; Locke's fairly conservative views on ethics and religion rule this out. Yet Locke's method suggested the rigorous explication of human knowledge in terms of experimental science. Hume, notoriously, saw the novelty of Locke's philosophical position in this way. Yet much less radical philosophers than Hume such as Hartley and Priestley saw Locke's thought as suggestive of the new empiricist science of man, as did the innovative apologist for religion Berkeley. After all, Locke was a friend of Robert Boyle, and came to be closely associated with Newton in the eighteenth-century imagination, and it was in Cambridge that Locke's thought exerted particular influence.[10] It was natural for writers such as Hume or the French intellectuals to see Locke as advancing with cautious steps towards a vision of human mental life in terms of experimental science.[11]

Whatever the precise upshot of Locke's own philosophy, the thrust of his reasoning was seen by many philosophers in the eighteenth century in terms of the attempt to explain human knowledge as a part of nature. The logical result of Locke's philosophy seemed to be 'naturalism': the thesis that human knowledge and activity can be explained as a scientifically intelligible part of an entirely natural process. Coleridge's counter-thesis is that *as* a spiritual being man cannot be explained in terms of 'nature'.

---

[9] cf. J. Yolton, *A Locke Dictionary* (Oxford: Blackwell, 1993), pp. 198–201; J. Mackie, *Problems from Locke* (Oxford: Clarendon, 1976), pp. 7–23.

[10] J. A. Gascoigne, *Cambridge in the Age of the Enlightenment* (Cambridge University Press, 1989).

[11] J. Yolton, *Thinking Matter: Materialism in Eighteenth-century Britain* (Minneapolis, Minn.: University of Minnesota Press, 1983).

Coleridge in *Aids to Reflection* is proposing an Idealistic philosophy. The term 'idealistic' is, of course, very broad and possibly misleading. Let us define it as the theory that *ultimate* reality does not consist of material objects but of consciousness or personality. It is not a *res* or thing but mind or spirit that constitutes his fundamental ontology. As W. R. Inge wrote: 'Idealism is most satisfactorily defined as the interpretation of the world according to a scale or value, or in Plato's phrase, by the idea of the Good.'[12] As such Coleridge's philosophy is opposed to a philosophical naturalism which explains reality by investigating the physical, that is 'natural', origins of objects, events, or persons. Hence Coleridge's metaphysics attempts to explain the 'lower' (nature) in terms of that which is higher (spirit) whereas the naturalist explains the higher in terms of the lower, the spiritual realm in purely natural terms. Berkeley in *Siris*, §263 writes:

Proclus, in his *Commentary on the Theology of Plato* observes there are two sorts of philosophers. The one placed Body first in the order of beings, and made the faculty of thinking depend thereupon, supposing that the principles of all things are corporeal; that Body most really or principally exists, and that all other things in a secondary sense, and by virtue of that. Others, making all corporeal things to be dependent upon Soul or Mind, think this to exist in the first place and primary sense, and the being of bodies to be altogether derived from and presuppose that of the Mind.

Coleridge belongs to an Idealistic tradition in Berkeley's sense of 'those who make all corporeal things to be dependent upon Soul or Mind', i.e. in the broad meaning of anti-naturalistic. He belongs, in an important sense, to the tradition that includes Plato, Plotinus, Aquinas, Leibniz, Berkeley, Hegel. Many theists are idealists in that they claim the dependency or derivation of the material realm upon or from the spiritual.[13] This is a view of idealism that has been contested, notably by Miles Burnyeat, but it does explain in part why Berkeley, Coleridge, Hegel and Schelling could see themselves as idealists within a Platonic tradition.[14]

We will not use the term 'Idealism' in this rather broad sense; however, it *is* a corrective to the misapprehension that idealism is the

---

[12] W. R. Inge, *Outspoken Essays* (London: Longmans, Green, and Co., 1919), p. 270.
[13] A. E. Taylor, 'Theism' in *Encyclopaedia of Religion and Ethics*, 13 vols., edited by James Hastings (Edinburgh, 1921–), vol. xii, pp. 261–87.
[14] M. Burnyeat, 'Idealism and Greek philosophy: what Descartes saw and Berkeley missed' in *Idealism Past and Present*, edited by G. Vasey (Cambridge University Press, 1982), pp. 19–50.

thesis that the world only exists in the human mind or is the product of human categories of thought. Although idealists use arguments to attack materialism, the major idealists tend to reject subjectivism or anti-realism. The best example is Hegel, who is quite adamant that the *Idee* is not subjective, a product of the finite mind, but is real per se and the presupposition of all finite subjective mental experience.[15]

Coleridge defines the spiritual as being not physical, and not passive. Mind cannot be identified with physical objects since the realm of objects presupposes some knower. The natural realm considered by itself is a realm of the chain of cause and effect: 'The moment we assume an Origin in Nature, a true *Beginning*, an actual First – that moment we rise *above* Nature, and are compelled to assume a *supernatural* Power' (*Aids*, p. 270). Characteristically Teutonic in Coleridge's Idealism is the distinction between 'nature' and 'spirit' that excludes the human spirit from the domain of nature. Whereas a Thomist would see human minds as created parts of nature, Coleridge exempts the human spirit, mind and will from what he defines as 'nature'; that is, in Kantian terms, 'the sum of all appearances'.[16] Transcendental idealism is precisely the theory that the understanding is the source of the laws of nature.

The second 'Teutonic' aspect is the link between knowledge as spontaneous and the fact of freedom. If knowledge is 'synthetic' in the Kantian sense, then a deterministic, reductionist philosophy of the sort commonly associated with the radical French Enlightenment, and to a lesser extent with Hume, cannot be true. If knowledge presupposes the a priori activity of the mind, knowledge cannot itself be explained as shaped from without, by 'natural' or 'mechanical forces'. All the Idealists, and Coleridge followed them on this point, held that Kant had produced the results of philosophy.[17]

These roughly correspond with the three critiques:

1. The principle of *subjectivity* qua spontaneity is the key to phil-

---

[15] G. W. F. Hegel, *Enzyklopädie der Philosophischen Wissenschaft* (Hamburg: Meiner, 1975), §213–44, pp. 182–97.

[16] cf A. Farrer, *The Glass of Vision* (Glasgow: Dacare, 1948), pp. 2ff.; Kant, *Critique of Pure Reason*, B163.

[17] See Schelling's letter to Hegel: 'Die Philosophie ist noch nicht am Ende. Kant hat die Resultate gegeben: die Prämissen fehlen noch.' *Materialien zu Schellings Philosophischen Anfängen*, edited by M. Frank (Frankfurt: Suhrkamp, 1975), p. 119.

osophy. If the mind is synthetic, and not merely reading off information from the world, determinism cannot be correct. A true philosophy must be a philosophy of freedom.

2. Freedom is the *ratio essendi* of morality. Morality is not the acceptance of alien codes and precepts, but is derived from the proper exercise of autonomous reason.

3. A teleological view of nature – not a mechanism but, rather as Schelling phrased it, 'slumbering spirit'.

These three principles were the basis of the idealistic interpretation of Kant, and the basis of their attempt to produce a systematic rational philosophy of the *super*natural in the strict but not superstitious sense. This project meant a radical critique of salient points in Kant's philosophy. It also meant the attempt to produce a monistic system that would overcome the dualisms of Kant's thought. The attempt to produce a unified system – inspired by Jacobi's critique – led to the renewal of almost precisely the kind of philosophising which Kant wished to abrogate.

The major issue was how the spiritual can be seen to relate to the material realm, mental to the non-mental, freedom to the laws of physics. Kant started from the description of the physical realm in natural science and then sought to find a place for the spiritual by means of his transcendental idealism. If the physical realm is transcendentally ideal, i.e. the product of the synthetic activity of the human understanding, Newton's physics is not a description of reality per se. Human freedom can be located 'beyond', as it were, the realm of appearances. Kant's concept of freedom was rooted in a dualism that the Idealists could not accept. This dualism seemed to be rooted in a compromise between the 'scientific' and 'spiritual' image of reality. Freedom in the Kantian system seemed to be an escape from the necessity of nature.

The central concern was to combine the spiritual principle of Kant's philosophy with a monistic system of thought on the model of Spinoza. All the Idealists were convinced that Kant had revolutionised philosophy through his establishment of a spiritual principle of freedom as the centre of philosophy; but they were equally determined that the dualisms of his system should be avoided. The Idealists rejected the resolute determinism and naturalism of Spinoza's system but the principle of a monistic system was accepted as the goal of a new philosophy. The idea of combining the insights of Kant and Spinoza was largely the result of the Idealist response to the philosophy of F. H. Jacobi.[18] Jacobi held the position that the 'fact' of freedom could not, without absurdity, be integrated into a philosophical system. Freedom, for Jacobi, is precisely that which is inexplicable for human reflection, and the attempt to explain the inexplicable leads to determinism and nihilism.[19] All the Idealists were convinced that Jacobi was wrong and that his challenge deserved serious attention and a decisive refutation.[20]

Jacobi's central thesis is that speculative thought cannot capture the 'fact' of the human experience, that which can only be accounted for by recourse to a personal extra-mundane God. Jacobi considers Spinoza to be supremely important because he reveals the pantheistic scheme in its true nature. The value of the rigour and clarity of Spinoza's pantheism is precisely its stark revelation of the impossibility of the compromise between

1. faith in God and the belief in the fact (*Tatsache*) of *freedom*
and
2. a philosophical *system* that attempts to deduce reality from an immanent ground.

This alternative between Spinozism and freedom presented by Jacobi was profoundly influential. One could say that the impetus of German Idealism was to develop a Spinozism *of freedom*.[21] Coleridge did not agree with Jacobi's presentation of an *alternative* between

[18] An excellent account of the period between Kant and Fichte is F. C. Beiser, *The Fate of Reason* (Cambridge, Mass.: Harvard University Press, 1987).

[19] Friedrich Heinrich Jacobi, *Werke* (Leipzig: Fleischer 1812–25), vol. iii. p. 70. cf. K. Hammacher, *Die Philosophie Friedrich Heinrich Jacobis* (Munich: Fink, 1969) and S. Peetz, *Die Freiheit im Wissen. Eine Untersuchung zu Schellings Koncept der Rationalität* (Frankfurt: Klostermann, 1995), pp. 18–76.

[20] Rolf-Peter Horstmann, *Die Grenzen der Vernunft. Eine Untersuchung zu Zielen und Motiven des Deutschen Idealismus* (Frankfurt am Main: Anton Hain, 1991), pp. 49–100.

[21] Spinoza's attempt to base freedom upon necessity was influential for the idealist attempt to base necessity upon freedom, evident in both Schelling's earlier thought and Hegel's dialectic. Although the influence of Spinoza upon Coleridge has been perhaps somewhat overemphasised by critics like McFarland, it is plausible to see Coleridge being attracted to several elements in Spinoza. The first part of the *Ethics* concerns the infinite and eternal divine substance. The conception of this unitary substance and its *modi* bears a very strong resemblance to Plotinus' philosophy of the One: it is certainly neither Cartesian nor Aristotelian. The conception of eternity and the distinction between *natura naturans* and *natura naturata* is Neoplatonic, as is the distinction between *intellectus* and *ratio*, the intellectual love of God, and the contrast between the bondage of the passions and the freedom of the intellect. cf. P. O. Kristeller, 'Stoic and neoplatonic sources of Spinoza's ethics', in *History of European Ideas* 5 (1985), pp. 1–15. See above, pp. 83–5.

either reflection or faith. Coleridge's lack of sympathy for Jacobi's alternative is evident from Coleridge's Jacobi marginalia:

Lessing insisted that he 'required everything to be natural'; and I (maintained) that there could be no natural philosophy of the supernatural and nevertheless both (natural and supernatural) evidently existed. (*Marg.* iii. 81)[22]

Coleridge writes opposite that 'there can be no natural', 'dass es keine natürliche'

This is a mere play on words, little better than a pun. By natürlich Lessing means vernunftmässig. Substitute this, viz *rationally*: and what becomes of Jacobi's repartee? That there can be no *rational* philosophy of the Supernatural ? (Ibid.)

The fact that Coleridge regards Jacobi's repartee as a pun reveals how little he shares Jacobi's basic position. On the contrary, philosophy is, according to Coleridge, the *rational* explication of the *super-natural*. Coleridge shares with the Idealists the deep impress of Jacobi's thought and the rejection of the 'philosophy of faith'. The parameters of Coleridge's thought are set by the Idealists, not by Jacobi. Nevertheless Coleridge was never the adherent of any one German Idealist. He comes closest to becoming an adherent of the most Platonic – Schelling. Yet even in this case Coleridge was never a slavish disciple, and becomes quite a powerful critic.

Coleridge's interest in Fichte seems entirely influenced by Schelling, who – though regarded as a pupil of Fichte – was from the earliest phases of his philosophy rather independent. Schelling's move was to reverse Fichte's 'The Subject is the Absolute' to 'The Absolute is Subject.' This move dispensed with subjective idealism and was the path to a revival of natural theology in German Idealism: the absolute is prior to the act of knowing.[23] Fichte wished to show that spirit is the key to nature, and freedom is the key to necessity. Notwithstanding Fichte's adamant insistence to the contrary, the constitution or 'positing' of the world or the 'not I' by the 'I' remained highly mysterious, and consequently his radical monism seemed no more attractive than the dualism of Kant. Furthermore,

---

22 'Lessing blieb dabey: dasz er sich alles "natürlich ausgebeten haben wollte"; und ich: dasz es keine natürliche Philosophie des Uebernatürlichen geben könnte, und doch beides (Natürliches und Uebernatürliches) offenbar vorhanden wäre.'

23 Even though Fichte violently attacked Schelling and Hegel for abandoning transcendental philosophy and reverting to metaphysics, Fichte himself, post-1801, places the absolute above the ego.

the tenor of Fichte's 'Science of Knowledge' or *Wissenschaftslehre* seemed to reduce nature to the condition of the moral development of humanity. If Kant's theory of freedom seemed like an escape from the chains of nature, Fichte's theory of freedom seemed to be based upon a curious denigration of nature: Coleridge takes over Schelling's mixture of admiration for, and impatience with, Fichte's thought (*BL* i. 158).

Coleridge was much more attracted to Schelling's philosophy. The latter's *Naturphilosophie* was dictated in part by a dissatisfaction with Fichte's Idealism. In the *Freiheitschrift* Schelling expounds the difference between Fichte and himself quite succinctly as follows: 'not solely that subjectivity is all but that, the other way around, everything is subjectivity' ('nicht allein die Ichheit alles, sondern auch umgekehrt alles Ichheit sei').[24] Schelling wished to integrate unconscious, natural processes with the activity of spirit: and to produce an *Ideal-Realismus*. In this, however, Schelling's philosophy barely remained an idealism at all. By insisting upon the polarity of nature and spirit as equal manifestations of the absolute, Schelling was denying the primacy of spirit that is characteristic for idealism (and Platonism). Despite the great shift in his thought in the *Freiheitschrift*, Schelling retains his concern to develop a *natural* or *physical* basis for freedom, a concern that links this middle period to the early *Naturphilosophie*. Coleridge criticises adamantly this aspect of Schelling, and his criticism has been well documented in scholarship:[25] nevertheless, whereas Fichte plays a very minor role for Coleridge, Schelling is a vitally important presence. Yet in a sense Coleridge's own drive to produce a natural theology can be seen in Schelling's attempt to adumbrate a philosophy that proceeds from the absolute rather than from the strictly transcendental/Kantian standpoint of knowledge: Fichte's *Ich*. This fact has led many Fichte scholars, notably Reinhart Lauth, to insist that Schelling never really appreciated Fichte's position properly.[26]

Coleridge does not seem to have found Hegel very congenial. His perfunctory *Marginalia* on Hegel's *Logik* suggest that Coleridge did

---

[24] F. W. J. von Schelling, *Über das Wesen der Menschlichen Freiheit*, edited by H. Fruhmans (Stuttgart: Reclam, 1983), p. 350.

[25] The best account is F. A. Uehlein, *Die Manifestation des Selbstbewußtseins im konkreten 'Ich bin'* (Hamburg: Meiner, 1982), pp. 108 ff.

[26] R. Lauth, *Die Entstehung von Schellings Identitätsphilosophie in der Auseinandersetzung mit Fichtes Wissenscaftslehre* (Freiburg: Karl Alber, 1975).

not consider Hegel as a serious alternative to Kant or Schelling. Although Coleridge considered the primacy of the spirit to have been firmly established by Kant, the *nature* of this realm and *its relation to physical phenomena* was very much open for discussion. Kant's dualism, Fichte's subjectivism, and the protean nature of Schelling's thought did not seem to offer a satisfactory spiritual philosophy, and Hegel's philosophy was not really considered in earnest. Thus Coleridge had more scope for his own philosophical work than is sometimes conceded by critics such as Wellek or Orsini.

THE REVIVAL OF NATURAL THEOLOGY

The phrase 'natural theology' strikes modern English readers as redolent of Paley, the 'Bridgewater Treatises', and the notoriously arid apologetic theology of Hanoverian England. Yet, this apart, it is an accurate term for Coleridge's thought that explains the link between the Cambridge Platonists and Hegel and Schelling, and, moreover, why Coleridge felt that his own dynamic philosophy was the 'system of Pythagoras and Plato revived' (*BL* i. 263): natural theology. The word 'system' is important. It is a favourite term of Cudworth, the 'real founder of British Idealism'.[27] Cudworth's 'system', moreover, is a defence of freedom against philosophical fatalism in which he invokes Pythagoras and Plato against Hobbes as the modern sophist.

The challenge presented by Jacobi led to a revival of natural theology: his objection, as a philosopher of *Empfindsamkeit*, to all kinds of system-building in philosophy as nihilistic, threw down the gauntlet to the neo-Kantians, and fired the Idealists' attempt to produce a true intellectual system that was grounded in freedom and a chain of reflections that culminate in the Platonic Trinity. Hegel and Schelling are perhaps the last great phase of the Platonic succession; not in the sense of being avowed disciples of Plato the thinker, but rather as proponents of the natural theology forged by Plato and especially the Neoplatonists.

The term 'natural theology' was employed by Cicero's contemporary the great antiquarian M. Terentius Varro to define the attempt to give an account of the divine that claims truth. The original

---

[27] John H. Muirhead, *The Platonic Tradition in Anglo-Saxon Philosophy* (London: Macmillan, 1931), p. 27.

distinction is not between natural and revealed but mythical and civil theology on the one hand, and natural on the other. Mythical theology consists of the stories of the gods and since the Periclean enlightenment the educated regarded these as the fantasy of the poets. Civil theology is the knowledge of the religious rituals of the state calendar. Again these matters were thought by enlightened Athenian intellectuals to be the product of (human) νόμος and not φύσις. Natural theology is a doctrine of God that belongs to a rational and comprehensive theory of φύσις or *natura*.[28] Unlike civil and mythical theology it claims to be ἐπιστήμη; or what the Germans call *Wissenschaft*. The Cambridge Platonist Ralph Cudworth provides a clear account of such a natural theology. He claims that true religion has *three* elements:

First, that all things in the world do not float without a head and governor; but there is a God, an omnipotent understanding Being, presiding over all. Secondly, that this God being essentially good and just, there is φύσει καλὸν καὶ δίκαιον, something in its own nature immutably and eternally just and unjust; and not by arbitrary will, law and command. And lastly, that there is something ἐφ᾽ ἡμῖν, or, that we are so far forth principles or masters of our own actions, as to be accountable to justice for them, or to make us guilty and blame-worthy for what we do amiss, and to deserve punishment accordingly.[29]

The real founder of natural theology as three things '(which are the most Important Things, that the Mind of man can employ it self upon) [and which] taken all together, make up the Wholeness and Entireness of that which is here called by us, The True Intellectual System of the Universe', is Plato.[30] He established the principles of God, providence, and judgement as the cardinal tenets of a philosophic theology. In the tenth book of the *Laws* he asserts that:

1. God is a good and wise spirit, and the source and designer of the realm of becoming, i.e. nature.
2. God controls nature according to his goodness.
3. God judges man according to his justice.

This, through the influence of Neoplatonism (in particular Proclus),

---

[28] cf. the *Periphyseon* of John Scot Eriugena, Coleridge's favourite, translated by I. P. Sheldon-Williams (Dublin: Dublin Institute for Advanced Studies, 1976–   ), known as *De Divisione Naturae*.

[29] Cudworth, The *True Intellectual System of the Universe*, 3 vols., edited by Harrison (London: Tegg, 1845), p. xxxiv.

[30] Cudworth, *True Intellectual System*, p. xxxiv.

is constitutive for St Thomas' thought.[31] The *Summa contra Gentiles* presents a vision of an exhaustive system of reality from God

1. in himself
2. in his procession in his creatures
3. in the return of the creatures to their Divine source.

The first book is devoted to the existence and attributes of God, the second book to the providential divine relationship with his creatures, and the third to God's ultimate relation to his creatures as their good: as their gracious judge. St Thomas constructs a broadly Neoplatonic edifice.[32] Schelling's *Freiheitschrift* has just the same *exitus–reditus* structure.

Cudworth's 'Philosophy of Religion' is an account of the true system because it is opposed to atheism; 'intellectual' to distinguish it from the 'other, Vulgarly so called, Systems of the World' :

Cogitation is, in order of nature, before local motion. Life and understanding, soul and mind, are no syllables or complexions of things, secondary and derivative, which might therefore be made out of things devoid of life and understanding; but simple, primitive, and uncompounded natures; there are no qualities or accidental modifications of matter, but substantial things . . . A perfect understanding Being is the beginning and head of the scale of entity; from whence things gradually descend downward, lower and lower, till they end in senseless matter.[33]

Cudworth's System is intellectual in the sense of being idealistic: 'cogitation' is before 'motion'.

In the mature *Religionsphilosophie* of both Hegel and Schelling we find an explicit avowal of natural theology; not in the sense of the Enlightenment 'evidences' of a designer but in the ancient, Cudworthian sense of a reasoned explication of the relation of God to world. Hegel opened his lectures on the philosophy of religion with the words: 'The object of these lectures is the philosophy of religion, which in general has the same purpose as the earlier type of metaphysical science, which was called *theologia naturalis*.'[34] Furthermore, this natural theology is explicitly a *Geistesmetaphysik* or meta-

[31] W. Hankey, *God in Himself* (Oxford: Clarendon, 1987), p. 8.
[32] A. E. Taylor, *The Faith of a Moralist* (London: Macmillan, 1930), vol. i. pp. 1–14 and C. C. J. Webb, *Studies in the History of Natural Theology* (Oxford: Clarendon, 1915), pp. 1–83.
[33] Cudworth, *True Intellectual System*, vol. iii. pp. 434–5.
[34] G. W. F. Hegel, *Lectures on the Philosophy of Religion*, edited by P. C. Hodgson, 3 vols. (Berkeley: University of California Press, 1984), vol. i. p. 83.

physics of the spirit or mind: the philosophy of religion of the
German Idealists is a phenomenology of self-consciousness.

Paul Tillich has distinguished between the 'ontological' and the
'cosmological' approaches in natural theology. The first, the Platonist and idealist method, approaches the divine through immediate
consciousness or awareness of the transcendent ontological ground.
The second, the Aristotelian or Thomistic path, tends to use
evidence of the cosmos as the basis for an inference to a Divine
architect.[35] Augustine's books IX and X of *De Trinitate* serve as an
example of the first kind that considers God through the spirit, and
the 'Five Ways' of Aquinas, which considers God through the world,
as an example of the second path. The Idealists follow the first
'interior' path. The absolute, or God, is not to be inferred from the
facts or the very contingency of the cosmos, but is intuited or
apprehended in consciousness or the structure of the spirit. The
distinction between the spiritual and material is such that the
transcendence of the divine is not conceived in materialistic terms as
remoteness. The refusal to envisage divine transcendence as 'out and
up there' and the absolute as the apex of a cosmic pyramid has
sometimes been mistakenly interpreted as pantheism; when in fact it
is the opposite. The enigmatic image of God as a circle whose centre
is everywhere and circumference is nowhere is the attempt to dispel
materialistic conceptions.

Tillich notes: 'Obviously German idealism belongs to the ontological type of philosophy of religion.'[36] We find in Hegel's *Philosophy of
Religion* and Schelling's writings the same use of the Neoplatonic
triadic structure in order to explicate the ground of subject and
object, an absolute *prius* that both thinkers identify with the Christian
doctrine of the Trinity. The revival of natural theology in Germany
was linked to the renewal of the *Trinitas Platonica*. Coleridge planned
his own great speculative work, but he speaks of his intent to
defend 'CHRISTIAN FAITH as THE PERFECTION OF HUMAN
INTELLIGENCE' (*Aids*, p. 6). This reflects Coleridge's interest in
natural theology, not in opposition to revealed theology but as a
speculative explication of the central doctrines of the Christian

[35] Paul Tillich, 'Zwei Wege der Religionsphilosophie' in *Gesammelte Werke*, 14 vols., (Stuttgart:
    Evangelisches Verlagswerk, 1959–74), vol. v (1964), pp. 122–37 and 'The two types of the
    philosophy of religion' in *The Theology of Culture* (New York: Oxford University Press, 1959),
    pp. 12–29.
[36] Tillich, *Culture*, p. 21.

religion. Coleridge could not have known the full-blown natural theology of Schelling and Hegel, but only fragments and outlines – of which Schelling's *Philosophie und Theologie, Vorlesungen über die Methode des akademischen Studiums, Bruno,* and the *Freiheitsschrift* were the most significant.

PLATONISM

In his *Marginalia* on Thomas Gray Coleridge writes of the 'little, according to *my* convictions at least, the very little of proper Platonism contained in the *written* books of Plato' (*Marg.* ii. 866). Until the eighteenth century 'Platonism' referred to Plato's dialogues, the commentaries of the Academy, the comments of certain Church Fathers, and often esoteric writings of vaguely Platonic provenance. The term 'Neoplatonism' arose precisely during the eighteenth century as this very catholic view of Platonism was in decline.[37] 'Platonism' in this context meant various metaphysical doctrines that had been distilled from the dialogues and made explicit within the tradition. The result was a tendency to allegorise certain passages.

Yet it was only really in the early nineteenth century with the great philological labours of Schleiermacher that a radically revised picture of Plato was developed. Influenced by the culture of sensibility, and the Romantic conception of the philosopher-artist-poet, Schleiermacher developed the idea that the literary form of Plato's writing was an essential part of the content of Plato's philosophy – his thought is not merely hinted at but contained in dialogues, and it is fruitless to try and discover a metaphysical 'system'. This was expressed most notably in Schleiermacher's *Introduction* to his translation of Plato in 1804.[38] Hegel and Schelling, however, remained within the limits of the older Neoplatonic vision of Platonism as a metaphysical system, of which Plato's dialogues form an introduction. Rüdiger Bubner notes: 'Despite the contemporaneous nature of both projects – Early Idealism and Early Romanticism, both expressed in the middle of the last decade of the 18th century,

[37] E. N. Tigerstedt, *The Decline and Fall of the Neoplatonic Interpretation of Plato: an Outline and some Observations* (Helsinki: Societas Scientiarum Fennica, 1974). Creuzer's translation of Plotinus' *Treatise* iii. 8 in 1805 marks a change towards a more positive reception of Neoplatonic thought in Germany.

[38] Printed in K. Gaiser, *Das Platon Bild* (Hildesheim: Olms, 1969), pp. 1–32.

they constituted wildly differing views of how to interpret Plato for their own age'.[39] Platonism remained, for both Schelling and Hegel, a model of systematic metaphysical speculation.

Coleridge claims in the *Biographia Literaria* of Schelling that 'I first found a genial coincidence with much that I had toiled out for myself, and a powerful assistance in what I had yet to do' (*BL* i. 160). This claim has been attacked, most notably by René Wellek, as mere subterfuge.[40] However, Schelling is much of a Platonist: Crabb Robinson speaks of him as the 'modern Plato' in 1802. Schelling wrote a commentary upon Plato's *Timaeus* as a boy at the Tübingen Stift and his Platonic dialogue *Bruno* of 1802 was, as Michael Vater remarks, 'Schelling's decision to turn back the history of philosophy and present himself as Plato risen from the grave'.[41] In this dialogue Schelling attacks Fichte in the guise of Giordano Bruno. Vater says of Schelling: 'Neoplatonism means for him above all *systematic* thought, speculation which reconciles, integrates, harmonizes and achieves a point of view transcending conflict and opposition. In this sense all systematic philosophy is "Neoplatonism," the conceptual ascent to the vision of the eternal or the Absolute.'[42] At this period Schelling had barely any direct acquaintance with Plotinus. However, in 1804 Franz Berg, a professor of church history, launched into an attack on Schelling's philosophy in a dialogue in which the proponent of Schelling's thought is called 'Plotin'. In the following year Friedrich Schlegel attacked Schelling's thought as merely an expansion of Spinoza and Plotinus.[43] Coleridge's sense of affinity with Schelling's Platonism is perfectly intelligible.

If we consider Coleridge's notebooks and letters, we can see the strong influence of late seventeenth-century Platonists upon his early thought. Cudworth's 'counterfeit infinity' or the motto for the

---

[39] 'Trotz der historischen Gleichzeitigkeit beider programme – des Frühidealismus wie der Füromantik, die beider nach der Mitte des letzten Jahrzehnts des 18. Jahrhunderts formuliert werden, handelt es sich doch um deutlich voneinander geschiedene Vorstellungen darüber, wie Platon aktuell zu lesen sie.' R. Bubner, 'Die Entdeckung Platons durch Schelling und seine Aneignung durch Schleiermacher' in *Innovationen des Idealismus*, (Göttingen: Vandenhoeck and Ruprecht, 1995), p. 33.

[40] Wellek, *Immanuel Kant in England*, pp. 78–9.

[41] Michael G. Vater, introduction in Schelling, *Bruno, or, On the Natural and the Divine Principle of Things* (Albany: State of New York Press, 1984), p. 73.

[42] Michael G. Vater 'Schelling's "neoplatonic system-notion"' in B. Harris (ed.), *The Significance of Neoplatonism* (Norfolk, Va: Old Dominion University Press, 1976), pp. 277 ff.

[43] cf. W. Beierwaltes, *Platonismus und Idealismus* (Frankfurt am Main: Klostermann, 1972), pp. 100 ff.

Ancient Mariner taken from Thomas Burnet are examples of the deep influence that the Christian Platonic metaphysical tradition exerted on Coleridge's mind before his acquaintance with German Idealism. The Cambridge Platonists play the central role not least because they were professional philosophers (unlike Hobbes and Locke) in eminent positions in the University of Cambridge: Whichcote was the Provost of King's, Cudworth was Master of Clare and Christ's. Their influence extended to major figures of the early eighteenth century such as Locke, Ray, or Shaftesbury. Furthermore, they were the first group of philosophers to develop the vernacular for philosophical writing: indeed, much of the terminology of modern English philosophy: 'consciousness', 'self-consciousness', 'philosophy of religion', 'theism', even 'Cartesianism', are coinages of the Platonists.[44]

Ralph Cudworth is the most important because his *True Intellectual System of the Universe*, a defence of metaphysical theism and the Christian Platonic Trinity, became a handbook of philosophical ideas: Cudworth's historiography provided the foundations for the German histories of philosophy of the eighteenth century. Traces of Cudworth's influence can be found quite clearly in the *Pantheismus-streit* between Jacobi and Lessing.[45] Albeit often indirect, Cudworth is a significant source for Schelling.

The importance of the Cambridge Platonists is quite overlooked if they are detached from the roots and ramifications of their Platonism. They are not an exotic growth that sprang up in Cambridge amid the turbulence of the Civil War that then withered and disappeared – leaving no mark on subsequent thought; a notion based on the erroneous assumption that British thought is unremitting empiricism. The Cambridge Platonists are rooted in the humanism that led to the discovery of the Platonic texts at the beginning of the fifteenth century.[46] Although 'Platonism' never displaced Aristotelianism and was never part of the philosophical curriculum in England, it did have powerful proponents: figures

---

[44] U. Thiel, 'Cudworth and seventeenth-century theories of consciousness' in *The Uses of Antiquity*, edited by S. Gaukroger (Dordrecht: Kluwer, 1991), pp. 70–99; N. Lash, *The Beginning and the End of Religion* (Cambridge University Press, 1996), p. 14; P. Harrison, *'Religion' and the Religions in the English Enlightenment* (Cambridge University Press, 1990).

[45] Jan Assmann, *Moses the Egyptian* (Cambridge, Mass.: Harvard [University Press], 1997) pp. 80–90; 204ff.

[46] I owe this point to Sarah Hutton. cf. W. R. Sorley, *A History of English Philosophy* (Cambridge University Press, 1920), pp. 8–10.

such as Everard Digby (1550–90) at St John's in Cambridge and Thomas Jackson (1579–1640) at Corpus Christi, Oxford. Such 'humanists' were deeply interested in theological problems, and had evident roots in medieval traditions and practices:[47] we find not only links with Florentine Platonism, but strong similarities to Nicholas of Cusa, the German Mystics, John Scot Eriugena, and the Alexandrian divines – the 'lofty' Platonist and mystical wing of Christian theology rather than the more conceptual and empiricist Aristotelian-scholastics. Such a 'Platonism' was philosophically syncretistic and strongly theological: in particular the desire to produce a rational theology with ancient pedigree, a *prisca theologia*, is best exemplified by Cudworth's philosophical historiography in the *True Intellectual System of the Universe* in which philosophy is presented as a perennial battle between the theists-cum-idealists and atheists-cum-materialists. The 'Platonism' of seventeenth-century Cambridge had a distinctively Florentine form. It bore the imprint of Ficino's fusion of Renaissance Neoplatonism and Christian theology.

THE PLATONIC TRINITY

The doctrine of the Trinity is the most important doctrine of the Christian church and despite the attempts of the Church Fathers to define and expound the doctrine it is still the *quaestio vexata* of Christian theology. How can God be one substance and three persons? The Nicaean Council of 325 forged the non-biblical term ὁμοούσιος ('of the same substance') to describe the identity of the Father and the Son. At the Council of Constantinople (381) this identity is extended to the Spirit.[48] At the beginning of the fifth century Augustine and Boethius developed the doctrines of the Councils. The root of the problem was the idea of an intelligible world of ideas that served as an intermediary between the transcendent God and the world. This idea of the Logos was taken by Christians on the authority of the speculative theology of John and Paul to refer to the pre-existent Christ. Prior to Nicaea and Constantinople the exact relationship of this Logos to the divine

---

[47] cf. John B. Gleason, *John Colet* (Berkeley and London: University of California Press, 1989). Gleason argues that John Colet's (1466/7–1519) influence in English Platonism seems to have been greatly exaggerated by nineteenth-century historiography.

[48] Adolf Martin Ritter, 'Dogma und Lehre in der Alten Kirche' in *Handbuch der Dogmen und Theologiegeschichte* i. (Göttingen: Vandenhoeck, 1982).

source remained a matter of debate. The doctrine of the coequal Trinity arose from asserting the unity of the Logos with its source.

The great Antitrinitarian N. Soverain in his anonymous, but momentous, text *Le Platonisme dévoilé, ou Essai touchant le Verbe Platonicien* in 1700 isolated the tendency to hypostasise the divine word or creative disposition as the core of the Platonic Trinity, and of course Plato's demiurge is a creator – in opposition to the entirely contemplative God of Aristotle's metaphysics.[49] Drawing on the Wisdom books of the Old Testament and in particular Philo's idea of the Logos, where the wisdom of God is not just an attribute but a kind of being which contains the divine ideas, as the intelligible plan of creation, the Church Fathers abandoned the notion that the Logos was inferior to its source. The relational unity of the Christian Godhead integrates the Platonic Forms: the divine ideas do not constitute an intermediate world between the primal divine unity and the world but *are* the self-expression of the Godhead: the ideas constitute the intellect of God, who is thus an absolute mind or subject. A. H. Armstrong notes:

The created universe then appears as an 'extra', a magnificent and purely superfluous expression of pure disinterested generosity, in the image and for the glory of the eternal *Logos*: and not, as it was for the pagan Platonists, the descending stages of divine self expression.[50]

Cudworth saw providence in pagan thought:

For that Plato and his followers held τρεῖς ἀρχικὰς ὑποστασεῖς, 'three hypostases in the Deity, that were the first principles of all things,' is a thing very well known to all; though we do not affirm, that these Platonic hypostases are exactly the same with those in the Christian trinity. Now Plato himself sufficiently intimates this not to have been his own invention; and Plotinus tells us, that it was παλαιὰ δόξα, 'an ancient opinion,' before Plato's time, which had been delivered down by some of the Pythagorics.[51]

There is a powerful precedent for Cudworth's views if we look at the classic statement of the Trinity in Augustine, for whom the Trinity is not primarily a biblical notion; nor, indeed, philosophically dubious. In fact the Trinity is one of his earliest obsessions and constitutes an important reason for conversion. Despite the subordinationism implicit in the descending levels of the self-unfolding of

---

[49] cf. Franz, *Schellings Platon-Studien*, pp. 28 ff.
[50] A. H. Armstrong, *Christian Faith and Greek Philosophy* (London: Darton, Longman, and Todd, 1960), p. 24.
[51] Cudworth, *True Intellectual System*, vol. i. p. 41.

the One qua Intellect and soul, the Neoplatonic triad of the three hypostases was often seen by the Church Fathers as a prelude to the Christian Trinity.[52] In his earliest work he uses triads such '*unum, species, bonitas*', or '*mensura, numerus, pondus*'.[53] One of the most important is God the Father and the mind of God and a mediator (*City of God* x. 23); a text which Cudworth quotes as a 'Platonick Hypothesis' wherein the Third Hypostasis is a 'Middle betwixt the First and Second'.[54] Here Augustine is referring to Plotinus v. 1 (10) *On the Three Primary Hypostases* via Porphyry.

The Trinity was particularly attractive to Platonists; not because of affinity with the triad of τὸ ἕν–ὁ νοῦς–ἡ ψυχή but because of the noetic triads. This is to say that the Neoplatonists used the model of *three* to give an account of the *divine spirit*.[55] For Augustine the Trinity is not merely the interpretation of biblical revelation but intimately related to the philosophical idea of mind. He rejects two cardinal principles of Neoplatonic metaphysics: a hierarchy of divinity and the superiority of the producer to the produced. These two principles are particularly evident in Plotinus' system of the divine intellect that proceeds from the ineffable One. The Christian theological tradition telescoped the two eminent members of the Platonic Trinity into a reflexive transcendent unity.[56] Plotinus has two models of unity – the One that is pre-eminent unity: the ground of all being, utterly transcendent and 'beyond being' and without any difference. The divine intellect is the perfect form of unity in difference: the divine mind which contains the ideas. The unity of the divine ideas is like light: ideas of the intellect are translucent. In their difference, the ideas mirror themselves and hence eternal perfect identity. Christian theology combined these two models of unity and formed a concept of God as a radically transcendent and yet a relational self-conscious unity.[57] The ideas inhere in the Word of the Father as his perfect expression and are thus coequal. The Spirit is a coequal expression

---

[52] Eusebius, *Praeparatio evangelica*, 15 vols., vols. 10–13; Augustine, *City of God*, § 5–11 and esp. 7.

[53] cf. Beierwaltes, 'Augustins Interpretation von "Sapientia" 11, 21', *Revue des Etudes Augustiniennes* 15 (1969), pp. 51–61.

[54] Cudworth, *True Intellectual System*, vol. ii. p. 430.

[55] Pierre Hadot, 'Etre, vie et pensée chez Plotin et avant Plotin' in *Les Sources de Plotin* (Geneva: Vandœuvres, 1960), pp. 105–41.

[56] Pierre Hadot has argued that Porphyry forged together the One and the intellect. This depends upon the attribution of an anonymous commentary on Plato's *Parmenides* to Porphyry. Pierre Hadot, *Porphre et Victorinus* (Paris: Etudes Augustiniennes, 1980) and W. Beierwaltes, *Denken des Einen*, pp. 198 ff.

[57] Beierwaltes, *Denken des Einen*, p. 65.

of the union of Father and Son. The Trinitarian Godhead is a relational unity akin to the finite mind: the difference among the three persons can only be expressed in terms of their *relations*, the Father to the Son, the Son to the Spirit, etc., and not in terms of *substance*.

Coleridge saw therein his *own* task as a *philosophical* defence of the Trinitarian metaphysical conception. Here he was following the steps of Cudworth, to whom Coleridge is deeply indebted. In *Aids to Reflection* he can refer to the *Plato Christianus* who propounded speculation about the Trinity and had intimations of incarnation:

> Nor was it altogether without grounds that several of the Fathers ventured to believe that Plato had some dim conception of the necessity of a Divine Mediator, whether through some indistinct echo of the patriarchal faith, or some rays of light refracted from the Hebrew prophets through a Phoenician medium, (to which he may possibly have referred in his phrase, θεοπαράδοτος σοφία, the wisdom delivered from God). (*Aids*, p. 41)

Typically, the word θεοπαράδοτος does not appear in Plato but in Proclus, and Coleridge seems to have derived the phrase θεοπαράδοτος σοφία from the British Platonists Cudworth and Berkeley (*Aids*, p. 41 n. 4).[58] Such a view of Plato as the 'divine philosopher' makes it evident that Coleridge's perception of 'Platonism' reflects a debate about Platonism and Christianity that was raging in Coleridge's intellectual environment.

In his marginalia on Luther Coleridge writes of the fears he has for the (typical Cambridge) young man reared on the 'Grotio-Paleyian Scheme of Christian Evidence' and reading Petavius, Locke, and Arminius (*CM* iii. 763–4). The distinguished Jesuit Denis Pétau (1583–1652) 'taxed' ancient Christians 'for Platonism' and 'having by that means corrupted the purity of the Christian faith', Cudworth remarks.[59] Pétau's *De Trinitate*[60] expounds the divergences between pre- and post-Nicaean Trinitarian theology. Pétau believed that the Christian heresy of Arianism was derived from Platonism. His *De Trinitate* starts with a consideration of Platonic triads, and Owen Chadwick notes that 'in reading the ancient Fathers, Pétau had formed in his mind a particular historical theory. He believed that Platonism was the bane of the Christian religion. He supposed

---

[58] *Greek Lexicon*, edited by H. G. Liddell and R. Scott, ninth edition (Oxford: Clarendon, 1968), p. 790.

[59] Cudworth, vol. ii. pp. 417–18.

[60] Denis Pétau, *Theologicorum dogmatum*, 5 vols. (Paris: Cramoisy, 1644), vol. ii.

that every ancient heresy, culminating in Arianism, derived from the Platonic infection. He began his treatise *De Trinitate* with a survey of the quasi-Trinitarian doctrines found amongst the Platonists.'[61] Lorenz von Mosheim refers to Cudworth's 'deference for the fathers':[62] Cudworth thought that by using Patristic sources he could dissuade those who saw the Trinity as the 'Choak-Pear' of Christianity.[63] Just like George Bull's *Defence of the Nicene Faith*,[64] Cudworth's attack upon Pétau was motivated by a defence of the Church of England and a Platonic metaphysical agenda. Coleridge was working in the tradition of Cudworth and a Christian Platonic metaphysics.

GERMAN IDEALISM AND THE PLATONIC TRADITION

The concepts which Augustine and Boethius used to defend the doctrine of the Trinity: 'unity', 'uniqueness', 'simplicity', 'difference', 'identity', 'substance', 'relation', and 'spirit' are, of course, all products of the Platonic-Aristotelian *Geistesmetaphysik*, especially Plato's *Timaeus*, *Sophist*, and *Parmenides*. It is largely through the prism of the theological debates in the Enlightenment about the Trinity and Greek philosophy, and their mutual relations or corruptions, that the young theologians Schelling and Hegel came to acquire their 'Platonism'.

Coleridge held that Schelling's thought is 'pura puta the Alexandrine Philosophy' (*CM* iv. 158), and Ernst Troeltsch writes of German Idealism that 'this form of idealism is, in reality, a revived Platonism or Neoplatonism'.[65] The Platonism that the young German theologians Hegel and Schelling encountered at the University of Tübingen was not just the Enlightenment Plato revived by Mendelssohn and Kant, but also the very syncretistic and theological Plato of the humanists Ficino and Cudworth. Michael Franz has

---

[61] Owen Chadwick, *From Bossuet to Newman*, second edition (Cambridge University Press, 1987), p. 58. cf. M. Hofmann, *Dogma und Dogmenentwicklung im theologischen Werk Denis Petaus* (Frankfurt: Lang, 1976).

[62] Cudworth, *True Intellectual System*, vol. ii. p. 282.

[63] D. W. Dockrill, 'The authority of the Fathers in the great Trinitarian debates of the sixteen-nineties', *Studia Patristica*, edited by E. A. Livingstone, xviii/4 (Leuven: Peeters 1990), pp. 335–47.

[64] Bishop George Bull, *Defensio Fidei Nicaenae* in vols. i. and ii. of *Bishop Bull's Works on the Trinity*, 3 vols. (Oxford: Parker, 1852).

[65] E. Troeltsch, article in *Encyclopaedia of Religion and Ethics*, 13 vols., edited by J. Hastings (Edinburgh: T. and T. Clark, 1908–26), vol. vii. p. 93.

investigated the context of Schelling's early work on Plato, in particular his commentary on the *Timaeus*, and demonstrates convincingly the extent to which the agenda established by Cudworth, in his attempt to demonstrate the compatibility of Platonic metaphysics and Christian theology, still provided the parameters of Plato interpretation in the Stift in the 1790s.[66] In the early and mid-eighteenth century the Church of England enjoyed considerable prestige amongst continental Protestants and Cudworth's *True Intellectual System of the Universe* of 1678 was translated and commented on by Johann Lorenz von Mosheim (1694–1755) in 1733. Mosheim's critique of Cudworth's fervent Christian Neoplatonism fired further consideration of the issues, but the picture of Plato remained dominated by Patristic/Neoplatonic and/or Middle Platonic themes and ideas; even though the Neoplatonic interpretation of Plato was no longer dominant. Dialogues such as the *Timaeus* or *Philebus* that were of particular importance for the Church Fathers were at the centre of any consideration of Platonic philosophy in the Stift.

Nietzsche writes with his characteristic mixture of venom and insight:

The Protestant Minister is the Grandfather of German philosophy, Protestantism is its *peccatum originale*. The definition of Protestantism is the semi-paralysis of Christianity and reason. One only need say the word Tübinger Stift in order to grasp what German Philosophy is: a cunning and deceitful theology.[67]

The extraordinary regional differences in the German Empire in the late eighteenth century are deeply significant. Clerical families had an inordinately important role in the constitution and administration of Württemberg,[68] and Tübingen played an important role in their training. The university also had an exceptionally strong philological tradition. Its foundation lay in the south-west-German Renaissance, which was marked by the influence of Ficino, Erasmus, Reuchlin, and Melanchthon. Perhaps even more important, its philosophy faculty was largely constituted from and dominated by

---

[66] Franz, *Schellings Tübinger Platon-Studien*, pp. 99–149.
[67] 'Der protestantische Pfarrer ist Großvater der deutschen Philosophie, der Protestantismus selbst ihr *peccatum originale*. Definition des Protestantismus: die halbseitige Lähmung des Christentums und der Vernunft . . . Man hat nur das Wort 'Tübinger Stift' auszusprechen, um zu begreifen, was die deutsche Philosophie ist: eine hinterlistige Theologie.' F. Nietzsche, *Der Antichrist* in his *Werke* (Berlin: Fischer, 1967–77).
[68] J. E. Toews, *Hegelianism, the Path Toward Dialectical Humanism 1805–1841* (Cambridge University Press, 1980).

theologians. The Chancellor of the University was professor primarius of theology, and 90 per cent of the students of the philosophy faculty were young theologians. John Toews notes that 'Higher education in Württemberg was virtually synonymous with theological training. Theologians were an important segment of the intellectual elite throughout Germany, but in Württemberg the clergy completely dominated the intellectual and cultural life of the society.'[69] Hegel, Schelling and Hölderlin all read philosophy in the euphoric revolutionary spirit of the 1790s; but also in an intensely *theological* context.

A number of contemporaries noted similarities between the German Idealists and Neoplatonist metaphysics, and some modern scholars, notably Harald Holz and Werner Beierwaltes, have emphasised the structural affinities.[70] Yet there is very little evidence of Schelling's or Hegel's direct contact with Neoplatonic thought, and those phrases or ideas that appear prima facie as evidence for Neoplatonism probably came from Spinoza. Yet by considering the link between a *theologia Platonica* and the doctrine of the Trinity forged by Cudworth and discussed through Souverain and Mosheim up to the late eighteenth century, we can appreciate how many Neoplatonic ideas were transmitted through a discussion of Plato dominated by patristic interests.[71] Thus, for reasons that have become obscure for the modern reader in the wake of Schleiermacher, both Schelling and Hegel read Plato in the light of Neoplatonic and patristic tradition: as a metaphysician who was concerned with the nature of the absolute One, the creation of the cosmos, and the immortality of the soul. Both Hegel and Schelling see the *Timaeus*, *Philebus*, and *Parmenides* as the heart of Plato. Much of this vision of Plato was conveyed to the young theologians by controversy about the doctrine of the Trinity: Cudworth's attempt to explain the harmony – in spirit if not letter – between the *Trinitas Platonica* and the orthodox Christian Trinity, Mosheim's translation and critique of Cudworth's *True Intellectual System of the Universe*, and the Unitarian rejection of the entire Platonic legacy.

Schelling wrote a commentary on the *Timaeus* as a boy in the Stift;

[69] Toews, *Hegelianism*, p. 19.
[70] cf. Beierwaltes, *Platonismus und Idealismus*, pp. 100 ff. H. Holz, *Die Idee der Philosophie bei Schelling* (Munich: Alber, 1977), pp. 19–63.
[71] Michael J. B. Allen, 'Marsilio Ficino on Plato, the neoplatonists and the Christian doctrine of the Trinity', in *Renaissance Quarterly* 37 (1984), pp. 555–84.

he used some of these materials in his Platonic dialogue on the Renaissance Neoplatonist *Bruno*. In this dialogue Bruno exclaims in a discussion concerning the absolute unity of thought and being (*'die absolute Einheit des Denkens und Seyns'*):

> The pure Subject-Object however, that absolute knowledge of the absolute I, the form of all forms, is the Son born of the Absolute, co-eternal, not differing in substance, but one.[72]

The link between Plato as the metaphysician of unity or identity and the patristic speculation concerning the tri-une identity of the *principium* was perfectly intelligible for Schelling, who wanted to develop a philosophy of the *Absolute Ich*. For both Schelling and Hegel the Trinity is an essential link between philosophy and theology. They consider the essence of Christianity to be reconciliation (*Versöhnung*), and the dogma of the essential and economic tri-unity as the expression of the reconciliation of the finite and infinite. In a sense Hegel's entire philosophy is Trinitarian; it is a reflection upon absolute spirit as a triadic unity.[73] Schelling in his Munich Lectures of 1827-8 made a point of criticising Schleiermacher's relative neglect of the doctrine of the Trinity.[74] R.W. Emerson remarked:

> The Germans believe in the necessary Trinity of God – The Infinite; the finite, & the passage from Inf. into Fin.; or the Creation. It is typified in the act of thinking. Whilst we contemplate we are infinite; the thought we express is partial & finite; the expression is the third part & is equivalent to the act of Creation. Unity says Schelling is barren.[75]

Hegel believes that the philology of Schleiermacher is 'quite irrelevant for philosophy and belongs to the excessively critical spirit of the age'.[76] The dialogue form is rather a weakness of Plato: 'the

---

[72] 'Das reine Subjekt-Objekt aber, jenes absolute Erkennen das absolute Ich, die Form aller Formen, ist der dem Absoluten eingeborne Sohn, gleich ewig mit ihm, nicht verschieden von seinem Wesen, sondern eins.' Schelling, *Schriften von 1801–1804* (Stuttgart: 1859–60, reprinted Darmstadt Wissenschaftliche Buchgesellschaft. 1988), p. 223. cf. M Vater, *Bruno*, p. 221.

[73] See W. Beierwaltes, *Identität und Differenz* (Frankfurt am Main: Klostermann, 1985). See my article 'Was Schleiermacher a Christian Platonist?', *Dionysius* 17 (1999), pp. 61–77.

[74] F. W. J. von Schelling, *System der Weltalter. Münchener Vorlesung 1827–28*, edited by S. Pcetz from lecture notes by Ernst von Lasaulx (Frankfurt am Main; Klostermann 1990), pp. 189–90.

[75] Quoted by J. L. Esposito, *Schelling's Idealism and Philosophy of Nature* (Lewisburg: Bucknell, 1977), p. 195.

[76] 'ist für die Philosophie ganz überflüssig und gehört der Hyperkritik unserer Zeit an'. G. W. F. Hegel, *Werke*, (Frankfurt am Main: Suhrkamp, 1971), vol. xix. p. 20.

Spirit does not appear [in Plato] in the form which we require. Plato's philosophical training was not sufficiently developed.'[77] Hegel is particularly scathing about Schleiermacher's interpretation of Plato: 'that which it calls philosophy and puts into Plato's mouth, betrays an utter ignorance of the nature of speculative thought, i.e. the contemplation of the Idea'.[78] Let us try to pursue what Hegel means here by 'the contemplation of the Idea'. Hegel believed that the genius of Plato lay in his inchoate dialectic; particularly *Parmenides*, 'the masterpiece of Platonic dialectic'. *Parmenides* was the eminent source of Plato's theology for Proclus, and the source of much Christian Platonic Trinitarian speculation.[79] It is clearly no accident that the evidently metaphysical Plato of the Christian Neoplatonic tradition revered by those two eccentric modern Neoplatonists Hegel and Schelling, the Plato who conjured over identity and difference in the *Sophist*, and the Divine triad in the *Parmenides* and *Timaeus*, was criticised by Schleiermacher. Nor is it fortuitous that Schleiermacher replaced the 'Attic Moses' with the much less speculative and more, as it were, Romantic Plato, one who believed that dialogue was the only proper way of communicating philosophical truth. Schleiermacher was the theologian who believed that 'we have no formula for the being of God in itself as distinct from the being of God in the world'.[80] Schleiermacher's criticism of the arcane (Neoplatonic) Plato was linked to his rejection of the essential Trinity and the Logos speculation of the Alexandrines and Hegelians alike.

It is of particular significance that the early Schelling commentary was on the *Timaeus*: one of those few texts that were a perpetual source of Platonic ideas within Christian theology from the Fathers through the School of Chartres up to the modern period, and which fired the sort of Trinitarian and cosmological speculation so congenial to the Idealists.[81] Those characteristically (and perennially)

---

[77] 'der Geist tritt aber nicht in der bestimmten Form hervor, die wir fordern. Die philosophische Bildung Platos war dazu noch nicht reif.' Hegel, *Werke*, vol. xix. p. 27.

[78] 'wo dasjenige, was sich Philosophie nennt und wohl den Plato immer im Munde führt, und auch keine Ahnung von dem hat, was die Natur des spekulativen Denkens, der Betrachtung der Idee, ist.' G. W. F. Hegel, *Sämmtliche Werke*, ed. H. Glockner, 26 vols (Stuttgart: Fromann Holzboog, 1968), vol. xx. p. 27.

[79] See Beierwaltes, 'Das seiende Eine' in *Denken des Einen*, pp. 201 ff.

[80] F. D. E. Schleiermacher, *Der christliche Glaube nach den Grundsäzen der evangelische Kirche*, edited by M. Redeker (Berlin: de Gruyter, 1984), §172 1, vol. ii. p. 470.

[81] R. Klibanski, *The Continuity of the Platonic Tradition during the Middle Ages* (London: Warburg, 1939); P. O. Kristeller, 'Renaissance Platonism' in his book *Renaissance Thought and its Sources*,

Schellingian problems of the relation of the absolute to the physical cosmos, the relation of myth to rational reflection, and an organic teleological vision of nature can now be seen to be rooted in the adolescent Schelling's reception and interpretation of Plato; especially as mediated through the theological concerns of Tübingen humanism. In the *Timaeus* the demiurge creates the world-spirit in accordance with the ideas, and there are three elements in the dialogue: an architect, ideas, and spirit. Furthermore, in Plato's *Epistles* there is a triad that is spoken of as three Gods – all of which attracted the interest of Justin Martyr and Clement of Alexandria.[82] Interestingly – despite his Herculean labours – Schleiermacher did not translate the *Timaeus*.[83] The omission is perhaps highly significant.

Schleiermacher sees Plato as an artist rather than as a prophetic theologian; as a conscious writer of dialogues and not an arcane mystagogue. Furthermore, Schleiermacher sees Plato's dialogues as the expression of a certain metaphysical agnosticism. Hegel's attempt to reconcile reason with religion is based upon the same foundation as Schelling's. The modern reader finds the leap from Plato to Hegel's *Wissenschaft* des 'göttlichen Begriffs' and 'des göttlichen Erkennens' via the *Trinitas Platonica* archaic and implausible; but this rests both upon Schleiermacher's massive philological labours and upon his rejection of Cudworth's view of Plato as forerunner of the Christian Trinity.

PALEY, LOCKE AND SOCIANIANISM

What relation does this revival of the Platonic Trinity bear, we may ask, to Coleridge's polemic throughout *Aids to Reflection* against William Paley (1743–1805)? Coleridge himself writes:

I have, I am aware, in this present work, furnished occasion for a charge of having expressed myself with slight and irreverence of celebrated Names, especially of the late Dr Paley . . . I believe myself bound in conscience to throw the whole force of my intellect in the way of this triumphal Car, on which the tutelary Genius of modern Idolatry is borne, even at the risk of being crushed under the wheels. (*Aids*, p. 408)

    edited by M. Mooney (New York and Guildford: Columbia University Press, 1979), pp. 50–65.

[82] C. Bigg, *The Christian Platonists of Alexandria* (Oxford: Clarendon, 1886), pp. 248–9.

[83] cf. Bubner, *Innovationen des Idealismus*, p. 21.

Coleridge's contemporaries were taken aback by the vehemence of his criticism of Paley, and it is at first difficult for the modern reader to follow the point of Coleridge's invective. Firstly, Paley's *Moral and Political Philosophy* and his *Evidences of Christianity* were very successful; in his lifetime there were fifteen editions. Secondly, Paley was a highly esteemed defender of Christian theology against the learned despisers of Christianity amongst the figures of the British Enlightenment. Paley's *Moral and Political Philosophy* was introduced in 1787 into the Cambridge syllabus; it remained significant until 1857, two years prior to Darwin's *Origin of Species*, when it disappeared from the syllabus. The *Evidences of Christianity* was prescribed in 1822 and was the subject matter of a compulsory examination for all undergraduates in their second year. All Cambridge students of the nineteenth century including Charles Darwin and many in the early part of the twentieth century knew Paley's *Evidences* as a textbook.

The mature Coleridge believed that the decline in English thought from 1688 coincided with the decline in Trinitarian theology and Platonic metaphysics and the increasing influence of John Locke's thought. In order to explain this prima-facie odd combination of dogmatic theology and empiricist epistemology, it is necessary to recognise the role of John Locke (1632–1704) in the development of Socinianism in England. The modern English reader tends to think of Locke as the philosopher: his attack on innate ideas, his theory of abstraction, and perhaps his contractual theory of society. Locke's theological opinions are largely ignored despite their massive influence upon the eighteenth century. When a writer such as Coleridge speaks of the lamentable influence of Locke upon the English mind he probably means Locke's theological and metaphysical opinions as well as his theory of knowledge and his social theories. Locke spent time in Holland and was well acquainted with Socinian literature. Indeed, Coleridge takes Locke's theology to be fundamentally Socinian.[84] In this Coleridge followed Leibniz's aversion towards the empiricism of the Socinians as 'a certain attenuated philosophy in which scarcely anything outstanding and sublime survives, God himself is almost reduced to the status of creatures and our mind degenerates into the nature of matter . . . And much more generous

---

[84] H. J. McLachlan, *Socinianism in Seventeenth-Century England* (Oxford: Clarendon, 1951), pp. 326–30 and J. Harrison and P. Laslett, *The Library of John Locke* (Oxford: Clarendon, 1965).

seem to me the opinions of Pythagoras and Plato who recognised that souls are incorporeal and immortal by their own nature, and that there is a supreme mind governing all things with great wisdom.'[85] Leibniz thought that Locke's theology was partly Socinian and contrasted Locke unfavourably with Plato because Locke 'minimises too much the generous philosophy of the Platonists'.[86]

Coleridge believed that the opinions of Gassendi and Hobbes spread during the 'licentious and abominable days of Charles II' and that the influence and authority of John Locke's philosophy contributed to the increasing acceptance of the idea that rational knowledge derived from sense experience (CL II p. 701). There is much insight in Coleridge's view – quite apart from the obvious fact of the prestige and influence of the Royal Society in England post-1688 (PL p. 381).

Coleridge's Christian Platonism explains both why he thinks of ideas in (his own) Trinitarian terms of the 'Pythagorean TETRACTYS' (*Aids*, p. 181 ff) and why he associates the ideas with 'spiritual platonic old England' (*Aids*, p. 182). Furthermore, it explains his horror of the view that an IDEA is 'an impression on the Senses' a 'definite Conception' or an 'abstract Notion'. As such it is a 'strangely misused word' (*Aids*, p. 179). Coleridge sees this misuse of the word 'idea' as rooted in the Lockean view of an idea as a mental image rather than as a living power, as rooted in human abstractions rather than in the creative pleroma of the tri-une Godhead. The Platonic ideas are, however, for Coleridge, not abstract entities. This is the mistake of those who employ the 'false antithesis between *real* and *ideal*' (*Aids*, p. 178).

Coleridge was convinced that the shift in English thought from the Christian Platonic view of the idea as a divine power to the Lockean view of an idea as a mental image meant that the traditional riches of Christian philosophical speculation about the nature of spirit and concept of God became increasingly unintelligible, and were duly replaced by the rational supernaturalistic apologetics on the common-sense anti-metaphysical Lockean model of miracles and evidences of Christianity.

---

[85] Quoted by Nicholas Jolley, 'Leibniz on Locke and Socinianism', in *Journal of the History of Ideas* 39 (1978), p. 235.

[86] Quoted by Jolley, ibid. It is of interest that Henry More thought that the metaphysics of Socinianism was too Aristotelian. cf. Luisa Simonutti, 'Reason and toleration' in *Henry More 1614–1687: Tercentenary Studies*, edited by Sarah Hutton with a biography and bibliography by R. Crocker (Dordrecht and Boston: Kluwer, 1990), pp. 201–218, p. 205.

The collapse of the Platonic view of spirit led to the neglect and misunderstanding of the distinctively Christian concept of God as tri-une, and the abeyance of a spiritual theology. Paley represents, for Coleridge, the hegemony of a Lockean-Socinian-empiricist tradition within the Church of England. Coleridge regarded the Lockean theology of Paley as a symptom of the decline of the national Church. The Platonism of Spenser or Cudworth was eroded and replaced after the Glorious Revolution of 1688 with the Socinian-empiricism of Locke and Paley. The effect of the corpuscular philosophy, Coleridge insists in the conclusion of *Aids to Reflection*, 'has been most injurious to the best interests of our Universities, to our incomparably constituted Church, and even to our National Character' (*Aids*, p. 407). Coleridge mentions *On the Constitution of the Church and State* and then launches into an invective against Paley. The popular success of Socinianism – in its diluted respectable form exemplified by Paley – is simply the product of the tacit acceptance of a philosophy incompatible with Christian tenets.

Coleridge judged Locke by the fruits which he bore, which had been much more evident in eighteenth-century Cambridge than Oxford: through writers such as Hartley and Paley. There is an amusing account of Paley's lecturing that is probably written by the Unitarian of Jesus College, William Frend. Paley is said to have used 'a dirty, cover torn ragged Locke' expounding points of Locke's philosophy of mind. In the Greek New Testament class there were 'no rigmarole stories about the Trinity' and the Thirty-nine Articles that were a source of controversy in Cambridge of the day. Nor were there disputes between Calvinists and Arminians like those that had dominated the seventeenth century. Paley used Locke's *The Reasonableness of Christianity* and Locke's comments on the Epistles, a theology based upon the belief 'that we should listen to God, not to man; that we should exert our faculties in understanding the language of holy men of old; that we should free ourselves, as much as possible, from all prejudices of birth, education and country; and we should not call any our master in religion but Jesus Christ'.[87]

Paley was suspected of Socinianism and of 'maintaining a very marked suspicious reserve on some points, more especially on the

---

[87] Quoted by M. L. Clarke, *Paley, Evidences for the Man* (London: SPCK, 1974), p. 16.

important issue of our Saviour's divinity'.[88] He was wary of dogmas and insists that 'The truth of Christianity depends upon its leading facts and upon them alone' (*Evidences*, p. 416). As a pupil of Locke Paley was very much a conventional Englishman of the eighteenth century, and because of the Socinian roots of Locke's theology Paley seems not just an empiricist but doctrinally close to Unitarianism. His doctrinal minimalism may have been part of a late eighteenth-century attempt to revive the older comprehensiveness of the Church of England, rather than the expression of any Socinian tendencies. Notwithstanding the plausibility of such a view of Paley's works, he was associated with Socinian-Unitarian radicals like Jebb and Frend who agitated to abolish the subscription to the Trinitarian Thirty-nine Articles of the Church of England. Paley's pupil Frend was expelled from the University in 1793, and *Moral and Political Philosophy* includes a chapter on subscription to the Thirty-nine Articles (pp. 134–5) which he defended. Thus Paley seemed an ambivalent – even hypocritical – figure. The Unitarian scholar Wakefield wrote: 'I blush for this degradation of my species . . . when I see that Author stain the pages of his incomparable book with such a shuffling chapter.'[89] Coleridge may have been unfair on Paley to accuse him of closet Socinianism, but the view of Paley as unorthodox on the Trinity was widely held in the period from 1809 to 1825, and contributed to the decline in the prestige of his work.[90]

PRIESTLEY, UNITARIANISM AND PLATONIC IDEALISM

How did Coleridge become embroiled in this debate? His father was a priest of the Church of England and incumbent of the imposing parish church of Ottery St Mary; Coleridge attended Christ's Hospital in London – a school designed for the sons of needy clergy. In the *Biographia Literaria* he describes how as a boy he particularly relished conversations with clergymen on theological topics (*BL* i. 16). At Cambridge it was necessary to subscribe to the Thirty-nine Articles in order to graduate and Oxford demanded Under-graduate subscription to the Thirty-nine Articles and communion once a term. It was only in 1854 in Oxford and 1856 in Cambridge that Dissenters could take degrees, and in 1871 that religious tests

---

[88] Ibid., p. 112; Paley, *Evidences of Christianity*, p. 146.   [89] Ibid., p. 22.
[90] cf. G. A. Cole, 'Doctrine, dissent and the decline of Paley's reputation 1805–1825', in *Enlightenment and Dissent* 6 (1987), pp. 19–30.

(apart from for those studying divinity) were abolished for academic degrees and for lay academic office.

The polemic of the Romantics apart, the historiography of the eighteenth century has generally stressed the liberal and rationalist nature of Augustan England in contrast to the ancien régime of continental Europe. The Oxford historian Jonathan Clark has recently attacked this 'Whig' view of the eighteenth century on the grounds that it generally overlooks the extent to which a *Trinitarian* orthodoxy bound to the established church was at least a central if not the dominant ideology of the age. The church was the prime source of values in Georgian England and functioned as the sanction of the existing political and social order.[91] Clark's argument is that England was, just like its continental neighbours, a confessional state until the Reform Act of 1832. The force of this argument as a whole need not detain us; however, we may well reflect upon the undoubted importance of the doctrine of the Trinity for everyday life in eighteenth- and early nineteenth-century England, a fact that is hard to appreciate in contemporary secular Britain.

One marginal product of Reformation theology was a strong rejection of the doctrine of the Trinity. This form of anti-Trinitarianism was Socinianism.[92] The Socinian movement is a product of the strongly nominalistic radical wing of the Reformation that goes back to the theology of the Italian Faustus Socinus (1539–1604). Since Socinianism was repressed as an institutional movement in Poland during the Counter-Reformation we cannot trace a direct line of influence. It became absorbed into the early Enlightenment. 'Unitarianism' usually denotes an eighteenth-century institutional development in England and America that has its intellectual roots in the radical Protestantism of Socinianism. Unitarianism embraced differences in its theological content and emphasis but was united in its opposition to the dogmas of the Trinity.[93] We will speak of the theological spirit of 'Socinianism'

[91] Jonathan C. D. Clark, *English Society 1688–1832: Ideology, Social Structure and Political Practice during the Ancien Régime* (Cambridge University Press, 1986).

[92] Gustav Adolf Benrath, 'Der Antitrinitarismus' in *Handbuch der Dogmen und Theologiegeschichte* (Göttingen: Vandenhoeck, 1984), vol. iii. pp. 49–66. Yet Socinianism had wider influence, on English deism, Dutch Arminianism in the seventeenth century, and on critical biblical scholarship in Germany of the eighteenth century. A useful collection of essays is *Socinianism and its Role in the Culture of the sixteenth to the seventeenth Centuries*, edited by L. Szczucki and others (Warsaw and Lodz: Polish Academy of Sciences Institutes of Philosophy and Sociology, 1983).

[93] cf. J. E. Carpenter, 'Unitarianism' in *Religion and Ethics*, vol. xii. pp. 519–27.

(following Coleridge) and eighteenth-century religious movements led by figures such as Priestley as 'Unitarianism'.[94]

During and after the reign of Elizabeth I radical members of the Church of England were convinced that the Reformation was far too mild. In the seventeenth century there were considerable secessions from the established church. With the draconian Act of Uniformity of 1662 a great number of clerics left the Church of England.[95] These became the Dissenters, and their interaction with the established church became a very significant factor in English life. With the Glorious Revolution of 1688 they were formally rehabilitated and given the right to exist under the Toleration Act of 1689. This toleration was not extended to Anti Trinitarians and it was only in 1813 that the Anti-Trinitarian laws were repealed.[96]

The doctrine of the Trinity is expressed in the *first* of the Thirty-nine Articles of the Church of England:

There is but one living and true God, everlasting, without body, parts, or passions; of infinite power, wisdom and goodness; the Maker and Preserver of all things both visible and invisible. And in the unity of this Godhead there be three Persons, of one substance, power and eternity: the Father, the Son, and the Holy Ghost.[97]

God here is a *spiritual* being without body or passions who is the causal source and sustainer of reality and is *tri-une*.

This controversy between the established church and dissenting Protestantism was an excellent basis for the development of Unitarianism as an institutional force. Although the majority of the Dissenters were orthodox in their tenets, the lack of dogmatic creeds among Protestant dissent meant that Anti-Trinitarianism was able to flourish in their ranks. Further, because the doctrine of the Trinity is a development of the scriptural position rather than a simple exposition of the Bible, it was easy for the Unitarian Dissenters to claim the genuine biblical and thus Protestant position to be that of Anti-Trinitarianism.

There is a further important point here. Whereas on the continent

---

[94] *Unitarius* is the word used since the sixteenth century in Transylvania for the ecclesiastical movement and Socinianism for the ideas which have their roots in the Italian Faustus Socinus.

[95] *From Uniformity to Unity 1662–1962*, edited by G. F. Nuttall and Owen Chadwick (London: SPCK, 1962).

[96] E. M. Wilbur, *A History of Unitarianism in Transylvania, England and America* (Cambridge, Mass.: Harvard University Press, 1952).

[97] *Book of Common Prayer.*

theological conflict was between Protestant and Catholic – or Calvinist and Lutheran – the struggle in England was between a Reformed church with strong elements of the older Catholic heritage and the dissenting party which existed without confessional dogmas. Whereas Socinianism in Europe lacked a confessional basis after the repression in Poland and was a movement of *theological* rather than *ecclesiastical* importance, in England the Dissenters were a potent social force and, through the channels of dissent, Socinianism was able to exert an increasingly powerful influence.

The identification of the Platonic νοῦς with the λόγος of the Johannine Prologue in the theology of men like Cudworth or Berkeley was an obvious source of polemic. The Trinity seemed the instance of a wilful Hellenising of the evidently 'unitarian' biblical gospel. This is expressed particularly powerfully by Joseph Priestley (1733–1804), one of the most influential English thinkers of the late eighteenth century and a prominent Unitarian.[98] Priestley was a convinced empiricist who believed that the doctrine of the Trinity was the product of Platonic corruptions. Priestley attempted to establish a connection between the corruptions of Christian doctrine and speculative metaphysics. The close link between Trinitarian theology and philosophy was exploited by Lessing, Schelling, and Hegel, but the situation in Coleridge's England was quite different. Firstly, the doctrines of the *Trinity* and the *Atonement* were not the subjects of confessional theological debates in Germany as they were in England. Notwithstanding their differences concerning justification, sacraments, the saints, etc., Roman Catholic, Lutheran, and Reformed churches all accepted the doctrines of the Trinity and the Atonement. These doctrines constituted, as it were, common ground between Roman Catholics and Protestants in continental Europe. In England Roman Catholicism played an insignificant role before the Catholic Emancipation Act (1829), and the very theological debate was between the established church and dissenting Protestantism. Given the rise of Unitarianism amongst the ranks of dissent, the discussion rested upon the issue of the Trinity. The established church could not afford to ignore the claims of a man like Priestley who spoke not as a cultured despiser of religion but as a fervent and sincere Christian.

Joseph Priestley is the subject of vigorous attack in *Aids to*

---

[98] Coleridge writes: 'Priestley was the author of the modern Unitarianism.' *TT,* i. 448.

Reflection. Priestley was an adherent of David Hartley, the Lockean philosopher of Jesus College, after whom Coleridge christened his first born.[99] Coleridge refers to Priestley as 'a good and benevolent man, as sincere in his love, as he was intrepid and indefatigable in his pursuit, of Truth' (*Aids*, p. 210), but 'Unitarianism is not Christianity' (*Aids*, p. 211) and 'evidences of Priestley' are incompatible with Paul's teaching (*Aids*, pp. 356–8) and a concept of God that effectively reduces the deity to 'a mere Anima Mundi' (*Aids*, p. 403). He was something of a Renaissance man: primarily a philosopher and theologian, he was a successful and respected scientist. He isolated oxygen (he called it dephlogisticated air), was a fellow of the Royal Society, and was familiar with men of the stature of Benjamin Franklin, Erasmus Darwin, Lavoisier, and Turgot. Priestley is now largely remembered as a natural scientist, but he saw his own work as primarily theological and philosophical.[100] It is an indication of his stature in late eighteenth-century Europe that Kant refers to him in his *Prolegomena*, Schelling discusses his scientific work, and Jeremy Bentham discovered the phrase 'the greatest happiness of the greatest number' in Priestley's work.[101]

Priestley admired Locke, Newton, and Hartley, and heartily opposed the religious scepticism of Voltaire and Hume. (Priestley suggests that most unbelievers not only have studied the object of their unbelief inadequately, but are men of profligate character.) Priestley's writing is ardently Christian and rather conservative in the sense that he wishes to reclaim primitive Christianity in opposition to its corruptions. Unitarianism was, he claims, the general opinion of the Christian church until the Council of Nicaea.[102] The growth of Trinitarian doctrine was the result of dabbling in Platonism and Gnosticism on the part of the Church Fathers, and their consequent development of a spiritual philosophy that deni-

---

[99] See Priestley, *Theological and Miscellaneous Works*, edited by John Towill Rutt (London: George Smallfield, 1817–31), vol. iii. p. 10.

[100] Basil Willey, *The Eighteenth Century Background: Studies on the Idea of Nature in the Thought of the Period* (London: Chatto and Windus, 1940), pp. 168–204.

[101] I. Kant, *Prolegomena to any Future Metaphysics*, edited by Beryl Logan (London: Routledge, 1996), p. 32, F. W. J. von Schelling, *Ideas for a Philosophy of Nature, as an Introduction to the Study of that Science*, translated by E. E. Harris and P. Heath (Cambridge University Press, 1988), pp. 110–11 and J. S. Mill and J. Bentham, *Utilitarianism and other Essays*, edited by A. Ryan (London: Penguin, 1979), p. 7.

[102] Jonathan Z. Smith, *Drudgery Divine, on the Comparison of Early Christianities and the Religions of Late Antiquity* (University of London Press, 1990), pp. 1–35.

grated the material world and developed a doctrine of the immateriality of the soul. This belief in the immateriality of the soul is, for Priestley, the root of almost every corruption of Christianity. This contagion led to the doctrine of the divine ideas. This led to the doctrine of the Logos as a second God and thus to the Trinity, as well as to a mysticism that pre-supposes an exaltation and divinisation of the mind: the idea of the divinity of the Son was first urged by men who were heathen philosophers and in particular by those who had admired Plato and believed in the doctrine of a second God or *nous*. As a result of these dark and mysterious Platonic beliefs, the doctrine of the divinity of the Son arose in the fourth century and replaced the previous Unitarianism of the church. Priestley insists that a little reflection shows that such a late development could not be genuinely Christian doctrine: that which became orthodox Christian doctrine after Nicaea was deeply influenced by Gnosticism but the real source was Plato.[103] Priestley sees the Platonic conception of intelligible forms smuggled into the historical God of Scripture. The development of the doctrine of the Trinity is, he claims, primarily an erroneous reflection upon the nature of the supreme mind. In this idealism Priestley sees the conception of mind as essentially immaterial and matter as evil as the foundation for the patristic view of redemption as *participation*. Redemption for the Platonic Fathers is primarily participation in the life of the spirit, νοῦς or λόγος. The corruptions of Christianity are based upon the development of a *spiritual* philosophy within the church which denigrates the material realm and envisages the founder of the Christian religion as the incarnation of the transcendent divine spirit which redeems men as spirit. Priestley believes that the doctrines of the Incarnation and the Atonement are metaphysical accretions and corruptions of a faith that originated in the ethical teaching and the miracles of Jesus of Nazareth.

The manifest absurdities of the Platonic philosophy were readily accepted as Christian orthodoxy, Priestley claimed, because the obscurities of this school flattered the philosophical ambitions of those theologians who were eager to give Christianity a philosophical cloak. The spirit of Stoicism was too rigorous, and Aristotelianism and Epicureanism were too worldly. The very lack of exactitude of the Neoplatonists together with the air of mystery and

---

[103] J. Priestley, *Works*, vol. vi. p. 152.

obscurity that pervades their writing meant that they were congenial company for the Church Fathers. (The scholastics are daylight in comparison, exclaims Priestley!) The Church Fathers were characterised, Priestley insists, by an overweening pride in their own learning and a profound contempt for the vulgar.[104]

Since the establishment of modern science, Priestley argues, it has become manifestly clear that these metaphysical accretions are both unscriptural and without scientific warrant. The failure of subsequent churchmen to recognise the Neoplatonic corruptions of Christianity means that the Christian religion is perpetually subject to the ridicule of atheists and agnostics. Consequently a person who is both a good Christian and a good philosopher will reject the false philosophy of the Fathers as corruption of the pristine faith.

For all Priestley's ridicule of the spiritualist metaphysics of Neoplatonism, he clearly sees this philosophy as of great import for the history of western thought, and a force that must be refuted by thinking men. The fact that Coleridge should identify a speculative idealistic metaphysics with the claims of orthodox Christian belief is readily comprehensible within the context of Priestley's attack upon the corruptions of Christianity. Coleridge denies Priestley's claim that the Idealistic metaphysics presents a corruption of the Christian faith. Yet he is in basic agreement with much of Priestley's diagnosis. For Coleridge, Christianity and an Idealist metaphysics stand or fall together. He believes that bad philosophy, i.e. empiricism, will lead to Socinianism or an outright hostility towards Christian tenets. Priestley exclaims:

Austin, speaking of the principles of *Plato, says*, that 'by changing a few words and sentences, the Platonists would have become Christians, as many of those of later times have done' . . . I am ready enough to join these Christian writers in their admiration of many things in the philosophy of *Plato* . . . But, unhappily, these admirers of Plato carried their admiration, much too far; and as we have seen, in the case of *Justin* and *Austin*, were more particularly struck with that very part of this system, namely, that concerning the doctrine of *ideas*, and the Divine intellect, *nous* or *logos*, in which the greatest darkness and absurdity belonging to it is found.[105]

Priestley's challenge that the doctrine of the Trinity sprang from the absurdity and mystery of *Platonism* forged for Coleridge the link

---

[104] Priestley, *Works*, vol. vi. p. 261.
[105] Priestley, *Works*, vol. vi. pp. 199 f.

between the speculative Trinity and Platonism and the essential antagonism of both towards materialism and empiricism.

Priestley is thus enormously significant because he associates *Empiricism* in philosophy with *Unitarianism* in religion. By contrast Platonism, that is, *Idealism* in philosophy, is linked with *Trinitarianism* in religion. Coleridge asserts that his Platonism led him back to the Trinitarian faith, and he was almost certainly negatively influenced by Priestley. Furthermore, the sheer mass of information and the lucidity of Priestley's doctrinal history are almost equally significant; Priestley attempts to show how Christian doctrine developed under the influence of the prevailing speculative metaphysics of late antiquity, and thereby presents in the most vivid and strident manner the Platonic tenets in much patristic thought:

> Having seen this strange confusion of ideas respecting the Divine nature, its operations and influences, we shall the less wonder at the mysticism of these Platonists with respect to the exaltation of the mind of man by a supposed union with the Divine nature, so as to be *supported* and *nourished* by it . . . as Jamblichus says 'The soul is perfected by the *nous*'.[106]

Priestley believes that the pristine Unitarian faith consists of 'evidences' of Christianity. The divine authority of the man Jesus was attested by the empirical evidence of his miracles that no man could have performed without God's 'presence and concurrence'.[107] The centre of the Christian religion is the eschatological conviction that Jesus Christ will, at a given time, resurrect all the dead to a future life, and judge men according to their deeds. Priestley's philosophy of religion is both biblical and empirical; his creed combines candidly and sincerely a resolute empiricism with a fiercely scriptural form of nonconformist Protestantism. Priestley envisages miracles as providing empirical evidence that Jesus of Nazareth is the Messiah of men. Such infringements are not only compatible with but presuppose a causally determined universe: the mechanics of Newton present the laws of what is habitually the case and the biblical story describes the unique infringements of them. The strictness of the former highlights the religious and metaphysical significance of the latter: if God can infringe the laws of the universe for his adopted Son, it is equally plausible to believe that God can raise believers in his Son to eternal life. This constitutes for Priestley

---

[106] Priestley, *Works*, vol. vi. p. 180.
[107] Priestley, *Works*, vol. ii. p. 228.

a theology without recourse to obscure, impious, and unscriptural speculations about the immortality of the soul.

The conflict between the rational Dissenters such as Priestley and the Georgian church seemed to compromise Paley, who had so many strong links with Socinian circles. A formative influence on Coleridge in his Unitarian days was William Frend (1757–1841). Frend was a fellow of Coleridge's college, Jesus, and a pupil of Paley. Frend resigned his living and tried to help the abolition of subscription to the Thirty-nine Articles in his 'Thoughts on Subscription' of 1788, upon which he was deprived of his fellowship at Jesus. His next publication was 'An address to the Inhabitants of Cambridge and its neighbourhood, exhorting them to turn from the false worship of Three persons, to the worship of the One True God' where he tries to show the unscriptural and irrational nature of the doctrine of the Trinity.[108] Coleridge was at Cambridge at a time when Paley's pupils were openly questioning the doctrine of the Trinity. In 1791 Priestley's house, laboratory, and library were ransacked by a mob in the midst of the anti-French hysteria, and Priestley emigrated to America. As is well known, Coleridge had plans to settle in the same part of America in the wake of Priestley's exile. The issue of the doctrine of the Trinity and its relation to both philosophy and the status of the established church was a central theme of Coleridge's early life and thought. I believe we can only understand the vehemence with which Coleridge attacks Unitarianism and Socininism in *Aids to Reflection* if we consider these seminal influences of Coleridge's youth.

Paley's pupil Caesar Morgan produced an attack upon the 'Platonic Trinity'. This was not just a philological exercise but a critique of the Platonic tradition of Cudworth and Berkeley that revered the *Plato Christianus*.[109] Caesar Morgan was a pupil at William Paley's college, Christ's Cambridge, was elected to a fellowship there in 1775, and left in 1776 – the same year in which Paley left. In 1795 Morgan published his essay *An Investigation of the Trinity of Plato and Philo Judaeus and of the Effects which an Attachment to their Writings had upon the Principles and Reasonings of the Fathers of the Christian Church*. Morgan argues in this work that the Fathers of the

---

[108] Frida Knight, *University Rebel: the Life of William Frend 1757–1841* (London: Gollancz, 1971).
[109] Caesar Morgan, *An Investigation of the Trinity of Plato and of Philo Judaeus, and of the Effects which an Attachment to their Writings had upon the Principles and Reasonings of the Fathers of the Christian Church* (Cambridge University Press, 1853).

Church had misapprehended the doctrines of Plato and erroneously thought both Plato and Philo to have had some doctrine of the Trinity.[110] The book is less polemical than Priestley's, but the tendency of Morgan's thought is the same. He wishes to attack the view of Cudworth that the metaphysical opinions of the Platonists were conducive to and point towards the Christian doctrine of the Trinity. The Socinian interest in such scholarly work is evident. A major element of Trinitarian apologetic in the seventeenth century was the essential harmony between the classical pagans and the doctrine of the Trinity. Pointing to the weakness of this harmony theory, Morgan is attacking a major apologetic strategy for the defence of the dogma; the reasoning of the Church Fathers is as obscure for Morgan as it is for Gibbon.

It is in the light of criticism of the 'obscurities' of the 'Platonic Trinity' that we should try to understand the single most important development in Coleridge's mind: *the move from Unitarianism to Trinitarian theology and metaphysics*. Coleridge writes:

The value of these writers, however, especially of Plato, in predisposing the mind to the reception of the Christian Faith, St Augustine himself elsewhere asserts on his own experience. (*Marg.* iii. 619.)

Coleridge's youth – 1780s and 1790s – was a period of renewed enthusiasm for Greeks and Platonism which was formative for the general development of British Romanticism.[111] The efforts of Thomas Taylor meant that much Neoplatonist material was translated into English much earlier than first German translations;[112] however, the real significance of Neoplatonism lies in the debates based upon the critiques of Pétau, Soverain, and Priestley, which identified Platonic-idealising metaphysical tendencies as the root of the errors of Trinitarian theology.

---

[110] 'The writings of Philo Judaeus furnished the Fathers of the Christian Church with the fatal means of deceiving themelves and others. The figurative language in which that author delivered himself concerning the Logos, whenever he meant by it either the divine intellect, its internal operation, the ideal object of its contemplation, or the external expression of it, led them to imagine that he attributed to it a real and essential personality . . . Hence was devised the metaphysical argument for the eternity of the second person of the Trinity, which was built upon this plain and incontrovertible maxim, that God could never have been destitute of reason. Hence the second person is called by Athanasius substantial *Logos* and substantial Wisdom.' Morgan, *Trinity of Plato*, p. 158.

[111] K. Raine, 'Thomas Taylor, Plato and the English Romantic movement', in *British Journal of Aesthetics* (1967), pp. 99–123 and R. Jenkins, *The Victorians and Ancient Greece* (Oxford: Blackwell, 1981).

[112] Beierwaltes, *Platonismus und Idealismus*, pp. 83 ff.

IDENTITY AND DIFFERENCE: HENOLOGY OR ONTOLOGY?

Priestley envisaged his philosophy of religion as both Newtonian and biblical and saw himself as a genuine heir of Locke. Coleridge speaks of being encouraged by the authority of our genuine divines and philosophers before the revolution to discriminate between Reason and Understanding, as opposed to

Hume, Priestley, and the French fatalists or necessitarians; some of whom had perverted metaphysical reasonings to the denial of the mysteries and indeed of all the peculiar doctrines of christianity . . . I would request such men to consider . . . that true metaphysics are nothing else but true divinity, and that in fact the writers, who have given them just such offence, were sophists, who had taken advantage of the general neglect into which the science of logic has unhappily fallen, rather than metaphysicians, a name indeed which those writers were the first to explode as unmeaning. Secondly, I would remind them, that as long as there are men in the world to whom the Γνῶθι σεαυτόν is an instinct and a command from their own nature, so long will there be metaphysicians and metaphysical speculations; that false metaphysics can effectively be counteracted by true metaphysics alone'. (*BL* i. 291)

'Γνῶθι σεαυτόν' or 'Know Thyself' is a sign of Platonism, but the topic of self-consciousness is also the central topic of German Idealism.[113] We shall try to explore what Coleridge means by 'true metaphysics' and how this relates to the topic of 'self-knowledge'. One of the abiding problems of ancient Greek metaphysics was that of the relations of identity and difference and the nature of the ἀρχή. Although many scholars have argued that the Nicaean definition of the relation of the Father to the Son as ὁμοούσιος constituted a rejection of pre-Nicaean Christian Platonism,[114] the role of the doctrine of the Trinity *within* natural theology is profoundly influenced by the tradition emanating from Plato's *Parmenides*; especially the question of the relation of identity to difference. The principle and fount of the intellectual system is the transcendent ἀρχή which constitutes a relational unity. The realm of ideas does not form an inferior intermediate realm between the causal source of the universe

---

[113] cf. Dieter Henrich, *Selbstverhältnisse. Gedanken und Auslegungen zu den Grundlagen der Klassischen Deutschen Philosophie* (Stuttgart: Reclam, 1982) and Robert B. Pippin, *Hegel's Idealism: the Satisfactions of Self-consciousness* (Cambridge University Press, 1989).

[114] A classic version of the view that Nicaea was a rejection of Platonism is F. Ricken, 'Nikaia als Krisis des altkirchlichen Platonismus', in *Theologie und Philosophie* 44 (1969), pp. 312–41. See also G. C. Stead, 'The Platonism of Arius', in *The Journal of Theological Studies* 15 (1964), pp. 341–58.

and the physical world but *is* the divine mind: the Logos is the perfect expression of its source. Arianism, with its belief that there was a time when the Logos did not exist, implied the sterility of the principle. Cudworth insists that while Christians denied polytheism, they did not 'make God a solitary and sterile being'.[115] His reasoning is:

For if the whole Deity, were nothing but one simple monad, devoid of all manner of multiplicity, as God is frequently represented to be; then could it not well be conceived by us mortals, how it should contain the distinct ideas of all things within itself, and that multiform platform and paradigm of the created universe, commonly called the archetypal world.[116]

The ἀρχή of Christian metaphysics is a relational *unity* – the self-explication or differentiation of the One as tri-une is an essential element of its nature.[117] Thus an element of *difference* is integrated within the divine *identity*; the divine unity is a relational identity in which the ideas are modes of divine self-consciousness. Hence intellection does not compromise the divine unity but constitutes it.[118] Cudworth could present the doctrine of the Trinity as essential to the true intellectual system in combining the contemplative God of Aristotle[119] (the Father contemplates himself in the Son as νοήσεως νόησις: the Trinity 'ad intra') with the creative God of Plato's demiurge: because the divine mind is 'ad extra' the *causal* source of the physical cosmos, the divine must be amenable to human apprehension; albeit imperfectly:

There must be a mind senior to the world, and all sensible things, and such as at once comprehends in it the ideas of all intelligibles, their necessary scheses and relations to one another, and all their immutable truths[120]

---

[115] Cudworth, *True Intellectual System*, vol. ii. p. 311.

[116] Cudworth, *True Intellectual System*, vol. ii. p. 400.

[117] It could be argued that the Christian metaphysics of absolute divine subjectivity has roots in Porphyry's telescoping the clear Plotinian division between the One and the intellect. This argument depends upon accepting Pierre Hadot's attribution of the anonymous commentary on Plato's *Parmenides* to Porphyry in Hadot, *Porphyre et Victorinus* and 'La Trias'. See Beierwaltes, *Denken des Einen*, pp. 198 ff. and M. J. Edwards, 'Being, life and mind: a brief inquiry', in *Syllecta Classica* 8 (1997), pp. 191–205.

[118] In particular see the work of Beierwaltes, especially *Identität und Differenz*, pp. 24–96 and J. Patrick Atherton, 'The Neoplatonic "One" and the Trinitarian "ΑΡΧΗ"' in *The Significance of Neoplatonism*, edited by R. Baine Harris (Norfolk, Virg.: Old Dominion University Press, 1976), pp. 173–85.

[119] cf. E. Booth, 'St Augustine's "de Trinitate" and Aristotelian and neoplatonist noetic', in *Studia Patristica*, edited by E. H. Livingstone, Berlin: Akademic Verlag, 1985), vol. xvi. pp. 487–90 and 'St Augustine's "notitia sui" related to Aristotle and the early neoplatonists', *Augustiniana* 27 (1977), pp. 70–132, 364–401; 29 (1979), pp. 97–124.

[120] Cudworth, *True Intellectual System*, vol. iii. p. 70.

Cudworth is wary of the language of the supreme Principle as 'beyond being', ἐπέκεινα τῆς οὐσίας, which language and conceit of Plato's, Cudworth avers, 'some of the Greek fathers seem to have entertained, yet so as to apply it to the whole Trinity, when they call God ὑπερούσιον or "super-essential." But the meaning of that philosopher was, as we conceive, no other than this, that this highest good hath no particular characteristic upon it, limiting and determining it, it being the hidden and incomprehensible source of all things.'[121] Such is Cudworth's dismissal of the negative theology derived from the strict henological tradition in Neoplatonism, and explains his lack of interest in later Neoplatonism where the negative theology of Plotinus is reinforced.[122] The tendency of later pagan Neoplatonism to insist upon the *radical* transcendence of the One is dismissed by Cudworth as 'a certain kind of *Mysterious Atheism*'. Cudworth's *philosophia Trinitatis* is part of a metaphysics of the absolute that is opposed to the 'one *Peculiar Arcanum* of the *Platonick* and *Pythagorick* Theology',[123] particularly in Proclus, Iamblichus, and most of all Damascius, that is the adamant rejection of any difference or relations within the ἀρχή.[124] There is a sense in which Cudworth is correct. Christian theology could develop a concept of absolute (divine) subjectivity (required by most forms of theism), a notion which was prohibited within Neoplatonism by the refusal to contemplate any difference *within* the supreme principle.

It is of particular significance, however, that Cudworth dwells upon a most unusual but decisive Ennead – vi. 8, *Free Will and the Will of the One*. This treatise is striking on account of Plotinus' apparent readiness to make positive claims about the supreme principle; where the strictness of Plotinus' affirmation that the ἀρχή is placed ἐπέκεινα τῆς οὐσίας is in fact modified by his speculation about the essence of the One. In Augustine's *The Trinity*, we can see a strong dependence upon the patrician Roman Neoplatonic-philosopher-turned-Christian Marius Victorinus in his work *Adversus Arium*. His work on the Trinity was part of an active engagement in the Arian controversy, using Platonist metaphysics *against* Arianism. In this very speculative treatment Victorinus takes

---

[121] Cudworth, *True Intellectual System*, vol. ii. p. 76.
[122] Cudworth attributes this excessive negative theology to Plotinus' rigid and superstitious exegesis of Plato's *Republic* 509. Cudworth, *True Intellectual System*, vol. ii. p. 397.
[123] Cudworth, *True Intellectual System*, vol. ii. p. 395.
[124] cf. C. J. de Vogel in *Greek Philosophy* (Leiden: E.J. Brill, 1964), vol. iii. p. 589.

up the Plotinian idea of the Absolute as αἴτιον ἑαυτοῦ (*causa sui*) in this treatise vi. 8:[125] God's self-constitution is an unfolding and returning to itself. The Father is the 'status', Son is 'progressio', Spirit is 'regressio': Victorinus strictly denies any ontological inferiority of the Son to the Father: he uses Plotinian ideas and terminology, *esse, vivere, intelligere*, in order to defend the ὁμοούσιος against the Arians.[126] Being is life, life is intelligence, intelligence is will: each of the qualities are not accidents but form an interpenetrating, mutually inclusive, relation. In this context, Victorinus employs the Platonic categories of ταὐτότης and ἑτερότης, identity and difference, in his philosophical theology for the purposes of formulating a concept of deity which, though soaked in the Neoplatonic tradition, is expressly meant to serve the cause of Nicaea.[127] Markus observes:

This central concern to vindicate the consubstantiality of the hypostases, which Neoplatonic thought would separate and subordinate, leads Victorinus to take considerable liberties with the philosophical framework within which he works . . . It amounts to a fundamental change about the unknowability of the absolute, and indeed we find the 'negative theology' characteristic of the Neoplatonic framework receding into the background with Victorinus . . . [he] telescopes into his conception of God what Neoplatonic ontology had separated among the hypostases[128]

Augustine uses Victorinus' speculations about 'identity', 'difference', and 'relation' to argue that God cannot have any qualities which do not constitute his being.[129] Cudworth, in discussion of Augustine's dependence upon Porphyry, states that the Platonists provided a model of hypostases 'not as accidents and qualities, but as all substantial' whereby 'it is more easy to conceive that all these are really but one and the same God, than how there should be any

---

[125] Plotinus, *Treatise* vi. 8 (39) 14, 41. cf. E. Benz, *Marius Victorinus und die Entwicklung der Abendländischen Willensmetaphysik* (Stuttgart: Kohlhammer, 1932).

[126] Paul Henry, 'The adversus arium of Marius Victorinus', *Journal of Theological Studies* 1 (1950), pp. 42–55. R. A. Markus, 'Marius Victorinus and Augustine' in *The Cambridge History of Later Greek and Early Medieval Philosophy*, edited by A. H. Armstrong (Cambridge University Press, 1967), pp. 331–7. See also the critical comments of P. Manchester, 'The Noetic Triad in Plotinus, Marius Victorinus and Augustine' in *Neoplatonism and Gnosticism*, edited by J. Bregman and R. T. Wallis (Albany: State of New York Press, 1992), pp. 207–22.

[127] Cudworth, for all his admiration of the Alexandrians, is very much a western theologian. For his scathing remarks about the Cappodocian Trinity cf. Cudworth, *True Intellectual System*, vol. ii. p. 605.

[128] Markus, 'Victorinus and Augustine', p. 335.

[129] For Augustine on Victorinus, see Augustine of Hippo, *Confessions*, translated by R. S. Pine-Coffin (Harmondsworth: Penguin, 1961), vol. viii. § 2ff.

considerable inferiority in them'.[130] The dilemma for Augustine was: either Father, Son, and Spirit are three substances: this destroys the divine unity and leads to tritheism; or the persons are mere accidents of the one divine substance: modalism. Augustine solved the problem by repudiating the substance–accident distinction for the realm of spirit.[131] For Augustine all the persons of the Godhead are equal in all: their differences reside exclusively in their *relations*–Fatherhood, Sonship, procession from Father and Son: 'they are mutually inexistent in each other, the *first* being in the second and both *first* and *second* in the *third*'.[132] So too the mind: we cannot distinguish between the substance of mind and its attributes such as memory, insight, and will. Mind just *is* constituted by the interrelation and interdependence of its constituents.[133] This metaphysics of a relational as opposed to a merely numerical identity is evident as Cudworth discusses the Athanasian images of fountain, stream, and river, root, stock, and branches of the tree, as expressing:

> not only for things agreeing in one common and general essence, as three men are co-essential with each other; but also for such as concurrently together make up one entire thing, and are therefore jointly essential thereunto . . . the root, stock, and branches are not only of one kind, but also all together make up the entire essence of one plant or tree. In like manner, those three hypostases, the Father, Son and Holy Ghost, are not only congenerous and co-essential, as having all the essence of the Godhead alike in them, but also concurrently making up one entire divinity.[134]

The unity of the Godhead is a relational unity: 'neither of these could be without the other'; further 'these are so nearly and intimately conjoined together, that there is a kind of συνέχεια, 'continuity', betwixt them; which yet is not to be understood in the way of corporeal things, but so as is agreeable to the nature of things incorporeal'. Thirdly, the hypostases are 'not only indivisibly cojoined with one another, but also to have a mutual inexistence in each other, which later Greek fathers have called ἐμπεριχώρησιν, their "circumincession".[135]

The relevant metaphysics rests upon the principle that *spiritual*

---

[130] Cudworth, *True Intellectual System*, vol. ii. p. 428.
[131] See K. Flasch, *Augustinus* (Stuttgart: Reclam, 1980), pp. 353 ff.
[132] Cudworth, *True Intellectual System*, vol. ii. pp. 597–8.
[133] A good account of Cudworth on the Trinity is to be found in Lydia Gysi, *Platonism and Cartesianism in the Philosophy of Ralph Cudworth* (Bern: Lang, 1962), pp. 99–119.
[134] Cudworth, *True Intellectual System*, vol. ii. p. 456.
[135] Cudworth, *True Intellectual System*, vol. ii. pp. 453–4.

unity is quite different from physical unity: the unity of an object consists of being distinguished from other single objects and thus numerically one chair or one table; however the unity of mind is characterised by a relation to *itself* not to others. Whereas one object stands over against another single object, the mind cannot be aware of its thoughts as objects standing over against itself. The mind only *is* insofar as it thinks. Coleridge states: 'we know indeed, that all mind are Subjects; but are by no means certain, that all Subjects are Minds. For a Mind is a Subject that knows itself, or a Subject that is its own Object' (*Aids*, p. 179). Thought, thinking, and thinker constitute an interpenetrating reality, a relational unity, which is quite distinct from any unity in the 'object' world. Cudworth notes that the relation is 'not to be understood in the way of corporeal things, but so as is agreeable to the nature of things incorporeal'.[136] The paradigm of this self-knowing unity is the perfect self-conscious unity of the tri-une Godhead. The persons of the Trinity are not to be thought of as akin to discrete substances with accidental qualities, but a unity constituted by *relations*. Unlike those philosophers such as Aristotle who insist that relations are not of any importance in the fabric of reality, Augustine is arguing for the ontological priority of 'relation'. As Cudworth notes: 'Though a corporealist may pretend to be a theist, yet I never heard that any of them did ever assert a trinity, respectively to the Deity. . .'[137]

In opposition to the Aristotelian doctrine of the manifold meanings of Being,[138] within the Platonic tradition unity is the privileged sense of 'being'. Yet the onto-theology created by Christian philosophical theology is not a strict henology. The unity of the divine tri-unity is not a numerical identity, and the general tendency of the Christian assimilation of Neoplatonism in Marius Victorinus or Augustine was to modify the strength of the ἐπέκεινα τῆς οὐσίας so that it did not mean that the supreme principle transcends being and thought, and hence to render it compatible with the doctrine of the ὁμοούσιος.[139] The doctrine of the ἐπέκεινα τῆς οὐσίας ultimately leads to a divine remoteness which is incompatible with theism. In short, it is not the doctrine of the radical transcendence of the One,

---

[136] Ibid.   [137] Cudworth, *True Intellectual System*, vol. i. p. 42.

[138] Aristotle, *Metaphysics* , revised translation by W. D. Ross (Oxford: 1942), v. 7, 18, 30; vi. 2–4: xi. 8.

[139] Markus , 'Victorinus and Augustine', pp. 335 ff.

but the Aristotelian doctrine of the divine intellect which Cudworth sees as the great bond between Christianity and Platonism, and he rejects the strict apophatic metaphysics of the later Neoplatonic tradition which was transmitted into Christianity through pseudo-Dionysius (or Denys the Areopagite). It is the fusion of supreme principle with the intellect and the vision of the supreme principle as consubstantial with the intelligible paradigm of the sensible world which provides the metaphysical foundations for a Platonic Christian.[140] 'Wherein we cannot but take notice of an admirable correspondency betwixt the Platonic philosophy and Christianity, in that the second hypothesis of both their trinities (called also sometimes λόγος by the Platonists, as well as νοῦς) is said to be the immediate cause of all things; and the Demiurgus, the architect, maker or artificer of the whole world.'[141]

This is a good example of how 'Christian Platonism' was often rather more Christian than Platonic, while simultaneously deeply dependent upon Platonic ideas. One important upshot of the complex relations between Christian and pagan Platonism is that Christian theologians developed a notion of God as absolute subjectivity; an essentially unPlatonic notion, and yet often formulated with tools and ideas taken from Neoplatonic metaphysics. Yet we can also see how this telescoping of the One and the intellect, which is essential to the Christian notion of divine subjectivity, provides the step between strict Neoplatonism and German Idealism. The apophatic or henological tradition in Neoplatonism means that the personal or subjective is either radically redefined or strictly denied, and the later Neoplatonists became increasingly sceptical about knowledge concerning the ultimate source. The fusing of the intellect and the One within Christian theology not only provided a metaphysics of the absolute I AM, as it were, but tended to reinforce the Aristotelian intellectualism implict in the vision of God as self-reflexive thought.

SUPREME BEING AND SELF-CONSCIOUSNESS

No man in his senses can deny *God* in some sense or other, as *anima mundi, causa causarum,* &c., but it is the *personal, living self-conscious* God which it is so

---

[140] Cudworth, *True Intellectual System*, vol. ii, p. 446.
[141] Cudworth, *True Intellectual System*, vol. ii. p. 76.

difficult, except by faith of the Trinity, to combine with an infinite being infinitely and irresistibly causative. (*Marg.* i. 242)

Coleridge was an admirer of Lessing; at one point he planned to write a biography of him.[142] Lessing was the beginning of the impulse towards a speculative theology which culminated in Hegel's and Schelling's philosophy of religion. The rediscovery of the dogma of the Trinity in the nineteenth century was a product of the philosophers and not, as one might expect, the theologians. This philosophical revival of the dogma was rooted in the development in German Idealism of the idea of absolute being as subjectivity. In order to pursue this idea we must consider the controversy between Mendelssohn and Jacobi known as the *Pantheismusstreit*.

Lessing was a central figure for the history of German Idealism and a deeply ambivalent theologian. It was Jacobi's 'revelation' of Lessing's alleged pantheism which sparked off the *Pantheismusstreit* of 1783 (cf. *BL* ii. 140).[143] Lessing edited *The Goal of Jesus and his Disciples* (*Vom Zwecke Jesus und seiner Jünger*) of 1778 in which Lessing's Hamburg teacher Hermann Samuel Reimarus (1694–1768) tried to explain the account of the resurrection and gospel of Jesus as a fraud. Although he distanced himself from the opinions of the author, Lessing's behaviour as editor aroused distrust and sharp criticism, particularly and famously with the Lutheran minister J. M. Goetze. Similarly radical was Lessing's tolerant attitude to Judaism expressed in his drama *Nathan the Wise* (1778–80), which describes a Jew of exemplary tolerance and benevolence.

Jacobi's *Über die Lehre des Spinoza* consists of the reconstruction of a discussion between Jacobi and Gotthold Ephraim Lessing (1729–81) about Spinoza.[144] The book is addressed to Lessing's friend Mendelssohn because Jacobi believed Mendelssohn wanted to publish a defence of Spinoza. At the same time, Lessing was intent upon defending two dogmas most ridiculed by the Enlightenment, the Trinity and Revelation, in *Christianity of Reason* (*Das Christentum der Vernunft*) and *The Education of the Human Race* (*Die Erziehung des Menschengeschlechts*) (1780). Lessing published Leibniz's *Defensio Trini-*

---

[142] R. Holmes, *Coleridge, Early Visions* (London: Hodder and Stoughton, 1989), p. 216.

[143] See Gordon E. Michalson, Jr., *Lessing's 'Ugly Ditch': a Study of Theology and History* (University Park, Penn., and London: Pennsylvania State University Press, 1985), pp. 23–59.

[144] H. Timm, *Gott und die Freiheit. Studien zur Religionsphilosophie der Goethezeit* (Frankfurt: Klostermann, 1974) and K. Christ, *Jacobi und Mendelssohn. Eine Analyse des Spinozastreits* (Würzburg: Königshausen und Neumann, 1988).

tatis under the title *Regarding Andrew Wissowatius' Objections to the Trinity.*[145] Lessing was at once an enlightened liberal theologian *and* fascinated by the doctrinal tradition of Christian theology. These three texts, *Christianity of Reason*, *The Education of the Human Race*, and *Regarding Andrew Wissowatius' Objections to the Trinity*, constitute the beginning of the revival of Trinitarian thought within German theology which culminated in Hegel and Barth.

Lessing, clearly, constituted a controversial and ambiguous figure; this inspired the desire to find out what Lessing really thought in theological matters, and Jacobi was intent upon exploding the false, even sinister, aspects of Lessing's theology. He notoriously reported Lessing as saying: 'The orthodox concepts of the deity are not for me any more. I cannot relish them. "Hen kai Pan!" I know of nothing else.'[146] Significant for our purposes is not Jacobi's thought per se but rather Jacobi's presentation of Spinoza's philosophy: he presents Spinoza's metaphysics as a philosophy of *being*. 'The God of Spinoza is the pure Principle in all that is real, the Being in all existence.'[147] The question which Jacobi poses is: can the speculative intellect be expected to be able to fathom being itself? His answer is that this is impossible and that genuine philosophy attempts not to explain or deduce being but to reveal the incomprehensible divine ground in existence.[148] In his discussion with Lessing Jacobi exclaims: 'In my opinion the greatest achievement of a scholar is the revelation of existence'. ('Nach meinem Urteil ist das größte Verdienst des Forschers, Dasein zu enthüllen'). One can trace the influence of this in Schelling's early texts. In *Vom Ich als Prinzip der Philosophie* (1795)[149] Schelling writes: 'The greatest achievement of the philosophical scholar is not the construction of abstract concepts, and building systems out of them. His aim is pure and absolute Being.'[150]

---

[145] G. E. Lessing, *Des Andreas Wisowatius Einwürfe wider die Dreyeinigkeit* in his *Werke*, edited by Paul Rilla (Berlin: Aufbau, 1957), vol. ix. pp. 607 ff.

[146] 'Die orthodoxen Begriffe der Gottheit sind nicht mehr für mich; ich kann sie nicht mehr genießen. "Hen kai Pan! Ich weiß nichts anderes".' F. H. Jacobi, 'Über die Lehre des Spinoza in Briefen an den Herrn Moses Mendelssohn' in *Die Hauptschriften zum Pantheismusstreit*, edited by Heinrich Scholz (Berlin: Kantgesellschaft, 1916), p. 76.

[147] 'Der Gott des Spinoza ist das lautere Prinzipium der Wirklichkeit in allem Wirklichen; des Seyns in allem Dasein.' Ibid., p. 101.

[148] Timm, *Gott und die Freiheit*, pp. 135–40 and Birgit Sandkaulen-Bock, *Ausgang vom Unbedingten. Über den Anfang in der Philosophie Schellings* (Göttingen: Vandenhoeck and Ruprecht, 1990), pp. 13–18.

[149] Horstmann, *Grenzen der Vernunft*, pp. 72 ff.

[150] 'Das höchste Verdienst des philosophischen Forschers ist nicht abstrakte Begriffe aufzustellen, und aus ihnen Systeme herauszuspinnen. Seine letzter Zweck ist reines

Immediately afterwards, Schelling states: 'The I contains all Being, all reality.'[151]

Schelling's philosophy may be described as an objective idealism of absolute subjectivity.[152] Objective idealism means that reason (or *Vernunft*) is thought of as an objective structure rather than as the capacity of finite beings for thinking. It is a philosophy of absolute subjectivity because 'the I contains all Being, all Reality' ('das Ich enthällt alles Sein, alle Realität'). Schelling combines the concept of *being* with that of *self-consciousness*. The issue of the nature of being should be explained with recourse to the principle of *self-consciousness*. The terminological connection between being and self-consciousness arises with German Idealism in the period of the Jacobi–Spinoza discussion. God is, in the tradition and spirit of Aristotle, absolute reflection: self-affirmation. Furthermore, true philosophy is theology because God is the highest object of philosophy.[153] At the beginning of *Aids to Reflection* we read that Coleridge sees his purpose in writing the book in the following manner:

To exhibit a full and consistent Scheme of the Christian dispensation, and more largely of all the *peculiar* doctrines of the Christian Faith . . . There are indeed Mysteries, in evidence of which no reason can be *brought*. But it has been my endeavor to show, that the true solution of this problem is, that these Mysteries *are* Reason, Reason in its highest form of Self-affirmation. (*Aids*, pp. 8–9)

The language which Coleridge uses concerning the philosophical importance of the Christian religion is both Trinitarian and influenced by the speculative theology from Schelling.[154] In the Godhead

---

absolutes Sein', F. W. J. Schelling, *Ausgewählte Schriften in 6 Bänden*, edited by M. Frank (Frankfurt: Suhrkamp, 1985), i. (1794–1800), p. 76.

[151] 'das Ich enthällt alles Sein, alle Realität.' F. W. J. Schelling, *Ausgewählte Schriften*, vol. i (1794–1800), p. 76.

[152] A good introduction is H. Knittermeyer, *Schelling und die romantische Schule* (Munich: Reinhardt, 1929). Much more difficult but a classic is Walter Schulz, *Die Vollendung des Deutschen Idealismus in der Spätphilosophie Schellings* (Stuttgart: Kohlammer, 1955). See also Bernard M. G. Reardon, *Religion in the Age of Romanticism: Studies in Early Nineteenth-Century Thought* (Cambridge University Press, 1985) and Robert F. Brown, *The Later Philosophy of Schelling: the Influence of Boehme on the Works of 1809–1815* (Lewisburg: Bucknell, 1977); Xavier Tilliette, *Schelling, une philosophie en devenir*, 2 vols., vol. i., *Le Système vivant 1794–1821*; vol. ii., *La Dernière Philosophie 1821–1854* (Paris: Vrin, 1970).

[153] See Peetz, *Die Freiheit im Wissen* and Sandkaulen-Bock, *Ausgang vom Unbedingten*.

[154] Schelling writes: 'Ein solches, welches sich selbst absolut affirmiert und also von sich selbst das Affirmierte ist, ist nur das Absolute oder Gott.' *Werke* (Stuttgart: Cotta, 1856–61), vol. vi. p. 148. 'Such a (being) that affirms itself and is that which is affirmed, is simply the absolute or God.' Reason is for Schelling 'worin Gott selbst sich das All – und Einheit aller

we find, according to Schelling, unity *and* difference in his self-affirmation. For Coleridge, unlike Schelling at this stage, the language of the self-affirmation of reason is unambiguously talk of the tri-unity.[155] For Coleridge the speculative tenet of the Trinity is the culmination of philosophy, not its denial or repudiation (*BL*, i. 204ff. and ii. 247ff.): the 'scriptural and only true Idea of God will, in its development, be found to involve the Idea of the tri-unity' (*Aids*, p. 177) because the Trinity is the solution to the problem of the 'LIVING GOD' (*Aids*, p. 168) as 'Being, Infinity and Personality' (*Aids*, p. 188).

The idea of God revealing himself as the great I AM leads to the question of personality and infinity. The revival of German Trinitarian theology was, we have noted, a product of the moderate Spinozistic school. This resulted in a purely economic Trinity: the identification of the world with the Son and, insofar as he follows Schelling, Coleridge reveals his affinity to the neo-Spinozistic idealistic school. In his *Biographia* Coleridge emphasises the importance of the problem of the relationship of the *personality* and *infinity* of the Godhead for his own intellectual development. This theme is a central topic in the *onto-theology* of German Idealism and is of vital concern for Coleridge: 'For a very long time indeed I could not reconcile personality with infinity; and my head was with Spinoza, though my whole heart remained with Paul and John' (*BL* i. 201).[156] In *Aids* Coleridge is determined to defend a concept of 'a God infinite, yet *personal*' (*Aids*, p. 283) as 'the living Fountain of Life . . . the Plenitude of Reality! the Absoluteness of Creative Will' (*Aids*, p. 401) in an age of reluctance 'to contemplate the Supreme Being in his *personal* Attributes' (*Aids*, p. 403; cf. p. 405).

This interest in Spinoza, as McFarland has rightly pointed out, is rooted in the German pantheism controversy (*Pantheismusstreit*), and Jacobi's attack upon systematic theology. Jacobi hit a nerve in his polemic: the relation of infinitude and personality has been a particular problem of modernity. If we are to think of the universe as

---

Folgen seiner Idea erkenne.' That is: 'wherein God himself recognises the all and unity of all consequences of his idea'. Quoted by Beierwaltes, *Identität und Differenz*, p. 216.

[155] See Uehlein, *Manifestation*, pp. 107–11 for a discussion of the issue. Augustine, *Confessions* xiii. § 11, 12. See Beierwaltes, *Identität und Differenz*, p. 217 n. 48.

[156] Austin Farrer describes his own experience of Spinoza liberating him from an unduly anthropomorphic sense of the deity in his Bampton Lectures, *Glass of Vision*, pp. 7–8. I owe this reference to Brian Hebblethwaite.

an infinite *explicatio Dei*, how can this be compatible with an extra-mundane personal God who is free and intelligent? From the other perspective, if the world is genuinely other than God, how can God be unlimited, i.e. infinite?

The Spinozistic solution was to reject or at least severely modify traditional theism and to posit a purely immanent cause: God as *natura naturans*. If traditional theism sacrifices God's infinity by conceiving God as being too much like a human agent, Spinozism sacrifices God's personality for the sake of his (as it were) infinity. God, for Spinoza, is in no sense limited by the world. Whereas traditional theism sees God opposed to the world, pantheism sees God and World as one.

The Idealist move (which influenced Coleridge) was the attempt to preserve both the idea of the infinity and of the personality of God by combining the Spinozistic (ultimately Neoplatonic) idea of 'hen kai pan' or all-unity with the concept of absolute *subjectivity*. Whereas Spinoza saw God as the absolute object, Schelling (and Hegel) wanted to see God as the absolute subject: as the great I AM. On this model the world is not 'outside God' but participates in God. Hence the younger Schelling employs the concept of 'intellectual intuition' for knowledge of the absolute in order to suggest a knowledge which is not a knowledge of an object but which is rather participation in the absolute subjectivity. If God is absolute, the process of his being, i.e. thought, must be incorporated in himself. In this sense God's infinity is preserved.

Personhood seems intuitively to involve an awareness of otherness and the idealists were convinced that a minimal requirement of being a person involves distinguishing *oneself* from *another self*. Yet this conflicted with the all-oneness tenet of Spinozism. If God is *all* he cannot be a person in any remote sense because logically there can be nothing which is 'other' to the 'all-oneness'. One of the Spinoz-ists, Herder, denied personality to God on the grounds that person-ality involves limitation,[157] and Fichte was thrown out of his position in Jena for denying that the absolute could be personal because person implies otherness and thus limitation.[158] Fichte did not wish

---

[157] J. G. Herder, *Gott* in his *Sämtliche Werke*, edited by B. Suphan (Hildesheim: Olms, 1967), vol. xvi. pp. 497 ff.

[158] Falk Wagner, *Der Gedanke der Persönlichkeit Gottes bei Fichte und Hegel* (Gütersloh: Bertelsmann, 1971), pp. 28–38.

to reject the concept of God but the concept of divine personality or personhood.

Schelling believed that the solution of this problem did not lie in the approach of Herder and Fichte, i.e. denying God's personality in order to preserve his infinity, but in the revival of the doctrine of the Trinity. The otherness necessary for the attribution of personhood rests in the Trinitarian relations: Father, Son, and Spirit. God's personhood and infinity are preserved insofar as the movement of the Trinitarian persons is identified with the dialectical relations of absolute subjectivity from infinity to finitude and back to infinity: from God (Father) to world (i.e. God as Son) and the *reditus* or reflection (Spirit) of the world to God. God can be said to be personal in the sense that his otherness *is* the Son *as the world*. In his *Vorlesung über das akademische Studium* Schelling refers to the thought of Lessing on the issue and criticises Lessing for not working out the 'idea' of the Trinity in relation to the history of the world:

The atonement of the finite which has fallen from God with God himself through his own birth into finitude is the primary idea of Christianity and the perfection of the whole purpose of the universe and the history of the same in the idea of the Trinity which is therefore thoroughly necessary. It is well known that Lessing in his *Education of the Human Race* already sought to reveal the philosophical significance of the tenet and what he said about it was perhaps the most speculative of all that he wrote. His account was lacking in the relationship of this idea to the history of the world. This resides in the fact of identity of the eternal son of the father of all and the finite world. The former is the latter in the eternal Divine sight and appears as suffering God who is subordinate to the harsh fate of time who at the summit of his appearance, in Christ, closes finitude and opens infinitude or rather the Supremacy of the Spirit.[159]

The answer, Schelling boldly claims, lies in the identity of the finite

---

[159] 'Versöhnung des von Gott abgefallenen Endlichen durch seine eigene Geburt in die Endlichkeit ist der erste Gedanke des Christenthums und die Vollendung seiner ganzen Absicht des Universum und der Geschichte desselben in der Idee der Dreieinigkeit, welche eben deswegen in ihm schlechthin nothwendig ist. Bekanntlich hat schon Lessing in der Schrift: Erziehung des Menschengeschlechtes, die philosophische Bedeutung dieser lehre zu enthüllen gesucht, und was er darüber gesagt hat, ist vieleicht das Spekulativste, was er überhaupt geschrieben. Es fehlte aber seiner Ansicht noch an der Beziehung dieser Idee auf die Geschichte der Welt, welche darin liegt, daß der ewige aus dem Wesen des Vaters aller Dinge geborene Sohn Gottes das Endliche selbst ist, wie es in der ewigen Anschauung Gottes ist, und welches als ein leidender und den Verhängnissen der Zeit untergeordneter Gott erscheint, der in dem Gipfel seiner Erscheinung, in Christo, die Welt der Endlichkeit schließt und die der Unendlichkeit oder der Herrschaft des Geistes eröffnet.' F. W. J. von Schelling, *Schriften von 1801–1804* (Darmstadt: Wissenschaftliche Buchgesellschaft, 1988, reprinted from Stuttgart: 1859–60).

realm – that is the world – and the Trinitarian Son. The Son resolves the antagonism between the finite realm and God which is expressed in the doctrine of the Fall and inaugurates the supremacy of the Spirit. In the divine intuition the Son *is* the world and atonement resides in the reconciliation between the infinite and the finite. The roots of this Trinitarian revival in German Idealist thought are to be found in Lessing's *Education of the Human Race* (*Erziehung des Menschengeschlechts*, §73ff.) and in Schelling's *Lecture on Academic Study* (*Vorlesung über das akademische Studium*).[160] Lessing follows Leibniz in his speculative rehabilitation of the Trinity of God as thought thinking itself; whereby the unity of God should not be thought of as the unity of finite things, but as the unity of that highest being – rapt in self-contemplation: having a 'complete idea of himself'.[161] Hence we can say that in this respect, at least, Lessing was not a Spinozist.[162] Lessing writes:

the doctrine of the Trinity – how can one bring the human Understanding on the path of recognising, after endless wandering left and right, that God cannot be unitary in the human Understanding for which finite things are unitary; that his unity must be transcendent – and of nature which does not exclude plurality? Should not God have at least the complete idea of himself? that is an idea in which everything is which is in him.

Lessing puts this thought about the higher unity of the divine Trinity into a historical framework: the recognition of revealed truths as truths of reason is necessary in order to aid humankind. The revealed truth of the Trinity is legitimised by speculative reason. Revelation is necessary in order to 'aid' mankind and once mankind

---

[160] 'die Lehre von der Dreieinigkeit. – Wie, wenn diese Lehre den menschlichen Verstand, nach unendlichen Verirrungen rechts und links, nur endlich auf den Weg bringen sollte, zu erkennen, daß Gott in dem Verstande, in welchem endliche Dinge *eins* sind, unmöglich *eins* sein könne; daß seine Einheit eine transzendentale Einheit sein müsse, welche eine Art von Mehrheit nicht ausschließt? Muß Gott wenigstens nicht die vollständigste Vorstellung von sich selbst haben das ist eine Vorstellung, in der sich alles befindet, was in ihm selbst ist.' G. E. Lessing, *Die Erziehung des Menschengeschlechts*, ed. L. H. Helbig (Bern: P. Lang, 1980, facsimile of Berlin: Boß, 1780), p. 22, cf. Coleridge *Marg.* iii. 660. 'die Ausbildung geoffenbarter Wahrheiten in Vernunftwahrheiten ist schlecterdings notwendig, wenn dem menschlichen Geschlechte damit geholfen sein soll. Als sie geoffenbaret wurden, waren sie freilich noch keine Vernunftwahrheiten; aber sie wurden geoffenbaret, um es zu werden.'

[161] Maria Rosa Antognazza, 'Die Rolle der Trinitäts und Menschwerdungsdiskussion für die Enstehung von Leibniz "Denken"', *Studia Leibnitiana* 1 (1994), pp. 56–75.

[162] Whether Spinoza's God might be deemed self-conscious is a contentious matter. Certainly Spinoza's pantheism and his denial of will to God militate against the idea. H. A. Wolfson argues for the attribution of self-consciousness to God in *The Philosophy of Spinoza: Unfolding the Latent Processes of his Reasoning*, 2 vols. (Cambridge, Mass.: Harvard University Press, 1962), vol. i. pp. 328 f.

is able to contemplate revealed truths as intelligible they become truths of reason. Lessing thus exhibits his deep knowledge of the Fathers and his debt to the Platonism of Leibniz.[163]

This idealistic defence of Christian dogma combined with the idea of progressive historical enlightenment exerted enormous influence upon Schelling. Yet Christian Trinitarian theology distinguishes traditionally between the essential and the economic Trinity. The *essential* Trinity is the Trinity regarded immanently; that is to say as the relationship between Father, Son, and Holy Spirit quite apart from their work in the world. The work of the Trinity *ad extra* is creation, redemption, and sanctification: this is designated the *economic* Trinity. The economic Trinity describes the supervention of the deity upon creation. The great signal difference between Coleridge and the early Schelling is that Schelling generally has merely an economic Trinity whereas Coleridge refers to the essential and the economic Trinity. In the middle and later period of his thought Schelling moves towards an *essential* Trinity. In the *Freiheit-schrift* of 1809 Schelling writes of 'the inner reflexive representation by means of which God can *as* God see himself in his image. This representation is the first wherein God, considered absolutely, is realised, although only within himself.'[164] This representation is described by Schelling as the *Word:* the Logos. God's relation to himself is described as a *visio absoluta* which precedes the economic relations of the Trinity.

Whether or not he was directly influenced by Schelling's middle phase, Coleridge chose to revive the idea of the immanent Trinity, i.e. immanent relations within the Godhead. The *otherness* which is requisite for personality lies in the relation between *Father and Son* without the world. The internal difference within the Trinitarian Godhead provides the possibility of conceiving of God as personal without envisaging the world as a necessary component of the divine nature. This consubstantial otherness, the Son, is called 'alterity', a

---

[163] cf. H. Schultze, *Lessings Toleranzbegriff* (Göttingen: Vandenhoeck, 1969) for the thesis that Lessing was influenced by the 'Spiritualisten', and the remarks of H. E. Allison in *Lessing and the Enlightenment* (Ann Arbor: University of Michigan Press, 1966), pp. 162 ff.

[164] 'eine innre reflexive Vorstellung, durch welche, da sie keinen anderen Gegenstand haben kann als Gott, Gott sich selbst in einem Ebenbilde erblickt. Diese Vorstellung ist das erste worin Gott, absolut betrachtet, verwirklicht ist, obgleich nur in ihm selbst.' F. W. J. von Schelling, *Philosophische Untersuchungen über Wesen der Menschlichen Freiheit und die Damit Zusammenhängenden Gegenstände* with an essay by W. Schulz, 'Freiheit und Geschichte in Schelling's Philosophie' (Frankfurt: 1975, reprinted 1984), pp. 360–1.

concept derived from Cudworth and Berkeley.[165] It means that God himself is *absolute reflection* or thought; not just in that God contemplates the world in or as the Son, but the Son as his Self:

that all-perfect Idea, in which the Supreme Spirit contemplateth itself and the plenitude of its infinity – the only begotten before all Ages! the beloved Son in whom the Father is indeed well pleased! (*Aids*, p. 312)

The problem for this position is how the three persons of the Godhead are compatible with personality.[166] Coleridge is aware of the difficulty and tends to speak of the *personeity* of the divine.[167] This language preserves the insight that God as the infinite source of human personality cannot be less than humanity, without rejecting the dogma of the three persons: 'the absolute Will, as the universal *Ground* of *all* Being, and the Election and purpose of God in the personal Idea, as the Father' (*Aids*, pp. 333–4). With this philosophical rehabilitation of the immanent Trinity one can sense the affinity to Plato's *Timaeus* and to Aristotle's *Metaphysics*. God is contemplated as pure thought thinking himself as Logos and wisdom. Thus the divine nature can be seen as both personal and infinite. God is infinite thought and yet in thinking himself as the Logos (his alterity) there is the difference in the unity which accommodates personhood.[168]

Absolute Idealism may be defined as the doctrine that reason (*Vernunft*) is the unity of thought and reality. Having rejected the view of revelation as supernaturally dictated facts contained within the Bible, the central idealistic principle was that 'revelation' constitutes the unveiling or disclosure of the divine essence. Since God reveals himself as a Trinity in his historical manifestation, this points to an ontological Trinity. The Trinity is thus not a way of discussing merely God's actions, but his nature.

The later Schelling came to mount a vigorous polemic against precisely this identification of reality with thought as 'essentialism'.

---

[165] Cudworth, *True Intellectual System*, vol. ii. p. 393. Bishop George Berkeley, *Siris*, § 329 in *The Works of George Berkeley, Bishop of Cloyne*, 9 vols., edited by A. A. Luce and T. E. Jessop (London: Nelson, 1967), vol. v. p. 150.

[166] One method is to replace talk of persons with talk of modes of being: this is the solution of the great nineteenth-century German theologian Dorner, and even Barth in the twentieth century is close to monarchism. cf. W. Pannenberg, *Systematische Theologie* (Göttingen: Vandenhoeck und Ruprecht, 1988), vol. i. pp. 321 ff.

[167] John H. Muirhead, *Coleridge as Philosopher* (London: Macmillan, 1930) and M. A. Perkins, *Coleridge's Philosophy: the Logos as Unifying Principle* (Oxford: Clarendon, 1994), p. 84.

[168] I differ on this point from John Beer: I do not think that 'personeity' means the impersonal ground of personality but the tri-une personality of the relation of the three persons of the Trinity. cf. *Aids*, p. lxxvi.

His 'existentialist' critique of both Hegel and the Platonic-Aristotelian metaphysical theology perceived a central error in constraining the absolute will by thought. The supreme principle, the later Schelling insists, must be thought of as absolute freedom, and as such prior to laws of thought. God is the 'unprethinkable', a principle 'beyond being'. Here we can see the issue which Cudworth isolated within the Neoplatonic metaphysical legacy of the idea of the principle as 'beyond being'. The notion of absolute mind in idealism, generally, has an obvious precedent in the Neoplatonic intellect, and the Christian employment of the intellect in its philosophical theology. Yet Neoplatonism also provides resources for a criticism of such an absolute unity of thought and reality with its doctrine of the absolute transcendence of the first principle or the One. The joint influence of Boehme and Jacobi, and his conflict with Hegel, seem to have driven Schelling to search for a principle beyond the noetic, which mirrors the apophatic tradition in Christian mysticism which derives from Pseudo-Dionysius.[169] In the *Freiheitschrift* one can see the first stage of this move towards the late philosophy of revelation, and it is instructive that Coleridge takes issue with Schelling on the same areas as the Cambridge Platonists censured Boehme.

'I AM WHO I AM'

Berkeley observes that 'Plato describes God, as Moses, from His being. According to both, God is He who truly is.'[170] German Idealist theology also drew upon the patristic tradition of a philosophical interpretation of Exodus 3: 14, 'God said to Moses, "I AM WHO I AM".'[171] It plays a particularly central role in Schelling's speculative theology.[172]

The Bible does not speak of God as 'spirit' in the manner of

---

[169] E. Booth, 'Tὸ ὑπερεῖναι of pseudo-Dionysius and Schelling' in *Studia Patristica* (Leuven: Peeters, 1989), pp. 215–25. cf. S. Hutton, 'Henry More and Jacob Boehme' in *Henry More, Tercentenary Studies* (Dortrecht: Kluwer, 1990) pp. 157–71.

[170] Berkeley, *Siris* § 342 in *Works*, vol. v. p. 155.

[171] Gilson tried to establish an 'existentialist' interpretation of this passage for his influential view of Thomas Aquinas, and objected to the deduction of God's existence from his essence. Gilson was motivated by anti-Platonic and anti-idealistic concerns. cf. W. Hankey, 'From metaphysics to history, from Exodus to neoplatonism, from scholasticism to pluralism: the fate of Gilsonian Thomism in English-speaking North America' in *Dionysius* 16 (1998), pp. 157–88.

[172] Beierwaltes, *Platonismus und Idealismus*, pp. 68 ff.

Aristotle and the ensuing metaphysical tradition, and this has encouraged the common cliché about the irreconcilable conflict between the Hebrew and Hellenistic traditions within Christianity.[173] However, the Church Fathers nevertheless used their philosophical concepts in the interpretation of scriptural passages. The most important instance is Exodus 3:14. The Septuagint translates the sentence as ''Εγώ εἰμι ὁ ὤν.' This is a participle construction using the verb for being: 'I am the one who is being.' Thus Scripture in the Greek Septuagint version speaks of God as 'being'. The philosophical question about the divine ground of reality, 'being' or the first principle, seemed entirely in accordance with Scripture.[174] Aristotle's first philosophy is theology: it is the exposition of God as supreme reality. In his *Metaphysics* Aristotle describes the first substance (πρώτη οὐσία) as the Principle (ἀρχή). This first divine substance is the best, and *as* the best enjoys the best form of life: pure thought. Indeed, it is thought thinking *itself* νοήσεως νόησις.[175] The Aristotelian idea of God as pure thought was effectively mediated by Philo of Alexandria. Philo interpreted the sentence to mean that God alone 'is' as opposed to the rest of being.[176] That is to say that God is real *being*. Philo is followed by Christian writers like Gregory of Nyssa and Gregory of Nazianzus. The Aristotelian idea of God as thought is intensified by the Christian reception of the Neoplatonic idea of the νοῦς as the identity of being and thought. When Augustine considers the sentence *Ego sum qui sum*, 'being' is the exclusive name of God and he uses the Plotinian thought that eternity is the life of the νοῦς. Augustine treats the exclusive being of God as his eternal life: his being is eternal and eternity is his being. The Christian insistence upon the reflexive identity of the Godhead meant the reinforcement of an Aristotelian intellectualism, the conviction that God is thought, which – despite the Plotinian influence upon Augustine – militated

---

[173] Christopher Stead, 'The concept of mind and the concept of God in the Christian Fathers' in *The Making of Orthodoxy*, edited by R. Williams (Cambridge University Press, 1989), pp. 39–54.

[174] W. Jaeger, *Die Theologie der frühen griechischen Denker* (Stuttgart: Kohlhammer, 1953), pp. 42 f. and Thomas Bonhoeffer, 'Die Wurzeln des Begriffs Theologie', *Archiv für Begriffsgeschichte* 34 (1991), pp. 7–26.

[175] Aristotle, *Metaphysics*, translated and edited by W. D. Ross (Oxford, Clarendon, 1924), vol. xii. 9 1074b34. J. Owens, *The Doctrine of Being in the Aristotelian 'Metaphysics'* (University of Toronto Press, 1951).

[176] Beierwaltes, *Platonismus und Idealismus*, pp. 12 ff.

against the apophaticism which followed from the Neoplatonic tenet of the supreme One as strictly beyond thought.[177]

The concept of the Logos is the key to the Christian metaphysical idea of the essential tri-une life. Philo's concept of logos as the immaterial, spiritual, transcendent, and mysteriously personified version of the *Timaeus* demiurge prepares the way for the identification of the Logos as the 'object' of divine self-consciousness. This philosophical tradition was the source from which the Christian Fathers could develop the idea of a unity which is a relational unity: the absolute self-contemplation or absolute *reflection*.[178] In the *City of God* Augustine, after admiring Plato's definition of the philosopher as the lover of God, and speaking of Plato's affinity to the biblical faith, claims that what impresses him most is the name of God in Exodus 3: 14. 'HE WHO IS'

implies that in comparison with him who really *is*, because he is unchangeable, the things created changeable have no real existence. This truth Plato vigorously maintained and diligently taught.[179]

Cudworth argues that this metaphysics of supreme being reveals the deep affinity of Platonism and the Christian doctrine of the consubstantiality of the Logos.

[Plato] does thus state the difference betwixt uncreated and created beings, or betwixt God and creature; namely that creature is that, whose duration being temporary or successive, once had a beginning; and this is his τὸ γιγνόμενον μὲν, ὂν δὲ οὐδέποτε, 'that which is made, but never truly is,' and that which ὑπ' αἰτίου τινὸς ἐξ ἀνάγκης γίγνεται, 'must of necessity be produced by some cause;' but that whatsoever is without beginning, and hath a permanent duration, is uncreated or divine; which is his τὸ ὂν μὲν ἀει,γένεσιν δὲ οὐκ ἔχον, 'that which always is, and hath no generation, nor was ever made.' Accordingly, as God is styled in the septuagint translation of the Mosaic writings, ὁ Ὤν, 'He that truly is.'[180]

Cudworth is following patristic tradition in deriving the Platonic idea of being from Exodus 3: 14 and proving this with Plato's *Timaeus* 27d5–28a1. He could have found this in Eusebius, but also in Justin

---

[177] cf. E. Booth, *Aristotelian Aporetic Ontology in Islamic and Christian Thinkers* (Cambridge University Press, 1983), pp. 36 ff.

[178] Middle Platonism incorporated the Aristotelian idea of the self-contemplating divinity, i.e. as mind, with the Platonic idea of the good. J. N. D. Kelly, *Early Christian Doctrines*, fifth edition (London: Adam and Charles Black, 1977), p. 20.

[179] City of God, vol. viii. § 11, p. 315.

[180] Cudworth, *True Intellectural System*, vol. ii. p. 366.

and in Athanasius.[181] E. P. Meijering has argued for a strong Platonic element in Athanasius' thought[182] on the grounds that Athanasius skilfully combines the Platonic insistence upon divine immutability and the biblical insistence that God can be trusted: Platonic ontology can buttress the biblical affirmation of divine faithfulness. He writes: 'if one places God ἐπέκεινα τῆς οὐσίας then one postulates a God who is different from or even superior to the God who reveals Himself as love and who is love'.[183] God is perfect, and the paradigm of the visible being, the Son, must, he thinks, be placed firmly on the side of the divine. The Arian Trinity, Cudworth argues, is a 'jumbled confusion of God and creature'[184] and hence a sort of 'paganic and idolatrous Christianity'. Maurice Wiles has shown with lucidity how Cudworth attempted to defend his place on the Trinitarian question 'within the bounds of accepted ortho-doxy'.[185] Cudworth is quite explicit in his defence of Nicaea:

. . . this was the very meaning of the Nicene Council itself, that the Son was therefore co-essential or con-substantial with the Father; merely because he was God and not a creature.[186]

John Donne observes :

. . . God declares to Moses, his bosome name, his viscerall name, his radical, his fundamentall name, the name of his Essence, *Qui sum, I am* . . . It is true, that literally in the Originall, his name is conceived in the future; it is there, *Qui ero*, I that shall be . . . Howsoever, all intend, that this is a name that denotes Essence, Beeing: Beeing is the name of God, and of God onely . . . The name of the Creator is, *I am*, but of every creature rather, I am not, I am nothing. (*Marg.* ii. 287)

Coleridge notes :

Rather, I should say – the Antecedent of Being – I that shall be in that I will to be – the absolute Will, the ground of Being – the Self-affirming Actus purissimus. (ibid.)

---

[181] The *Cohortatio ad Graecos* of Pseudo-Justin now *Ad Graecos de vera religione* 20, 2ff., which was translated by Pico della Mirandola and until 1551 was the only work of Justin to be circulated in print. Christoph Riedweg, *Pseudo-Justin (Markell von Ankyra!) Ad Graecos De Vera Religione (bisher 'Cohortatio ad Graecos')*, 2 vols., (Basel: Reinhardt, 1994), vol. ii. pp. 556 ff.; for Athanasius on Exodus 3:14 see E. P. Meijering, *Orthodoxy and Platonism in Athanasius: Synthesis or Antithesis?* (Leiden: Brill, 1974), p. 125.

[182] Ibid.   [183] Meijering, *Athanasius*, p. 187.

[184] Cudworth, *True Intellectual System*, vol. ii. p. 389.

[185] M. Wiles, *Archetypal Heresy: The Rise and Fall of British Arianism* (Oxford: Clarendon, 1996), pp. 64 ff.

[186] Cudworth, *True Intellectual System*, vol. ii. p. 420.

Coleridge is reflecting this Augustinian tradition. God is 'an existing and self-subsisting reality' (*Aids*, p. 178), 'even the *Person*, the I AM, who sent Moses to his Forefathers in Egypt' (*Aids*, p. 183).[187] This is the great I AM and the 'filial WORD that re-affirmeth it from Eternity to Eternity, whose choral Echo is the Universe' (*BL* ii. 246): the Ἐγώ εἰμι ὁ ὤν of Christian Platonic metaphysics, the eternal self-affirmation of the Father in the Logos and the Spirit which is echoed in the universe. Hence the repeated references in Coleridge to the living personality of God (*Aids*, pp. 183; 188; 213; 240). Schelling also appeals to Exodus 3: 14, but there is a profound difference in his approach; despite the superficial similarity. For Schelling, God is free to choose what he wishes to be.[188] Although Coleridge has no access to the Exodus speculation of the later work of Schelling, he was quite aware of its basis: the essay on freedom of 1809.

The key to Coleridge's own disgreement with Schelling can be seen in Schelling's move to a voluntaristic metaphysics under Jacobi's influence. Coleridge was in agreement with Schelling that philosophy cannot remain satisfied with Kant's restrictions upon metaphysics. Yet Schelling's own conception of the absolute was changing around the period of his move from Jena to Bavaria (1803) and was quite novel by the time of the *Freiheitschrift* of 1809. At this period Schelling was influenced by the Catholic Bavarian Romanticism of thinkers like Görres, von Baader, and Eschenmeyer.[189] It was in this period that Schelling was developing an increasingly positive attitude to Christianity and especially to the mystics and the German spiritual reformers such as Boehme. In the *Freiheitschrift* Schelling develops an explicitly Trinitarian metaphysical system in which Christ as the cosmic Logos plays a central role. It is quite intelligible why Coleridge found this work fascinating, but he had quite specific (largely Platonic) reasons for rejecting some of the central ideas.

Schelling's *Freiheitschrift* was written with the intention of demonstrating, in reply to Jacobi's criticism, that it was not Spinoza's monism or pantheism which led to the fatalism of the Spinozistic system, but the basic *ontology*. Schelling believes that an adequate monist ontology can be reconciled with the fact of freedom. Schel-

---

[187] *Confessions*, xii. 7 270, 5–7; xii. 8 270, 20–2. Beierwaltes, *Identität und Differenz*, pp. 92 ff.
[188] Schelling, *Werke*, vol. iii. pp. 269–70.
[189] Knittermeyer, *Schelling*, pp. 348 ff.

ling presents being qua reflective will in opposition to the unreflective *substance* of Spinoza as the basis of an adequate ontology.
Freedom is rooted – albeit obscurely – in the Trinitarian will of the
supreme being. Schelling's *Freiheitschrift* of 1809 is a nodal point in
Schelling's philosophical development and Coleridge considered it
Schelling's best work.[190] Written in Munich, with the physical
proximity of F. H. Jacobi and Franz von Baader, it contains the seeds
of Schelling's powerful and influential attack upon Hegel.

The roots of the *Freiheitschrift* can be seen fairly clearly in the text
Philosophie und Religion (1804). In this work Schelling first uses the
concept of 'God' for the absolute;[191] he considers the source of finite
things in the absolute, and thinks that these can only be thought of
as a fall (*Abfall*) from the absolute. This fall explains the reality but
not the possibility of finite things. The possibility presupposes
difference within God. In order to give some account of this difference
within the Godhead, Schelling considers the divine ideas as part of a
visionary theogony. The Trinity in the *Freiheitschrift* comprises two
additional elements, derived from Boehme. Schelling distinguishes
between divine *ground* and the divine *existence*: the ideal and real
principles in God. The unity of the ideal and the real in God
constitute 'highest personality' and creation is an act of this personality. This means, of course, that Schelling cannot be described as a
pantheistic in any simple sense of the word. On the contrary, he
insists upon the idea of God as personal and he sees creation as the
free product of this personal being; one could describe Schelling's
philosophy as a '*philosophia trinitatis*'.[192]

Why did Coleridge regard Schelling's middle period with suspicion? Although Schelling develops his thinking in response to the
vehement criticism of Hegel and Jacobi, he does not give up the
basic principles of his earliest thought. We can describe these as

1. the attempt to produce a 'system' of freedom
   and
2. the attempt to produce a 'real'-idealism: i.e. nature must be
   integrated into the system and not taken as a by-product of spirit.

[190] Coleridge claimed that 'Schelling . . . appears greatest in his last work on Freiheit.' *Diary,
Reminiscences, and Correspondence of Henry Crabb Robinson*, third edition, edited by T. Sadler,
2 vols. (London: Macmillan, 1872), vol. i. p. 107 (13 August 1812).
[191] Schelling, *Bruno*, pp. 150 ff.
[192] E. Coreth, *Trinitätsdenken in neuzeitlicher Philosophie* (Salzburg: Pustet, 1986).

The influence of Jacobi can be seen in the increasing emphasis in Schelling's middle and late period upon

3. Divine sovereignty

and

4. the 'fact' of freedom.[193]

Jacobi's influence coincides with Schelling's move to Munich in 1806. He became a member of the Munich Academy of which Jacobi was the President.[194] From 1806 onwards Schelling had personal contact with Jacobi, and this seems to have played a decisive role in the change in Schelling's thought between 1804 and 1809. Furthermore, The *Freiheitschrift* is marked by Schelling's attempt to attack the rising star of Hegel. Hegel caustically ridiculed Schelling's concept of the absolute as the night in which all cows are black.[195] The pivotal concept which Schelling employs in his attempt to hold 1 and 2 together with 3 and 4 is the concept of 'division' (*Scheidung*). Jacobi sees freedom as *unmediated spontaneity (unmittelbarer Selbstätigkeit)*; a fact and feeling which is by definition inexplicable for human reflection, which explains by mediation.[196] In Hegel's system freedom is precisely the dialectical (triadic) *mediation (Vermittlung)* of the Spirit.[197] Schelling wishes to emphasise the fact of evil in freedom in the division or rupture of forces in God which enables both finite freedom and evil. Schelling's Trinitarian positing of difference within the mind of God becomes the self-division or rupture of the divine forces within the Godhead. Whereas Hegel's idea of freedom is based on the concept of mediation (*Vermittlung*), Schelling's is based upon the idea of rupture or division (*Scheidung*). In effect, the controversy with Hegel, and the influence of Jacobi, were driving Schelling's thought into voluntarist or even irrationalist metaphysics. Coleridge is most fascinated, but also rather disturbed, by the Munich Schelling. And his motives are intimately linked to Cambridge tradition; the Cambridge Platonists were doughty opponents of the idea, which they perceived in

---

[193] My account of Schelling is deeply indebted to Siegbert Peetz, *Die Freiheit im Wissen*.
[194] M. Brüggen, 'Jacobi und Schelling' in *Philosophisches Jahrbuch* 75 (1967–8), pp. 419–29.
[195] G. W. F. Hegel, *Phenomenology of Spirit*, translated by A. V. Miller, sixth edition (Oxford: Clarendon, 1952), p. 9. The text was published in 1807.
[196] cf. Peetz, *Die Freiheit im Wissen*, pp. 18–72.
[197] M. Negele, *Grade der Freiheit. Versuch einer Interpretation von G. W. F. Hegels 'Phänomenologie des Geistes'* (Würzburg: Königshausen und Neumann, 1991) and J. O'Donohue, *Person als Vermittlung. Die Dialektik von Individualität und Allgemeinheit in Hegel's 'Phänomenologie des Geistes'* (Mainz: Grünewald, 1993).

Calvinism, of an arbitrary deity. For all his fascination with the Trinitarian metaphysics of Schelling and his speculative predilections, Coleridge was not prepared to follow that path which made Schelling a forerunner of Kierkegaard, Schopenhauer, and Nietzsche.

Arguing from the nature of mind as self-retaining and self-containing power to a self-causing power, Coleridge sees

Causa sui αἰτία ὑπερούσιος. Here alone we find a problem which in its very statement contains its own solution – the one self-solving power, beyond which no question *is possible*. Yet short of this we dare not rest; for even the ʽΟ ˮΩΝ, the Supreme *Being*, if it were contemplated abstractly from the Absolute WILL, whose essence it is to be causative of *all* Being, would sink into a Spinozistic Deity. That this is not evident to us arises from a false notion of Reason (ʽΟ Λόγος) as quality, property, or faculty of the Real: whereas reason *is* the supreme reality, the only true *being* in all things visible and invisible! the Pleroma, in whom alone God loveth the world! Even in man *will* is deeper than *mind:* for mind does not cease to be mind by having an antecedent; but Will is either the first (τὸ ἀεὶ πρόπρωτον, τὸ nunquam *positum*, semper *sup*ponendum) or it is not WILL at all. (*CCS*, p. 182)

The idea of the supreme principle of being as *causa sui* is to be found in Plotinus:

And one ought perhaps to understand that it was in this sense that the ancients spoke of 'beyond being' with a hidden meaning, not only that he generates substance but that he is not a slave to substance or to himself, nor is his substance his principle, but he, being principle of substance, did not make substance for himself, but when he had made it left it outside himself, because he has no need of being, he who made it . . . he himself is primarily his will.[198]

This treatise is somewhat more positive in its account of the good than elsewhere in the *Enneads*, in particular the use of language of thought, love, and *will*. The creative activity of the One is only necessary in the sense that it could not *not happen* but it is absolutely *spontaneous* in its creative perfection. There is, Plotinus insists, no possibility of constraint from without or within. The One is not determined by necessity but establishes necessity: the essence of the freedom of the One is his own *will* – the One or the Good creates himself (αἴτιον ἑαυτοῦ).[199] For Plotinus the freedom of the One resides in his not being subject to any extrinsic causal power. The

[198] Plotinus *Treatise* vi. 8 (39) 19, 13–20; 21,16.
[199] Plotinus *Treatise* v. (39) 8 14, 41.

One is not free in the sense of having choices or deliberating, and is not necessitated in the sense of being determined from without. In this sense all the 'actions' of the One are 'necessary' in so far as they ensue from his immutable essence. It was this concept of divine 'necessity' that Spinoza employed in his *Ethics*. F. H. Jacobi denounced vehemently Spinoza's vision of divine necessity as incompatible with the Christian faith. But, as Kolakowski observes, it is not at all clear that Spinoza's conception of divine freedom differs radically from mainstream Christian theology.[200] Augustine and Aquinas largely inherited the Plotinian vision of the supreme being as *actus purus*, as perfect actuality: there is no potentiality in the divine – nothing that God could become. This Platonic tradition rejected adamantly the anthropomorphism which imagines God as *capable* of *choosing* evil. Such a capacity for choosing evil would be in conflict with the divine essence. As Richard Hooker observes, 'The being of God is a kinde of lawe to his working: for that perfection which God is, geveth perfection to that he doth.'[201]

Let us consider what Schelling seeks to achieve with his concept of division or rupture (*Scheidung*). Whereas thinkers in the Platonist tradition like Kant and Hegel define freedom as the freedom for the good, Schelling sees freedom as the freedom for good *and evil*.[202] He consciously rejects the view that freedom is the sovereignty of the intellectual principle over sensual lusts and desires (*Freiheit in der bloßen Herrschaft des intelligenten Prinzips über die sinnlichen Begierden und Neigungen besteht*).[203] Here he departs radically from traditional (Platonic) metaphysics, which maintains that there can be no bad without good, but which insists emphatically that there can be good without bad: in God. For Schelling the darkness is a principle within God who is the indivisible unity of both principles (*Gott als Geist (ist) die unzertrennliche Einheit beider Prinzipien*)[204] and this corresponds to

---

[200] L. Kolakowski, *Religion* (Glasgow: Fontana, 1982), pp. 27 ff.
[201] *The Works of Richard Hooker*, 3 vols., ed. W. Speed Hill (Cambridge, Mass.: Harvard University Press 1981), vol. i. p. 59. I owe this reference to Wayne Hankey. See his article 'Augustinian Immediacy and Dionysian mediation in John Colet, Edmund Spenser, Richard Hooker and the Cardinal de Bérulle' in *Augustinus in der Neuzeit, Colloque de la Herzog August Bibliothek de Wolfenbüttel 14–17 octobre 1996*, edited by K . Flasch and D. de Courcelles (Turnhout: Brépol, 1998).
[202] 'The real and living concept is that of a capacity for good and evil' ('Der reale und lebendige Begriff aber ist, daß sie ein Vermögen des Guten und des Bösen sei'). Schelling, *Freiheit*, pp. 352–3.
[203] Ibid., pp. 371–2.   [204] Ibid., pp. 373–4.

the *Grund* within humanity: the ego as the principle of contraction and love as the principle of expansion. Although Schelling is struggling to avoid a dualism which presumes primordial evil, he nevertheless suggests that inchoate evil is the fundamental force of existence (*das Böse ist nicht anders als der Urgrund zur Existenz*[205]). Mankind has the capacity to elevate its selfishness into a leading and dominating principle rather than merely a basis and tool of life (*der Mensch seine Selbstheit anstatt sie zur Basis, zum Organ zu machen, vielmehr zum Herrschenden und zum Allwillen zu erheben*).[206] Concrete evil (*das Böse*) is the abuse of the vital dynamic principle which actually is the motor of life. The vision of human freedom which permeates the text is that it is a state of permanent menace of the dark principle of will and selfishness in creation, which perpetually breaks loose from the ideal intelligible principle, and constitutes a continual challenge to human life.[207]

How should we understand the 'vitalism' of this stage of Schelling's thought? In one sense Schelling wishes to explain human freedom in terms of divinity. The fact of freedom is seen as rooted in the divine nature and self-explication or rupture. The essential model of divinity is biological or, as Jacobi said, 'naturalistic'. Schelling writes:

God is something more real than a mere moral world order and possesses quite different and more vital dynamic powers than the feeble subtlety attributed (to Him) by the abstract Idealists. The revulsion towards all that is real, as if the ideal would be contaminated by each contact with the former has blinded philosophers with respect to the origin of evil. Idealism, if it does not possess a vital realism as its basis becomes just as empty and distant a system as the Leibnizian, Spinozistic, or any dogmatic system. The entire modern European philosophy since its inception (by Descartes) shares this common weakness: the absence of nature and hence the lack of this as the vital fundament.[208]

---

[205] Ibid., p. 378.　　[206] Ibid., pp. 389–90.

[207] See the introductory essay by Horst Fuhrmans in Schelling, *Freiheitschrift*, pp. 3–38, especially pp. 36ff., and Brown, *Later Philosophy of Schelling*, pp. 114–50.

[208] 'Gott ist etwas Realeres, als eine bloße moralische Weltordnung, und hat ganz andre und lebendigere Bewegungskräfte in sich, als ihm die dürftige Subtilität abstrakter Idealisten zuschreibt. Der Abscheu gegen alles Reale, der das Geistige durch jede Berührung mit demselben zu verunreinigen meint, muß natürlich auch den Blick für den Ursprung des Bösen blind machen. Der Idealismus, wenn er nicht einen lebendigen Realismus zur Basis erhält, wird ein ebenso leeres und abgezogenes System als das Leibnizische, Spinozistische, oder irgendein andres dogmatisches. Die ganze neu-europäische Philosophie seit ihrem Beginn (durch Descartes) hat diesen gemeinschaftlichen Mangel, daß die Natur für sie nicht vorhanden ist, und daß es ihr am lebendigen Grunde fehlt.' *Freiheitschrift*, pp, 355–6.

Coleridge's critique of Schelling's speculative Trinitarian theology is exactly what one would expect from a Christian (Neo)Platonist: the great weakness of Schelling is the 'establishment of Polarity in the Absolute' (cf. *Notebooks* iii. 4449; *CL* iv. 874). Coleridge's favourite symbol of the divine is the (Platonic) image of light: and he frequently employs mirror imagery in *Aids to Reflection*. In contrast to the Behmian and Schellingian idea of a dark element in the Godhead, Coleridge insists that the divine is translucent light.

As absolute Identity: 'is not the *Will* of God identical with his nature? Is it not naturally good or beneficent? Is there in Eternity a distinguishable moment, that one moment should possibly be preferred to another?' (*Inquiring Spirit*, p. 385). Coleridge's conviction is that *polarity* at the level of *divine being* is inadequate: the distinctions between light and darkness, love and hate as finite opposition cannot be legitimately projected into the divine life.

Schelling's proposition that: 'each being can only be revealed in terms of its opposite, love only in hate, unity in conflict' (*jedes Wesen kann nur in seinem Gegenteil offenbar werden, Liebe nur in Haß, Einheit in Streit*)[209] is rejected adamantly by Coleridge, for whom truth certainly does not depend upon the existence of falsehood. Hence, for Coleridge, evil or falsehood is not a *principle* of true being, but the absence or privation of the good: Spinoza expressed this with his dictum that truth is the index of itself and falsehood: 'just as light shows itself and darkness also, so truth is a standard of itself and falsity'.[210] In his *Logic* Coleridge maintains that the question of the nature of truth in relation to God 'has either no meaning or admits of one reply, viz. "God Himself". God is truth, the identity of thing and thought, knowing and being . . . Truth, therefore is its own criterion and, in the language of Augustine, at once discovers itself and detects its opposite, even as we discover darkness by light and light by its own evidence' (*Logic*, pp. 111–12).

Coleridge's conviction is that the self-explication is not a *rupture* within the Godhead but an absolute eternal self-affirmation. Trinitarian theology tends to subordinationism in that the Father is the *source* of the Trinity. For Coleridge the Father *is* only in relation to the Son and the Spirit. The Father is the Ipseity, the Son the Alterity,

---

[209] Ibid., pp. 373–4.
[210] Spinoza, *Ethics*, vol. ii. § 43, translated by A. Boyle (London: Dent, 1986), p. 70. cf. Wolfson, *Spinoza*. vol. ii. p. 100.

the Spirit the Community.[211] The very notion of an opposite requires duality, so that there cannot be an opposite to the One. That is to speak of the super-categorical relational *unity* of the three elements; the super-categorical unity of the Godhead *is* Itself without process or rupture.

The real problem with Schelling's system for Coleridge is not its pantheism; God and world are certainly not identical for Schelling because the polarity in the Godhead is sustained in harmony, whereas in the world it forms the basis for evil and conflict. What is disturbing for Coleridge is the denial of the Christian Platonic vision of God as identical with and 'constrained' by the logos. An arbitrary God, the divine will without the divine wisdom (i.e. the archetype of the world) is no better than atheism. In a letter to Charles Tulk Coleridge writes:

All that exists has a beginning – and God whose essence is the ground of all things, is by his Will, thro' the *utterance* of his Will [= the Word, Λόγος] the Beginner of their existence; God *createth* all things. He not only *formeth* them, i.e. establisheth their relativity and correspondent relations, but he likewise *groundeth* them – *in* him they have their Being, *from* him they receive their *existence*. (*CL* iv. 1077, p. 767)

The fact that the intellect or Word or Logos belongs to God's essential being – in the language of Nicaea, is consubstantial with the Father – means that his creation reflects God's own rational nature. Divine power has no arbitary dominion over 'understanding, truth and knowledge.' Cudworth writes:

Truth is not factitious; it is a thing which cannot be arbitarily *made*, but *is*. The divine will and omnipotence itself hath no imperium upon the divine understanding . . . though the truth of singular contingent propositions depends upon the things themselves existing without, as the measure and archetype thereof, yet as to the universal and abstract theorems of science, the terms whereof are those reasons of things which exist nowhere but only in the mind itself (whose noemata and ideas they are) the measure and rule of truth concerning them can be no foreign or extraneous thing without the mind, but must be native and domestic to it, or contained within the mind itself, and therefore can be nothing but its clear and distinct perception. In these intelligible ideas of the mind whatsoever is clearly perceived to be is; or, which is all one, is true.[212]

---

[211] S. H. Ford, 'Perichoresis and interpenetration: Samuel Taylor Coleridge's Trinitarian conception of unity' in *Theology* 89 (1986), pp. 20–40; J. W. Clayton, 'Coleridge and the logos: the Trinitarian unity of consciousness and culture' in *The Journal of Religion* 70 (1990), pp. 213–40.

[212] Cudworth, *True Intellectual System*, vol. iii. pp. 33–4.

The emphasis in Coleridge's thought upon the personal Godhead and the metaphysical Trinity is intimately linked to the natural theology of the post-Kantians. Coleridge could see Kant as the initiator of the dynamic philosophy in that his pupils were led to revise their Spinozism and develop a speculative Trinitarian theology by virtue of their desire to preserve the Kantian tenet of man's spiritual nature as his rational freedom within a monistic metaphysical system. Coleridge does not accept the strictly idealistic idea that both God and world are dialectically one subject and that the world is part of a divine process or theogony: he distinguishes much more strongly than Schelling or Hegel between divine and finite thought.[213]

Furthermore, Coleridge's Platonism mitigated against an acceptance of some of Schelling's central tenets, particularly the latent materialism of Schelling's philosophy and the idea of a primordial principle in the Godhead that becomes active evil in the finite realm. Here Coleridge's Platonism resists the voluntaristic tenets of Schelling's middle period. Schelling asserts in the *Freiheitschrift*: 'In the last and final stage there is no Being other than Will. Will is original being, and for this the following predicates alone are fitting: aseity, eternity, independence of time, self-affirmation. Philosophy in its entirety strives solely thither: to find this highest expression.'[214] Coleridge reveals Schelling's influence in his preface to *Aids to Reflection* when he speaks of his attempt to show that the mysteries of the Christian faith are reason in its highest form of self-affirmation: the concept of God as self-affirming will is central for *Aids to Reflection*. But this should not, in the case of Coleridge, be understood as theological or metaphysical voluntarism (will is primordial being) but self-affirming actus purus. Coleridge does not envisage the divine 'will' in opposition to nature – and thus shows his deep affinity with Cudworth and Hooker (*Aids*, p. 141). Perhaps, Coleridge's metaphysical building, with its part of a room from Schelling and a roof from Anglican theology, is not as untenable as critics such as Wellek have assumed.

---

[213] cf. Augustine, 'si enim comprehendis, non est Deus', *Sermon* cxvii § 3, 5 in *Sancti Aurellii Augustini*, 12 vols., edited by J.-P. Migne (Paris, 1861–3), 38, p. 663.

[214] 'Es gibt in der letzten und höchsten Instanz gar kein andres Sein als Wollen. Wollen ist Ursein, und auf dieses allein passen alle Prädikate desselben: Grundlosigkeit, Ewigkeit, Unabhängigkeit von der Zeit, Selbstbejahung. Die ganze Philosophie strebt nur dahin, diesen höchsten Ausdruck zu finden.' Schelling, *Freiheitschrift*, pp. 350–1. Ernst Benz's book on Plotinus and the roots of the metaphysics of the will in mystical thought, *Marius Victorinus*, is deeply Schellingian.

CHAPTER 2

Inner word: reflection as meditation

Our hearts find no peace until they rest in you.   (Augustine, *Confessions* 1.1)

In the beginning was the Word, and the Word was with God, and the Word was God.   (John 1:1)

Exclusive of the abstract sciences, the largest and worthiest portion of knowledge consists of *aphorisms*: and the greatest and the best of men is but an aphorism.   (*Aids*, p. 34)

Aids to Reflection is permeated by the literary tendencies of an age which encouraged a conversational tone on the part of the author. In the 'Age of Sensibility' friendship was a particularly common literary motif. Biographical confessions of a seemingly private nature were, prior to Romanticism, both rare and thought undesirable: Rousseau's *Confessions* (1782) and Gibbon's *Memoirs of my Life* (1796) were published posthumously. However their publication constitutes instances of a developing European trend towards autobiography culminating in Goethe's *Dichtung und Wahrheit* (1811–33). Coleridge's *Biographia Literaria* (1817) was published long before Wordsworth's *Prelude* (1850) and Newman's *Apologia Pro Vita Sua* (1864). Thomas de Quincy's *Confessions of an Opium Eater* (1822) is a good instance of the novel and rather scandalous resonance of autobiographical confessions in this period.

The eighteenth century was a period in which letters or aphorisms assumed a particular importance in the wake of the salon culture, and in which biographical elements, travel news, and intellectual gossip were often integrated into a book form.[1] An obvious example is Friedrich Heinrich Jacobi's *Concerning the Teaching of Spinoza in Letters to Mr Mendelssohn* (*Ueber die Lehre des Spinoza, in Briefen an den Herrn Mendelssohn*) in which Jacobi reports on his visit to Lessing and his conversation with him.

---

[1] e.g. Laurence Sterne, *The Life and Opinions of Tristram Shandy, Gentleman*, 1759–67, edited by I. C. Ross (Oxford University Press, 1983).

Coleridge addresses the reader at the beginning of *Aids to Reflection*, and describes his own frame of mind at the time of writing.[2] These are aspects which are characteristic for the epistolary and rather sentimental temper of the age. *Aids to Reflection* also has dialogues, parables, and, throughout, a personal tone. The titles of his works, *The Friend, Lay Sermons, Confessions of an Inquiring Spirit* are part of the enthusiasm for the 'confessions' (e.g. Rousseau) and 'lives and opinions' (e.g. *Tristram Shandy, Gentleman*).

The final form of *Aids to Reflection*, with its long passages of Coleridgean metaphysics, does not cohere easily with the original intent to produce a collection of 'beauties', that is, short excerpts of striking prose from Leighton. The final product was much more than a homage to Leighton, and in fact many of the most important quotations come from other writers. Coleridge shows some discomfort in his attempt to maintain the aphoristic plan of the work while evidently attempting something much more ambitious than the original concept, and much more difficult to sustain as aphoristic. The fact that *Aids to Reflection* started as a relatively minor project and became something close to the projected 'Assertion of Religion' is of considerable importance for our judgement of the real significance of the aphorism. The change in plan took place while the work was being printed, and this led to Coleridge employing rather artificial devices – 'Preliminary' or 'Note Prefatory' or 'Comment' – to sustain the impression that the aphoristic structure had been maintained (cf. *Aids* lviii–lxxi). Nevertheless, we cannot simply attribute Coleridge's use of the aphorism to contemporary fashions and his problems with the technical production of his text.

APHORISM

What is an aphorism? Though akin to a proverb, it is the work of an author. The writer of aphorisms practises a precise manner of writing whereby sentences are not bound logically to each other but are self-contained. Coleridge uses the etymological roots of the word, *ap* and *horizein* (to limit), to make this point, and he uses the example of cutting up the county boundaries of England and considering them apart from the rest: 'This twofold act of circum-

---

[2] 'Since the preceding pages were composed, and during an interim of depression and disqualification', *Aids*, p. 242.

scribing, and detaching, when it is exerted by the mind on subjects of reflection and reason, is to *aphorize*, and the result is an *aphorism*' (*Aids*, p. 33).

The aphorism is, however, an odd vehicle for philosophy because of the generally argumentative nature of philosophical writing; an aphorism precludes discursive argument because it becomes hard to produce a chain of continuous reflection with deliberately discrete and disjointed reflections.[3]

Aphorisms constitute memorable maxims for behaviour: aids based upon the conviction that experience teaches fools (*eventus stultorum magister!*) and books teach the wise. The seventeenth century was a period which encouraged the making of notes of such observations:[4] acute but unsystematic wisdom. One might compare *Aids to Reflection* with Benjamin Whichcote's classic *Moral and Religious Aphorisms* or George Berkley's *Siris*. The aids which Coleridge offers are didactic: they should instruct the reader and help to form the character. Inge notes that 'The good aphorism is an essay or sermon in miniature, and the beauty of it is that it leaves us to think out the essay or sermon for ourselves'.[5] This certainly fits the didactic nature of the *Aids to Reflection*: the aphorism is an ideal form for the meditative intent of the work; the aphorisms constitute *spiritual exercises*.

There is no consensus concerning the literary identity of the aphorism; particularly not in England because Bacon was *the* great writer of aphorisms in the English language, yet the concept of an aphorism was determined largely by the French moralist tradition. The interest in aphorisms and proverbs has its roots in the classical *sententiae* and the biblical proverbs. There are examples in Erasmus (*Institutio principis christiani*, 1515) and Bacon (*Novum Organum*, 1620), Pascal and La Rochefoucauld; however, there was virtually no determinate idea about the literary identity of the aphorism. The aphorism enjoyed massive prestige in the Renaissance. Marlowe's Dr Faustus says that his common talk is taken to be aphoristic, and Richard Mulcaster, Spenser's schoolmaster at Merchant Taylors School, states that he cannot present his thoughts in the form of the

---

[3] The aphorising philosopher is sometimes a strident irrationalist: Nietzsche is the philosopher who philosophises in aphorisms, and Adorno is a more modern instance of a writer who sees the aphorism as a revolt against system.

[4] Brian Vickers, *Francis Bacon and Renaissance Prose* (Cambridge University Press, 1968), p. 77.

[5] W. R. Inge, *More Lay Thoughts of a Dean* (London: Putnam, 1932), p. 154.

aphorism since they do not warrant such a dignified status.[6] Bacon writes:

It is generally to be found in the wisdom of the more ancient times, that as men found out any observation that they thought good for life, they would gather it and express it in parable or aphorism or fable.[7]

The aphorism becomes particularly important in Romanticism[8] and would seem to be a point of intuitively obvious affinity between Coleridge and the literature of German Romanticism.[9] The question is whether aphorism and irony belong together here. A number of Coleridge scholars have insisted that we must consider Coleridge's thinking as generally influenced by the German Romantic view of irony. The German concept of the relation of aphorism to irony is particularly shaped by Friedrich Schlegel. It appears in his writings from 1797 onwards: not as a rhetorical device but as philosophical capacity, a 'philosophisches Vermögen'.[10] For Friedrich Schlegel the aphorism has an *epistemological* function and an aphoristic philosophy is constantly aware of the limits of linguistic expression. The main point of contact between F. Schlegel and Coleridge is the conviction expressed in Plato's seventh letter that genuine enlightenment cannot be achieved through formal argument but through special insight.[11] Yet we should be cautious with respect to direct dependence. The scholars who present an ironic Coleridge wish to assert just this: they wish to establish that Coleridge was consciously using irony in the tradition of the German Romantics. If that is the case it would be obvious that he is using irony in *Aids to Reflection* through

[6] Vickers, *Francis Bacon and Renaissance Prose*, p. 62.
[7] Bacon, *Works*, 3 453, quoted by Vickers, *Francis Bacon*, p. 70.
[8] *Historisches Wörterbuch der Philosophie*, edited by J. Ritter (Darmstadt: Wissenschaftliche Buchgesellschaft, 1971–), vol. i, p. 438 and Gerhard Neumann, *Der Aphorismus. Zur Geschichte, zu den Formen und Möglichkeiten einer literarischen Gattung* (Darmstadt: Wissenschaftliche Buchgesellschaft, 1976).
[9] The standard work in German is: Gerhard Neumann, *Der Aphorismus. Ideenparadiese Aphoristik bei Lichtenberg, Novalis, Friedrich Schlegel und Goethe* (Munich: Fink, 1976).
[10] F. N. Nennemeier, 'Fragment und Ironie beim jungen F. Schlegel' in *Poetica* 2 (1968), pp. 348–70. Hegel was a severe critic of the 'infinite absolute negativity' of irony ('unendliche absolute Negativität), Hegel, *Ästhetik* in his *Werke*, 20 vols. (Frankfurt: Suhrkamp, 1986), vol. xiii. pp. 93–9.
[11] 'Wer irgend eine höhere Überlieferung der Wahrheit und Quelle der Erkenntis zugibt, der berührt eben damit auch den Plato und betritt das Gebiet seiner Philosophie, die ja ohnehin kein beschränktes System, sondern eine sokratische Kunst und ein freier, alle Erweiterung fähiger Geistesweg ist.' F. Schlegel, *Kritische Ausgabe*, 35 vols, edited by H. Eichner (Paderborn: Schöningh, 1967–) vi. p. 95 in his *Ausgabe*, 35 vols., edited by H. Eichner (Paderborn: Schöningh, 1967–). Novalis also considered fragment to be a particular mode of thought. See Neumann, *Der Aphorismus. Ideenparadiese*, pp. 265–416.

the medium of the aphorism; however, there is very little evidence for this assumption. Firstly, Coleridge was much closer to Schelling and the idealistic school than to the German Romantics.[12] Secondly, Coleridge is using 'aphorisms' from other writers. The ambiguity in the text is more like that between an editor and original author such as Reimarus and Lessing than the consciously ironic self-presentation in Schlegel. Furthermore, Leighton is neither a poet nor even an aphoristic writer.[13]

The most important inspiration for Coleridge was Francis Bacon, the most distinguished writer of aphorisms in the late Renaissance. Bacon, moreover, enjoyed a revival in the late eighteenth and early nineteenth centuries, and seems to have been an important precedent for Coleridge; the length of Coleridge's aphorisms is more easily appreciated by the reader of Bacon's long aphorisms. Brian Vickers shows the extent to which Bacon combines the traditional Renaissance view of the aphorism as prestigious, flexible, empirical, and practical with the insistence that aphorisms are the 'pith and heart of sciences'.[14] Bacon writes:

But as young men when they knit and shape perfectly, do seldom grow to a further stature, so knowledge, while it is in aphorisms and observations it is in growth, but when it once is comprehended in exact methods, it may perchance be polished and illustrate, and accommodated for use and practice, but it increaseth no more in bulk and substance.[15]

The mind is thus free to work on the materials given: aphorisms 'representing a knowledge broken, do invite men to enquire farther, whereas Methods, carrying the shew of a total, do secure men as if they were at furthest'.[16] Vickers also stresses the imaginative power of the aphorism. Bacon has a clear vision of aphorism stimulating further inquiry and, correspondingly, of *discovery* through aphorism; he declares that 'discoveries are as it were new creations, and imitations of God's works':[17] an image of growth, closely related to

---

[12] e.g. Schleiermacher, F. Schlegel, and Novalis. Ernst Behler, *Unendliche Perfektibilität. Europäische Romantik und die Französiche Revolution* (Paderborn: Schöningh, 1989), and *Studien zur Romantik und zur idealistischen Philosophie* (Paderborn: Schöningh, 1988), pp. 9–45. cf. M. Frank, *Unendliche Annährung. Die Anfänge der philosophischen Frühromantik* (Frankfurt: Suhrkamp, 1997), pp. 921–44.

[13] His works consist largely of biblical commentary.

[14] Bacon, *New Organon*, iv. 85, quoted by Vickers, *Francis Bacon*, p. 73.

[15] Bacon, F., *Advancement of Learning*, vol. iii. p. 292 in *The Works of Francis Bacon*, edited by James Spedding, R. L. Ellis, and D. D. Heath (London: Longman and Co., 1857–74), vol. iii. p. 297.

[16] Bacon, *Works*, vol. iii. p. 405, quoted by Vickers, *Francis Bacon*, p. 72.

[17] Bacon, *Works*, vol. iv. p. 113.

the inductive process. Perhaps it is odd that the name of Bacon which is so closely associated with the virtues of strict science should have laid such a weight upon an imaginative form of expression, one which often revolves around a striking image. The aphorism, for Bacon, is likely to make the reader think about that which he reads and try to apply it; as such, it is a literary form ideally designed for the scientific endeavour: firing development, openness, and hence genuine research. The aphorism is an unsystematic method of pointing to a deeper system or pattern which the mind has yet to explore. Bacon was a passionate advocate of devising systems, and the interest in the form of the aphorism does not entail a rejection of system per se. Bacon, like Schelling, uses the aphorism with a systematic intent. One might consider Schelling's aphorism: 'Science has ever been searching for the point where Knowledge includes Being.'[18] Aphorisms express the universal in a fragment.

Coleridge shares Bacon's belief that the aphorism may point to system but is himself critical of the 'corruption, introduced by certain immethodical aphorisming Eclectics . . . dismissing not only all system, but all logical connection (*BL* i. 292). Coleridge combines Baconian confidence in the aphorism as a harbinger of systematic insight with the Platonic conviction that reflection upon the nature of the mind is a means of access to the divine. Bacon claims that his aphorisms 'are *seeds* only, not *flowers*'.[19] Such seminal aphorisms are well suited to the aims of *Aids to Reflection*. It is perhaps no coincidence that Bacon was a great admirer of seventeenth-century theology: 'the best work in divinity which had been written since the apostles' times'.[20]

MEDITATION AND AWAKENING: SPIRITUAL EXERCISES

Leighton did not himself write aphorisms. However, the seventeenth century was an age in which schoolboys were encouraged to keep notebooks in which they recorded aphorisms or particular passages. Coleridge's collection of 'beauties' of Leighton is an interesting reflection of this habit. A form of writing which is designed to

---

[18] 'Von eher sucht die Wissenschaft nach dem Punkt, wo das Seyn das Erkennen einschließt' (no. 61). F. W. J. von Schelling, 'Aphorismen zur Einleutung in die Naturphilosophie' in *Ausgewählte Werke. Schriften von 1806–1813* (Darmstadt: Wissenschaftliche Buchgesellschaft, 1968), p. 139.
[19] Bacon, *Works*, vol. iv. p. 492.   [20] Bacon, *Works*, vol. iii. p. 488.

encourage meditation is aimed at the *will* and employs metaphors
and images which have a strongly emotional and conative component. The aim is to try to point to the religious dimension in
experience: Leighton is not, strictly speaking, a philosopher. Nonetheless, his theological writings are unintelligible without reference
to his philosophical sources, all of which are clearly part of what
Coleridge refers to glowingly as the 'spiritual platonic old England'
(*Aids*, p. 182 n. 71).

Leighton was a scholar of a mild temperament who was consecrated bishop during the unhappy period of the conflict between
Charles II and the Scottish Presbyterians. Leighton had strong
sympathies with presbyterianism and his church was very close to
the discipline of John Knox. Leighton's acceptance of a see, first at
Dunblane and then at Glasgow, seemed to many a betrayal of the
Scottish Reformation, and Leighton resigned his see in the wake of
much strife and discord. He has been described as an ineffectual
saint, and it is quite possible that Coleridge felt an affinity with this
man of a profound Christian spirituality embroiled in difficulties and
adverse circumstances, a failure in worldly terms. Leighton was a
Christian Platonist and a mystic who was a contemporary and
admirer of Henry More and the Cambridge Platonists.[21] He was
profoundly familiar with the Neoplatonists and the Christian mystics
and spiritual tradition in Christianity and seemingly indifferent to
scholasticism. Coleridge describes Leighton as 'Plato glorified by St
Paul' (*Marg.* iii. 511). Coleridge could almost consider his soul to be
an emanation from Leighton (*Marg* ii. 523) and in the same passage
Coleridge remarks that in reading Leighton he seems to be 'thinking
my own thoughts over again'.

We have access to the nature of Leighton's library and it is clear
from his books that Leighton was primarily interested in the
Neoplatonists. He possessed works by Plotinus, Proclus, and Iamblichus, and speaks of Plotinus as 'the philosopher'. Scholastic works
are conspicuously absent. Leighton belongs to that tradition of
western mysticism which derives primarily from Augustine and

---

[21] John Forbes of Corse, *Spiritual Exercises*, Henry Scougall, *Life of God in the Soul of Man*, and
James Garden *Comparative Theology, or, the True and Solid Grounds of a Pure and Peaceable Theology.*
North-east Scotland was a stronghold of episcopalianism at the end of the seventeenth
century. This Aberdonian episcopalian tradition was marked by an interest in mysticism.
See W. W. Ward, 'Anglicanism and assimilation, or mysticism and mayhem in the
eighteenth century' in *Faith and Faction* (London: Epworth, 1993), pp. 385–96.

Bernard and which uses Neoplatonic conceptual tools in its description of the ascent of the soul to God.[22] This is, furthermore, a
tradition of thought which is intensely biblical. Augustine moves
effortlessly between Platonist metaphysics and the exegesis of biblical
texts: especially St Paul and St John, the Psalms, and Genesis.

> It was customary with religious men in former times, to make a rule of
> taking every morning some text, or aphorism, for their occasional
> meditation during the day, and thus to fill up the intervals of their attention
> to business. (*Aids*, pp. 32–3)

Coleridge's interest in the aphorism as a form reflects further his
admiration for seventeenth-century English literary and philosophic
culture. On 25 January 1830 his contemporary Goethe was reported
to have said, 'Folk do not know what time and effort it requires to
learn to read. I have required eighty years, and I cannot say that I
have yet reached my goal.'[23] The apparent paradox is dispelled if
Goethe means by 'reading' reflections or spiritual exercises upon
those truths which 'lie bed-ridden in the dormitory of the soul' (*Aids*,
p. 11). The point of Goethe's observation is most relevant for
Coleridge's concept of reflection: to ponder is not at all the same as
'cleverness' or 'quick'-wittedness; on the contrary – it is more a
matter of *slowing* down and achieving a deliberate, ruminative frame
of mind. Real discovery is often the product of raising questions
which others have thought silly or obvious. Equally, it is the product
of slow and painstaking labours, toils for which the 'quick' wit may
be too impatient. Most importantly, originality 'consists in thinking
for ourselves, not in thinking differently from other people'.[24] The
real novelty of ideas lies in their having been digested and assimi-
lated by the mind, and not just passively and timidly accepted.

Coleridge was concerned that discursive prose might encourage
the reader to pass over points which require thought rather than
attention, and aphorisms encourage a reflective pondering upon the
specific points discussed. The distinguished Neoplatonism scholar
Pierre Hadot notes:

> I sincerely believe that our most urgent and difficult task today is, as

[22] Bishop E. A. Knox, *Robert Leighton, Archbishop of Glasgow: a Study of his Life, Times and Writings* (London: James Clarke, 1930), p. 224. See further J. B. Craven, *The Esoteric Studies of Leighton* (Selkirk: Scottish Chronicle Press, 1918).

[23] Goethe, W. *Gespräche mit Eckermann, in den letzten Jahren seines Lebens*, edited by Ludwig Geiger (Leipzig: Insel, 1902), p. 570.

[24] W. R. Inge, *Faith and Knowledge* (Edinburgh: T. and T. Clark, 1904), p. 246.

Goethe said, to 'learn to believe in simplicity'. Might it not be the case that the greatest lesson which the philosophers of Antiquity – and above all Plotinus – have to teach us is that philosophy is not the complicated, pretentious, and artificial construction of a learned system of discourse, but the transformation of perception and life, which lends inexhaustible meaning to the formula – seemingly so banal – of the love of the Good?[25]

The lectures of Coleridge's pupil Hort were described in the following manner, which is fascinatingly close to Hadot's depiction of the impact of a genuinely philosophical mind, where assent to ideas can genuinely shape lives towards the good:

There is something mysterious about those lectures. I do not think there is anyone in Cambridge whose lectures are so utterly simple as yours are: language, ideas, reasoning, everything is simple in them. One does not at the time always feel that there is any particular depth in what you are saying; and yet when the hour is over and the notebook shut, and we are out in our silly world again, we find that at least one point you have been telling us about has become a sort of living creature in our minds, has made itself a home in us, and will not leave off talking to us. The one childishly simple idea runs on in a chain of beautiful thoughts that illustrate and explain everything we come across for days and months.[26]

It is perhaps with such a notion of ideas becoming 'a sort of living creature in our minds', making 'a home in us', that Coleridge draws on the 'beauties' of Leighton – as attempts to awaken in the conscious mind the awareness of the inward Christ. Coleridge quotes Leighton: 'Plotinus thanked God, that his Soul was not tied to an immortal Body' (*Aids*, p. 91). This curious remark is meant to point to a spiritual vigilance[27] in Plotinus' efforts to contemplate the good; a philosopher who would not speak of his parents, birth, or home, and who refused to have a portrait made of himself. The reference points to Leighton's and Coleridge's approval of the 'otherworldliness' of Plotinus' meditations.

Louis Martz in his book *Paradise Within* distinguishes between the Roman Catholic meditative tradition, which has its complex analytic method, and the relative formlessness of the Protestant type. Whereas Ignatian meditation concentrates upon the passion and eschatology, this Protestant Augustinian meditation is rather like 'an

---

[25] Pierre Hadot, *Plotinus, or the Simplicity of Vision*, translated by M. Chase with an introduction by A. I. Davidson, revised and augmented second edition (Chicago and London: University of Chicago Press, 1993), p. xi.

[26] Inge, *Faith and Knowledge*, p. 246.

[27] Perhaps a reference to Plotinus, *Treatise* iv. 3 (27) 12, 8 ff. cf Augustine, *City of God*, ix. §11.

intuitive groping into the regions of the soul that lie beyond sensory memories'.[28] Leighton's meditation is based upon the three books of Christ: the Bible, nature, and conscience. Of these three books the Bible plays a particularly important role, and in the Bible particularly the psalms. The psalms had been put into English for the purposes of singing, and the word meditation occurs often within them. In the literature of this period a common metaphor for meditation is digestion. As the body needs physical nutrition, so the soul needs spiritual sustenance by meditating on the three books: nature, the soul, and the Bible.[29]

He [says Archbishop Leighton] who teaches men the principles and precepts of spiritual wisdom, before their minds are called off from foreign objects, and turned inward upon themselves, might as well write his instructions, as the Sibyl wrote her prophecies, on the loose leaves of the trees, and commit them to the mercy of inconstant winds. (*Aids*, p. 13)

God is to be found both immanent within the soul and beyond the soul. However much emphasis is laid upon the inwardness of the divine, this is always balanced by the insistence that the divine is transcendent. Leighton insists that one should live more by the soul than by the body: 'What a full Confession do we make of our dissatisfaction with the Objects of our bodily senses' (*Aids*, p. 92). Leighton avers that 'immoderate use of the world' renders the soul 'heavy in spiritual exercises, and obstructs the way and motion of the Spirit of God, in the soul' (*Aids*, p. 99).

Although the style of *Aids to Reflection* is closely bound to the epistolary and incipiently autobiographical mode of the age, Coleridge is pursuing the ancient vision of philosophy as a spiritual exercise (cf. *Aids*, p. 99 on 'spiritual exercises'): he is intent upon awakening genuine thought in his reader rather than merely conveying information, and his use of aphorisms is aimed at encouraging a contemplative frame of mind. Pierre Hadot argues that contemporary philosophers are inclined to overlook the practical or spiritual nature of philosophy in antiquity. Philosophy did not mean abstract technical theories produced by professionals but the living wisdom of a life led according to reason.[30] Hadot calls the Platonic

---

[28] L. Martz, *The Paradise Within: Studies in Vaughan, Traherne and Milton* (New Haven: Yale University Press, 1964) p. 23.

[29] For a standard account of the motif of the book see Robert Curtius, *Europäische Literatur und Lateinisches Mittelalter*, second edition (Bern: Francke, 1954), pp. 306–52.

[30] Pierre Hadot, *Exercices spirituels et philosophie antique* (Paris: Etudes Augustiniennes, 1987).

dialogues spiritual exercises for the *philo-sophos* rather than for the *sophos*, for the one who is seeking wisdom rather than for the sophist.[31] Philosophy is the task of seeking objectivity by stripping away the distortions of subjective desires. In Neoplatonism the idea of spiritual progress plays a particularly prominent role. Marinus' *Life of Proclus*, a work from which Coleridge culled one of his mottos (*Aids*, p. 4), arranges the works of Proclus according to the stages of his spiritual life.[32] Hadot insists that philosophy was thought of as the conscious reflective transformation of life. Given this concept of philosophy, it is entirely intelligible why Church Fathers could see the Christian religion as the fulfilment of philosophy or as the one true philosophy. Coleridge defines PHILOSOPHY as the 'doctrine and discipline of ideas' (*CCS*, p. 47). In speaking of philosophy as not just the 'doctrine' but also the *'discipline'* of ideas, he is drawing upon a concept of philosophy as a spiritual exercise.[33] The seventeenth-century theologian Bishop Burnet writes of Whichcote that:

being disgusted with the dry systematical way of those times, he studied to raise those who conversed with him to a nobler set of thoughts, and to consider religion as a seed of a deiform nature, (to use one of his own phrases.) In order to this, he set young students much on reading the ancient Philosophers, chiefly *Plato, Tully* and *Plotin*, and on considering the Christian religion as a doctrine sent from God, both to elevate and sweeten humane nature, in which he was a great example, as well as a wise and kind instructor.[34]

Burnet wrote that Leighton expressed a sense of the purpose of religion as a divine life in the soul that carried a man far above mere opinions.[35] In Whichcote and Leighton we find the emphasis upon the practical aspect of Christian divinity as philosophy in the sense of the ancients: a spiritual discipline, a tending of the soul and the

---

[31] Plato, *Phaedrus* 278d, insists tht 'wise' is a name for God alone. The humble title for a man is 'lover of wisdom'.

[32] Coleridge's copy was the Proclus edition of Aemilius Portus (Hamburg, 1618).

[33] A. H. Armstrong writes in respect of Plotinus: 'It would be anachronistic and wrong to consider his thought, or that of any other late Greek philosopher, in terms of the disassociation of moral and intellectual concerns characteristic of our way of thinking, which would lead us to consider it absurd and impertinent, for instance, to inquire closely into the degree of moral virtue possessed by a candidate for a Chair of philosophy *The Cambridge History of Later Greek and Early Medieval Philosophy*, ed. A. H. Armstrong (Cambridge University Press, 1967), pp. 195–271, p. 228.

[34] Quoted in G. Burnet, *History of his Own Time*, 2 vols., vol. i edited by G. Burnet Jr. and vol. ii edited by Sir T. Burnet (London: Ward, 1724), vol. i. p. 187.

[35] Ibid., pp. 134–9.

love of God. John Smith wrote that 'Were I indeed to define divinity, I should rather call it a *divine life*, than a *divine science*.'[36]

The natural link between the mystical and the Idealistic tradition can be seen in Fichte's use of the spiritual address in his *Instructions for (the Attainment of) a Blessed Life* (*Anweisung zum seligen Leben*, 1806). Ernst Benz has pointed out in his work *Les Sources mystiques de la philosophie romantique allemande* that Fichte is deliberately utilising the literary style of mysticism, especially the spiritual guide. In German pietism, spiritual guides, modelled on Franke's translation of Miguel de Molinos' *The Spiritual Guide*, were widely read.[37] As a spiritual guide *Aids to Reflection* not only has Platonist precedents, but idealistic analogues.

The title *Aids to Reflection*, we suggest, reveals the *practical nature* of the work. It is certainly not transcendental; it is not concerned with establishing necessary conditions of knowledge or the nature of reality in an abstract manner, but in giving practical assistance or aids: spiritual exercises. The introductory aphorisms are largely dedicated to the need for meditation: to 'awaken both the faculty of thought and the inclination to exercise it' (*Aids*, p. 14). The central distinction between energy of 'thought' and indolence of 'attention' is rooted in a Christian Neoplatonic view of genuine thought as meditative and contemplative. This is the basis of Coleridge's conviction that philosophy itself is pre-eminently practical – aimed at the transformation of the *will*. Coleridge is drawing upon a tradition of spiritual writing: Robert Leighton, John Smith, and Henry More belong to a tradition of spiritual aids to reflection in which philosophy, the search for genuine wisdom, is closely allied to prayer.

It may seem unduly paradoxical to deem the practical and experiential component of Coleridge's writing Platonic, since Platonism is often regarded as a doctrine of abstract transcendent forms, and blank hostility to mere appearances. Yet Plato himself is much less of an intellectualist than Aristotle; ultimately the good can only be gestured at, and finds its vindication in the moral and political life; the doctrine of the forms, after all, is most famously expressed in a treatise about government called the *Republic*. Unlike the rigorous first philosophy (i.e. metaphysics) presented by his

---

[36] John Smith, *Select Discourses* repr. (London: 1660, New York: Garland, 1978), p. 3.
[37] E. Benz, *The Mystical Sources of German Romantic Philosophy* (Allison Park, Pa: Pittsburgh Theological Monographs, 1983), p. 25.

greatest pupil, Plato bequeathed a number of memorable philosophical images of experiential and emotional power of that which is
'beyond being'. Plotinus intensifies the experiential component in
Platonism because he maintained that the central tenets of philosophy had been irrefutably established by Plato and Aristotle, and
the real task for the active philosopher was essentially the recovery,
through exegesis and meditation, of the ancient vision and experience – as a guide to the good life and an aid to following Plato's
injunction in the *Theaetetus* (176b) to 'become like God'. Plotinus'
writings are essentially a guide and invitation to mystical experience.[38] He uses conceptual reflection with the goal of reaching an
experience which transcends conceptuality. Philosophically, Plotinus invokes
the principle of the reciprocity of experience and reflection; experience must be disciplined and shaped by reflection and reflection
must be infused with experience. The concept of 'experience' is also
not without ambiguities.[39] Certainly irrelevant for our purposes is
the notion of 'experience' in the empiricist philosophical sense of
experiencing 'sense data'. There are two important colloquial meanings of the word, however, which are entirely relevant. The root of
our word 'experience' is the Latin verb which means 'to try'. This is
the *active* sense of having experience which means that one has
become expert through active trial. A teacher who has experience
with children, a doctor who is well established in practice; such
people have 'experience' in this active sense. Yet there is also a
strong *passive* sense in which we think of experiences as endured or
given. Both senses of the concept 'experience' are relevant for
Plotinus' philosophy. His writings are (active) spiritual 'exercises',
and their goal is the (passive) experience of the ineffable.[40]

We can perhaps explain this double sense of 'experience' with the
help of a suggestion of the Swiss Plotinus scholar H. R. Schwyzer.
Schwyzer has argued that one has to consider Plotinus' thinking
from two perspectives.[41] One perspective is the metaphysical hier-

---

[38] Beierwaltes, 'Henosis' in *Denken des Einen*, pp. 125–54.

[39] J. R. Lucas, *The Principles of Politics* (Oxford: Clarendon, 1985), § 78, pp. 357–9.

[40] This is a considerable and impressive body of literature which casts doubt upon the validity
of the concept of 'religious experience', and its applicability to the philosophical mystics,
e.g. Nicholas Lash, *Easter in Ordinary: Reflection on Human Experience and the Knowledge of God*
(London: SCM, 1988) or Denys Turner, *The Darkness of God: Negativity in Christian Mysticism*
(Cambridge, Cambridge University Press, 1995). I cannot deal with such objections to the
concept here, but for the purposes of expounding Coleridge's views I think the notion of
'religious experience' is ineluctable.

[41] H. R. Schwyzer, 'Die zwiefache Sicht in der Philosophie Plotins' in *Museum Helveticum* 1

archy of unity: ἕν – νοῦς – ψυχή. The other perspective is from the subjective experience of these levels of unity.[42] This latter *experiential* perspective is crucial for understanding Plotinus' thinking. 'Reflection' (a central term for Plotinus), the turning of the soul to the One, is achieved by the turning of the soul into itself; the return of the soul into itself leads to its own noetic ground. Speaking of the soul in the context of a reflection upon the chariot myth of *Phaedrus* 246a ff., Plotinus says: 'as long as there is anything higher than that which is present to it, it naturally goes on upwards, lifted by the giver of its love'.[43] The conative aspect of the drive to the One, the soul's reflection, is given by the One itself. The experience of a higher unity is simultaneously *awareness of the gift of the One*. This is one reason why Augustine's anti-Pelagianism has a Platonist aspect: the radical dependence upon divine 'giving' in Plotinus is certainly not Christian, but it is a metaphysical idea which Augustine could exploit for Christian purposes.[44]

When Plotinus starts his discussion of time and eternity, an involved and highly abstract argument which was so influential in late antiquity, he immediately appeals to experience. Armstrong notes:

This passage gives a clearer idea of Plotinus's way of philosophising than any other in the *Enneads*. He starts by reflecting on his own experience and trying to clarify it. In doing this his respect for tradition leads him naturally to seek help from the ancient philosophers, but he is never satisfied simply to repeat their statements; they are for him helps to further reflection leading to clearer understanding.[45]

Similarly, Augustine lays enormous weight upon the *experience* of God's presence. This is the central and pervading topic of the *Confessions*. It would be a mistake to see here a diffuse sentimentality; the analysis of experience in the first eight books of the *Confessions*, the 'flame of love' which carries the soul to God, is followed by an analysis of memory and happiness where God is presented as the *presupposition* of the self's yearning for the transcendent good. The psychology of Augustine is determined by the numinous sense of the

---

(1944), pp. 87–99. Schwyzer is developing an idea of P. O. Kristeller, *Der Begriff der Seele in der Ethik Plotins* (Tübingen: Mohr, 1919).

[42] Schwyzer speaks of these differing views of reality as the 'gegenständlich' and the 'aktuale' viewpoint.

[43] Plotinus, *Treatise*, vi. 7 (38), 22, 19 ff.

[44] Hadot, *Plotinus*, pp. 50–1 and 59–60.

[45] *Plotinus Enneads*, vol. iii, p. 297.

sovereign *transcendence* of the Creator who impinges upon his creation most profoundly and intimately at the point of the human heart.[46] Coleridge wrote to his friend Thomas Poole in 1801 that 'deep Thinking' is only possible in a man of deep feeling (*CL* ii. 709), and in the *Biographia Literaria* he defines philosophy itself as an 'affectionate seeking after truth' (*BL* i. 142). This thought too has its tradition; Denys the Areopagite states that the divine matters must be not just known but felt: 'οὐ μόνον μαθὼν ἀλλὰ καὶ παθὼν τὰ θεῖα'.[47]

REFLECTION, RECOLLECTION AND RESTLESSNESS

In his stimulating and instructive biography, Richard Holmes lays great stress upon the restlessness of Coleridge's life: his disturbed childhood and schooldays, his desultory university career; his broken marriage and dwelling in a series of households as a guest. He never established a conventional home, and this restlessness seems reflected in his spiritual yearning. Perhaps it explains his particular fondness for Robert Leighton whose wish it was to die in an inn – because they reminded him that mortal life is a stage on a pilgrim's path to God.[48] The sense of the soul in a state of exile, and the restlessness of the pilgrim spirit, is a deeply Neoplatonic-Augustinian idea.

Though the heart once gone from God turns continually further away from Him, and moves not towards Him till it be renewed, yet, even in that wandering, it retains that natural relation to God, as its centre, that it hath no true rest elsewhere, nor can by any means find it. It is made for Him, and is therefore still restless till it meet with Him. (*Aids*, p. 128)

This is the Neoplatonic-Augustinian concept of the absolute as rest in itself and rest for all created being.[49] If unhappiness is linked to the vanity of the empirical world, happiness in its deepest sense is linked to God,[50] religion is, at it were, instinctual. In 'Every rank of

---

[46] Anton Maxsein, *Philosophia Cordis* (Salzburg: Müller, 1966).
[47] Ysabel de Andia, 'παθὼν τὰ θεῖα' in *Platonism in Late Antiquity*, edited by S. Gersh and C. Kannengiesser (University of Notre Dame Press, 1992), pp. 239–58.
[48] E. A. Knox, *Robert Leighton, Archbishop of Glasgow: A Study of his Life, Times and Writings* (London: James Clarke and Co., 1930), p. 214.
[49] Plotinus' Homeric, 'For it is "the easy life" there', *Treatise* v. 8 (31) 4, 1.
[50] 'God hath suited every creature He hath made with a convenient good to which it tends, and in the obtainment of which it rests and is satisfied. Natural bodies have all their own natural place, wither, if not hindered, they move incessantly till they be in it . . . Sensitive

Creatures, as it ascends in the scale of Creation, leaves Death behind it or under it' Coleridge is pointing to an analogy between the instinctual drives of animals for security and development, and the religious aspirations of humanity. Plotinus describes the One as the most sufficient and independent of all things;[51] while all created things seek their intelligible source just as Odysseus sought his home: 'We shall put out to sea, as Odysseus did . . . our country from which we came is there, our Father is there.'[52] Augustine, commenting on this passage, presents the incarnate Word as the means to that rest which is sought by the uneasy or restless heart.[53] In the *City of God* Augustine writes that 'in this situation of weakness and in these times of evil such anxiety is even not without its use in leading them (saints and worshippers of God) to seek, with more fervent longing, that state of serenity where peace is utterly complete and assured'.[54] This very Augustinian concept of the restlessness of the heart which is unconsciously longing for eternal happiness pervades *Aids to Reflection*: 'While you labour for anything below your proper humanity, you seek a happy life in the region of death' (*Aids*, p. 119).[55] The energy of religion, on this instinctual model, is drawn from sources *beneath* consciousness and discursive reflection.

Coleridge insists in the preface that *Aids to Reflection* belongs to 'the class of didactic works' and can prepare the way for theology as the contemplation of the divine: 'At the annunciation of *principles*, of *ideas*, the soul of man awakes' (*LS*, p. 25). Coleridge sees philosophy

---

creatures are carried to seek a sensitive good, as agreeable to their rank in being, and attaining that, aim no further. Now, in this is the excellency of Man, that he is made capable of a communion with his Maker, and because capable of it, is unsatisfied without it: the soul, being cut out (so to speak) to that largeness, cannot be filled with less' (*Aids*, p. 128). The movement of created things towards their creator is driven by an immanent gravitation (*pondus*) towards its true place (*locus*): 'Omnia in mensura et in numero et in pondere disposuisti', Wisdom 11. 21. Augustine, *City of God* v, ii. W. J. Roche, 'Measure, number and weight in Saint Augustine', *New Scholasticism* 15 (1941), pp. 350–76., Oliver du Roi, *L'Intelligence de la Foi en la Trinité selon Saint Augustin*, (Paris: Etudes Augustiniennes, 1966).

[51] Plotinus, *Treatise* vi. 9 (9) 6, 17 f.

[52] Plotinus, *Treatise* i. 6 (1) 8, 17 ff.

[53] Augustine, *City of God*, ix. 17 and his: 'you made us for yourself and our hearts find no peace until they rest in you', *Confessions* i. 1 (Harmondsworth: Penguin, 1961), p. 21.

[54] Augustine, *City of God* xix. 10.

[55] The phrase 'region of death' is Augustinian, see Augustine, *Confessions* iv. 12, 2 and W. Beierwaltes, 'Regio Beatitudinis. Zu Augustins Begriff des glücklichen Lebens', *Sitzungsberichte der Heidelberger Akademie der Wissenschaften, Philosophisch-historische Klasse* 6 (1981). *Regio beatitudinis: Augustine's Concept of Happiness*, translated into English by Bernard Barsky (Villanova: Augustinian Institute, 1981).

as the *awakening* to those truths which lie 'bed-ridden in the soul'
(*Aids*, p. 11) and Leighton is he who 'perhaps of all our learned
Protestant Theologians best deserves the title of a spiritual Divine'
(*Aids*, p. 155) because his writing is inclined to awaken a conscious-
ness of the presence of the spiritual as the basis of the phenomenal
realm.

Your blessedness is not, – no, believe it, it is not where most of you seek it,
in things below you. How can that be? It must be a higher good to make
you happy.

COMMENT

Every rank of Creatures, as it ascends in the scale of Creation, leaves Death
behind it or under it . . . Behold the shadow of approaching Humanity, the
Sun rising from behind, in the kindling Morn of Creation! Thus all lower
Natures find their highest Good in semblances and seekings of that which is
higher and better. All things strive to ascend, and ascend in their striving.
And shall man alone stoop? Shall his pursuits and desires, the *reflections* of
his inward life, be like the reflected Image of a Tree on the edge of a Pool,
that grows downward, and seeks a mock heaven in the unstable element
beneath it, in neighbourhood with the slim water-weeds and oozy bottom
grass that are yet better than itself and more noble, in as far as Substances
that appear as Shadows are preferable to Shadows mistaken for Substance!
No! it must be a higher good to make you happy. While you labor for any
thing below your proper Humanity, you seek a happy Life in the region of
Death. Well saith the moral Poet –

> Unless above himself he can
> Erect himself, how mean a thing is man. (*Aids*, pp. 116–19)

In the wake of the empiricist concentration upon material phenomena and their sensualist epistemology, Coleridge wishes to call
his readers to reflect upon the mystery of the human mind, confident
that the dimension of reality which natural science investigates is in
continuity with and, indeed, is the symbol of a higher spiritual
realm. Like Augustine, Coleridge wishes to concentrate upon the
nature of the human mind which will point to the reality and
influence of the transcendent divine mind; both believed that
philosophy could have a pastoral effect in refutation of scepticism
and materialism.[56] The best philosophies, Coleridge avers, are those
which encourage a retreat from the sensual world and a concentration upon the intelligible. The nature of reality is disclosed in the

---

[56] cf. Augustine, *Against the Academics*, translated by J. J. O'Meara (Westminster, Md: Newman
Press and London: Longman, Green, and Co., 1950), p. 386.

mind's dissatisfaction with sensible experience and the soul's longing for the intelligible realm. In the very first aphorism of *Aids to Reflection* Coleridge insists that philosophy has the task of rescuing 'admitted truths from the neglect caused by the very circumstance of their universal admission' (*Aids*, p. 11). He is employing a very particular concept of philosophy: Plotinus' metaphysics is a technique for meditation. Reflection is the condition of the soul's return to her source and metaphysics is a technique for *waking up* the soul.[57] Coleridge writes:

One excellence of the Doctrine of Plato, or of the Plotino-platonic Philosophy, is that it never suffers, much less causes or even occasions, its Disciples to forget themselves, lost and scattered in sensible Objects disjoined or *as* disjoined from themselves. It is impossible to understand the Elements of this Philosophy without an appeal, at every step & round of the Ladder, to the fact within, to the mind's Consciousness – and in addition to this, instead of lulling the Soul into an indolence of mere attention . . . but rouses it to acts and energies of creative Thought & Recognition – of conscious re-production of states of Being. (*Notebooks* iii. 3935)

Coleridge's emphasis upon the *psychological* acumen of the Platonists is acute and well grounded: the great twentieth-century scholar of the Platonists E. R. Dodds suggests that Plotinus was 'the first to have clearly distinguished the concepts of soul . . . and ego'. Dodds points to the fact that for Plotinus the soul is a 'continuum extending from the summit of the individual ψυχή, whose activity is perpetual intellection, through the normal empirical self right down to the εἴδωλον, the faint psychic trace in the organism; but the ego is a fluctuating spotlight of consciousness. This picture is a great advance on Aristotle's . . . These are some of my reasons for regarding Plotinus as primarily a great psychologist.'[58] Referring to the Delphic Oracle 'Know Thyself!' Plotinus sees the oracle as relevant for those who do not know what constitutes their real principle[59] and links this to 'the command of the god who urged us

---

[57] G. J. P. O'Daly, *Plotinus's Philosophy of the Self* (Shannon: Irish University Press, 1973). *Aids*, p. 351, 'spiritually awakened natures'. See Stephen R. L. Clark, *God's World and the Great Awakening* (Oxford: Clarendon, 1991), pp. 145–68 for a modern discussion of this philosophical idea.

[58] E. R. Dodds, R. Schwyzer, et al., *Les Sources de Plotin* (Geneva: Vandœuvres, 1957), p. 385. See the critical remarks of H. Oosthout, *Modes of Knowledge and the Transcendental: An Introduction to Plotinus Ennead v.3. (49) with a Commenatary and Translation* (Amsterdam: Grüner, 1991), pp. 33 ff.

[59] Plotinus, *Treatise* vi. 7 (38) 41, 42.

to know ourselves':[60] the conscious mind is in a state of slumber, preoccupied with false objects, and such a preoccupation means a loss of identity. Berkeley, commenting on Proclus, writes: 'if the soul look abroad, she beholds the shadows and images of things, but returning into herself she unravels and beholds her own essence. At first she seemeth only to behold herself, but having penetrated farther she discovers the mind. And again, still farther advancing into the inmost sanctuary of the soul, she contemplates the θεῶν γένος.'[61] Berkeley is describing the Neoplatonic doctrine that the individual soul must reject its natural environment and, by abstracting the false realm, become aware of its unconscious self in its kinship with the divine.[62] Coleridge writes:

If any reflecting mind be surprised that the aids of the Divine Spirit should be deeper than our Consciousness can reach, it must arise from the not having attended sufficiently to the nature and necessary limits of human Consciousness. (*Aids*, p. 79)

This is not an irrational or emotional retreat within the self – the awakening is linked to the reflection upon the act of knowledge, and to the awareness of the divine ground of knowledge. Reflection has an epistemic element: returning within the soul is a means of gaining certainty. Writing of the Neoplatonists in his literary life *The Confessions*, Augustine states:

These books served to remind me to return to my own self. Under your guidance I entered into the depths of my soul, and this I was able to do because *your aid befriended me*. I entered, and with the eye of my soul, such as it was, I saw the Light that never changes casting its rays over the same eye of my soul, over my mind . . . And, far off, I heard your voice saying *I am the God who IS*. I heard your voice, as we hear voices that speak to our hearts, and at once I had no cause to doubt. I might more easily have doubted that I was alive than that truth had being. For we catch sight of the Truth, as he is known through his creation.[63]

'These books' are those of the Neoplatonists. We can see the

[60] Plotinus, *Treatise* vi. 3 (27), 1, 8 f
[61] Berkeley, *Siris* § 333, *Works*, vol. v. p. 152.
[62] H. R. Schwyzer, ' "Bewusst" und "Unbewusst" bei Plotin' in Dodds, Schwyzer, et al., *Sources de Plotin*, pp. 343–90. One should be circumspect in regard to the details of Plotinus' view of the soul. Plotinus believed that a part of the soul remains in the intelligible realm. This was formally rejected by all Christian and later pagan Neoplatonists. See Armstrong, *Christian Faith and Greek Philosophy*, p. 55 ff.
[63] Augustine, *Confessions*, translated by Pine-Coffin (Harmondsworth: Penguin, 1961), pp. 146–7.

Neoplatonic structure: withdrawal within and illumination by the divine light.[64] In Augustine the alienation of the natural man from the divine is perceived as a state of sinfulness, and the renewal of the soul is only possible on the basis of grace.[65] Yet, despite the difference of nuance, there is a considerable similarity with Plotinus: Augustine sees the unregenerate soul as characterised by its desire to revel in its own strength and to rove in the *region of death* (*Aids*, p. 119). The disappointments which arise and frustrate the longing for happiness have a providential function whereby God admonishes the soul and induces the soul to seek happiness elsewhere.[66] In a note on Kant Coleridge calls these 'Providential Aids' such as 'shocks of Sickness forcing the attention backward in upon the state of our collective consciousness' (*Aids*, p. li). The source of this awakening may be a 'sermon, a calamity, a sick bed, or a providential escape' (*Aids*, p. 35). It is a duty of conscience to 'form the mind to a habit of distinct consciousness' (*Aids*, p. 25), and the most frequent 'impediment to men's turning their mind inward upon themselves, is that they are afraid what they shall find there' (*Aids*, p. 24).

The goal of the 'experimentative faith' which Coleridge invokes by quoting Augustine in his preface to *Aids* is to re-mind the soul of its intelligible source. The very seeking of the divine presupposes a *faint or an unconscious* knowledge. Such an issue is developed by Augustine in chapter X of the *Confessions*, where he tries to raise the reader above the habitual sense of memory to the sense of *memoria* as the ground of the soul. Coleridge quotes Leighton to the effect that the human mind retains some 'faint idea' of the good it has lost. It is nonetheless difficult to fix the attention of men upon 'the world within them' and to 'awaken' in them the faculty and exercise of thought. Here Coleridge expresses quite explicitly the Platonic-Augustinian conviction that the natural man must be awoken in order to become aware of his alienation from the supreme good. We have seen that Coleridge praises the Platonists for their meditative philosophy which 'instead of lulling the Soul into an indolence of mere attention . . . rouses it to acts and energies of creative Thought & Recognition' (*Notebooks* iii. 3935). He employs exactly this language

---

[64] Augustine's mentor St Ambrose explicitly compares the ecstasies of St Paul and Plotinus in the language of the awakening. See Hadot, *Plotinus*, p. 25.

[65] Mary Clark, *Augustin, Philosopher of Freedom* (New York: Descalée, 1958).

[66] R. Holte, 'Glück' in *Reallexion für Antike und Christentum*, 11 (1979), pp. 264–8.

when he defines the distinction between thought and attention in
Aids to Reflection:

In ATTENTION, we keep the mind *passive*: In THOUGHT, we rouse it into
activity. In the former we submit to an impression – we keep the mind
steady in order to *receive* the stamp. In the latter, we seek to *imitate* the artist,
while we ourselves make a copy or duplicate of his work. We may learn
arithmetic, or the elements of geometry, by continued attention alone; but
self-knowledge, or an insight into the laws and constitution of the human
mind, and the *grounds* of religion and true morality, in addition to the effort
of attention, requires the energy of THOUGHT. (*Aids*, pp. 14–15)

Coleridge's distinction between attention and thought is not an
exercise in psychological phenomenology but reflects his Platonist
metaphysics. The soul must be awoken from slumbers and natural
indolence and redirected to its transcendent source.

Stephen R. L. Clark observes (contra Heidegger) that for Greek
philosophy it is the *forgetfulness* rather than the hiddenness of being
which is central.[67] Eternal life is the awakening from the dreamlike
existence within the phenomenal world to the presence of the
logos, and the philosophical life is the recollection or making
aware of the illuminating principle.[68] Coleridge asserts this quite
emphatically:

Now I do not hesitate to assert, that it was one of the great purposes of
Christianity, and included in the process of our Redemption, to rouse and
emancipate the Soul from this debasing Slavery to the outward Senses, to
awaken the mind to true Criteria of Reality, viz. Permanence, Power, Will
manifested in Act, and Truth operating as Life. (*Aids*, pp. 406–7)[69]

Hence it is no accident that *Aids to Reflection* begins with this Christian
Platonic motif of *awakening*, of 'truths the most awful and interesting'
within the 'dormitory' of the soul (*Aids*, p. 11). Perhaps he had in
mind Berkeley's description of the Platonic a priori – that the mind
needs 'sensible occasions . . . only for awakening, rousing or exciting

---

[67] Clark, *God's World*, pp. 51 ff.
[68] Stephen R. L. Clark, 'Waking-up: a neglected model for the afterlife' in *Inquiry* 26 (1983),
pp. 209–30 and Clark, *God's World*, pp. 145–68.
[69] Coleridge: 'The sense of Before and After becomes both intelligible and intellectual when,
and *only* when, we contemplate the succession in the relations of Cause and Effect, which
like the two poles of the magnet manifest the being and unity of the one power by relative
opposites, and give, as it were, a substratum of permanence, of identity, and therefore of
reality, to the shadowy flux of Time. It is Eternity revealing itself in the phaenomena of
Time.' The soul's perceptions 'prove to the afflicted Soul that it has not been deprived of
the sight of God . . . though through a darkened glass' (*BL* ii. 234).

into act what was already pre-existent, dormant and latent in the soul'.[70]

It is at once the disgrace and the misery of men, that they live without fore-thought. Suppose yourself fronting a mirror. Now what the objects behind you are to their images at the same apparent distance before you, such is Reflection to Fore-thought. (*Aids*, p. 12)

Coleridge readily and expressly identifies 'reflection' with the Delphic Oracle:

there is one art, of which every man should be master, the art of REFLECTION. If you are not a *thinking* man, to what purpose are you a *man* at all? In like manner, there is one knowledge, which it is every man's interest and duty to acquire, namely SELF-KNOWLEDGE: or to what end was man alone, of all animals, endued by the Creator with the faculty of *self-consciousness*. Truly said the Pagan moralist, E coelo descendit, Γνῶθι Σεαυτόν. (*Aids*, pp. 9–10)

Coleridge does not explain, however, how he interprets this notor-iously cryptic oracle. The term 'reflection' can also mean mirroring. The reflection of the mind upon itself is like a light – hence the metaphor – which sheds light upon itself. The mirror analogy is a familiar topic in the writings of antiquity and the metaphor of mirroring can have a number of quite different meanings: what sort of material is mirroring? Who is looking into the mirror? Further-more – what does the mirror reveal? Clarity or opacity, truth or illusion?

The image of the mirror in Plato is not very prominent; his hints are taken up and developed by the Neoplatonists. Yet the distinctive point of the mirror imagery – the communion of God and man through the spirit – is reinforced, or even intensified, within the Christian Platonist tradition. The Cambridge Platonist John Smith writes:

We cannot see . . . in Speculo Lucido; here we see but in a glass, and that darkly too. Our own Imaginative Powers, which are perpetually attending the highest acts of our Souls, will be breathing a grosse dew upon the pure

---

[70] Berkeley, *Siris* §309 in his *Works*, vol. v. p. 309. Augustine rejects the strict Platonic notion of knowledge as recollection from a past life (*De Trinitate*, 12, 15, 24), but memory plays a very significant role in his theory of mind (*City of God*, viii. 7). Cf. BL ii. p. 147.

Glasse of our Understanding, and so sully and besmear it, that we cannot see the Image of Divinity clearly in it.[71]

The English word 'reflect' is derived from the Latin *reflectere*, which means to bend or to turn back (cf. Coleridge's *Logic*, p. 70, ('*reflecto* = turn back or turn inwardly upon')).[72] This is a rendering of the Neoplatonic philosophical notion of the return of the soul to the Divine principle or ἐπιστροφή. Coleridge thought that the 'belles esprits' (sic) contemporary philosophers had an impoverished theory of mind and stood in need of a study of Plato, Plotinus, and Proclus (*Notebooks* i. 3820). The importance of the Delphic oracle 'Know Thyself!' for Coleridge lies in the call to reflect upon the nature of mind as self-conscious spirit.[73] This task is the awakening of the mind to its real nature as a *reflection* of the divine. Coleridge explicitly associates reflection with '*self consciousness*' (*Aids*, p. 10). Ralph Cudworth's discussion of Plotinus was probably the source of the term 'self-consciousness' as a distinct philosophical concept in English.[74] Udo Thiel observes that 'at least in England, the term "consciousness" came onto the scene not primarily as a Cartesian influence . . . but much more as part of a revival of the Platonic tradition'.[75] The specific concept of *reflection* was first brought into prominence in the general English philosophical discussion by Locke, who was much influenced by the Cambridge Platonists in his terminology. 'Reflection' is 'the *Perception of the Operations of our own Minds* within us, as it is employ'd about the *Ideas* it has got'.[76] The ideas of reflection provide the understanding with '*Ideas* which could not be had from things without'.[77] Reflection is thus contrasted with 'sensation': whereas

---

[71] Smith, *Discourses*, p. 22.

[72] Aquinas uses *reflectere* instead of *reditio*. cf. Aquinas, *De Veritate* i. 9: 'cognoscitur autem ab intellectu secundum quod intellectus reflectitur super actum suum . . . unde secundum hoc cognoscit veritatem intellectus quod supra se ipsum reflectitur.' F.-X. Putallaz, *Le Sens de la réflexion chez Thomas d'Aquin*, with a preface by R. Imbach (Paris: Vrin, 1991), pp. 11–15 and R. L. Fetz, *Ontologie der Innerlichkeit. Reditio completa und Processio interior bei Thomas von Aquin* (Universitätsverlag Fribourg 1975). The image of the human soul as turning upon itself is a central theme in Plato's work. In Plato's *Republic* 518c Socrates argues that just as the physical eye must rurn from darkness to light, so too must the whole soul turn (στρέφειν) from the realm of *becoming* to the realm of the good. Similarly in Plato's *Timaeus* (37a) the metaphor is used to describe the soul as a sphere which turns upon herself. I owe these observations to Robert Griffin's unpublished paper 'Reflection in Locke and Coleridge'.

[73] cf. Coleridge, *BL* i. 252, 279, and 291 and *BL* ii. 240.

[74] U. Thiel, 'Cudworth and seventeenth-century theories of consciousness' in *The Uses of Antiquity*, edited by S. Gaukroger (Dordrecht: Kluwer, 1991), pp. 79–99.

[75] Ibid., p. 80

[76] J. Locke, *An Essay Concerning Human Understanding* (Oxford: Clarendon, 1975), 2.1.4.

[77] Ibid.

sensation conveys the contents of thought, reflection constitutes the internal operations of the mind.[78] A. E Taylor sees Locke's usage as due to the 'widespread influence of Neo-Platonism on the English philosophical writers contemporary with Cudworth and Henry More'.[79] Thomas Stanley is a good instance of the Platonic revival; he translates Pico della Mirandola's Platonic discourse concerning the contemplation of intelligible beauty:

> Reflecting upon her Operation, the knowledge of universal Beauty, and considering that every thing founded in matter is particular, she concludes this universality proceeds not from the outward Object, but her Intrinsical Power: and reasons thus: If in the divine Glass of Material Phantasms this Beauty is represented by virtue of my Light, it follows, that beholding it in the clear Mirrour of my substance divested of those Clouds, it will appear more perspicuous: thus turning into herself, she finds the Image of Ideal Beauty communicated to her by the Intellect, the Object of Celestial Love.[80]

The decisive development of the concept of reflection is Neoplatonic and self-knowledge is explicitly linked to the Delphic Oracle in the dialogue *Alcibiades I* – generally the starting place in late antiquity for any discussion of the nature of mind, and the single most important philosophical source for speculation about self-knowledge. *Alcibiades I* was the introductory text in philosophy at the Platonic Academy and there are commentaries by Proclus and Olympiodorus extant.[81] Within the Platonic school, pagan or Christian, proper self-knowledge is inextricably bound to knowledge of one's 'proper *being*, truest *self*, *the* man *in* the man' (*Aids*, p. 15).[82] Coleridge's use of the term 'reflection' springs from his interest in the Neoplatonist terminology rooted in the tradition of the interpretation of *Alcibiades I*.

Since Schleiermacher, scholars have tended to regard the dialogue as a product of the Platonic school.[83] *Alcibiades I* was, however, a

---

[78] Yolton, *Locke Dictionary*, pp. 208–12.

[79] Quoted by Douglas I. Rabb, *John Locke on Reflection* (Washington: University Press of America, 1985), p. 8 from A. E. Taylor, *Philosophical Studies* (London: Macmillan, 1934), pp. 185–6.

[80] T. Stanley, *The History of Philosophy* (London: Thomas Bassett, Dorman, Newman, and Thomas Cockerill, 1687), p. 207, cf. Rabb, *John Locke*.

[81] A. J. Festugière, 'L'ordre de lecture des dialogues de Platon au Vème et VIème siècle' in *Museum Helveticum* 26 (1969), pp. 281–96. cf. Berkeley, *Siris*, § 333, 334: Works v. pp. 152–3. For these reasons the great Alcibiades is more important for the history of philosophy than the *Charmides*, where self-knowledge is discussed in relation to the issue of temperance.

[82] cf. Smith, *Discourses*, p. 61 on ΓΝΩΘΙ ΣΕΑΥΤΟΝ'. Further, see Einar Molland, 'Clement of Alexandria and the origin of Greek philosophy' in *Symbolae Osloenses* (1936), pp. 57–85.

[83] Schleiermacher, *KGA i. 3. Schriften und Entwürfe. zum Platon*, p. 346. He thinks it is from

dialogue of massive importance in late antiquity. Socrates attempts
to show young Alcibiades that he should be wary of his ambition.
Socrates argues that just as the body is more important than
possessions, the soul is more important than the body. Consequently
one cannot care for others when one does not care for one's own
soul. Alcibiades is intent upon engagement in politics; Socrates
wishes to show Alcibiades that insight into the nature and well-being
of the city state is requisite for responsible political action, and this
requires insight into one's own soul in order to know where virtue is
to be found. Virtue is to be found in the divine: self-knowledge is
self-vision in the sense that the rational part of the soul *mirrors* the
divine.

The command Γνῶθι σεαυτόν, 'Know thyself!' is structurally akin
to 'see your own self'. It can only be done through objects like
mirrors through which the eye can see both the object and itself. An
eye, in order to see itself, needs to look into another eye and its best
part, the pupil, and similarly a soul knows itself by looking into the
best part of another soul: the divine part of the soul. Achilles in
Shakespeare's *Troilus and Cressida* uses precisely the imagery of the
Great Alcibiades:

> Nor doth the eye itself,
> That most pure spirit of sense, behold itself,
> Not going from itself; but eye to eye opposed
> Salutes each other with each other's form.
> For speculation turns not to itself
> Til it hath travelled and is mirrored there
> Where it may see itself. This is not strange at all.[84]

It is not strange that true personal identity is broader than particular
individuality, but consists in exchange with others – a purely secular
mind can concede this point; but the essential claim is that self-
knowledge and knowledge of the divine are intextricably related:
contemplating the rational part of the soul we come to experience
the divine within ourselves. In the first *Alcibiades* the command
'Know Thyself!' is interpreted as 'ἰδὲ σαυτόν,' 'Look at Thyself',[85]

Xenophon's school. This is not conclusive, cf. W. Beierwaltes' remarks in his *Selbsterkenntnis und
Erfahrung der Einheit. Plotins Enneade v. 3* (Frankfurt: Klostermann, 1991), pp. 81–2 and R.
Wiggers, 'Zum großen Alcibiades 132d–133c' in *Philologische Wochenschrift* 25 (1932), pp. 700–3.

[84]   W. Shakespeare, *Troilus and Cressida*, III. iii. 105–11.

[85]   Plato, *Alcibiades I*, 132d–133d in *The Dialogues of Plato*, translated by B. Jowett, fourth edition
(Oxford, 1953), pp. 670 f. cf. Proclus, *Commentary on the First Alcibiades of Plato*, translated by
W. O'Neill (The Hague: Nijhoff, 1965) p. 87.

and this is what Coleridge means when he says 'This *seeing* light, this *enlightening* eye is Reflection' (*Aids*, p. 15). As Berkeley notes, in this dialogue

the contemplation of God is the proper means to know or understand our own soul. As the eye, saith he, looking steadfastly at the visive part or pupil of another eye, beholds itself, even so the soul beholds and understands herself while she contemplates the Deity[86]

Rather than the modern intuitive idea of one's self as being a unique and exclusive monad, the mirror imagery should suggest that the soul becomes a better knower of her nature as *subject* by becoming more *objective*: she knows what she is by seeing her identity with the divine.[87] The salient points of the dialogue are that the real self is the soul and not the body, and that the meaning of 'Know Thyself!' is 'Know God!' The two thoughts belong together; the point of Plato's dialogue is not that of preserving the self as a *soi-disant* ghost within the machine but rather to establish a more objective reality than one's bodily existence. The Neoplatonists interpreted this as referring to a rational common soul.[88]

Plotinus connects the Delphic Oracle with the idea of *self-consciousness*. In the great treatise on 'Self Knowledge' (v. 3 (49)) sense perception is described as dianoetic because νοῦς enlightens discursive thought.[89] The self-knowledge of the soul is knowing that it is illuminated by the νοῦς.[90] Yet, as Hankey remarks, 'no pagan obeyed more completely than Augustine the Delphic Command Know Thyself'.[91] Augustine's great treatise on the Trinity is the locus classicus of his reflection on the Delphic Oracle: 'Why then is the mind commanded to know itself? I believe it means that it should think about itself and live according to its nature.'[92] Furthermore: 'How will it see to act on the command it hears, *Know thyself*, if it does not know what "know" is or what "thyself" is? If however it

---

[86] Berkeley, *Siris* §334 in his *Works*, vol. v. p. 152.

[87] Julia Annas, 'Self-knowledge in early Plato' in *Platonic Investigations*, edited by Dominic O'Meara (Washington: Catholic University of America, 1985), pp. 111–38.

[88] O'Daly, *Plotinus's Philosophy of the Self*, pp. 18–19.

[89] Plotinus, *Treatise* v. 3 6, 22 ff.: the discursive power of reasoning is called such because it 'has its power through and from Intellect'. Plotinus is playing on the putative etymology of discursive reasoning, διάνοια, from the preposition διά which can mean 'through' and ὁ νοῦς, Reason or Intellect.

[90] Plotinus, *Treatise* v. 3 (49) 3, 45–6.

[91] W. Hankey, 'Mens' in *Saint Augustine through the Ages: an Encyclopedia*, ed. A. Fitzgerald, (Grand Rapids, Mich.: Erdmans, forthcoming).

[92] Augustine, *The Trinity* x. 7 translated by E. Hill (New York: New City Press, 1996), p. 292.

knows both, then it knows itself.'[93] Self-knowledge is an intellectual self-knowledge which should culminate in the unity of thought and thinker, knower and the known.[94] At this stage self-knowledge means no longer knowing oneself as a particular person but being united with the divine reason, the knower is transformed by the object of contemplation. This doctrine of the unmediated knowledge of God is an assertion of the unique affinity and communion of the rational part of the soul with the divine. The tradition of *Alcibiades I* together with St Paul's reference to seeing through a glass darkly (1 Cor. 13: 12) meant that the mirror symbol became the central image of the relationship of rational soul to God, and hence a central element of Christian Platonic speculation: 'For now we see through a glass, darkly; but then face to face.' Another important passage is 2 Cor 3: 18.

Now the Lord is that Spirit: and where the Spirit of the Lord is, there is freedom. And we all, with unveiled face, beholding the glory of the Lord, are being changed into his likeness from one degree of glory to another; for this comes from the Lord who is the Spirit.

It is possible to interpret 'beholding' – κατοπριζόμενοι (Lat. *spec-ulantes*) – as looking in a mirror or looking with the aid of a mirror,[95] and such an interpretation emphasises the indirect and incomplete nature of this knowledge in contrast with the future clear vision. The mystical interpretation, however, takes κατοπριζόμενοι or *speculantes* to mean 'reflecting' or 'mirroring': the glory of God is reflected in the believer. The Genesis account of the creation of man in God's image, 'Let us make man after our image and likeness', and the Pauline notion of 'being changed into his likeness' in 2 Cor. 3: 18 converge. These texts provide a basis for much metaphysical speculation about the 'image' in Christian thought. Instead of 'beholding the glory of the Lord' the mystics read it as 'mirroring the glory of the Lord'.[96] Hence Coleridge construes the passage as expressing man's essential nature as a partaker of the divine – in the all-pervading Logos – and 'capable of being transfigured from glory to glory, in accordance with the varying circumstances and outward

---

[93] Augustine, *The Trinity* x. 12 (New York: New City Press, 1996), p. 295.

[94] Augustine, *Confessions*, pp. 196–9.

[95] B. McGinn, *The Foundations of Mysticism* (London: SCM, 1992), p. 71 and K. E. Kirk, *The Vision of God* (Cambridge University Press, 1991), pp. 47 ff.

[96] cf. A. Model, *Metaphysik und reflektierende Urteilskraft bei Kant. Untersuchungen zur Transformierung des Leibnizschen Monaden Begriffs in der 'Kritik der Urteilskraft'* (Frankfurt am Main: Hain, 1987), pp. 174 ff.

relations of its moving and informing spirit' (*Aids*, p. 32).[97] In this mystical interpretation the glorious mirroring of the divine in the human soul is emphasised rather than the distance between human and divine: it expresses the *rational* spirit of man' (*LS*, p. 20). For Coleridge, personhood at its deepest level is fostered by seeking its good in God, in deification (cf. *Aids*, pp. 40; 41; 274 n).[98]

The very word 'speculation' was taken to be derived from *speculum* (mirror). Thomas says that Augustine speaks of *speculation* in conscious dependence upon the underlying sense of *speculum* (mirror) and not *specula* (observation point). To see something in a mirror means to see the cause through the effect, the former appearing in the image of the latter. Thus, concludes Thomas, we can reduce speculation to meditative vision. The mirror analogy coheres with the common Greek doctrine that only 'like can be known by like'[99] and through the mirror of thought mankind reflects its divine source; an idea which can be seen in the 'living mirrors' of Leibniz, a thinker for whom[100] knowledge depends upon illumination and souls are mirrors of divinity.[101]

The mind is the source of the capacity for union with the divine; it is not a contingent characteristic of humanity but the defining element. In true self-knowledge, God is *in* man, and man is *in* God. The ideas within the divine Word provide the instrument by which the finite mind can ascend to the divine. These ideas are the rational principles and laws which the finite mind must employ in order to judge or understand. The characteristically *Christian* component in Coleridge's Christian Platonism has to do not so much with the biblical faith as (paradoxical as it may seem) the intellectualist shift

---

[97] A. Zimmermann, *Der Begriff der Representatio im Mittelalter. Stellvertretung, Symbol, Zeichen, Bild* (Berlin: de Gruyter, 1971) and W. Beierwaltes, 'Visio Facialis Sehen ins Angesicht. Zur Conincidence des endlichen und unendlichen Blicks bei Cusanus' in *Sitzungsbericht der Bayerischen Akademie der Wissenschaften* (Munich: Beck, 1988).

[98] Plato, *Republic*, 613b: 'the gods will never neglect the man whose heart is set on justice and who is ready, by pursuing excellence, to become as like god as man is able'. cf. Plato, *Timaeus*, 90d, 3.

[99] Originally Empedocles, Plato, *Timaeus*, 45 c4 ὅμοιον πρὸς ὅμοιον. Plotinus *Treatise* i. 6, 9: 'No eye ever saw the sun without becoming sun-like.'

[100] cf. H. Leisegang, 'Die Erkenntnis Gottes im Spiegel der Seele und der Natur' in *Zeitschrift für philosphische Forschung* 4 (1949–50), pp. 161–83 and R. Konersmann, *Spiegel und Bild* (Würzburg: Königshausen und Neumann, 1988).

[101] George Macdonald Ross, 'Leibniz und Renaissance Neoplatonism' in *Leibniz et la Renaissance: Colloque du Centre national de la recherche scientifique (Paris), du Centre d'etudes supérieures de la Renaissance (Tours) et de la G. W. Leibniz-Gesellschaft (Hannover)*, edited by A. Heinekamp (Wiesbaden: Steiner, 1983), pp. 125–34.

in Augustine. Both Plotinus and Augustine agree in the view that mind must turn from external objects to the interior realm of the mind, to a domain of pure thought. But Augustine maintains that this ascent culminates in thought about a God who is, in himself, pure thought; whereas Plotinus holds that the ascent of the mind must move beyond this stage to the union with the One which is strictly 'beyond thought'. In this sense, Coleridge's Christian, Trinitarian, Platonism drives him closer to Idealism than a strictly Hellenic Neoplatonist could properly admit.

THE ASCENT OF THE MIND AND THE INNER WORD

Seek thou the derivation of thy Soul . . . whence and from what rank having fallen into slavery to the Body, to that rank, from which thou wert precipitated, Thou mayest re-ascend, uniting thy energy with the Holy *Word*. (*Friend* i. 2)

Hans Aarsleff has pointed out the centrality of Locke's insistence that the origin of language is human and not divine.[102] He remarks that 'the most spectacular and pervasive influence of the *Essay* occurred in the new philosophy of language that was developed during the eighteenth century'.[103]

One of the four purposes of *Aids to Reflection* is to 'direct the Reader's attention to the value of the Science of Words'. Coleridge refers to Horne Tooke's

Ἔπεα πτερόεντα Winged Words: or Language, not only the *Vehicle* of Thought but the *Wheels*. With my convictions and views, for ἔπεα I should substitute λόγοι, i.e. Words *select* and *determinate*, and for πτερόεντα ζώοντες i.e. *living* Words. The Wheels of the intellect I admit them to be; but such as Ezekiel beheld in the 'visions of God'. (*Aids*, p. 7)

Tooke was an avowed and enthusiastic Lockean who developed the empiricist approach to language, and conversely, developed Locke's thought in an exclusively linguistic mode.[104] Coleridge says that he prefers the word λόγοι with its obvious connection to the second person of the Trinity and the divine root of language because all words have their 'ground and highest source in the 'Word' that was

---

[102] H. Aarsleff, *From Locke to Saussure* (Minneapolis: University of Minnesota Press, 1982), pp. 42–83.

[103] H. Aarsleff, *The Cambridge Companion to Locke* (Cambridge University Press, 1994), p. 271.

[104] cf. H. Aarsleff, *The Study of Language in England, 1780–1860* (Princeton University Press, 1967), pp. 44–114.

from the beginning' (*Logic*, p. 120). John Beer notes that 'C no doubt chose λόγος for its further connotations, particularly as conveying meaningfulness' (*Aids*, p. 551). The question of language is immediately linked to the problem of the intelligibility of the universe through the choice of the word λόγοι. In this passage Coleridge uses the image of Ezekiel's vision of the divine chariot. Tim Fulford observes that 'Coleridge's use of this passage was significant because merkabah mystics interpreted the wheels as the letters of God's name, turning Ezekiel's vision into a commentary on language's literal symbolising of the divine.'[105] 'Winged words' should convey the mind in its ascent back to its divine source. Quite clearly, we have an attack on the Lockean (represented by Tooke) legacy in the philosophy of language, and a reassertion of the divine origin of language.

Coleridge's view of philosophy is dictated by the idea of the ascent of the mind. This ascent is aided by the conscious concentration upon the original logos which is mirrored in the specific λόγοι. The ascent is conceived of Platonically – in the tradition of the spiritual exercises:

> it is obvious that in order for its realisation the several faculties of the mind should be specially disciplined, and as (if I may be allowed the illustration) the muscles of the leg and thigh are brought out and made prominent in the exercises of the riding school, that *so* should the intellectual powers be called forth from *their* dormant state . . . a subject perfectly answering this character is provided for us in the privilege and high instinct of language. (*Logic*, p. 12)

The method of awakening, discipline, and purification – of stripping away error and confusion – is a propaedeutic for the contemplation of the ideas. The purification secures the emancipation from the despotism of the eye. It means that one can use the language of sight without being enslaved by its affection (*BL* i. 107), and it thus avoids the delusive notion that that which is not *imaginable* is likewise not conceivable. Such a Platonic concept of analysis is closely linked to the model of insight which pervades Coleridge's thought about language. Language is, for Coleridge, *a living power which enables men to improve their vision of the truth* – it brings unconscious elements lying in the dormitory of the soul into an intelligible light. This is why the aphorism is so important: the aphorism is an obvious instrument of and aid to active reflection, is the right instrument to awaken a slumbering soul.

---

[105] T. Fulford, *Coleridge's Figurative Language* (Basingstoke: Macmillan, 1991), p. 149: Coleridge's language perhaps suggest Plato's Phaedran Charioteer, *Aids*, p. 7 n4.

Coleridge sees the *midwifery* of Plato's dialogues and the aphorisms of Bacon as models for the encouragement of active thought in his readers. But it is a matter of difficulty to awaken 'the faculty of thought' in men (*Aids*, p. 14). Coleridge defines thought as the voluntary reproduction in our minds of those states of consciousness to which, as to his best and most authentic documents, the teacher of moral and religious truth refers us (*Aids*, p. 14). The teacher of moral or religious truth is not just the historical person Jesus of Nazareth but Christ as the Logos or *Magister interior* or *Verbum interius* as a perpetual source of illumination.[106] In *Marginalia*, on Leighton Coleridge writes:

We say; 'Now I see the full meaning, force and beauty of a passage, – we can see them through the words.' Is not Christ the Word – the substantial, consubstantial Word . . . not as our words, arbitrary; nor even as the words of Nature phenomenal merely? If even through the words [of] a powerful and perspicuous author – (as in the next to inspired Commentary of Archbishop Leighton, – for whom God be praised!) I identify myself with the excellent writer, and his thoughts become my thoughts: what must not the blessing be to be thus identified first with the Filial Word, and then with the Father in and through Him? (*Marg.* iii. pp. 522–3)

The issue of language is linked by Augustine to both the idea of creation and the *principle* of genuine thought. Christ is the principle of creation and connected to this idea, as the inner teacher, the principle of *intelligibility.* Whether direct or indirect, Coleridge is following (via the inner word) Augustine's interweaving of the Platonic themes of the recollection[107] and the divine craftsman[108] with the Christian idea of Christ as the cosmic and the indwelling Logos. Language for Augustine is linked to the question 'by what means did you make heaven and earth. What tool did you use for this vast work?[109] The tool is the Word; yet it is certainly no instrument in the sense that it might be divided from its source and there is no matter or space or time which the Word can utilise. The Word is consubstantial: 'God with God, your Word uttered eternally in whom all things are uttered eternally . . . it is by a Word co-eternal with yourself that you say all that you say.'[110]

---

[106] cf. Theo Kobusch, *Sein und Sprache. Historische Grundlegung einer Ontologie der Sprache* (Leiden: Brill, 1987), pp. 23–78.
[107] Plato, *Meno*, 80a–85a.   [108] Plato, *Timaeus*, 28a ff.
[109] Augustine, *Confessions*, p. 257.   [110] Augustine, *Confessions*, p. 259.

> Mind! Co-eternal Word! forth-breathing Sound!
> Birth and Procession; Ever re-incircling Act![111]

It is God *himself* who creates the World as the second person of the Trinity, as the WORD. 'Earth and the heavens also proclaim (*clamant*) that they did not create themselves. "We exist", they tell us, "because we were made . . ." And the fact that they plainly do exist is the voice which proclaims this truth.'[112] The *evidence* of the creative eternal Word lies in the beauty and order of things. They *proclaim* or *call* – in Augustine's metaphor – because they are rooted in the creation of the Word.

Coleridge knows that the summoning power of the good is illustrated by the discussion of the etymology of beauty in the Platonic school: 'the Greeks called a beautiful object καλον, quasi καλοῦν, i.e. *calling on* the soul' (*SW* i. 383). Plato himself traces the beautiful (καλόν) to 'bid', 'summon', or 'call' (καλεῖν) in his *Cratylus*.[113] Plotinus writes:

. . . one need not wonder if that which the soul pursues and which gives light to the Intellect and in falling upon it stirs a trace of itself has so great a power, and draws to itself and calls back from all wandering to rest beside it. For if there is something from which all things come, there is nothing stronger than it, but all things are less than it. How can the best of realities possibly not be the Good?[114]

The use of the language of 'calling' in relation to the Platonic etymology of the word for beauty is a standard Platonic topos. Speaking of the 'One' or the 'good', Proclus, too, derives beauty from 'to bid' and his Christian pupil Denys the Areopagite writes of God: 'Beauty "bids" all things to itself (whence it is called "beauty").'[115] Augustine is employing a fairly conventional Platonic tenet – that language is rooted in the intelligibility and beauty of the cosmos, and that the articulation of thought in human speech presupposes the true intellectual system of the universe, of which the physical cosmos is merely an expression. Language is the mode and organ of thought: it provides the wheels of thought, but the intelligibility of the cosmos is the ground or basis of language.

Coleridge wrote to his son Derwent encouraging him to pursue

---

[111] Quoted by J. Beer, *Coleridge's Poetic Intelligence* (London: Macmillan, 1977), pp. 59 ff.

[112] Augustine, *Confessions*, xii. 4, 'Et vox dicentium est ipsa evidentia.'

[113] Plato, *Cratylus*, 426d4–10   [114] Plotinus, *Treatise* vi. 7 (38) 23, 1 ff.

[115] Proclus, *Alcibiades*, 328, 12 and Pseudo-Dionysius, *The Complete Works*, translated by Colm Luibheid (London: SPCK, 1987), p. 76.

his classical studies 'under the guidance and in the light of PHILOLOGY, in that original and noblest sense of the term, in which it implies & is the most *human*, practical, and fructifying Form & (what is of no small moment in the present state of Society) the most popular *Disguise* of Logic and Psychology – without which what is man?' (*CL* v. 141). The meaning of the passage is very concentrated. The original and noblest meaning of the term is the science of the Logos; not merely the science of language as such. The logos which *fructifies* is at the centre of logic and psychology and it is the divine spark which invests man with his distinctive humanity. This eternal Word is unlike the word of human speech which is temporally limited.[116] This Word is the eternal reason which speaks to us[117] and the a priori basis of human communication. Thus it coheres with the anti-naturalistic thrust in Coleridge: in a discussion of immortality he uses the expression 'ingrafted word'; partly biblically motivated but partly used in the sense of a priori knowledge (*Aids*, p. 353). When we consider language philosophically, Coleridge believes, we are considering the immanent, divine, and a priori ground of human nature.[118]

Coleridge is not concerned to describe a language as a complex existing entity but rather to explore the root and source of language, the metaphysics of language. Unlike the Lockean empiricists who envisage the mind as a *tabula rasa* receiving impressions, and who trace *passively* the route from external verbal signs to interior impressions, Coleridge wants to see words as 'living growths, offlets, and organs of the human soul' (*Logic*, p. 126).

He wishes to explain the sort of fact which makes noises or signs convey meaning. How particular sounds can transmit meaning is perhaps the most serious question one can ask (*Logic*, p. 120). The empiricist answer is that utterances are or should be traced back to basic sensory items, 'impressions', to which sounds or letters refer. Language is thus envisaged as constructed out of such simple elements, whereby more complex words refer to combinations of simple items or abstractions on the foundations of empirical discrete data. Coleridge thinks that such an account cannot generate

---

[116] *Confessions*, xi. 7.   [117] *Confessions*, xi. 8.

[118] G. Watson, 'St Augustine and the inner word: the philosophical background' in *Irish Theological Quarterly* 54 (1988), pp. 81–92. Noam Chomsky appeals explicitly to Coleridge's thoughts on language in support of his thesis that language acquisition presupposes innate capacities. Noam Chomsky, *Cartesian Linguistics* (London: Harper and Row, 1966), p. 69.

meaning because there is no natural link between certain visible shapes and audible sounds and insight or comprehension. He thinks that the empiricist has misconstrued the problem. Meaning is not parasitic upon sensory experience, although our sensory experience has a different quality by virtue of language. Meaning presupposes another realm, quite unlike the sensory; a domain of the human spirit, its culture and traditions. Hence instead of seeing language primarily in terms of primitive ostensive definitions and these as gradually subject to the refinement of the learned, language is primarily the product of the schools: 'Among the *aids to* reflection, place the following maxim prominent: let distinctness in expression advance side by side with distinction in thought' (*Aids*, p. 47). Coleridge developed a term for the distinctness in expression which promotes distinction in thought: desynonymy. This term denotes the separation or refinement of meanings with respect to words which were hitherto identical in meaning. This separation of meaning is a necessary part of the process of the gradual refinement of thought in a culture:

there are few modes of instruction more useful or more amusing than that of accustoming young people to seek for the etymology, or primary meaning, of the words they use. There are cases, in which more knowledge of value may be conveyed by the history of a *word* than by a history of a campaign. (*Aids*, p. 17)[119]

Locke proposes that concepts 'have for the most part, in all Languages, received their Birth and Signification, from ignorant and illiterate people, who sorted and denominated Things, by those sensible Qualities they found in them, thereby to signify them, when absent, to others, whether they had an occasion to mention a Sort, or particular Thing.'[120] Coleridge is not merely rejecting the Lockean view of the purely human origin of language; he is equally opposed to the view of its source in 'ignorant and illiterate people'. Coleridge insists: 'as Alchemy went before Chemistry, and Astrology before Astronomy, so in all countries of civilized Man have Meta-

---

[119] Richard Chenevix Trench (1807–86), the author of the *Study of Words* (1851), was influenced by Coleridge on this point. cf. Beer in *Aids*, p. cxlvi, and K. M. E. Murray, *Caught in the Web of Words: James A. H. Murray and the 'Oxford English Dictionary'*, with a preface by R. W. Burchfield (New Haven and London: Yale University Press, 1995), p. 135. George Watson observes poignantly, and in a Coleridgean mood: 'Much of *OED* from the historian's point of view, looks like a rusting armoury that has never been taken from the wall' in his *Writing a Thesis* (Harlow: Addison, Wesley, and Longman, 1987), p. 47.

[120] Locke, *Human Understanding*, pp. 452–3.

physics outrun Common Sense' (*Aids*, p. 261). In the *Biographia
Literaria* Coleridge uses the vivid analogy of organisms which divide
themselves in order to illustrate the tendency towards differentiation
in a language: 'master' and 'mister' are both derived from an
identical root, *magister*. Once the words become divided, the community forgets their original source 'till at length all trace of the
original likeness is worn away' (*BL* i. 83) and 'in all societies there
exists an instinct of growth, a certain collective, unconscious good
sense working progressively to desynonymize those words originally
of the same meaning' (*BL* i. 82–3).

In the *Philosophical Lectures* Coleridge emphasises the extent to
which the development of language and of philosophy belong
together. In the *Biographia* he states explicitly: 'The best part of
human language is derived from reflection on the acts of the mind
itself. It is formed by a voluntary appropriation of fixed symbols to
internal acts, to processes and results of the imagination, the greater
part of which have no place in the consciousness of uneducated
man? (*BL* ii. 54). This is the sense of calling words λόγοι: the logos is
the evolving power of the ideas.

Desynonymizing is thus the conscious *awakening* of the unconscious
resources of the language. This awakening process is primarily the
task of the philosophers and the poets: to press forward the
desynonymizing.

The creed of true Common Sense is composed of the *Results* of Scientific
Meditation, Observation, and Experiment, as far as they are *generally*
intelligible. It differs therefore in different countries and in every different
age of the same country. The Common Sense of a People is the movable
index of its average judgement and information. Without Metaphysics
Science would have no language, and Common Sense no materials. (*Aids*,
p. 261)

Terms which had their roots in the philosophical schools become
part of the general stock of common sense through their widespread
acceptance; the more industrious philosophy is, the larger the sphere
of common sense, for whenever philosophy is so intelligible that all
men admit it, it becomes part of their common thoughts and
language. Common sense is the repository of the learning of previous
ages: ideas which in the period of their inception and development
are sources of controversy become common property. Just as a
mechanic's slide-rule is a safe substitute for arithmetical knowledge,
the subtleties of common language guide the mind. A schoolboy who

can distinguish the meaning of the words *compulsion* and *obligation* is in an excellent position to avoid any confusion between natural and legal laws without having to reflect philosophically on the strength of the 'must' in the instances of natural compulsion and legal obligation. Hence that which 'was born and christened in the schools passes by degrees into the world at large, and becomes the property of the market and the tea-table' (*BL* i. 86). In this way language is the 'growth and emanation of a People, and not the work of any individual Wit or Will' (*Aids*, p. 244).[121] Language is often inadequate but not delusive:

We have only to master the true origin and original import of any native and abiding word, to find in it, if not the *solution* of the facts expressed by it, yet a finger-mark pointing to the road on which this solution is to be sought. (*Aids*, p. 244)

Coleridge wishes to encourage reflection upon metaphors and etymologies for philosophical rather than philological reasons. Human thought is not just the instinctual reaction to a given environment, but is embedded in the language of a culture. Language is not just a collection of signals which serves the need to co-operate and communicate within a community, but rather serves to forge a community by giving expression to its spiritual or personal being. In this sense, language is less a pragmatic instrument which is ultimately incapable of resolving our inevitable ignorance of the private ideas of other thinkers than the characteristic mode in which human identity is nurtured and cultivated. Coleridge is pointing to the fallacy of thinking that words as 'articulated sounds are things of moral indifference' (*F* i. 49): on the contrary, they are 'LIVING POWERS'. Iris Murdoch expresses exactly this thought when she argues that:

Words are the most subtle symbols which we possess and our human fabric depends on them. The living and radical nature of language is something we forget at our peril . . . We are men and we are moral agents before we are scientists, and the place of science in human life must be discussed in *words*.[122]

The capacity for language expresses the intelligible nature of the soul and its capacity to rise above the obscurity of the empirical

---

[121] R. C. Trench observed: 'the love of our own language, what is it . . . but the love of our country expressing itself in one particular direction?', 'language may be regarded as "a moral barometer", which indicates and permanently marks the rise or fall of a nation's life.' Quoted in Murray, *Web of Words*, p. 135.

[122] Iris Murdoch, 'The idea of Perfection' in *Existentialists and Mystics: Writings on Philosophy and Literature*, edited by P. Conradi (London: Chatto and Windus, 1997), p. 326.

realm to the vision of God: language is the mirror of the human soul inasmuch as it reflects the personal core of humankind which subsists in the divine Logos. The Delphic command 'Know Thyself!' has a quite strict application: Words are 'LIVING POWERS, by which the things of most importance to mankind are actuated, combined and humanised' (*Aids*, p. 10). Hence, without explicitly returning to an Adamic theory of language, Coleridge is attacking the anti-essentialism of the Lockean language theory.

That is to say, rather than seeing language as a medium of the causal relation between world and mind a posteriori where language picks off and names items which the mind observes in the world, Coleridge wishes to see language as rooted in an a priori capacity for articulate insight. Speech is the vehicle of thought, but language presupposes intentionality. Carlyle wrote:

The meaning of life here on earth might be defined as consisting in this: To unfold your self, to work what thing you have a faculty for. It is a necessity for the human being, the first law of its existence. Coleridge beautifully remarks that the infant learns to *speak* by this necessity it feels.[123]

Augustine is the source of speculation about the metaphysics of language in his attempt to develop a theory of the 'inner word' as the explanation of the capacity to invest signs with significance. The a priori in human nature which is the root of language is love. Love is the source of communication: the inner word is *cum amore notitia*, it is the judicious approval which binds mind and knowledge. Just as the Son is begotten through the love of the Father, the inner word is begotten through the love of, through the yearning for, articulate insight.

The language of the 'birth' of the inner word is part of the tradition of the spiritual love of God and the soul; metaphors of fertility, pregnancy, and generation are quite evident in Plato, Philo, and Plotinus.[124] Socrates is described as a midwife and Plotinus speaks of the 'birth-pangs' of the soul as it is illuminated by the intellect.[125]

Coleridge's appeal to the a priori foundation of language can be evinced in his recourse to the Augustinian concept of the inner

[123] Carlyle, quoted by C. R. Sanders in *Coleridge and the Broad Church Movement* (Durham, NC: Duke University Press, 1942), p. 155.
[124] The locus classicus is Plato's *Symposium*, 203b, which deeply influenced Philo, and thence the Christian Platonic tradition. cf. Plotinus, *Treatise* vi. 9 (9) 9, 20.
[125] Plotinus, *Treatise* iii. 8 (30) 5, 3–12.

word. In a manuscript note on John Hunter, Coleridge remarks: 'Still did he seem to miss the compleating WORD that should have reflected the Idea, . . . and have . . . placed it at the disposal of his conscious and voluntary Contemplation for the word is the first birth of the Idea, and its flexible organ' (*F* i. 474). In a much earlier passage, which dates from the initial phase of his Trinitarian thoughts, he speaks of

Reason, Proportion, communicable Intelligibility intelligent and communicant, the WORD – which last expression strikes me as the profoundest and most comprehensive Energy of the human Mind, if indeed it be not in some sense ενεργημα Θεοπαραδοτον [*sic*] the moment we conceive the divine energy we co-conceive the logos. (*Notebooks* ii. 2445)

Here Coleridge is punning on the dual meaning of the word 'conceive':

To me (why do I say to me?) to Bull, to Waterland, Gregory Nazianzen, Basil, Athanasius, Augustine, the terms Word and generation have appeared admirably, yea, most awfully pregnant and appropriate. (*NED* ii. 136)

Augustine's theory of the 'inner word' is part of his Trinitarian theology, and the attempt to draw an analogy between the human mind and the Godhead; the act of knowledge is envisaged as the *bearing* of an interior 'word'. Knowledge is the result of *process* in which that which is inchoately already 'thought' is brought to articulate expression. Augustine uses the term 'word' to express the relation between the conceived word and the conceiving thought, the fruition of an *innate* capacity for articulate insight prior to any concrete, historical language; what Coleridge refers to as the 'sermo interior' (*BL* i. 290). The inner word is the real word: being incarnate is inessential to it, even though we cannot think of it except as the discarnate analogue of the embodied word. The linguistic sign merely reminds or even admonishes; the real teacher is the inner word (*foris admonet, intus docet*).[126] Meaning is generated by the interior Master or Word (i.e. the indwelling Logos) and external conventional linguistic signs merely serve to point to the internal truths. Augustine considers the problem of how he might question Moses about creation:

how should I know whether what he said was true? If I knew this too, it could not be from him that I got such knowledge. But deep inside me, in my most intimate thought, Truth which is neither Hebrew nor Greek nor

---

[126] Augustine, *On Free Choice of the Will*, translated by Thomas Williams (Indianapolis, Ind.: Hackett, 1993), p. 58.

Latin nor any foreign speech, would speak to me, though not in syllables formed by lips and tongues. It would whisper 'He speaks the truth'.[127]

The priority of the interior to exterior, the a priori *verbum* to the concrete *vox*, reflects the priority of the intelligible over the sensible. The inner word is begotten by the divine light shining upon the finite mind; articulate insight is the product of the perception of the objects of the world in the light of the divine standard. Augustine's appeal to the 'generation' or 'conception' of the inner word is an index of his debt to the Platonic doctrine of recollection; in an interpretation of Matthew 10: 20: 'For it is not ye that speak but the spirit of your father which speaketh in you'. Augustine develops the idea that both language and insight are properly speaking divine gifts (*Confessions.* xiii. 31, 46): this is his development of Plato's insight in the *Meno* (80e ff.) that one must know what is true in order to judge falsity, and such a knowledge of the truth is recognition that 'we are like explorers who rejoice in what they have discovered, not like inspectors who have to put things right'.[128] Philosophical reflection is the attempt to pursue the traces of the divine word, and thus to reflect the divine ground. Arthur Hallam, a friend of the pioneer philologist Richard Trench, was struck by Coleridge's power to take human thought to 'Being's dim foundations' (cf. *Aids*, p. cxlvi). Indeed, Coleridge's thoughts upon language are not just philological exercises, but are meant to lead to the dim foundations of being.

Coleridge is quite aware of those Enlightenment philosophers like Hume who argue that we have little reason for assuming that the universe is a rational cosmos, and even less for assuming that this 'little agitation' of the human brain might be a model for the underlying structures and recesses of the world. Why not assume the absurdity of being? The Latin root of the word 'absurd' is the word meaning 'deaf' – 'surdus'. The contemporary philosopher of religion Lesek Kolakowski makes a Coleridgean point when he observes:

And is it not a plausible suspicion that if 'to be' were pointless and the universe void of meaning, we would never have achieved not only the ability to imagine otherwise but even the ability to think precisely this: that 'to be' is indeed pointless and the universe void of meaning?[129]

---

[127] Augustine, *Confessions*, p. 256.   [128] Augustine, *On Free Choice*, p. 55.
[129] L. Kolakowski, *Metaphysical Horror* (Oxford: Blackwell, 1988), p. 120.

THE COMMUNICATION OF TRUTH AND BIBLICAL SYMBOLS

Coleridge sees the empiricist view of language as incapable of explaining the fact of *meaning or communicative intelligence* and envisages the scriptural meditations of Leighton as providing the means for his reader to meditate upon that 'inner word' which is the ground and source of all meaning in the cosmos – the Logos which is the communicative intelligence of the Godhead.

John Beer notes that Coleridge distinguishes between λόγος and ῥῆμα in connection with Swedenborg's use of correspondences: 'the Noumenon, I say, is the Logos, the WORD. The Phaenomenon, or visual and literal Apprehension is ῥῆμα – a fluxion' (*Aids*, p. 551). This λόγος–ῥῆμα distinction was also used in the 1825 edition but removed from the second edition of 1831 (*Aids*, p. 534). Nevertheless, it is a useful key to Coleridge's Platonic reflections about language and scripture.

The noumenal meaning of the scriptural λόγος is best expressed through the symbol of light: language conveys insight and such insight is possible because language sheds light upon and points to the intelligible transcendent reality; scriptural language is that which pre-eminently illuminates the hidden intelligibility of being. God created the world through the Word, and the world, Scripture, and the soul are the books of the Word.

What a mine of undiscovered treasures, what a new world of Power and Truth would the Bible promise to our future meditation, if in some gracious moment one solitary text of all its inspired contents should but dawn upon us in the pure untroubled brightness of an IDEA, that most glorious birth of the God-like within us, which even as Light, its material symbol, reflects itself from a thousand surfaces, and flies homeward to its Parent Mind enriched with a thousand forms, itself above form and still remaining in its own simplicity and identity! (*LS*, p. 50)

The language of Scripture points back beyond itself – like *light* – to its source as the Creator of being, the Word: *verbum ante tempora* which is the self-explication of the Father and as such is the *splendor Patris*.

An IDEA, in the *highest* sense of that word, cannot be conveyed but by a *symbol* . . .Veracity does not consist in *saying* but in the intention of *communicating* truth; and the philosopher who can not utter the whole truth without conveying falsehood . . . is constrained to express himself *mythically* or equivocally. (*BL* i. 156–7)

We should consider the metaphysical context of communicating truth through myth or equivocally: symbols are expressions of *ideas* which cannot be expressed in discursive terms without apparent contradiction (*BL* i. 156). These ideas are living powers (*BL* i. 97; *LS*, p. 61) of the all-pervading Logos (*LS*, p. 97). Words reflect and partake in the communicative intelligence of the Logos.

With his distinction between 'truth' and 'veracity' Coleridge reveals his adherence to the tradition of philosophising from Plotinus to Schelling which envisages artistic and imaginative expression as a key to reality. Plato himself tends to employ pictures and images in order to speak of the good. Whereas Aristotle's metaphysics consists of analysing the various meanings of the word 'is' in the attempt to explicate the 'principles' of the natural world, Plato thinks that the goal of thought is 'beyond being' and he eschews the attempt to categorise that which is transcendent. At this point he tends to employ a 'likely tale': a myth. These myths are philosophical and purged of the immoral and irrational aspects of the received myths and legends in the poets. But they remain enigmatic and evade strict discursive treatment.[130]

The material universe, saith a Greek philosopher, is but one vast complex MYTHOS (i.e. symbolical representation): and mythology the apex and complement of all genuine physiology . . . WHAT COMES FROM THE HEART, THAT ALONE GOES TO THE HEART; WHAT PROCEEDS FROM A DIVINE IMPULSE, THAT THE GODLIKE ALONE CAN AWAKEN. (*F* i.524)

The Greek philosopher is presumably the Neoplatonist Sallustius, and Coleridge's symbol theory is Neoplatonic. The concept of imagination in Coleridge lies rooted in Neoplatonism and, specifically, in the Romantic reception of late antique metaphysics of nature and mythology. The concept of imagination or φαντασία, particularly in Porphyry's hands, is the mode of the embodied soul in using images because it cannot attain to purely noetic or discursive thought.[131] On the other hand nature itself is the product of the the world-soul's lower part, a bridge between the intelligible and the visible. Nature is mythic for the Neoplatonists because it simultaneously manifests figures and shapes and signs whose real significance remains hidden – unless, of course, the

---

[130] cf. Luc Brisson, *Einführung in die Philosophie des Mythos, I Antike, Mittelalter und Renaissance* (Darmstadt: Wissenschaftliche Buchgesellschaft, 1996) pp. 26–38.

[131] Hadot, *Porphyre et Victorinus*, vol. i. pp. 182–9.

observer employs φαντασία, the fount of both myth and nature.[132] This Neoplatonic theory had a great impact via Paracelsus and Boehme up to the Romantics, whereby 'Phantasie' or 'fancy' was reserved for the much inferior faculty contrasted by Coleridge with 'imagination'.[133]

Plotinus was eager to emphasise the symbolic presence of the intelligible in sensible reality, and insisted against Plato – who had so notoriously banished the artists from the city state – that true art is a reflection of the real presence of the divine reality; the artist has privileged access to the ideas, and creates a mirror in which the divine is reflected.[134] When an object is thus seen as a mirror, it is not banished to a shadowy semi-reality: the complaint often raised against Platonism by 'realists' who claim that this metaphysics is 'dualistic' or that it allegorises the hard facts of reality. This view of a spatio-temporal item as mirror of the intelligible does not mean that the object *loses* its own character in order to reflect something else. Hort said of Coleridge: 'the visible world was most thoroughly substantial to him, *because* he believed it to be sustained by an unseen world'.[135] Armstrong notes: 'It is important, if you are to understand Platonism at all, to understand that it *is* by being themselves that things image their archetypes.'[136] In 'being themselves', objects possess a value which is bequeathed by God, but which is not extraneous to them. The symbol 'partakes of the Reality which it renders intelligible' (*LS*, p. 30). This value constitutes that perfection of finite items which abides when they themselves have perished. As Coleridge observes in his *Biographia Literaria*, Plotinus supposes nature to veil her mysteries: 'Should any one interrogate her, how she works, if graciously she vouchsafe to listen and speak, she will reply, it behoves thee not to disquiet me with interrogatories, but to understand in silence, even as I am silent, and work without words' (*BL* i. 241). Goethe's paradoxical phrase 'das offenbare

---

[132] Sallustius, *Concerning the Gods and the Universe*, edited with prolegomena and translation by A. D. Nock, (Cambridge University Press, 1926), p. 5: 'The universe itself can be called a myth, since bodies and material objects are apparent in it, while souls and intellects are concealed.' Cf. Coleridge, *Notebooks*, iii, § 3, 902.

[133] James Engell, *The Creative Imagination: Enlightenment to Romanticism* (Cambridge, Mass. and London: Harvard University Press, 1981).

[134] Plotinus, *Treatise* iv. 3 (27) 11, 1–8.

[135] *Cambridge Essays*, p. 334.

[136] A. H. Armstrong, 'Platonism' in *Prospects for Metaphysics: Essays of Metaphysical Exploration*, edited by Ian Ramsey (London: George Allen, 1961), p. 108.

Geheimnis' (the open secret)[137] expresses the Plotinian conviction that the philosopher or scientist has to learn to see *that* mystery in the phenomenal reality which *lies open before his eyes* and this is a spiritual or meditative exercise as much as a purely academic enterprise. The philosopher-poets Goethe and Coleridge used Plotinus to attack an unreflective and dogmatic instrumentalism which simply wished to 'unveil' nature. Their counter point is that nature inevitably resists such disclosure, a thought expressed by Angelus Silesius:

> The Rose is without why, she blooms because she blooms;
> She does not care about her self, and does not ask whether she is seen.[138]

Herein lies the significance of the symbolic as opposed to the merely metaphoric: the former *reflects* in the sense of pointing beyond itself *while being itself*; in other words, the image of the mirror stands in a relationship of dynamic continuity with its source.[139]

This essentially Neoplatonic idea was employed by Schelling in his reflections about the nature of art.[140] Schelling's philosophy of art is rather protean, as is its function within his system:[141] generally speaking, art became progressively less important within Schelling's philosophy. Nature for Schelling is never simply an objective realm of 'fact' but it is a stepping-stone to the spiritual realm (*Staffel zur Geisterwelt*)[142] and art removes the veil between the natural and spiritual by expressing the spiritual in the natural.[143]

---

[137] Pierre Hadot, 'Zur Idee der Naturgeheimnisse', *Akademie der Wissenschaften und der Literatur, Mainz, Abhandlungen der Geistes und Sozialwissenschaften Klasse Jahrgang* 8 (1982), pp. 29 ff.

[138]   Die Ros ist ohn Warum: sie blühet, weil sie blühet,
                   Sie acht nicht ihrer selbst, fragt nicht, ob man sie siehet.
                   (Angelus Silesius, *Cherubischer Wandersmann* (Zürich: Manesse, 1989), p. 96.

[139] There is an obvious analogy with the theology of Paul Tillich who wrote both dissertations and licenciate on Schelling.

[140] F. W. J. von Schelling, *Texte zur Philosophie der Kunst*, edited with introduction by W. Beierwaltes (Stuttgart: Reclam, 1982.), pp. 3–35. An important link between Schelling and Plotinus was Friedrich Creuzer, *Symbolik und Mythologie der alten Völker, besonders der Griechen* (Leipzig und Darmstadt: Carl Wilhelm Leske, 1822): Creuzer translated Plotinus' Treatise iii. 8 (30), 'On Nature and Contemplation' in 1805. cf. Beierwaltes, *Platonismus und Idealismus*, pp. 100 ff.

[141] Balthasar, *Herrlichkeit*, iii. pt. 1, pp. 889–904; H. Freier, *Die Rückkehr der Götter. von der Aesthetischen Überschreitung der Wissensgrenze zur Mythologie der Moderne. Eine Untersuchung zur systematischen Rolle der Kunst in der Philosophie Kants und Schellings* (Stuttgart: Reclam, 1976); E. L. Fackenheim, 'Schelling's philosophy of literary arts' in *Philosophical Quarterly* 4 (1954), pp. 310–26.

[142] F. W. J. von Schelling, *Die Weltalter Fragmente. In den Urfassungen von 1811 und 1813*, ed. M. Schröter (Munich; Beck, 1946), p. 234.

[143] F. W. J. von Schelling, *Sämmtliche Werke* (Stuttgart, Augsburg: Cotta, 1859), vol. v. pp. 368 ff.

Yet for Schelling the body of art consists of *myths*. Myths are not relics of primitive humanity – the illusions and ignorance of dark ages – but the enigmatic expression of profound truths. Myths, in particular, provide art with materials with which the spiritual aspect of nature can be suggested: art expresses the (divine) ideas through images of gods. These ideas are, as Coleridge puts it, 'CONSTITU- TIVE, and at one with the power and life of Nature according to Plato and Plotinus' (*LS*, p. 114).[144] Each idea is represented by a god, and mythology is a story of the gods.[145] In this manner art is closely linked to the philosophical articulation of the Absolute via mythology.[146] C. S. Lewis expresses the philosophical significance of myth in the Platonic tradition when he writes:

We feel it to be numinous. It is as if something of great moment had been communicated to us. The recurrent efforts of the mind to grasp – we mean chiefly, to conceptualise – this something, are seen in the persistent tendency of humanity to provide myths with allegorical explanations. And after all allegories have been tried, the myth itself continues to feel more important than they.[147]

Such a vision of the cognitive content of myth explains why Schelling came to envisage Christian symbols as structurally related to the cognate myths of the Hellenistic world, without wishing to reduce or relativise their truth content.[148]

The Neoplatonic-Schellingian metaphysics of the symbol express- ing divine ideas provides the basis of Coleridge's momentous difference between *analogous* and *metaphorical* language delineated on pp. 205–206 of *Aids*:

Analogies are used in aid of *Conviction*: Metaphors, as means of *Illustration*. The language is analogous, whenever a thing, power, or principle in a higher dignity is expressed by the same thing, in a lower but more known form. Such for example is the language of John iii 6 *That which is born of the*

---

[144] Coleridge claims: 'It seems to me plain enough, that the Ground of the Plotinian Philosophy . . . is a *clear* and *positive* exposition of Ideas. The doctrine rather hinted by Plato in his *writings* than set forth.' *PL*, p. 426.

[145] It is worth noticing that Schelling's earliest and latest philosophical work was on the nature of myth. Hence one might say that the philosophy of mythology (*Philosophie der Mythologie*) is an abiding concern.

[146] A. Hilary Armstrong, 'The divine enhancement of earthly beauties: the Hellenic and Platonic Tradition' in *Eranos* 53 (1984), pp. 49–81.

[147] C. S. Lewis, *An Experiment in Criticism* (Cambridge University Press, 1961), p. 44.

[148] Robert F. Brown, *Schelling's Treastise on 'The Deities of Samothrace'* (Missoula, Mont.: 1974) and Paul Tillich, *The Construction of the History of Religion in Schelling's Positive Philosophy: its Presuppositions and Principles*, translated and edited by Victor Nuovo (Lewisburg: Bucknell, 1974).

Flesh, is Flesh; that which is born of the Spirit, is Spirit. That latter half of the verse contains the fact *asserted*; the former half the *analogous* fact, by which it is rendered intelligible. (*Aids*, p. 205)

The phrases 'born again' and 'spiritual life' are not metaphorical or figurative but express a symbolic fact. 'Symbols and symbolical expressions; the nature of which is always *taute*gorical (i.e. expressing the *same* subject but with a *difference*) in contra-distinction from metaphors and similitudes, that are always *alle*gorical (i.e. expressing a *different* subject but with a resemblance) (*Aids*, p. 206). Coleridge wishes to insist upon the 'wide difference between *symbolical* and *allegorical*' (*Aids*, p. 314). Symbols are 'born' of the reconciling and mediating power between the images of sense and the ideas of reason. These symbols are 'harmonious in themselves, and consubstantial with the truths, of which they are the *conductors*'. In the preface to *Aids to Reflection* living words are described as the '*Wheels* of the intellect . . . such as Ezekiel beheld' (*Aids*, p. 7). The full account is given in the *Stateman's Manual*:

These are the Wheels which Ezekiel beheld, when the hand of the Lord was upon him, and he saw visions of God as he sate among the captives by the river of Chebar. *Withersoever the Spirit was to go, the wheels went, and thither was their spirit to go: for the spirit of the living creature was in the wheels also.* The truths and the symbols that represent them move in conjunction and form the living chariot that bears up (for *us*) the throne of the Divine Humanity. Hence, by a derivative, indeed, but not a divided, influence and though in a secondary yet in more than a metaphorical sense, the Sacred Book is worthily intitled *the* WORD OF GOD. (*LS*, p. 29)

As '*living educts*' of the imagination the words of the history of Scripture – unlike the abstractions of the Enlightenment historians – bear us up to the throne of the divinity humanity. The wheels symbolise a philosophical-religious ascent of the mind to God. If the link between the Platonising view of symbols as a means of ascent of the mind and the Christian devotion to Scripture seems incongruous, it is worth considering that the greatest Christian Platonists Origen and Augustine were primarily biblical exegetes. The pagan Platonists developed complex philosophical accounts of Homeric myths, and the Christian Platonists shared this concern for exegesis, even if its immediate object was different. Origen is clearly an exegete of the Alexandrine school,[149] and Augustine describes

---

[149] Bernhard Neuschäfer, *Origenes als Philologe* (Basel: Reinhardt, 1987), vol. i. pp. 57–84.

poignantly how listening to Ambrose's philosophical sensitive exegesis of Scripture in Milan removed the veil of mystery (*mysticum velamentum*) and disclosed the spiritual meaning of the sacred text.[150] Many of the most philosophically interesting thoughts of Augustine are contained in his analysis and exposition of the psalms; most notable perhaps the elucidation of the divine name 'ego sum qui Sum'.[151]

Self-conscious thought requires an organ in order to make actual the spiritual realm which it possesses *unconsciously*. This organ is language, and the highest expression of the spritual is that of Christian scripture. Hence it is with a particular Platonist metaphysic that Coleridge can assert:

The Bible alone contains a Science of *Realities*: and therefore each of its Elements is at the same time a living GERM, in which the Present involves the Future, and in the Finite the Infinite exists potentially. (*LS*, p. 49)

The central biblical idea of redemption expresses in symbolic terms a cosmic event: 'the process which began in the separation of light from Chaos . . . and has its end in the union of life with God'. Christ is the 'Logos or Word that was in the beginning, by whom all things *became* . . . who in and by the Creation commenced that great redemptive Process, the history of *Life* which begins in its detachment from Nature and is to end in its union with God' (*CCS*, p. 113). The Bible is not a forensic record of attested miracles, 'proofs of Christianity', but the symbolic and figurative expression of a cosmic event: the life, death, and resurrection of Jesus of Nazareth as the divine renewal of creation. Dietrich Mahnke suggests:

the fundamental Christian dogma of Divine incarnation can express the substantial transcendence of the Godhead through the real immanence of his personality in earthly affairs far more than is possible for the Jewish and Islamic theologies of Divine remoteness or Plotinus' doctrine of intelligible hierarchies. It is for this reason that it was primarily Christian mysticism which developed a *genuine Symbolism* in which the physical realm is not merely a superficial allegory or analogy of the Divine reality, but the terrestrial is a σύμβολον, a mark of the self revelation of the heavenly, indeed a 'sacrament sent and consecrated by God', which administers invisible values in the midst of the visible.[152]

[150] Augustine, *Confessions*, p. 116.
[151] cf. W. Beierwaltes, *Platonismus und Idealismus*, pp. 26–37.
[152] 'Denn das christliche Grunddogma der Menschwerdung Gottes vermag die substantielle Transcendenz des göttliche Wesens durch die wirkliche Immanenz seiner Schöpferkraft und die unmittelbare Offenbarung seiner Persönlichkeit im irdischen Geschehen doch viel

Scripture expresses the reaction of human beings to divine revelation: it is not, for Coleridge, a miraculous dictation from above. Yet it is *not merely human* and its language is *not merely figurative.* The words of Scripture are 'living powers' and thus vehicles of truths about the sacred – not merely rhetorical or ornamental, they convey insight and bear truths. The language of Scripture is most deeply *symbolic* rather than allegorical. Symbolic means for Coleridge *tautegoric* – it expresses *itself* in that it expresses its divine source. Instead of the plenary inspiration of Scripture as a whole, Coleridge presents a theory of the *plenary inspiration of symbolic images* which are con*substantial* with that which they symbolise.[153] A symbol is defined as 'a sign included in the Idea, which it represents' (*Aids*, p. 263); a '*lower* form or species of a higher in the same *kind*': *pars pro toto* rather than a merely figurative expression.

The decisive term 'tautegoric' is rooted in the Platonic *Sophist* where Plato uses the categories of identity and difference (ταυτότης and ἑτερότης) along with the categories of rest and movement.[154] Coleridge may have been influenced by Smith in his *Select Discourses*:

The soul's 'Operations about Truth . . . are the true badges of an Eternal nature, and speak a ταυτότης and στάσις (as Plato is wont to phrase it) in man's Soul'.[155]

'Tautegorical' expresses the thought that the symbolic imagination has a luminous quality and provides special access to spiritual realities and conversely, in Swiatecka's memorable phrase, that symbols are 'visible tips of an ontological iceberg'.[156] Schelling once remarked to the great Victorian Platonist and biblical critic Benjamin Jowett that 'Coleridge had expressed many things better than

---

wesentlicher zu ergänzen, als dies in der jüdischen und islamischen Erhabenheitstheologie oder in Plotins übersinnlicher Weltstufenlehre überhaupt möglich ist. Deshalb hat auch erst die christliche Mystik einen echten Symbolismus ausbilden können, der in der sinnlichen Realität nicht bloß äusserliche Allegorien oder Analogien der höheren, göttlichen Wirklichkeit findet, sondern dem alles Irdische eine wahres σύμβολον, ein Erkennungszeichen des sich offenbarenden Himmlischen ist, ja ein von Gott persönlich "eingesetztes und geweihtes Sakrament", das im Sichtbaren selbst unsichtbare Werte spendet.' Dietrich Mahnke, *Unendliche Sphäre und Allmittelpunkt. Beiträge zur Genealogie der Mathematischen Mystik* (Halle: Max Niemeyer, 1937), pp. 214–15.

[153] See Alan Richardson's brief but pertinent discussion of Austin Farrer's theory of revelation in *The Cambridge History of the Bible*, edited by S. L. Greenslade (Cambridge University Press, 1963), vol. iii. p. 334.

[154] W. Beierwaltes, *Identität und Differenz*, pp. 24 ff.

[155] Smith, *Discourses*, p. 97.

[156] M. Jadwiga Swiatecka, *The Idea of the Symbol: some Nineteenth-Century Comparisons with Coleridge* (Cambridge University Press, 1980), p. 59.

he could himself, that in one word he had comprised a whole essay, saying that mythology was not allegorical but tautegorical' (cf. *LS*, p. 30 n. 3).

The concept 'tautegoric' links insight and the Platonist maxim, ὅμοιον ὁμοίῳ 'like is known by like'. Discussing the 'vision and faculty divine' in connection with Plotinus' great treatise v. 5 (32) 'That the Intelligibles are not Outside the Intellect', Coleridge writes:

They and they only can acquire the philosophic imagination, the sacred power of self-intuition, who within themselves can interpret and understand the symbol, that the wings of the air-sylph are forming within the skin of the caterpillar . . . all the organs of sense are framed for a corresponding world of sense; and we have it. All the organs of spirit are framed for a correspondent world of spirit; tho' the latter organs are not developed in all alike. But they exist in all, and their first appearance discloses itself in the *moral* being. (*BL* i. 241–2)

Imagination is famously a 'repetition in the finite mind of the eternal act of creation in the infinite I AM' (BL i. p. 304).[157] The theological-metaphysical resonance of the *imago Dei* in Coleridge's use of the word 'imagination', especially in his critique of a 'hunger-bitten and idea-less philosophy' which cannot recognise a 'medium between *Literal* and *Metaphorical*' (*LS*, p. 30) is not simply fortuitous.[158]

The scrutiny of, and attention to, language is not a tedious hair-splitting scholasticism but an intellectual task of religious significance. In his *Logic* Coleridge quotes Henry More's poem *Psychozoia* where More uses the Narcissus motif:

> And this I wot is the soul's excellence,
> That from the hint of each self-issuing glance
> In shadows se(nsible) she doth from hence
> Her inward life and radiant hue advance
> To higher pitch and good governance
> May weaned be from love of fading light
> In outward forms having cognizance
> That 'tis not these that are the beauty bright
> Which takes men so, but they cause in human sprite.
>
> (*Logic*, p. 96)

The image which Henry More uses is that of the 'self-issuing glance' or the 'radiant hue', the inner light which enables the soul to ascend

---

[157] cf. the excellent discussion by Engell, *Creative Imagination*, pp. 328–66.
[158] cf. editors' Introduction in *BL*, pp. lxxiii–ciii.

from the shadows of the sensible realm – the fading light of the outward forms – to the intelligible realm. Words are thus for Coleridge vital elements in the contemplation of the intelligible since they reflect and partake in the communicative intelligence of the divine Logos. A mind comes to know itself as such through language. The latter is a medium by which the divine light may be communicated: it partakes of both the pure spiritual and the material realm. Coleridge refers, in a remark about Plato's *Symposium*, to the living Words which are envoys and interpreters between heaven and earth (cf. *CCS*, pp. 166, 184).

THE PHILOSOPHIC AND THE BELOVED APOSTLE

The philosophical theology of William Paley rested upon a clearly literalist and forensic approach to Scripture. The Christian Scriptures can be treated like legal documents: the miracles were publicly attested signs of the validity of the teaching of Jesus, and even if we would usually be wary of claims to miraculous powers, the testimony and behaviour of the witnesses serve as sufficient evidence for the accuracy of the biblical account. The coherence of incidental persons and facts reported in the Acts of the Apostles and the letters of St Paul provide sufficient evidence that these are authentic.[159] It is easy to mock Paley; however, his was a subtle response to both libertines and sceptics who presented Christianity as based upon an impostor and forgeries, and Roman Catholic apologetics which encouraged doubts about the literal meaning of the text as a means of attacking Protestantism and showing the necessity of the church as buttress of the faith.

Coleridge, however, reacts from this forensic and public view of the biblical text of Paley, and returns to the approach of the Cambridge Platonists who wished to judge Scripture in terms of its spiritual power rather than as a quarry for particular tenets or facts. As Ralph Cudworth writes: 'Scripture faith is not a mere believing of historical things, and upon artificial arguments or testimonies only, but a certain higher and diviner power in the soul, that peculiarly correspondeth with the Deity.'[160] Thomas Browne, a

---

[159] cf. Neil Hitchin's superb article 'Probability and the Word of God: William Paley's Anglican Method and the Defence of the Scriptures in *Anglican Theological Review* 72/3 (1997), pp. 392–407.

[160] Preface in Cudworth, *True Intellectual System*, p. xiv.

seventeenth-century Platonist, writes in his *Religio Medici* of the two books from which he collects his divinity, the Bible and nature, 'that universal and public manuscript'. In his marginal note Coleridge states 'All this is very fine Philosophy, + the best + and most ingenious defence of Revelation' (*Marg.* i. 747). The best and most ingenious defence of revelation envisages Scripture as an enigmatic disclosure of supernatural reality, akin to the oblique revelation of the realm of spirit in nature. Leighton writes:

In this elementary world, light being (as we hear) the first visible, all things are seen by it, and it by itself. Thus is Christ, among spiritual things, in the elect of the Church; *all things are made manifest by the light* says the Apostle, Eph. v.13.

Coleridge notes: 'On the true test of the Scriptures. Oh . . . I seem to myself to be only thinking my own thoughts over again' (*Marg.* iii. 523). Christianity is not a merely historical *opus operatum* but connected to the interior light of the spiritual life: the inward Christ. The Christian Platonists of the seventeenth century could draw upon the allegorising tendencies of the Church Fathers while defending this practice by reference to the 'spirit'. Whereas strict Calvinists identified revelation with the Bible, the 'spiritualists' could appeal to evidence in revelation quite unlike the proofs of Locke or Paley. Scripture, Leighton avers,

carries the lively stamp of Divine inspiration, but there must be a spiritual eye to discern it. He that is blind, knows not that the sun shines at noon, but by the report of others; but they that see, are assured they see it, and are assured by no other thing but its own light. To ask one who is a believer, 'How know you the Scriptures to be Divine?' is the same as to ask him, 'How do you know light to be light?'

The soul is nothing but darkness and blindness within, till that same Spirit that shines without in the word, likewise shines within it, and effectively make it light; but that once done, then it is the word read with some measure of the same Spirit by which it was written, and the soul is ascertained that it is Divine: as in bodily sight, there must be a meeting of inward light, *viz.* the visual spirits with the outward object.

The Spirit of God within brings evidence with it, . . . and makes itself discernible in the word . . .[161]

Leighton lays great stress upon the transforming, or spiritual, power of Scripture 'The Gospel is called *light,* and the children of God are

---

[161] Robert Leighton, Commentary on 1 Peter 1: 10–12 in *The Whole Works*, with a life of the author by J. N. Pearson, 2 vols. (London: Duncan, 1849), vol. 1. p. 167.

likewise called *light,* as being transformed into its nature.'[162] This
elevated sense of the workings of the spirit meant that some of the
spiritualists felt free from the fetters of the literal text, and able to
pursue the deeper spiritual meaning. The more extreme figures
posed a very real threat to Christian orthodoxy with their perfec-
tionism and illuminatist ideas, and flourished in the mid-seventeenth
century. It was often in such groups that the heritage of German
mysticism flourished in England. John Everard (1582?–1640) of Clare
College, Cambridge and Giles Randall (BA at Lincoln College,
Oxford, 1625–6) translated the *Theologia Germanica,* Nicholas of Cusa,
and the central German spiritualist theologian Sebastian Franck
(1499–1542).[163]

Of course, Leighton or the Cambridge Platonists were innocent of
modern biblical criticism and had little of what might today be
called a 'historical sense'. Coleridge, by way of contrast, was well
aware of German developments and raises the question: 'Is the
fourth Gospel authentic? And is the interpretation, I have given,
true or false?' (*Aids,* p. 386).[164] Coleridge's distinction between the
conviction that the Bible contains the religion revealed by God and
the superstitious assumption that whatever is contained in the Bible
is religion and revealed by God is based on the precept that the
Bible is of all the 'conservatives of Christian Faith' the 'surest' and
'most reflective of the inward Word'.[165] Nevertheless, we should be
wary of assuming that biblical criticism is entirely an invention of the
Enlightenment. Antony Grafton has argued persuasively that the
pioneering Renaissance and Enlightenment scholars were disposed
to exaggerate the gulf between their work and their medieval and
ancient predecessors.[166] The great Christian Platonist Origen was a
skilled philologist, and a product of the source of philology in the
ancient world: Alexandria.[167] The influence of Origen and the

[162] Leighton, 1 Peter, 2: 1, 2 *The Whole Works,* vol. i. p. 228.
[163] cf. Rufus Jones, *The Spiritual Reformers in the Sixteenth and Seventeenth Centuries* (London: Macmillan, 1914). Nigel Smith, *Perfection Proclaimed: Language and Literature in English Radical Religion, 1640–1660* (Oxford: Clarendon, 1989). I am grateful to Lewis Owens for pointing out the importance of Everard and Randall.
[164] A. J. Harding, *Coleridge and the Inspired Word* (Kingston and Montreal: McGill, Queen's University Press, 1985).
[165] *SW* ii 1145.
[166] A. Grafton, *Defenders of the Text: the Traditions of Scholarship in an Age of Science* (Cambridge, Mass.: Harvard University Press, 1991).
[167] cf. Rudolf Pfeiffer, *Geschichte der Klassichen Philologie von den Anfängen bis zum Ende des Hellenismus* (Munich: Beck, 1978) and Neuschäfer, *Origenes als Philologe.*

Alexandrine school upon the Cambridge Platonists and the mystics militated against a crude view of Scripture as dictating supernatural facts.

In Coleridge's eyes Paul is the 'philosophic Apostle' (*Aids*, pp. 146, 235). Paul divides humanity into the spiritual and the natural: the former are members of a new order, a new creation (*Aids*, p. 146 n. 2). John similarly distinguishes between those who have and those who have not received the spirit (cf. *Aids*, p. 301). Christ as the Logos incarnate is the exclusive principle of freedom and life; a cosmic principle active in the creation of the universe and source of spiritual renewal in the life of men. The metaphysical aspect of the nature, work, and effects of Christ is much more prominent in Paul and John than in those documents which New Testament scholars call the 'Synoptic Gospels'.

Coleridge's Pauline emphasis upon the Son's unity with the Father is intended to counter the view that Jesus of Nazareth was simply a historical figure: that Jesus was the *Christ* means for Paul quite unequivocally that the man Jesus of Nazareth is the incarnation of the universal man of Alexandrine Platonism, the eternal discarnate Son.[168] The dying and rising of the Jewish rabbi is also the dying and rising of the eternal son of God and the paradigm of the dying of every man to sin and rising to a new life, 'a Spiritual Conception of the Messiah, and of his Communion with the Soul' (Coburn, p. 150). Coleridge exclaims in a note on the French mystic Fénelon: 'Wear at your bosoms that precious amulet against all the spells of the antichrist, the 20th verse of the 2nd chapter of Paul's Epistle to the Galatians: – *I am crucified with Christ, nevertheless, I live; yet not I but Christ liveth in me: and the life, which I now live in the flesh, I live by the faith of the Son of God, who loved me and gave himself for me*' (*Marg.* ii. 592).

The logos theology in John has a rather different emphasis. Whereas Paul emphasises the crucifixion and resurrection, John lays more weight upon incarnation and revelation. All the specific events

---

[168] Heraclitus' λόγος is the rational principle which unifies the world and through whom we come to learn our real nature. Seen alongside Plato's doctrine in his *Timaeus* that the world is the living and rational image of the good, and the Stoic principle that the logos is the organic goal and directing principle of the universe, it is easy to see how Jewish and Christian thinkers came to envisage the *logos* as the *communicative* aspect of the Godhead. In St Paul the idea of a cosmic principle which communicates the transcendent deity is evident; even if he does not use the concept λόγος. Christ is the 'image' of the Father (2 Cor. 4: 6), image of the invisible God (εἰκὼν τοῦ θεοῦ τοῦ ἀοράτου), and all is created through him (τὰ πάντα δι' αὐτοῦ) (Col. 1: 15–17). Although in the form of God (ἐν μορφῇ θεοῦ) he took on the form of a slave (Phil. 2: 6).

in the narrative gospel point to the activity of the eternal Logos breaking into history: the light of the world heals the blind; the sustainer of the universe feeds his followers with bread and fish. The history serves as a parable and symbol (John 6: 51: 'I am the bread'). Jesus is the Christ, i.e. the Messiah, because he is the light which enlightens all men. Coleridge uses the mystical language of the Cambridge Platonists when he speaks of the indwelling Logos as the infant Christ. The 'birth' of the Logos within the soul is the beginning of the process of participating in the dying and rising Christ. The Christian doctrines 'all must converge to one point, and with them all the essential faculties and excellencies of the human being – so that Christ in the Man, and Man in the Christ will be *one* in *one*' (*Notebooks* iii. 3803): deification.

To those who see Christianity primarily through the first three gospels, Coleridge's emphasis upon the intense Christ mysticism of Paul and John with its central tenet of the eternal cosmic status of Christ and his communion of the soul is rather alienating. It is tempting to put this mysticism down to the Hellenistic influences upon Paul and John (a policy which was vigorously pursued by the Ritschl school at the end of the nineteenth century and imitated throughout the twentieth century). The difference between John and Paul and the synoptic gospels seems to such minds the difference between obscure and plain Christianity. Coleridge, like most Platonists and idealists, sees the issue quite in the opposite way. He sees John and Paul as the key to the riddle presented by the other New Testament writers. The solution to the puzzle of the extraordinary claims of the Evangelists concerning Jesus of Nazareth rests in the Logos theology of John and Paul. John insists that Christ was a divine person before creation as the Logos and presents the activity of the Spirit as the perpetuation of the Incarnation: it is expedient that Jesus should leave earth and be replaced by the Spirit who will reveal Christ and continue his work. This aspect of the continuation of the incarnation in the community of believers is a point of contact with Paul. Coleridge sees the idea of the mystical participation in the body of Christ through the spirit as the centre of Paul's theology:

Exactly (as in all other points) consonant with the Pauline doctrine is the assertion of John, when speaking of the re-adoption of the redeemed to be Sons of God, and the consequent resumption (I had almost said, re-absorption) of the Law into the Will. (*Aids*, p. 301)

In short, Coleridge sees John and Paul as philosophical theologians who give Christian belief its Logos theology and thereby its Trinitarian structure. Christ is not just the greatest of all prophets, a supreme teacher, but the visible expression of a spiritual principle:

> Did Christ come from Heaven, did the Son of God leave the Glory which he had with his Father before the World began, only to *show* us a way to life, to *teach* truths, to tell us of a resurrection? Or saith he not, I *am* the way, I *am* the truth, I *am* the Resurrection and the Life! (*Aids*, p. 316)

The events of the life of Jesus of Nazareth recounted in the gospel constitute the 'sacramental Acts and Phaenomena, of the *Deus Patiens*, the visible Words of the (invisible) Word that was in the Beginning, Symbols in time & historic fact of the redemptive functions, passions and procedures of the Lamb crucified from the foundation of the World . . . the whole life of Christ in the flesh . . . on this account proper SYMBOLS of the acts & passions of the Christ dwelling *in* man, as the Spirit of Truth . . . ' (*Marg.* ii. 279–80). The centre of Coleridge's theology is the Incarnation of the Word rather than atonement. The Incarnation is not the contingent answer to the Fall of man but the expression of the eternal divine love of creation: 'Lamb of God, slain from the foundation of the World! thou art my Strength' (*Aids*, p. 309). The idea of the Logos is intimately connected to the idea of divine creation and salvation which involves not merely the regeneration of the individual human soul but the order and harmony of that creation.[169]

> Respecting the redemptive act itself, and the Divine Agent, we know from revelation that he 'was made a quickening (ζωοποιοῦν, *life-making*) Spirit': and that in order to this it was necessary, that God should be manifested in the flesh, that the eternal Word, through whom and by whom the World (κόσμος, the Order, Beauty, and sustaining law of visible natures) was and is, should be made flesh, assume our humanity personally, fulfil all righteousness, and so suffer and so die for us as in dying to conquer Death for as many as should receive him. (*Aids*, p323)

The 'inner Word' (*verbum interius*) among Coleridge's beloved seventeenth-century divines is probably a legacy of German mysticism. Coleridge is drawing upon the Logos speculation of Christian theology, in particular that of St Augustine which links the source of

---

[169] The emphasis upon the link between creation and salvation is particularly strong in mystical English thought. cf. G. Dowell, *Enjoying he World: the Rediscovery of Thomas Traherne* (London: Mowbray, 1990). See also R. Murray, *The Cosmic Covenant* (London: Sheed and Ward, 1992), and A. Galloway, *The Cosmic Christ* (London: Nisbet, 1951).

language as spoken or written word with the cosmic Word: the Logos.

These – the whole VIth of John to wit – are indeed hard sayings, alike for the disciples of the crude or dead *Letter*, and for the Doctors of abstractions & mere moral meanings . . . the manifest object (of this chapter) . . . is to reveal to us that Spiritual Things differ from Objects of Sense by their *greater reality*, by being more truly and literally *living substances*. (*Aids*, p. 386 n. 13)

Coleridge's pupil J. H. Green, in the 1849 edition of the *Confessions of an Inquiring Spirit*, had to fend off the charge that Coleridge had pillaged Lessing. Yet the emphasis upon the 'inner word' in Lessing is derived ultimately from the same sources as the mysticism of Leighton. In Lessing the mystical emphasis upon the *spiritual* reading of scripture becomes a part of his Enlightened criticism of orthodoxy, but Coleridge is perhaps less eccentric than we imagine in his avowal of Lessing. The Bible should be seen, for both Coleridge and for Leighton, in the context of the *spiritual life* rather than as a mine of otherwise inaccessible facts. Lessing, as a proponent of the doctrine of the Trinity and amongst the leading figures of new biblical criticism, seemed to provide materials for Coleridge's own invective against Socinianism. The common mystical roots of German Spiritualism which influenced Lessing and the German Idealists and the Platonic theology of Robert Leighton are evident.[170]

Yet, equally, Coleridge wishes to avoid the other extreme of taking the symbolic language of the renewal of the soul as merely figurative. The Son of God, for Kant, is a *metaphor* for every man who has gained a genuine moral will though the revolution of his ethical temper. But Coleridge denies emphatically that the dogma of redemption is merely metaphorical in this Kantian sense:

The Gospel it is not a system of Theology . . . it is a History, a series of Facts or Events related or announced. These do indeed involve, or rather I should say they at the same time *are*, most important doctrinal Truths; but still *Facts*, and Declaration of *Facts*. (*Aids*, p. 205)

The use of the word 'fact' is striking. We have emphasised the internal or spiritual aspect of Coleridge's view of religion. Yet

---

[170] Leighton's pupil Scougall's book *Life of God* is said to have had a potent effect upon the Wesleys and Methodism. John Wesley was also deeply influenced by German pietism during his stay in America. See Knox, *Robert Leighton*, p. 159.

Coleridge is adamant that a 'spiritual' interpretation of the Christian religion does not denigrate the historical aspect. The insistence upon the archetypal character of the Christ figure does not necessarily dislodge the historical content. There are many archetypal figures who were also historical persons. Historical persons are often moulded by particular paradigms: of the king-figure, or the saint, the fact that the depiction of Jesus of Nazareth conforms to a certain archetype of the dying and rising saviour does not strictly mean that we are dealing with a myth; though this is how Strauss viewed the matter in his *Life of Jesus*,[171] and Coleridge's views on the historical dimension of Christianity were regarded with suspicion by many.[172]

Coleridge distances himself from the 'errors of the *Familists, Vanists, Seekers, Behemists*, or by whatever names Church History records the poor bewildered Enthusiasts, who in the swarming time of our Republic turned the facts of the Gospel into allegories, and superseded the written Ordinances of Christ by a pretended Teaching and sensible Presence of the Spirit' (*Aids*, p. 142) and quotes Henry More against them:

These things I could not forbear to write. For *the Light within me*, that is my *Reason* and *Conscience*, does assure me, that the Ancient and Apostolic Faith according to the *historical* Meaning thereof, and in the *literal* sense of the Creed, is solid and true: and that Familism in its fairest form and under whatever disguise, is a smooth Tale to seduce the simple from their Allegiance to Christ. (*Aids*, pp. 142–3)

Coleridge's allegiance to Henry More is significant, as is the emphasis upon the 'historical Meaning of the Ancient and Apostolic Faith and the literal meaning of the creeds'. Some of these radical reformers or 'spiritualists' laid so great a stress upon the experience of the indwelling spirit that they tended to relegate the historical meaning of the faith and creeds of Christianity to a very insignificant role. The Enlightenment reception of spiritualism often led to a corresponding indifference to the historical and institutional element in Christianity. Coleridge's insistence that a symbol 'partakes of the Reality which it renders intelligible' (*LS*, p. 30) is partly directed against the 'spiritualist' manner of reducing the gospel to an allegory

---

[171] Hans Frei, 'David Friedrich Strauss' in *Nineteenth-Century Religious Thought in the West*, 3 vols., edited by J. P. Clayton, S. Katz, and N. Smart (Cambridge University Press, 1985), vol. i. pp. 215–60.

[172] cf. B. M. G. Reardon, *Religious Thought in the Victorian Age: a Survey from Coleridge to Gore* (London: Longman, 1980), pp. 79 ff.

of the inner life. The events of the life of Jesus of Nazareth are not figurative, but part of what they enunciate. The historical events bring mankind into contact with that spiritual reality which they incarnate: the reconciliation of God and creation.

Coleridge accepts the idea of Higher Criticism, and the idea of revelation as revelation of divine reason rather than the Scripture itself as an infallible oracle of propositional truths, as an immanent evolving power with the history of a people with their prophets and apostles, revealing the Word which is the indwelling light and life of mankind. It is to accept the legitimacy of the application of critical methods to Christian Scripture in the confidence that they evince the communion with the divine spirit. This is the difference between inspiration and dictation. Hence Coleridge could both harness tradition and face the challenge of sceptics in a rational manner. A modern writer observes:

> The allegorical interpretation had done for the cultured and philosophi-
> cally minded Fathers of the ancient Church what the historical method was
> to do for the Victorians and their successors: both methods helped to
> reconcile the scriptural teaching with the changed views of the Universe,
> whether Ptolemaic or Copernican, whether Stoic or Darwinian, and they
> made it possible to explain away ethical injunctions which no longer
> commended themselves to the enlightened conscience.[173]

The symbolic language of Scripture is not the figurative expression of a *deus absconditus*, but is rooted in the divine word: the Logos. In these symbols of Scripture the divine being is not merely gestured at; it becomes translucent: the symbol participates in the Logos. It was natural for Coleridge to address the issue of plenary inspiration: the Socinians and Unitarians encouraged the critical study of the Bible because they felt that this would support a Unitarian position inasmuch as the gulf between the Unitarian gospel message and the Trinitarian corruptions can be made evident through critical study of Scripture. Coleridge's reply is to place not just the content but also the reading of the Bible within a Trinitarian context. Those who try to maintain a 'supernatural diction' confound the revelation of the Word in Jesus of Nazareth and the 'actuation of the Holy Spirit'.[174] Hence Coleridge's famous defence of Scripture as finding 'me at greater depths of my being' is not a pragmatic-existentialist

---

[173] *Cambridge History of the Bible*, p. 302.
[174] *Confessions*, p. 61.

justification of Scripture, but a part of his attempt to revive the doctrine of the Trinity as the foundation of rational theology.[175] 'To discourse rationally it behoves us to derive strength from . . . [the] DIVINE WORD' (*Aids*, p. 219). The Logos is the dynamic informing principle within human thought and language. It is the life-making spirit (cf. *Aids*, p. 323) and the 'spirit of adoption' in Paul (*Aids*, p. 367), the evolving Logos: a dynamic principle which links Christ with the world process. Although, as we have noted, Paul does not use the term 'Logos', Coleridge speaks explicitly of 'St Paul's Christ (as the Logos) the eternal Yea' (*Aids*, p. 217).

REFLECTION AND RATIONAL DISCRIMINATION

There are two very bad things in this resolving of men's Faith and Practice into *the immediate suggestion* of a Spirit not acting on our Understandings, or rather into the illumination of such a Spirit as they can give no account of, such as does not enlighten their reason or enable them to render their doctrine intelligible to others. First, it defaces and makes useless that part of the Image of God in us, which we call REASON: and secondly, it takes away that advantage, which raises Christianity above all other Religions, that she dare appeal to so solid a faculty. (*Aids*, pp. 147–8)

This robust logocentrism is taken from Henry More's *Explanation of the Grand Mystery of Godliness*, of 1708. Coleridge believes that his contemporaries have been misled by the superficial writing of the Anglo-Gallican style. These authors have the unfortunate effect of exciting curiosity and sensibility without inducing effort. Those who confine their reading to such books diminish their capacities; Coleridge likes the analogy of morning guests who drop in and out of a household in regular succession leaving the mistress of the house superficially occupied but exhausted and unfit for her own concerns or those of more rational guests (cf. *F* i. 21). Elegant sceptics like Hume encourage a superficial activity which hides intellectual lethargy. The urbane coffee-house essay style is wholly inadequate given the necessity of prevailing upon the reader to retire within and to make one's own mind the object of 'stedfast attention'. The 'stately march and difficult evolutions' of the seventeenth-century English philosophers and divines were far more appropriate for the habituation, discipline, and *exercise* of the mind.

The modern 'asthmatic' style is characteristic for the eighteenth-

---

[175] *Confessions*, p. 70.

century empiricists. In *The Friend* Coleridge attacks the 'plenteous crop of Philosophers and Truth-trumpeters' who arose during the reigns of Louis XV and XVI. They have diffused their truths so clearly and forthrightly that the Parisian ladies and their hairdressers have become 'fluent Encyclopedists'. The only price for this knowledge, Coleridge notes with bitter irony, is the acknowledgement of the falsehood of Christianity (*F* i. 46). Underlying this enthusiasm is a naivety concerning the communication of truth. The *philosophes* cannot recognise the difference between truth as verbal accuracy and the higher sense of veracity. Coleridge writes:

By *verbal* truth we mean no more than the correspondence of a given fact to given words. In *moral* truth, we involve likewise the intention of the speaker, that his words should correspond to his thoughts in the sense which he expects them to be understood by others . . . The conscience or effective reason, commands the design of conveying an *adequate* notion of the thing spoken of, when this is practicable: but at all events a *right* notion or none at all. (*F* i. 42–3)

The *philosophes* and the Anglo-Scots who followed them prided themselves on having exposed superstition, and having destroyed the rational edifice of moral and religious truth. It is of little help for the French peasant to be corrected in his beliefs about 'ghosts, omens, dreams, etc. at the price of abandoning his faith in Providence and the continued existence of his fellow creatures after their death' (*F* i. 46). Truth in the sense of *veracity*, Coleridge avers, can never be damaging. Yet truth in the inferior sense of a formal correspondence of a particular fact to given words can create considerable harm: 'IT IS NOT EXPRESSIBLE HOW DEEP A WOUND A TONGUE SHARPENED TO THIS WORK WILL GIVE, WITH NO NOISE AND A VERY LITTLE WORD' (*Aids*, p. 111). The sceptics of the Enlightenment, who recognise no medium between the literal and metaphoric, dismiss and ridicule the symbolic truths of Christianity as in conflict with common sense and intuitive morality. They fail to see the power of these symbols as the expression of spiritual truths which cannot be treated as if they were *quasi*-historical explanations. The real conflict, Coleridge insists, is not between religion and enlightenment; belief and secularity; reason and ignorance – as the *philosophes* would maintain – but between a spiritual and a materialistic metaphysics. Once one accepts that our organs of sense are framed for a sensory world and our organs of spirit for a spiritual (cf. *BL* i. 242), one can see that the real conflict concerns metaphysics and values. Furthermore, the best critique of the naturalistic-sceptical despisers of religion lies in exposing their sophistries.

Coleridge is quite adamant: 'We want *thinking* Souls, we *want them*' (*Aids*, p. 151) and insists that 'it is a short and downhill passage from errors in words to errors in things' (*Aids*, p. 253). We should not imagine that the idiosyncrasies of Coleridge's style and address are an indication of lax thought. The 'excellence, the imitable but alas! unimitated excellence, of the Divines from Elizabeth to William IIIrd' was 'giving importance to the single words of a text' (*Marg.* ii. 294; cf. *Marg.* iii. 257). John Donne is dismissed as a 'poor Metaphysician, i.e. never closely questioned himself as to the absolute meanings of his words' (*Marg* ii. 316). Here metaphysics is linked with the scrupulous attention to meaning. It is clearly Coleridge's intention in *Aids to Reflection* to direct the reader to active thought about the meaning of particular words: 'Reflect on your own thoughts, actions, circumstances, and – which will be of especial aid to you in forming a *habit* of reflection, – accustom yourself to reflect on the words you use, hear or, read, their birth, derivation and history' (*Aids*, p. 10). The contemporary age of intellectual darkness – a falsely called enlightenment – has been partly caused by 'an aversion to all the toils of reflection' (*FI*, p. 124) of which ignorance of terms plays a central part. Coleridge's criticisms of 'the contemptuous Sneers' of merely verbal analysis (*Aids*, p. 126) are based upon his critique of the intellectual indolence of the age. He sees the aversion to philosophical and verbal analysis as a symptom of intellectual decay. He remarks upon Leighton's failure to distinguish conscience from consciousness, saying that the criticism of the *soi-disant* fruitless verbal debate is reminiscent of the attacks upon Bentley (cf. *Aids*, p. 126). Yet precise linguistic meaning is quite essential for philosophical and theological thought.

I am by the law of my nature a reasoner . . . I can take no interest whatever in hearing or saying anything merely as a fact – merely as having happened. It must refer to something within me . . . I require in everything . . . a reason, why the thing *is* at all, and why it is there or then rather than elsewhere or at another time. (*TT* i. p. 464)

For any instance of scholastic hair-splitting Coleridge claims he can find ten instances of legerdemain which have confirmed prejudices, and stood in the path of the advancement of truth 'in consequence of the neglect of *verbal debate*' (*Aids*, p. 126). In a note about *Aids to*

Reflection, especially the remark that the book is a *'proper brain-cracker'*, Coleridge discusses his own aims in writing the text. He wishes to compel the reader to reflect as to whether:

he has been hitherto aware of the mischief and folly of employing words on questions, to know the truth of which is both his interest and duty, without fixing the one meaning which in that question they are to represent? . . . In short I would fain bring the cause I am pleading to a short and simple yet decisive test. Consciousness, mind, life, will, body, organ, machine, nature, spirit, sin, habit, sense, understanding, reason: here are fourteen words. Have you ever reflectively and quietly asked yourself the meaning of one of these, and tasked yourself to return the answer in distinct terms . . . Or have you contented yourself with a vague floating meaning . . . or, if you have the gift of wit, shelter yourself under Augustine's equivocation, 'I know it perfectly well till I'm asked.' Know? Ay, as an oyster knows its life. But do you know your knowledge? (Coburn, p. 205)

Aids to Reflection consists to a large extent in reflection upon the meaning of certain words. *Conscience* is distinguished from *consciousness*; *Nature* is distinguished from *Spirit*, *sensibility* from *prudence*, *prudence* from *morality* and *morality* from *religion*, *regret* from *remorse*, *value* from *worth*, *will* and *volition*. In specific arguments in the text verbal distinctions play a considerable role; *original* sin is distinguished from *hereditary* sin; *symbols* are distinguished from *metaphors*; *reason* is distinguished from the *understanding*; *veracity* and *truth*; *deed* and *act*; *regret* and *remorse*. Coleridge admits that the scrupulous use of language sounds strained for the untrained ear. Yet the botanist, chemist, and the anatomist use terms which are technical, difficult to learn, and unattractive.

On the other hand, it is important to distinguish between philosophical accuracy and exhaustive definition. Consider the fact of the will, the *'Spiritual* in Man' (*Aids*, p. 135), which can be divided into the facts of the 'LAW OF CONSCIENCE'; the existence of a RESPONSIBLE WILL . . . and . . . the existence of EVIL' (*Aids*, p. 138); these are facts of consciousness, reason, and history (*Aids*, p. 139). These facts are the opposite of insubstantial or vague, although they resist exact definition or proof. Here Coleridge claims: 'I assume a something, the proof of which no man can *give* to another, yet every man *find* for himself' (*Aids*, p. 136). Such *indefinable* spiritual facts are nevertheless facts and not vague abstractions, and demand philosophical attention. The materialist and necessitarian ignore such indefinable facts, in opposition to the greatest philosophical minds and the 'vast majority of the Human race in all ages' (*Aids*, p. 138).

It has been said, that the Arabic has a thousand names for a Lion; but this would be a trifle compared with the useless Synonimes that would be found in an Index Expurgatorius of any European Dictionary constructed on the principles of a consistent and strictly consequential Materialism! (*Aids*, p. 138)

Much of the appeal of reductive materialism, Coleridge believes, rests upon a confusion between the indefinable and vagueness. On the contrary, the most indisputable facts, starting with phenomenal perception, cannot be exactly and exhaustively defined:[176] 'mere analysis of terms is preparative only, though as a preparative discipline indispensable' (*BL* i. 235). Whether in reflection or debate, one should as a rule, Coleridge maintains, ask the meaning of the word on which the issue depends, and if it can be used in several meanings, ask which meaning the word has in the specific case. In this way one will acquire the necessary skill to detect the fallacies of the *quid pro quo* which are the basis for exposing and disarming the great majority of irreligious philosophies: 'For the *quid pro quo* is at once the rock and quarry, on and with which the strong-holds of disbelief, materialism, and (more pernicious still) epicurean morality are built' (*Aids*, p. 47).

Coleridge seems concerned to attack the loss of metaphysical language in the English eighteenth century.[177] In an essay on Proclus A. E. Taylor notes the prevalence of Neoplatonic terminology in the seventeenth century and writes:

The eighteenth century saw the gradual decrease of this influence; in its latter third, writers like Gibbon lost all sense of the meaning of Neoplatonic language, and we thus find the *Decline and Fall of the Roman Empire* treating as gibberish doctrines which are referred to, for example, by Bacon as perfectly familiar and intelligible.[178]

Coleridge often writes of the seventeenth century as the great age of philosophy, poetry, and preaching in England. In philosophy and theology ideas do not need to be invented but merely rescued from abuse or oblivion (*Aids*, pp. 46–7). The desire to rescue 'admitted truths' (*Aids*, p. 11) lies in his loathing of the development described by A. E. Taylor and the desire to recover the lost ideas and language

[176] I owe this point to George Watson.
[177] His insistence that the use of reason cannot be considered in abstraction from language is reminiscent of Herder's thoughts about language. Coleridge thought little of Herder. cf. G. A. Wells, 'Man and future: an elucidation of Coleridge's rejection of Herder's thought' in *Journal of English and Germanic Philology* 51 (1952), pp. 314–25.
[178] A.E. Taylor, *Philosophical Studies*, p. 186.

of the seventeenth century. Coleridge's talk of the enrichment of the language by the philosophical schools should not be taken to mean any philosophical schools. On the contrary he eschews the idea-less empiricism of his age that leads to an impoverishment of society. His model of language as a treasure-house of past reflection and specula-tion which needs to be brought before a conscious mind, of metaphysics as a vital source of linguistic development, is in deliberate contrast to the reductive critique of metaphysics in empiricist philosophers. His model of the philosopher's task as awakening the mind to the riches in language as the 'embodied and articulated Spirit of the Race' (*Aids*, p. 244) is both a robust and an ingenious response to enlightened philosophers' critique of metaphy-sics as opposed to both science and common sense. Whereas the Anglo-Gallic Lockeans saw metaphysics as a product of a misunder-standing of language, Coleridge replies that language requires metaphysics for its very evolution and development.

Coleridge felt that his best allies in the struggle against pernicious empiricism were Kant and the German Idealists. In a note on Solger's *Erwin*, he writes:

Generally indeed I complain of the German Philosophers (as we are most apt to complain of dearest Friends) – of the Post-Kantians at least – for the precipitance with which they pass to their own determination of what the *thing* is, without having first enquired what the *word* means when it is used *appropriately* (Coburn, p. 99)

This is also significant with respect to Schelling. Schelling started to use an obscure terminology in the middle period of his thought, and in the treatise *Freiheitschrift*. In his marginalia on this treatise Coleridge remarks upon the 'many just and excellent observations'. Nonetheless he complains of the 'even more *over*meaning or unmeaning Quid pro Quos' and '*Thing*-phrases, (such as Licht, Fisterniss, Feuer, center, circumference, Ground . . . which seem to involve the dilemma, that either they are similies, when that, which they are meant to illustrate, has never been stated; or that they are *degrees* of a *Kind*, which Kind has not been defined' (*Marg.* iv 443).

Coleridge's interests and aims are clearly Idealist; but he does not simply repeat or translate the terminology of either Hegel or Schelling. This is particularly obvious when one compares Coleridge with minor German Idealists of the period such as Marheineke who employ exactly Hegel's terminology.[179] It is in general surprising that Coleridge in *Aids to Reflection* should endeavour to employ Kant's terms when one notes the freedom which Schelling or Fichte felt in revising the scrupulous conceptual distinctions in Kant's thought. Coleridge, however, was much impressed by the 'novelty and subtlety, yet solidity and importance, of the distinctions' which Kant employed (*BL* i. 153). Throughout *Aids to Reflection* we can note this influence. The distinctions between 'Reason' and 'understanding', 'prudence' and 'morality', 'person' and 'thing' reflect Coleridge's high estimate of Kant's terminology, even if he tends to use them in a rather different way. Kant's philosophy is conceptually extremely rich; the distinctions between 'legality' and 'morality', the 'empirical' and the 'pure' will, 'will' and 'volition', 'technical', 'pragmatic', and 'moral' imperatives are examples of the wealth of conceptual reflection in the Kantian corpus. Yet this high estimate of Kant is most revealing. Hamann famously subjected Kant to a metacritique in which he argued that the critical philosophy failed to engage with the linguistic and historical preconditions of thought. Coleridge's intense interest in language was not just borrowed from the anti-Kantians of the Jacobi–Hamann counter-Enlightenment – any Hamann influence is hard to trace – but reflects his own ingenuity and originality.[180]

Coleridge maintains much of Kant's conceptual apparatus, while trying to show that this is compatible with a metaphysical boldness which Kant eschewed. This meant primarily, for Coleridge, a rejection of Kant's concept of God as 'an unknown Something which is to answer the purpose of a Will' (*Marg.* iii. 358). Coleridge's sense of Kant's excessive coyness in his metaphysical theology, and his distrust of its inherent 'dogmatism', are perhaps justified by the fact that Kant's exposure of theoretical metaphysics was of the rather arid baroque scholasticism of the eighteenth-century German university. Coleridge's conviction that Kant was in fact much closer to the spirit of Platonism than his system sometimes suggested may be supported by the observation that Coleridge's perception of the

[179] P. Marheineke, *Die Grundlehren der christlichen Dogmatik als Wissenschaft*, 2nd edition (Berlin: Dunker and Humblot, 1927) is almost contemporary with *Aids*. A glance at Marheineke's 'Introduction', pp. 3–72 reveals how closely Marheineke follows his master Hegel in his terminology. Coleridge's relative independence towards the German Idealists revealed by his insouciance about following their terminology does not show that he is not an idealist but merely his originality.

[180] Johann Georg Hamann, *Schriften zur Sprache*, edited J. Simon (Frankfurt: Suhrkamp, 1967).

'metaphysical tradition' was broader and richer than that of Kant. For Coleridge – nurtured on the Cambridge Platonists, and their spiritual metaphysics – metaphysics was not a dogmatic illusion based upon the application of concepts beyond their legitimate range, but meant a life-forming vision, and a manly resistance to the 'pugnatious dogmatism of *partial* Reflection' (*Aids*, p. 241). Here were the seeds of Coleridge's belief in the great affinity between Kant and the Platonists; in the emphasis upon practical reason. We shall attempt to explore the grounds for this profound sympathy with Kant in the next chapter.

3

The image of God: reflection as imitating the divine spirit

Let us make man in our image, after our likeness. (Genesis 1: 26)

Truth endows men's purposes with somewhat of immutability.
(A. J. and Julius Hare)[1]

In *The Friend* Coleridge discusses William Paley's utilitarianism in some detail. The weakness of this theory, Coleridge avers, is that it confuses morality with law and 'draws away attention from the will and from inward motives and impulses which constitute the essence of morality, to the outward act' (*F* i. 314).[2] In *Aids to Reflection* Coleridge begins by considering the meaning of the word *happiness*. For Coleridge morality and religion belong inextricably together: religion is morality with reference to that which is permanent, i.e. God and the soul, and morality is religion in respect of the circumstances in which mankind *happens* to be placed (cf. *Aids*, p. 26). Morality is the attempt to organise that which *happens*, that is, the contingent, with principles which are timeless. Godlikeness or at-one-ment with the divine is the goal of the highest human ethical aspiration. The genuinely religious component in morality lies in the conviction that this aspiration towards *reflection* of the divine draws upon supernatural *aids*. Leighton sees the religious life in Augustinian terms of *pondus* or weight or gravity. This metaphor is used by Augustine to express the teleological striving of creation, and in particular the human soul, towards God[3] and denotes the dependence of the mirroring object upon its source, and the vanity of the finite: 'I assert that there is such a thing as human happiness, as *summum bonum*, or ultimate good' (*Aids*, p. 45). The leading question

---

[1] *Guesses at Truth* (London: G. Routledge, 1866), p. 148.
[2] Much useful information on Coleridge's ethics can be found in L. S. Lockridge, *Coleridge the Moralist* (Ithaca, NY: Cornell, 1977).
[3] Plotinus, *Treatise*, vi. 9 (9) 9, 15–16. 'its true life is there' (τὸ ἀληθῶς ζῆν ἐνταῦτα).

in *Aids to Reflection* is, in a sense, that of the nature of happiness, and yet this is a metaphysical rather than a psychological or an ethical question. Coleridge speaks of 'happiness' and 'blessedness' or 'felicity'. William Paley defined happiness in terms of prudence.[4] It is for this reason that Coleridge thinks that this word has been abused. Coleridge believes that true happiness is linked to *contemplation* rather than to prudence, to vision rather than to calculation.

Leighton is quoted to the effect that most men live 'at hazard' (*Aids*, p. 45) because Coleridge thinks that the word happiness is inappropriate for a state which should exclude 'hap' or 'chance'. The Greek εὐδαιμονία is a better word – conveying etymologically the influence of a 'good spirit'; ethics must be based upon fixed, that is *eternal*, principles rather than *hap*piness. John Beer refers to a note in which Coleridge quotes the sentence Ἡ εὐδαιμονία ἡδονή ἀμεταβλητός (*Aids*, p. 50 n. 8). Beer renders this in English as 'uninterrupted pleasure' but 'uninterrupted' is a correct but misleading translation. The root verb μεταβάλλω means 'I change' (hence the word 'metabolism' in English) and the *alpha privativum* ἀ points to the absence of change: ἀμεταβλητός really means 'immutable' – a characteristically *divine* attribute for the Greeks. This view of happiness as immutable pleasure is exactly the goal of ethics for Plotinus: it is 'θεὸν εἶναι' to 'to be god' and hence unchanging. Ethics must be based upon the 'spiritual state, in which the Humanity strives after Godliness and, in the name and power, and through the prevenient and assisting grace, of the Mediator, will not strive in vain' (*Aids*, p. 52).[5] The 'ought' of ethical obligation is derived from that which really 'is' – exists in the strong Platonic sense of exists, i.e. *unchanging form*. Paley is not a moralist because 'Scientia non est nisi de Universalibus et Eternis' (Science or knowledge is only about Universal and Timeless things) (*Aids*, p. 293) and Paley fails to contemplate Morality in its timeless aspect. Hence Coleridge – as a good Platonist – lays great emphasis upon the essential timelessness

---

[4] William Paley, *Principles of Moral and Political Philosophy* in *The Works*, 4 vols., edited by R. Lynam (London: Dove, 1827), vol. ii. pp. 35 ff.

[5] 'But this is always laudable, and worthy of the best minds, to be *imitators of that which is good*, wheresoever they find it; for that stays not in any man's person, as the ultimate pattern, but rises to the highest grace, being man's nearest likeness to God, His image and resemblance, bearing his stamp and superscription, and belonging peculiarly to Him, in what hand soever it be found, as carrying the mark of no other owner than Him.' *Aids*, p. 119, cf. pp. 40 and 98.

of ethics.[6] Coleridge, like Cudworth before him, wishes to defend an 'Eternal and Immutable Morality'.[7]

Coleridge believes, for reasons of meta-ethics, that ethics cannot subsist alone. Either it becomes subsumed into prudence or it becomes religion (*Aids*, p. 292). Coleridge employs the example of Sophron and Constantia: although prudence is not incompatible with morality, and is a necessary condition of the moral, it cannot be confused with it. Sophron knows that his marriage with Constantia will extend his wealth and influence yet this is not his motive in wanting to marry her (*Aids*, p. 53). The example of Sophron and Constantia should prepare the reader for Coleridge's dictum that the man makes the motive and not the motive the man (*Aids*, p. 74). Prudence is a necessary but not a sufficient condition of morality. Yet prudence is an aspect of the natural rather than the spiritual man. Its proper purpose is to prepare the mind for the reception of the higher light of conscience: the imprudent person will be hindered from accepting this light.

> We should distinguish between the *conditions* of our possessing good, and the goods themselves. Health, for instance, is ordinarily a condition of that working & rejoicing in and for God, which are *goods* in the end of, *themselves.*
>
> Health, Competent Fortune, & the like, are good, as negations of the preventives of Good, as *clear Glass* is good in relation to the Light, which it does not exclude. Health & Ease without the love of God are crown Glass in the Darkness. (*Marg.* ii. p. 325)

The passage is a discussion of remarks by John Donne on St Augustine, and the entire tenor of Coleridge's remarks on the difference between prudence and religious morality recall Augustine's distinction between *uti* and *frui*, between the considered and cautious use of the 'world' and the delight in God and the intelligible realm.[8]

Coleridge is appalled by the relation of religion to ethics in William Palcy's philosophy:

---

[6] 'Ethics, or the *Science* of Morality, does indeed in no wise exclude the consideration of *Action;* but it contemplates the same in its originating spiritual *Source*, without reference to Space or Time or Sensible Existence', *Aids*, p. 293.Cf. Plotinus, Treatise i. 2 (19) 6, 3.

[7] Ralph Cudworth, *A Treatise Concerning Eternal and Immutable Morality*, with *A Treatise of Free Will*, edited by Sarah Hutton (Cambridge University Press, 1996).

[8] cf. Markus, 'Marius Victorinus and Augustine', pp. 331–419, esp. p. 390.

Schemes of conduct, grounded on calculations of Self-interest; or on the average Consequences of Actions, supposing them *general*; form a branch of Political Economy, to which all due honor be given . . . But however estimable within their own sphere, such schemes or any one of them in particular, may be, they do not belong to Moral Science, to which both in kind and purpose, they are in all cases *foreign*, and when substituted for it, *hostile*. (*Aids*, p. 293)[9]

While considering and criticising Hume's attack upon the union between theology and ethics, Paley asserts that Hume cannot produce sufficient motives to avoid wickedness: further sanctions are necessary. Paley claims: 'But the necessity of these sanctions is not now the question. If they be *in fact established*, if the rewards and punishments in the gospel will actually come to pass, they *must* be considered.'[10] The emphasis upon the '*in fact established*' is Paley's positivism: Christianity is a 'divine religion, coming with full force and miraculous evidence upon the consciences of mankind'.[11] Coleridge is adamant that such a theological ethic is wholly inadequate:

where Religion is valued and patronized as a supplement of Law, or an Aid extraordinary of Police; where Moral SCIENCE is exploded as the mystic jargon of Dark Ages; where a lax System of Consequences, by which every iniquity on earth may be (and how many *have* been!) denounced and defended with equal plausibility . . . where the Mysteries of Religion and Truths supersensual, are either cut and squared for the comprehension of the Understanding . . . or desperately torn asunder from the Reason. (*Aids*, pp. 297–8)

When Coleridge speaks of moral science being exploded as the 'mystic jargon' of the dark ages, he is gesturing towards the mystical and Platonic roots of his own ethics, where the Christian revelation is not the supernatural *guarantee* of the advantages of a moral life, but the revelation of what genuine happiness is: the life of god-like-ness in the imitation of Christ. Hence his objection to theories of ethics where religion is a necessary appendage to utility, where 'Religion is . . . a supplement of Law, or an Aid extraordinary of Police' (*Aids*, p. 297).

One of the central aims of *Aids to Reflection* is the establishment of the difference between prudence, morality, and religion. Socinian thought and deism tended to assume the *rationality* of ethics. The reasonableness of Christianity, for the Socinians and the deists,

---

[9] cf. Paley, 'MORAL PHILOSOPHY, Morality, Ethics, Casuistry, Natural Law, mean all the same thing; namely, *that science which teaches men their duty and their reasons of it*', *Moral and Political Philosophy I: 1*, in *Works*, vol. ii. p. 15.
[10] Ibid., p. 52.   [11] Ibid., p. 151.

resides in its being *essentially* an ethical religion. In Paley's case this depended upon a utilitarian account of ethics. William Paley was a utilitarian moralist, and the onslaught upon utilitarianism is not so much an attack upon the political and legal utilitarianism of writers like Jeremy Bentham as the theological utilitarianism of Paley.

Paley starts from the conviction that God 'wills and wishes the happiness of his creatures'. And once this principle is established, we are at liberty to go on with the rule built upon it, namely, 'the method of coming at the will of God, concerning any action, by the light of nature, is to inquire into "the tendency of that action to promote or diminish the general happiness."'[12] According to this ethical theory, actions are to be estimated by their tendency: 'Whatever is expedient is right. It is the utility of any moral rule alone, which constitutes the obligation of it.'[13] Paley defines virtue as *'doing good to mankind, in obedience to the will of God, and for the sake of everlasting happiness'*.[14] God's will can be seen to be the happiness of his creation, the contrivances of nature reveal the benevolent disposition of the designer deity.

Moral obligation is grounded in what Paley calls a 'violent' motive, that constraint which can be obtained by the command of a senior, and where refusal would be too exacting.[15] The concept of obligation leads naturally to the sanction of heaven and hell. Paley in fact distinguishes between prudence and duty as the former considers gain or loss in this world, whereas the latter contemplates also profit or loss in the next world.[16] The appeal to utility is not an attempt to define philosophically the summum bonum, but simply to point out how we might ascertain God's will.

Coleridge's metaphysical view of the pursuit of genuine happiness as the basis of any ethics contrasts with Paley's pragmatic view of ethics as the perception of happiness as revealing the divine will. Paley openly eschews any subtle metaphysical discussion: ethics is *supported* by revealed religion: 'a divine religion, coming with full force and miraculous evidence upon the consciences of mankind'.[17] Religion provides special incentives for morality through the promise of eternal life which is proved by the miracles of Christ. 'A man who is in earnest in his endeavours after the happiness of a future state, has, in this respect, an advantage over all the world: for,

---

[12] Ibid., p. 52. [13] Ibid., p. 55. [14] Ibid., p. 38.
[15] Ibid., p. 47. [16] Ibid., pp. 49–50. [17] Ibid., p. 151.

he has constantly before his eyes an object of supreme importance.'[18] Paley's approach to Christian ethics is resolutely external and empirical. The Christian knows how to act by observing the words of Scripture, and by observing that which is ostensibly conducive to the general happiness. Coleridge is much more 'interior' in his approach to Scriptures. Ethical truths are derived by turning within, and the principles which this reflection obtains will be mirrored and illustrated by Scripture.

SENSIBILITY

Coleridge defines sensibility as 'a constitutional quickness of Sympathy with Pain and Pleasure, and a keen sense of the gratifications which accompany social intercourse, mutual endearments, and reciprocal preferences' (*Aids*, p. 57). It is further defined as for the greater part a 'quality of the nerves' (*Aids*, p. 58). Sensibility means the sensitivity of an intelligent organism with respect to its environment. Coleridge thinks that the idea of sensibility has been the source of philosophical errors far worse than those of Hobbes and the materialists. Far worse than the conviction that obligation collapses into compulsion, is the conviction that sensibility is the root of, or identical with, morality. The profanation of the word 'love' means the reduction of love to instinctive appetite; an idea which was greatly stimulated by the biological research of Carolus Linnaeus (1707–78) and Erasmus Darwin (1731–1802).

Coleridge describes the popularity of the concept of sensibility in the French Enlightenment and particularly amongst the 'sentimental novelists'. Rousseau's *sentiment intérieur* is the native feeling for the good which leads to virtue,[19] and the inspiration for a broader critique of the decadence of the French court and corrupting influence of civilisation generally. Rousseau's cultivation of sensibility, his critique of overweening and stifling civilisation (and even

---

[18] Ibid., p. 34.
[19] The term denotes primarily a litarary genre. E. Eräsmetsä, *A Study of the Word 'Sentimentalism' and other Linguistic Characteristics of Eighteenth-Century Sentimentalism in England* (Helsinki Press: 1951). It is the period of lavish diplays of melancholy in the young Werther and Chatterton. Our interest lies primarily in the philosophical importance of the concept. The English philosopher William Godwin (1756–1836) believed virtue to be a feeling of sympathy reduced to principle.

his penchant for a fur hat!) exerted enormous influence throughout Europe.[20]

In the exclamation: 'Can anything *manly* . . . proceed from those, who for Law and Light would substitute shapeless feelings, sentiments, impulses' (*Aids*, p. 63) Coleridge is objecting not just to the 'sentimental philosophy of Sterne', but to the tradition of moral thought evident from about 1740 onwards and particularly rooted in Lord Shaftesbury. The sentimentalists are writers who oppose both naturalism and intellectualism in ethics. A naturalist like Hume resolves moral ideas into non-moral natural concepts like *sympathy*, *habit*, or *self-interest*.[21] Coleridge is an intellectualist in that he sees ethical judgements as matters of *rational insight*. The sentimentalist rejects both the reductionist naturalism of the Humean and the intellectualism evident in Coleridge (and before him Ralph Cudworth or Henry More). The sentimentalist maintains that virtue is the fullest expression of the natural benevolence of man.[22] In the culture of sensibility, the topic of Platonic love flourished. Inspired by Shaftesbury, and Mendelssohn's *Phaedo*, writers such as F. H. Jacobi and Hemsterhuis presented a Platonism which was untrammelled by arcane theological problems, and a source of literary delight to quite a broad audience in the late eighteenth century. Yet this is not a strand of Platonism ('the Disciples of SHAFTESBURY' (*Aids*, p. 139)) to which Coleridge is drawn.

Coleridge does not argue against any sentimentalist: he is convinced that benevolent sentiment can no more furnish moral ideas than mere sympathy or selfishness. His reasons are Platonic. Plato presents man as composite: a child of the marriage of poverty and plenty; divided into the strictly physical organism which is orientated towards physical needs and desires, and a soul which longs for spiritual realities.[23]

These spiritual realities are *objective*, and Plato uses the term 'the good' to express the *force* which they exert upon the soul; he tries to describe the transforming character of the good upon those souls,

---

[20] Jean Staborinski, *Jean-Jacques Rousseau: la transparence et l'obstacle* (Paris: Editions Gallimard, 1971).

[21] It may seem paradoxical to deem the discoverer of the so-called 'naturalistic fallacy' an ethical naturalist, but it is fair to assume that Coleridge would have seen Hume in these terms.

[22] L. A. Selby-Bigge, *British Moralists* (New York: Dover, 1965), vol. i. p. xli.

[23] Plato, *Symposium*, 202a, translated by W. Hamilton (Harmondsworth: Penguin, 1988), pp. 79 ff.

and the capacity of the good to bestow something of its own reality upon those who reflect or bend back to it. One might consider the following passage:

The Greek word parakypas signifies the incurvation or bending of the body in the act of *looking down into*; as for instance, in the endeavour to see the reflected image of a star in the water at the bottom of a well. A more happy or more forcible word could not have been chosen to express the nature and ultimate object of reflection, and to enforce the necessity of it, in order to discover the living fountain and spring-head of the evidence of the Christian faith in the believer himself, and at the same time to point out the seat and region, where alone it is to be found, Quantum *sumus, scimus*. That which we find within ourselves, which is more than ourselves, and yet the ground of whatever is good and permanent therein, is the substance and life of all other knowledge. (*Aids*, p. 30)

Quantum sumus, scimus is a rather paradoxical-sounding tag for the idea expressed by Plotinus: 'different souls look at different things and are and become what they look at'[24] or Inge commenting on the passage: 'We are what we love and care about.'[25] The inherent sense of the incongruence of the mixture of finite and infinite in human nature – 'That which we find within ourselves, which is more than ourselves' – fires a longing for the good which Plato calls 'love'.[26] Secondly, the transformation of the self through the good is the goal of the ethical life. Hence the object of the soul's longing is *itself* at a deeper level; reborn in the good which is 'the ground of whatever is good and permanent therein, is the substance and life' of the soul. Coleridge presents in this manner the parameters of idealistic ethics up to T. H. Green's *Prolegomena to Ethics* and Bradley's *Ethical Studies*. Bernard Bosanquet articulates this tradition when he speaks of love as 'the supreme law or nature of experience, the impulse towards unity and coherence . . . by which every fragment yearns towards the whole to which it belongs'.[27] Coleridge is drawing on the Platonists and St Paul. Denys the Areopagite explicitly links the theme of the soul's longing for a transformation of itself into the image of the object of its love with St Paul's Christ mysticism:

This divine yearning brings ecstasy so that the lover belongs not to self but

[24] Plotinus, *Treatise* iv. 3 (27) 8, 15 ff.
[25] W. R. Inge, *Plotinus*, 2 vols. (London: Longmans, Green and Co., 1923), vol. ii. p. 25.
[26] Plato, *Symposium*, 201d ff.
[27] B. Bosanquet, *Principle of Individuality and Value* (London: Macmillan, 1912), pp. 340–1.

to the beloved . . . This is why the great Paul, swept along by his yearning for God and siezed of its ecstatic power, had this inspired word to say: 'It is no longer I who live, but Christ who lives in me.' Paul was truly a lover and, as he says, he was beside himself for God, possessing not his own life but the life of the One for whom he yearned, as exceptionally beloved.[28]

It is on the lines of this Platonic–Idealistic–Mystical concept of the division of self which characterises man's self-conscious rationality, and the correlated idea of ethics as a process of unification, that we should read Coleridge's moral philosophy. In *The Friend* Coleridge describes how 'men are ungrateful to others only when they have ceased to look back on their former selves with joy and tenderness. They exist in fragments . . . The whole energies of man must be exerted in order to [sic] noble energies; and he who is not earnestly sincere, lives in but half his being, self mutilated, self paralysed' (*F* i. 40–1). Sensibility has its source in '*parts* and *fragments* of our nature' (*Aids*, p. 60) and hence cannot provide the unifying force of the moral life. The path to unity and manly energy is that of purification as a process of freeing the soul in order to be able to become what it *actually* is:

The Bodings inspired by the long habit of selfishness, and self-seeking cunning, though they are now commencing the process of purification into that fear which is the *beginning* of wisdom, and which, as such, is ordained to be our guide and safeguard, till the sun of love, the perfect law of liberty is fully arisen. (*Aids*, p. 36)

Thus Coleridge is suggesting that the will is the abiding intentionality of the soul. The will is not a faculty within the mind or the isolated reflex of the body towards objects in its proximity, but a tending of the soul towards either its self-destruction through self-assertion, or self-realisation in the deeper selfhood *revealed* by conscience. Conscience as the free will 'with its Law within itself and its motive in the Law – and thus bound to originate its own Acts' (*Aids*, p. 98) is both the imitation of God and the 'Dawning of this inward Sun the perfect Law of Liberty' (*Aids*, p. 98), i.e. the revelation of the divine in man. Coleridge remarks:

In irrational Agents, viz. the Animals, the Will is hidden or absorbed in the Law. The Law is their *Nature*. In the original purity of a rational Agent the uncorrupted Will is identical with the Law. Nay, inasmuch as a Will perfectly identical with the Law is one with the *divine* Will, we may say, that in the

---

[28] Pseudo-Dionysius, *The Divine Names*, 712a in his *Complete Works*, p. 82.

unfallen rational Agent, the Will *constitutes* the law. But it is evident that the holy and spiritual Power and Light, which by a *prolepsis* or anticipation we have *named* Law, is a grace, an inward perfection, and without the commanding, binding and menacing character which belongs to a Law, acting as a Master or Sovereign distinct from, and existing, as it were, externally for, the Agent who is bound to obey it. Now this is St Paul's sense of the Word: and on this he grounds his whole reasoning. (*Aids*, pp. 300–1)

This, Coleridge asserted, is the Logos doctrine of St Paul, the creative principle of the cosmos is also the divine spirit which dwells in the renewed human soul.

THE TWO WORLDS

One of Coleridge's central aims is the repudiation of the 'animalizing tendency' of an Epicurean ethical naturalism: 'the insidious title of "Nature's noblest *Animal*"' (*Aids*, p. 135). The most obvious exponent of such a philosophy is Hume[29] who claims that reason alone cannot drive a man to act: 'first, that reason alone can never be the motive to any action of the will; and secondly, that it never can oppose passion in the direction of the will'.[30] Hume argues that reason cannot produce action because it always presupposes a propensity to a certain end and reason merely provides guidance towards this end. Propensities or aversions are the causes of all actions. The idea is that one does not act through reason because reason represents states of *facts* in the world which may be deemed true or false. Reason grasps a state of affairs and passion provides the motivational element. For example, the belief that cholesterol is harmful will not of itself explain the avoidance of animal fats. What is required is the *desire* to avoid harm. Here the will is seen as that component of the mind which provides the motor for action. Coleridge thinks that such a concept of the will which is essentially divorced from the rational component of the mind is inadequate. Goodness is compelling as reason, but the link between the two in 'practical pure reason' is not to be found in the external realm but in the domain of the inner and the 'otherworldly'. Pure reason is not empirical or instrumental; it is not a question of prudential 'know-how', of how to get by in the world when confronted by particular

[29] On Coleridge's relationship to Hume cf. A. Taylor, *Coleridge's Defense of the Human* (Columbus: Ohio University Press, 1986), pp. 40 ff.

[30] Hume, *Treatise of Human Nature*, second edition, edited by P. H. Niddich and L. A. Selby-Bigge (Oxford: Clarendon, 1978), bk. ii. pt. iii. sect. iii.

problems, but is an attitude to the world which transcends the physical cosmos: 'Two things fill the mind with ever new and increasing admiration and awe, the more often resolutely we reflect upon them: the starry sky above me and the moral law within me'.[31] The ultimate source of this passage seems to be Plato's *Laws*, where it is said that it is impossible to become steadfastly godfearing without grasping the two principles of the immortality of the soul and the beauty of cosmic world order.[32]

Coleridge, in effect, is deeply attracted to the 'two world' doctrine in Kant. The link is in the metaphysic of morals – in which Kant, like Plato, envisages the essence of morality to be otherworldly; and in a sense expressive of a religious perspective. In the first chapter of the seminal *Moral Law* Kant asserts that 'It is impossible to conceive anything at all in the world, or even out of it which can be taken as good without qualification, except a *good will*.' It is not entirely clear what Kant means by the 'good will', but for Coleridge Kant's meaning resides in the conviction that a good will is not good because of its utility but as the organ of a spiritual being: one who belongs to both the interior realm and to the exterior world. R. F. Holland observes:

To know, in so far as you can know it, that your will is good is not to know that this in particular is to be done or that in particular avoided: to search in the outer word, which is the wrong direction. Instead you are required to look inward; to know yourself, to ensure that your motive is not one of inclination, i.e. that you are not doing whatever you do for the sake of something to be got out of it, but rather for its own sake.[33]

Holland draws an illuminating analogy between Kant's insistence in the *Moral Law* that the 'good will' is the only unconditioned good and Socrates' claim in the *Gorgias* (469b) that inflicting harm is worse than being harmed.[34] Both Plato and Kant assert in effect that 'goodness' cannot be measured in terms of external or measurable utilities. It is rather a state of the soul.

Kant's view that only the 'good will' deserves the status of the supreme good is linked to the thesis that virtue is not a craft which

---

[31] I. Kant, *Kritique der praktischen Vernunft*, 288, in his *Werke*, 12 vols. (Berlin: de Gruyter, 1968), vol. v. p. 161.

[32] Plato, *Laws*, 967d. cf. L. Spitzer, *Classical and Christian Ideas of World Harmony* (Baltimore: Johns Hopkins University Press, 1963), p. 223.

[33] R. F. Holland, *Against Empiricism, on Education, Epistemology and Value* (Oxford: Clarendon, 1980), p. 82.

[34] Holland, *Against Empiricism*, p. 89.

can be learnt and acquired through practice and custom, but resides in acting upon *principles* derived from duty. These principles, or 'maxims' cannot be reduced to pragmatic considerations or utilities.

The real target of Kant's strictures against mere inclination is philosophical naturalism. In this sense Schiller's celebrated objection °I serve my friends with delight – oh but unfortunately with inclination' (*Gerne diene ich den Freunden, doch tue ich es leider mit Neigung*) misses the point. It is not the person who helps those dear to him who lacks proper ethical motivation, rather it is the person who *only* helps his friends.[35] The autonomous agent is just and fair even where friendship, inclination, and society exert no pressures. Onora O'Neill says of Kant's conception:

Autonomy is not a special achievement of the most independent, but a property of any reasoning being. The capacity for autonomy goes with the capacity to act on principles even when inclination is absent, with being able to adopt maxims of actions that do not sit well with our desires.[36]

This anti-naturalistic thrust in Kant's argument in the *Moral Law* and his other writings is equally powerful against utilitarianism, which is, if anything, even more naturalistic than Aristotelian ethics.

Certainly, Kant's 'paean to the good will' (Henry Allison) is a pietist legacy, a tradition which was critical of the scholastic legacy in Protestant orthodoxy and much institutional Lutheranism and which laid enormous emphasis upon the interior aspect of the Christian religion and especially the will and good action (*praxis pietatis*); there is a sense in which it pursues and develops the anti-intellectualism in the (largely) Franciscan-mystical medieval tradition with its dislike of scholasticism, its stress upon the will rather than the intellect. Combined with the democratic influence of Rousseau and the French Revolution, we can see a marked emphasis upon the interior as opposed to the insistence upon community and perform-ance in Aristotelian ethics. The ramifications for Kant's metaphysics, morever, are enormous.[37] As he emphasises in the preface to the second edition of the *Critique of Pure Reason* he has 'found it necessary to deny *knowledge*, in order to make way for *faith*'[38] and this coheres

---

[35] cf. H. J. Paton, *The Categorical Imperative: a Study in Kant's Moral Philosophy*, third edition (London: Hutchinson, 1958), pp. 48 ff.

[36] Onora O'Neill, *Constructions of Reason: Explorations of Kant's Practical Philosophy*, (Cambridge University Press, 1989), p. 76.

[37] Roger J. Sullivan, *Immanuel Kant's Moral Theory* (Cambridge University Press, 1989), pp. 95 ff.

[38] Kant, *Critique of Pure Reason*, p. 29. cf. Coleridge, *CM* iii. 956.

with the notion of supremacy of the good will. Kant is arguing for the priority of practical over theoretical reason. Whereas the theoretical intellect has access only to the transcendentally ideal realm, practical reason has access to the intelligible, objective, underlying reality: the intelligible world contains the ground of the sensible world and therefore also of its laws. 'Hence, in spite of regarding myself from one point of view as a being that belongs to the sensible world, I shall have to recognise that, *qua* intelligence, I am subject to the law of the intelligible world.'[39] Such is the 'pale, northerly, Königsbergian' Platonism[40] which Nietszche rebukes and mocks.

Significantly, the first philosophical use of the word 'autonomy' in English is that of Coleridge in the *Biographia Literaria* of 1817.[41] His favourite, the medieval Christian Platonist, John Scot Eriugena (circa 800–77), interprets St Paul, 1 Cor. 2: 15. 'The spiritual man judges all things, but is himself to be judged by no one', in a way which exults in man's rational nature; much like those Renaissance humanists Marsilio Ficino and Pico della Mirandola.[42] Kant's concept of autonomy is quite the descendant of the Christian-Platonic conviction in the indwelling logos: that the dignity of man lies in the capacity for being the subject of rational self-determination and not merely the object of external compulsion. Stephen Darwall has convincingly argued that Cudworth is an important precursor of Kant's doctrine of autonomy.[43] And just as Cudworth was defending freedom against Hobbes, so too Kant was defending freedom against the naturalism and determinism of the French Enlightenment.

Although Kant's insistence upon the priority of practical reason is an attack upon the Platonic-Aristotelian privilege of contemplation, his concentration upon the will and the interior dimension of the ethical has much in common with Platonism; albeit derived from

---

[39] I. Kant, *The Moral Law,* translated by H. Paton (London: Hutchinson, 1981), p. 114.
[40] F. Nietschze, *The Twilight of the Idols,* translated by R. J. Hollingdale (Harmondsworth: Penguin, 1968), p. 40.
[41] *The Compact Edition of the Oxford English Dictionary* (Oxford: Clarendon, 1985), vol. i. p. 575. Quoted by S. Darwall, *The British Moralists and the Internal 'Ought' 1640–1740* (Cambridge University Press, 1995), p. 110.
[42] 'Spirtualis homo judicat omnia, ipse vero a nemine dijudicatur.' *De Divisione Naturae,* edited by Migne, in *Patrologiae Cursus Completus* (Paris: Migne, 1853), vol. cxxii. pp. 753 a–b. I owe this reference to Dermot Moran's book *The philosophy of John Scottus Eriugena* (Cambridge University Press, 1989), p. 164. cf. D. Mahnke, 'Die Rationalisierung der Mystik bei Leibniz und Kant', *Blätter für Deutsche Philosophie* 13 (1939), pp. 1–73, esp. pp. 67–9.
[43] Darwall, *The British Moralists,* pp. 109–48.

pietism rather than from Plato or the Platonists. In particular, the 'good will' comes very close to a Platonic view of ethics where the will is not so much unimpeded activity as concentrated attention. Freedom, for both Kant and Plotinus, is ultimately the attainment of a state of rational being. Plotinus sees the goal of ethics neither as the *fulfilment of moral obligation* nor as the *avoidance of wrong-doing* but as the *achievement of a state of the soul*:[44] the person who acts out of a motive of lust or drunkenness exercises freedom in a trivial sense. Real freedom for Plotinus is purely rational determination and this occurs in accordance with one's proximity to the good which is free from all thraldom.

Coleridge's concept of freedom is Plotinian in the sense that it is a purely spiritual freedom: the highest freedom is absolute self-determination, i.e. absolute will. This means that human or finite freedom is necessarily impure: 'Woe to the man, who will believe neither power, freedom, nor morality; because he nowhere finds either entire, or unmixed with sin, thraldom and infirmity' (*Aids*, p. 32). Yet if freedom entails following the good one might ask whether this is a form of determination? Plotinus makes the point that alien determination only makes sense where one finds actuality and potentiality: where it is possible to distinguish between what one is and what one can do. Since the highest ontological level is constituted by pure actuality, the question is quite false.[45]

The ethical task, according to Plotinus, is essentially that of raising oneself to the level of the νοῦς (and somewhat more mysteriously to the level of the One). The will has more the quality of steadfastness than isolated resolve; Coleridge uses his model of the magnetic needle which continues to waver after a disturbing influence has been removed: the will is the fundamental orientation and the motives are without (*Aids*, p. 35). Whenever by subjection to the universal light, the individual will becomes a will of reason: this regeneration is a product and token of the contemplation of the νοῦς (cf. *Aids*, p. 217). Motives are symptoms of weakness, and 'supplements for the deficient Energy of the living PRINCIPLE, the LAW within us' (*Aids*, p. 97); morality is not a matter, for Plotinus or Coleridge, of moral behaviour but of vision: 'The more consciousness in our Thoughts and Words, and the less in our Impulses and

---

[44] This idea is reflected in the scholastic tag 'operari sequitur esse'.
[45] See John M. Rist, 'Plotinus and moral obligation' in *The Significance of Neoplatonism* (Norfolk, Va.: Old Dominion University Press, 1976), pp. 217–33.

general Actions, the better and more healthful the state of both head and heart' (*Aids*, p. 96). The image of the blindfold Cupid is used to express poetically the Plotinian idea of ethical obligation as the spontaneous by-product of a spiritual or contemplative state. This image seems *prima vista* opposed to the images of vision and contemplation which dominate Coleridge's ethics, but the idea is quite in keeping with the rest of Coleridge's thinking in its opposition to the concept of moral calculus: as Bradley, later observed, whosoever ' "deliberates" may be "lost" '.[46]

The model can perhaps be understood on the analogy of a skill such as playing a musical instrument. Unlike the beginner who has to think through and deliberate over particular hand movements, the particular resolve to act seems lacking in the expert – the playing of the instrument just seems to flow. This would seem to be the point of the Platonic geometer analogy. In the case of real knowledge we find a reduction of conscious deliberation.[47] If, perhaps because of nervousness, however, even the expert musician thinks about her tone or rhythm, she may spoil it; an example which can be reinforced by the colloquial English usage of 'being self-conscious' meaning to be ill at ease. Similarly with happiness: if *consciously* sought, happiness is notoriously elusive; it is usually found during concentration upon something else.

The thesis that the 'Man makes the motive, and not the motive the Man' (cf. *Aids*, p. 74) is linked to a *metaphysical* discussion of ascending *unity* in the natural realm:[48] Coleridge points to the evolution in nature from protozoa or polypi which 'are all from without' to human beings where 'the material and animal means are prepared for the manifestation of a free will, having its law *within itself* and its motive in the law – and thus bound to originate its own acts, not only without, but even against, outward stimulants. Coleridge states that motives are 'symptoms' of *weakness*: the most primitive animals do not possess brains or nerves; the driving powers are sun, light, etc. (*Aids*, p. 97). Higher forms of life have nerves which transmit an external influence. At the next level creatures

---

[46] F. H. Bradley, *Ethical Studies* second edition (Oxford: Clarendon, 1927), p. 195.

[47] This analogy should not be confused with the reductionist thesis that understanding is really just 'knowing how' in G. Ryle's *The Concept of Mind* (Harmondsworth: Penguin, 1980), pp. 26–60.

[48] Coleridge: 'a power that acts upon appetites and passions cannot be called a spiritual power'. *CCS*, p. 124.

possess centres of agency but not a centre as such. It is only with man that the reservoir of sensibility and the imitative power which informs the muscles are taken inward and appropriated. Thus the spontaneous rises to the voluntary and provides the possibility of the will; Coleridge is presenting a picture of reality as an ascending hierarchy of interiority: the human will has it own law; that of conscience, *within* itself. Free will is that which 'originates its own acts': it is a mirroring of the divine. Thus creation is an ascending reflection of God as *causa sui* (cf. *CCS*, p . 182); this means that the 'Thy will be done' of the Lord's Prayer does not simply express the resignation of an essential, servile spirit, but rather the willingness to bring one's self-will into harmony with the divine will.

Here Coleridge is arguing like the mystics, especially Meister Eckhart.[49] But the idea is rooted in Plotinus who thinks that really *free* action does not depend upon motives consisting of appetites or pressures resulting from external factors but – as he puts it – τοῦ ἀγαθοῦ χάριν, 'for the sake of the Good'.[50] The more virtuous the soul, for Plotinus, the less it is aware of any sense of obligation: once a man has attained the life of the νοῦς he has no consciousness of moral obligation: the man living the good life is one whose acts are dictated by the νοῦς. Living ethically does not mean the avoidance of imprudence and wickedness but the positive imitation of the divine.[51] The obligation of the moral life is conformity to reason. This is exactly what Coleridge means when he writes that motives are symptoms of weakness and the lack of the living principle, that is, the divine Logos. The really moral, that is, godlike life has no *external* but only an *internal* determination.

In his *Gorgias* 508a Plato criticises those Sophists who fail to see the absolute and independent power of ethical claims as lacking geometrical insight. This is an image of the unconditional independent power and beauty of ethical norms: the laws of geometry exert a power over the student of mathematics quite independent of his or her desires or inclinations.

---

[49] cf. Rolf Schönberger, 'Secundum rationem esse. zur Ontologisierung der Ethik bei Meister Eckhart' in ΟΙΚΕΙΩΣΙΣ *Festschrift für Robert Spaemann*, edited by R. Löw (Weinheim: Acta Humaniora, 1987), pp. 252–72, in particular 'Signum der Subjektivität scheint für Eckhart der Wille zu sein', p. 265.

[50] Plotinus, *Treatise* vi. 8 (38) 4, 37.

[51] Plato, *Theaetetus*, 176a/b where Plato speaks of escaping and becoming godlike is a central text for Plotinus' ethics. cf. Coleridge, *Aids*, p. 274 on the connection between righteousness and godliness.

Now the Spirit in Man (that is, the Will) knows it own State in and by its Acts alone: even as in geometrical reasoning the Mind knows its constructive *faculty* in the act of constructing, and contemplates the act in the *product* (*i.e.* the mental figure or diagram) which is inseparable from the act and co-instantaneous. (*Aids*, p. 94)

This image of the unconditional binding nature of goodness as akin to geometrical laws is of course linked to the image of the sun as the absolute transcendent source of ethical demands: we can turn towards the light, but we are not its source, notwithstanding the arguments of the Sophists that morality is the creation of human conventions. The good is the origin of obligation: we can only intuit ethical demands – as geometers intuit geometrical truths.

Plotinus is fond of the image of the work of the geometer as copying intelligible models of purely mental geometrical figures just as a painter can be seen as producing a visible form of a mental construction.[52] In the *Biographia Literaria* Coleridge writes: 'The words of Plotinus in the assumed person of nature, hold true of the philosophic energy' (*BL* i. 251). Immediately after quoting Plotinus and discussing the contemplative production of the geometrician Coleridge writes that 'the postulate of philosophy' and the test of philosophical ability is the 'heaven-descended KNOW THYSELF! . . . And this at once practically and speculatively' (*BL* i. 252). This Delphic imperative, the 'noblest of Sciences, the Scire teipsum' (*Aids*, p. 178) is the very centre of *Aids to Reflection* (cf. the Preface).[53] The determining idea is that specific ethical choices resolve at bottom into questions concerning the kind of *self* which the moral agent wishes to become, and the nature of this self is constituted by a conformity to either the divine or the sensual realms.

'KNOW THYSELF!'

It is the chiefest of Good Things, for a Man to be *Himself*. (Whichcote)[54]

---

[52] Plotinus, *Treatise* iii. 8 (30) 4, 1ff. cf. Plato, *Republic*, 510c-513. There is an interest in geometry as a model of contemplation in the Platonic-Pythagorean tradition, e.g. Nicholas of Cusa, *On Learned Ignorance*, edited by Jasper Hopkins (Minneapolis: Arthur Banning, 1981), pp. 61 ff.

[53] E. G. Wilkins, *The Delphic Maxims in Literature* (University of Chicago Press, 1929); Hermann Tränkle, 'ΓΝΩΘΙ ΣΕΑΥΤΟΝ: zu Ursprung und Deutungsgeschichte des delphischen Spruchs', *Würzburger Jahrbücher für die Altertumswissenschaft Neue Folge* 2 (1985), pp. 19–31. See further the bibliography listed in Beierwaltes, *Selbsterkenntnis und Erfahrung*, p. 262, and the discussion on pp. 77–93.

[54] *Moral and Religious Aphorisms* (London: Mathews and Marrot, 1930), no. 416.

... we may seek within us, what we ever can find elsewhere, that we may find within us what no words can put there, that one true religion, which elevateth Knowing into Being, which is at once the Science of Being, the Being and the Life of all genuine Science. (*LS*, p. 93)

Coleridge speaks of the value of prudence as encouraging a frame of mind which 'might prepare one for the sense and acknowledgement of a principle differing, not merely in degree but in kind, from the faculties and instincts of the higher and more intelligent species of animals . . . and which principle is therefore your proper humanity'. The aim of ethics, for Coleridge, is the awakening of a genuine *self-love* which is the 'groundwork and pre-condition of the spiritual state, in which humanity strives after godliness, and in the name and power, and through the prevenient and assisting grace, of the Mediator will not strive in vain'. Coleridge wishes to show that the philosophic apostle was right to speak of the 'Spirit which beareth witness with our spirit': the dictates of the divine spirit are not juridical or external pressures, but the principle of our personality: not heteronomy but autonomy (cf. *Aids*, p. 77).

Paley's attempt to construct both ethics and religion on the basis of self-love, leads logically to a philosophy quite as egoistic as Hobbes and as hedonistic as Epicurus. Paley's philosophy is overtly 'otherworldly' but unspiritual. Consequently it collapses into the very worldliness of those philosophies which Paley opposed. It is Kant's achievement to have shown that self-love cannot be a substitute for the recognition of the moral law: as subjects of moral action we cannot put aside our social and sensual natures. Morality, as opposed to prudence, is imperative-categorical because human nature struggles to follows its dictates. This difficulty, however, does not diminish the important fact that physical needs and inclination, the forces of environment, custom, and habit do not *determine* human life. The capacity for autonomy means that ethics is *more* than a craft and man is *more* than nature: Kant's provocative claim is that man can only follow the exhortation to 'Know Thyself!' in the reverence and fulfilment of that 'more' – 'he can look upon himself only with the greatest wonder . . . And if he takes it to heart, the very incomprehensibility of this self-knowledge must produce an exaltation in his soul which only inspires it the more to keep its duty holy, the more it is assailed.'[55] Coleridge speaks of prudence as an '*active*

---

[55] Sullivan, *Kant's Moral Theory*, p. 94.

Principle and implies a sacrifice of Self, though only to the same Self *projected*, as it were, to a distance' (*Aids*, p. 58). What does Coleridge mean by 'only' the same self projected at a distance? In a footnote concerning the 'individual's inherent desire of happiness' Coleridge notes: 'this depends on the exact meaning attached to the term *self*, of which more in another place' (*Aids*, p. 37). John Beer notes that Coleridge is presumably hinting at a longer discussion in the *Opus Maximum* and that the account of Paley can be read intelligibly in conjunction with Coleridge's remarks about the character Iago in Shakespeare's *Othello* in the *Opus Maximum*.[56] *Othello* is an instance of the 'dreadful habit of thinking moral feelings and qualities only as prudential means to ends.' Worse, the theological utilitarian aims at the wrong self.

Coleridge's most interesting attack upon morality conceived as prudence rests upon his concept of the *self*. Self-consciousness is, philosophically at least, a puzzling sort of knowledge. Self conscious-ness seems to be consciousness of a curious object. Is consciousness a bipolar awareness whereby I recognise myself as such? But this *presupposes* what is supposed to be discovered: if self-knowledge is effected by *reflecting* or *turning* upon oneself the act of turning presupposes an existent self. The constitution of the self on this model presupposes the very 'I' which should be constituted. Further there is an obvious asymmetry between knowledge of first-person states and justified belief. How can we speak of knowledge of oneself when there is no possibility of mistake?

The self cannot be intuited as an immaterial substance or bundle but has to be assumed as the *prior unity* of experience. Yet this minimal requirement does not reveal much of selfhood. We do not know ourselves through introspection and then know other minds by analogy. On the contrary human individuality requires social intercourse for its development.The relationship to others deter-mines our gradual and difficult acquisition of knowledge of our-selves.

Coleridge writes that the voluptuary seeks his self in 'that which is

---

[56] I suspect 'another place' might refer to the passage concerning conscience and consciousness within *Aids*. The discussion of Iago in the *Opus Maximum* elucidates a point made in *Aids*. I am much indebted to the excellent discussion by Graham Davidson in *Coleridge's Career* (Basingstoke: Macmillan, 1990), pp. 117–79 and the article by Elinor S. Shaffer, 'Iago's malignity motivated: Coleridge's unpublished "opus magnum"' in *Shakespeare Quarterly* 19 (1968), pp. 195–203.

only the common soil of his animal Life, i.e. in his Nature . . . And having given this false meaning to the *Self*, he offends by *seeking* it, when he should [be] seeking and finding a nobler Self in the love and service of his neighbor.'[57] In another passage Coleridge compares the self-love of the voluptuary to a hungry animal moving towards its food trough: 'we ought to say that the food in the trough is the temporary self of the hog'. The phenomenal self wallows in a pointless self-assertion which is both fragmentary and futile. The character Iago is an instance of this. His malignity is subject to outside pressures and his barren self-love has transformed him into a husk of a man. This is the self which is driven by the competitive impulse of personal aggrandisement and advantage. Coleridge wishes to contrast this primary inclination with the impulse which actually enlarges and forms the self; that of liberating oneself from the self in ethics or science. Justice or charity means trying to consider a state of affairs from another person's perspective. Knowledge means criticising opinion – how things seem to be to me – on the basis of what really is the case; whether through experiment, consultation, or debate. C. S. Lewis observes: 'Obviously this process can be described either as an enlargement or as a temporary annihilation of the self. But that is an old paradox; "he that loseth his life shall save it." '[58]

The Cartesian 'I' is a chimera which all idealists reject adamantly. Hegel's *Beisichselbstsein in einem Andern*', 'being with onself in another', expresses the idea that spiritual identity is in fact a mediated identity and not an object of immediate awareness, and this is the point of the justly celebrated master–slave dialectic.[59] This is the resolution of the duality of the actual self and ideal self (the 'Maxims of Interest' and 'Laws of Duty' (*Aids*, p. 52)). The great symbol of this mediation between the actual and the ideal, the lower and the higher self, is the cross and resurrection of Christ. The eminent Victorian idealist T. H. Green writes:

A death unto life, a life out of death, must, then, be in some way the essence of the divine nature – must be an act which, though exhibited once for all in the crucifixion and resurrection of Christ, was yet eternal – the act

---

[57] Coleridge, *MS*, N. 42. f. fos. 27v, 28. Quoted from Davidson, *Coleridge's Career*, p. 156.
[58] Lewis, *Experiment in Criticism*, p. 138.
[59] Hegel, *Phenomenology of Spirit*, § 178–96, pp. 111–19. A. Wood, *Hegel's Ethical Thought* (Cambridge University Press, 1990), p. 45.

of God himself. For that very reason, however, it was one perpetually re-enacted and to be re-enacted by man.[60]

In this way Paul's images of 'dying to live', crucifying the old man, rebirth 'in' Christ, the Church as a 'body' or a building of living stones, are the expression of the spiritual truth that being distinct individuals is a necessary but not sufficient condition of the mediate identity of genuine selfhood; and it is hardly fortuitous that idealist philosophers such as Hegel, T. H. Green, and Josiah Royce saw Paul, as Coleridge says, as 'the philosophic apostle' (*Aids*, p. 146). In an annotation on a copy of *Aids*, Coleridge describes a passage on the Pauline argument that the 'Spirit aids our infirmities', that is, by 'uniting and becoming one with our will and spirit' (*Aids*, p. 78) as the 'Vestibule to all the Reasoning in this Volume' (*Aids*, p. 74n. 4).

How should we understand this argument about spiritual identity 'even at the porch and threshold of Revealed Truth' (*Aids*, p. 78)? Self-knowledge, for Coleridge, is self-vision in the sense that the rational part of the soul *mirrors* the divine. In *Alcibiades* the command 'Know Thyself!' is interpreted as ἰδὲ σαυτόν, 'Behold Thyself!':[61] just as an eye in order to see itself needs to look into another eye and its best part the pupil and similarly a soul knows itself by looking into the best part of another soul: the divine part of the soul. The oddity of this 'Platonic' language is perhaps mitigated if one observes that the concept of 'deity' is much more fluid in the Hellenistic milieu and there is no clear concept of the person in Greek. The model of the mirror presents a fine paradigm of the apparent paradox of self which is constituted by wider correspondences, not by its particularity. This is only a paradox to theories of the self as inherently impervious or atomic. Coleridge holds that the self as a relatively isolated item is a rather poor and abstract phenomenon. The real self is permeated by the existence of other selves. And however paradoxical, the true or good self is in communion with the Divine. T. H. Green remarks:

Our formula then is that God is identical with the self of every man in the sense of being the realisation of its determinate possibilities . . . that in being conscious of himself man is conscious of God, and thus knows that God is, but knows what he is only in so far as he knows what he himself really is.[62]

---

[60] T. H. Green, *Collected Works*, edited by R. L. Nettleship, 3 vols. (London: Longman and Co., 1885–8), vol. iii. p. 233.

[61] Plato, *Alcibiades*, 132d6.

[62] Green, *Collected Works*, vol. iii. p. 227.

This idea explains why Coleridge attacks 'this AGE OF PERSON-ALITY, this age of literary *Gossiping*' (*F* i. 210); the contemporary age of sentimentality and biography irritates Coleridge because it concentrates upon the wrong self – the lower self which should be sacrificed for the realisation of the higher self.[63] T. H. Green's pupil John Muirhead expresses Coleridge's idea of personality with unusual pertinacity:

> In reality personality becomes more perfect in proportion as a man rises above the negations and privations by which the finite is differentiated from the Absolute, the human will from the divine, man from God . . . [it is] a circumference continually expanding through sympathy and understanding, rather than . . . an exclusive centre of self-feeling.[64]

Personality is a much broader notion than individuality, and requires a domain of recognition and mutual exchange: it is only this sense of personality which is compatible with the Christian doctrine of God as a unity of mutually reciprocating 'persons'.

The crudity of the empiricist concept of reflection as simple introspection is, as we have seen, rejected: there is no self which is transparent in self-reflection in inward scrutiny but only an inchoate self. Paley defines man, in terms strongly redolent of Hume, as 'a bundle of habits'.[65] Yet Coleridge would insist that the disparate drives, impulses, and habits which form the raw materials of a person's character must be subjected to the unifying will. There is no Cartesian luminosity in introspection: personal identity is that which is induced or drawn forth from the awareness of justice which is dormant within consciousness. Thus circularity is avoided because genuine self-knowledge does not presume that which it is supposed to discover:

> How do you define the *human mind?* the answer must at least *contain*, if not consist of, the words, 'a mind capable of *Conscience*' . . . For Conscience properly human (i.e. *Self*-consciousness), with the sense of moral responsibility, presupposes the Conscience, as its antecedent Condition and Ground. (*Aids*, p. 125)

---

[63] On the topic of 'person' in Coleridge there is much excellent secondary literature. cf. A. J Harding, *Coleridge and the Idea of Love* (Cambridge University Press, 1974), Taylor, *Coleridge's Defense of the Human*, and Davidson, *Coleridge's Career*.

[64] Muirhead, *Coleridge as Philosopher*, pp. 228–9.

[65] Paley, *Principles* in *Works*, vol. ii. p. 41. Neil Hitchin has noted the striking affinity between Hume and Paley; despite much disgreement, Paley obviously read Hume with care and interest, and shares much of the sceptical and pragmatic conservatism of Hume: N. Hitchin, 'Probability and the Word of God', p. 403.

Coleridge, in a note on this 'aphorism on the equivocal meaning of the term Consciousness' gives the following explanation: 'the identity or co-inherence of Morality and Religion, as the Transcendent containing both *in* one and *as* one' (*Aids*, p. 125 n. 5). In the same passage Coleridge goes on to say that this is the true meaning of *election*. The meaning of these rather cryptic suggestions becomes clear in the light of the exploration of the Delphic Oracle. Election, Coleridge avers, does not mean an eternal divine decree damning the many and choosing the elect, but the realisation of the indwelling Christ within man's conscious being and his constituting man's *real* identity. The 'birth into a new and spiritual life' (*Aids*, p. 204), which Coleridge sees as the centre of ethics and religion, is – as the mystics put the matter paradoxically – the birth of Christ in the soul.

The language which he uses in order to describe the religious significance of morality is Christological. Man can make himself into a better or worse mirror of Christ: the creative Word which is the measure and foundation of mankind's attempts to attain truth.[66] In a very early notebook entry (*Notebooks* i. 2167) Coleridge notes the Cambridge Platonist John Smith writing of the 'infant-Christ' formed in the human soul. The passage reads:

The true Metaphysical and Contemplative man . . . endeavours the nearest union with the Divine Essence that may be, κέντρον κέντρῳ συνάψας, as *Plotinus* speaks; knitting his owne centre, if he have any, unto the centre of the Divine Being . . . This life is nothing else but God's own breath within him, and an *Infant-Christ* (if I may use the expression) formed in his Soul, who is in a sense . . . *the shining forth of the Father's glory.*[67]

The passage finishes with the note εις εαυτον επιστεφων εις αρχην επιστρεφει. Reflecting into oneself is to bend back to the 'Living PRINCIPLE' (ἀρχή or *principium* cf. John's Prologue) – again a Plotinus quote from John Smith. The topic is knowledge of God, 'not so much'

That he is as *What he is.* Both which we may best learn from a Reflexion upon our own Souls, as *Plotinus* hath well taught us, ἐις ἑαυτὸν ἐπιστρέφων,εις αρχην ἐπιστρέφει *He which reflects upon himself, reflects upon his own Originall*, and finds the clearest impression of some Eternal Nature and Perfect Being stamp'd upon his own soul.[68]

---

[66] Karsten Harries, 'The infinite sphere: comments on the history of a metaphor' in *Journal of the History of Philosophy* 13 (1975), pp. 5–15.

[67] Smith, *Discourses*, pp. 20–1.

[68] Ibid., p. 123.

St Paul, the philosophic apostle, in Colossians 1: 15 refers to Christ as 'the image of the invisible God'. Only in the Son who is identical with the Father, only in seeing him, can mankind come to see its own identity, what Paul calls 'this mystery, which is Christ in you' Colossians (1: 27). The idea is that any given human being is not an impermeable atom but a member of a wider body: in exactly St Paul's sense of the word. The real self should not be confused with the immediate ego of conscious experience.

Coleridge's pupil F. D. Maurice, in a letter to his mother, relates this idea of Christ's indwelling to Acts 17: 28 'in him we live and move and have our being' and Paul's cosmic Christology: Christ is the Head of *every* man.[69] Maurice writes: 'What, then, do I assert? Is there no difference between the believer and the unbeliever? Yes, the greatest difference. But the difference is not about the fact, but precisely in the belief of the *fact*.' Those who disbelieve it, Maurice argues, walk after 'the flesh'. Indeed, 'we are forbidden by Christian truth and the Catholic Church to call this the real *state* of any man. On the contrary, the phrases which Christ and His Apostles use to describe such a condition are such as these: "They believe a *lie*. They make a *lie*. They will not believe the *truth*." The truth is that every man is in Christ; the condemnation of every man is, that he will not own the truth.' Here Maurice is drawing upon St Paul's distinction between living by the standard of men and the standard of God which Augustine employs in the *City of God* xiv 4 as the basic distinction between the two cities:

So when man lives by the standard of truth he lives not by his own standard, but by God's. For it is God who has said, 'I am the truth.' By contrast, when he lives by his own standard, that is by man's and not by God's standard, then inevitably he lives by the standard of falsehood.[70]

This, Coleridge insists, is the mystery of the indwelling Christ, and the fulfilment of the Delphic Oracle. 'Know Thyself!' means to know that truth which illuminates all men whether they are conscious of it or not. This truth will only make them free if they acknowledge and recognise it (*Aids*, p. 160). Coleridge writes:

By the phrase 'in Christ,' I mean all the supernatural Aids vouchsafed and conditionally promised in the Christian Dispensation: and among them the

[69] *The Life of Frederick Denison Maurice*, edited by Frederick Maurice (London, Macmillan, 1884), vol. i. pp. 154–7.
[70] Augustine, *City of God*, p. 552.

Spirit of Truth which the world cannot receive, were it only that the knowledge of *spiritual* Truth is of necessity immediate and *intuitive:* and the World or Natural Man possesses no higher intuitions than those of pure *Sense*, which are the subjects of *Mathematical* Science. (*Aids*, pp. 157–8)

The reference to life 'in Christ' is the culmination of a complex metaphysical consideration of the nature of selfhood: a Platonic and idealistic interpretation of the Pauline and Johannine writings.

Coleridge insists that consciousness is rooted in conscience. Coleridge did not believe that conscience is the product of repressed consciousness (although he thought about these issues long before Freud[71]), nor did he think of conscience as a faculty of the soul. Coleridge thinks of conscience rather, as the modern Platonist philosopher Stephen R. L. Clark has argued, as the voice of a spirit which is our real self and yet deeper than the intuitively obvious sense of self.[72] Clark quotes the distinguished Dutch Plato scholar Cornelia de Vogel:

It would be too easy just to say that for Plato, a divine spirit given to man by God was indwelling in man too, and that man's proper life-task was honouring and cultivating that divine spirit that dwells within himself. Yet it should be noted that this was literally what Plato said.'[73]

Coleridge's ethic has a religious basis but it is not a divine command theory. As in Butler, conscience is the 'candle of the Lord', the supreme authority in man; but by right not power. Authentic moral aspiration is fired by a dissatisfaction not with the environment but with *oneself*: 'All true remedy must begin at the heart; otherwise it will be but a mountebank cure, a false imagined conquest' (*Aids*, p. 111). Paley appeals to the interests of men who remain unenlightened: the satisfaction of inchoate or confused desires will not produce genuine happiness. Ultimately Paley's ethics is quite as egotistical as that of Hobbes and as hedonistic as neo-Epicureanism – notwithstanding the strident supernaturalism of Paley's theological buttress.

It is possible to see why Coleridge regards Kant as an aid in the face of Paley's utilitarianism in British (especially Cambridge) philosophy and theology, even though the structure of Coleridge's language and much of his explicit terminology is Christian Platonic

[71] Kathleen Coburn, *The Self-Conscious Imagination* (Oxford University Press, 1974), pp. 21 ff.
[72] Stephen R. L. Clark, *A Parliament of Souls* (Oxford: Clarendon, 1990), pp. 160 ff.
[73] Ibid., p. 164. cf. Cornelia J. de Vogel, 'The soma-sema formula' in *Rethinking Plato and Platonism* (Leiden: Brill,, 1986), pp. 233 ff.

rather than Kantian in the strict sense. Whereas Paley sees the prudential conformity to divine will as the corner-stone of ethics, Kant has an ethics which sees obedience to the moral law in terms of the perfection of human nature. When Coleridge writes that the opposition of morality to prudence is 'essentially religious'; implied and 'grounded' in 'an awe of the Invisible and a Confidence therein beyond (nay, occasionally in apparent contradiction to) the inductions of outward Experience' (*Aids*, p. 104), he is quite convinced that the establishment of the teleological and religious dimension to morality as opposed to prudence is an achievement of the Kantian philosophy. Further evidence for Coleridge's conviction that he is fully Kantian is his insistence that morality including 'the *personal* being, the I AM, as its subject' is a mystery and 'the ground and *supposition* of all other Mysteries, relatively to man' (*Aids*, p. 292). It is clear from Coleridge's language that he feels himself to be a follower of Kant in the sense that he believes the fact of conscience to be a matter of the deepest metaphysical significance.[74]

The will *as* intelligence is man's proper *self*. The core of Kant's ethics is the recognition that a rational agent is a member of an intelligible community: a *corpus mysticum* of moral agents. Kant's answer to the question of what man essentially is is that of St Paul or Plotinus: spirit.[75] Philip Merlan points to Herder's accusation that Kant was an Averroeist, i.e. monopsychist, who fails to distinguish between the destiny of the human race and that of the individual. Merlan argues that in fact Kant's theory of ethical universalisation was a rediscovery of the classical thought of participating in the νοῦς.[76] How can we explain that we can value the welfare of others, or, in other words: what is the cause of altruism? Kant's response to the question is: Human beings are citizens of two worlds: of matter and of spirit. As the latter we are conscious of our kinship with all spirits. Coleridge writes:

---

[74] There is a significant affinity between Bishop Butler's conscience as the 'principle of reflection', an 'inward principle' by virtue of which man is a 'law to himself' and Kantian autonomy. See Butler's *Fifteen Sermons* II 8 p. 45. cf Coleridge *LS* p. 187.

[75] M. B. Foster, ' "We" in modern philosophy' in *Faith and Logic*, edited by B. Mitchell (London: George Allen and Unwin, 1957), pp. 194–220, esp. pp. 215–16. Kant printed a letter as an appendix to his *Streit der Fakultäten* in which C. A. Wilmans pointed to the similarity between Kant's religious thought and that of a mystical group called the 'Separatists'. See Philip Merlan, *Monopsychism, Mysticism, Metaconsciousness* (The Hague: Nijhoff, 1963), p. 131.

[76] Kant is an ambiguous figure – on the one hand he is the critical philosopher and on the other he continues the rationalist or idealist tradition with his vision of man as the link between the intelligible and sensual realm.

What the duties of MORALITY are, the apostle instructs the believer in full, comprising them under the two heads of negative and positive. Negative, to keep himself pure from the world; and positive, beneficence from loving-kindness, *i.e* love of his fellow-men (his kind) as himself. (*Aids*, p. 40)[77]

The point is that altruism depends upon a recognition of and reverence for common humanity rather than a calculation of collective interests. Indeed, the consciousness of this kind-ness is the only intelligible explanation of altruism.[78] Coleridge interpreted this as uniting the private with the universal, i.e. divine, will. The Neoplatonist scholar Merlan contrasts Kant's universalising tendency with Schleiermacher's insistence that the ethical life is one which expresses one particularity.[79] Speaking of Kant's categorical imperative, Philip Merlan wrote: 'Indeed, it seems that it was only for reasons of style that Kant did not say "Whoever wants to divinize himself should, as much as possible try to unite his private will with that of the universal will".'[80] This expresses the affinity of the mystical doctrine of the will, the *imago Dei*, and Kant's ethical universalisation. The rational soul is an image of the Divine and it yearns for its archetype.

What Coleridge finds attractive about Kant is precisely the appeal to the universal and the timeless, which some modern commentators – notably Alasdair MacIntyre – find most objectionable. The critique of writers in the wake of MacIntyre, Williams, and Nussbaum, communitarians or virtue-ethics theorists envisages Kant's ethics as the expression of a Platonic-Stoic attempt to overcome contingency and particularity and the inability to countenance human frailty: all of which contrasts unfavourably, it is argued, with Aristotle's ethics of human flourishing within particular contingent traditions and communities. This Aristotelian option is widely perceived in contemporary thought as more attractive in the fragmented 'post-modern' environment than Kantian ethical universalism.

Paton claims that Kant's moral law 'ranks with the Republic of Plato and the Ethics of Aristotle; and perhaps – partly no doubt through the spread of Christian ideals and through the long

---

[77] I disagree with Beer's suggestion that 'Coleridge is presumably thinking of James', *Aids*, p. 40 n. 1. Firstly, *the* apostle is almost always Paul. Secondly, in the related passage of p. 227 on the nature of genius Coleridge refers to the Pauline idea of 'this world' in relation to the idea of kind- and unkindness.

[78] cf. Dietrich Mahnke, 'Die Rationalisierung der Mystik bei Leibniz und Kant', pp. 1–73.

[79] cf. Merlan, *Monopsychism*, pp. 135–6.

[80] Ibid., p. 121.

experience of the human race during the last two thousand years – it shows in some respects a deeper insight even than these'.[81] Perhaps Kant genuinely is the inheritor of the Stoic-Christian synthesis which developed after the breakdown of the rather narrow confines of the Athenian city state – a synthesis which, as a system of thought, was both *universalistic* and *individualistic*, and founded upon the desire to transcend both the empirical self and the immediate environment. Yet he shares the puritanical rigour of Plato. Aristotle's *Nichomachean Ethics* is sane and persuasive, and on the topic of friendship even moving; yet his ethics is primarily conceived of as the execution of duties which arise from a due consideration of the needs of the city state, and the desire to flourish. There is little of the radically internal sense of ethical obligation which we find in Plato's *Gorgias* (469b) where Socrates claims that it is a greater evil to inflict than to suffer injustice, or where he insists upon the fact that the lover of truth has to shake off the irreality and sophistry of popular opinion and strive for 'the reality rather than the appearance of goodness'.[82] Coleridge, as a sturdy Platonist, would be alarmed by the idea that virtues can and should be contingently embodied in communities, because ethics for him is stamped with the eternal: moral action is the outward sign of an adherence of the soul to the absolute good.

An adequate account, for Coleridge, of the nature of moral aspiration, of the ascent from uprightness to godliness, demands metaphysical reflection upon the nature of spirit. A richer concept of mind and spirit than that of contemporary empiricism is needed for this task, and it is understandable why Coleridge turns to Kant; if the natural man is radically estranged from the good, a view which Plato often hints at and which Kant explicitly maintains, the mere correction of bad habits and general waywardness is inadequate: something like the Pauline putting down the old man and taking up the new man is required.[83]

---

[81] H. J. Paton, introduction in Kant, *The Moral Law*, p. 7.

[82] Plato, *Gorgias* 527 B6 (Harmondsworth: Penguin, 1988), p. 148.

[83] Kant uses the language of rebirth. The change in a man cannot be achieved through a gradual reformation if the basis of his maxims is corrupt. Hence a revolution in mankind's disposition is required and this must be a new birth, a new creation and a change of heart. Kant supplements this language with the Pauline terminology of laying off the old man and putting on the new. See G. E. Michalson, *Fallen Freedom: Kant on Radical Civil and Moral Regeneration* (Cambridge University Press: 1990).

SPIRITUAL AIDS

F. J. A. Hort thought that the most striking fact about Coleridge's moral philosophy is the fact that there is 'so little to say about it' despite the evident importance of the subject matter.[84] Muirhead, another sympathetic and very able interpreter of Coleridge, remarks upon the almost entire absence of any attempt to develop the science of ethics.[85] Yet the absence of a separate ethical system which can be distinguished from the metaphysical is characteristic for both Platonist and German Idealist thought. There are no separate ethical treatises in German Idealism. Similarly, Plato's metaphysics and ethics can barely be separated: his most famous account of the relation of the mind to its intelligible objects is in his *Republic*, which is a treatise about moral and constitutional philosophy. Coleridge is producing a meta-ethics: not in the modern sense of a deliberation about the status of moral concepts, etc. but in the classical Platonic (and idealistic) sense of probing the metaphysical roots of ethical beliefs.

Coleridge distinguishes between the outward flux of events and the inward source of action. He presents the moral life through the imagery of light and mirroring as not so much an expression of *appetite* as *insight*. A vital element in Coleridge's ethics is the idea of *happiness* related to *seeing* and *knowing*. This Christian Platonic view of ethics as tied to the vision and imitation of the good is fundamentally opposed to the idea of ethics as a matter of calculating the results of any given act, the consequentialism of Paley. Coleridge's rejection of utilitarianism and sentimentalism is founded upon his Platonic ontology, which itself is buttressed by Kant's ethical rationalism. Coleridge states emphatically that ethics must be based upon the spiritual core of mankind – upon conscience – and its relation to the transcendent principle of being, and this is supported by Kant's denial that only the empiricist criterion of reality can decide what is really 'there':

Ethics, or the *Science* of Morality, does indeed in no wise exclude the consideration of the *Action*; but it contemplates the same in its spiritual *Source*, without reference to Space or Time or Sensible Existence. Whatever springs out of 'the perfect Law of Freedom,' which exists only by its unity with the Will of God . . . *that* (according to the principles of

---

[84] F. J. A. Hort, 'Coleridge' in *Cambridge Essays*, vol. ii. p. 336.
[85] Muirhead, *Coleridge as Philosopher*, p. 139.

Moral Science) is GOOD – it is light and Righteousness and very Truth.
(*Aids*, p. 293)

Coleridge's repeated reference to reason as the source of necessary
and universal 'Principles' (*Aids*, p. 232) and the scientific (i.e. rational)
nature of genuine ethics (*Aids*, p. 293, esp. n. 2) is inextricably tied to
his metaphysical theism. He is claiming ethics derives its rationality
from 'contemplating' its 'spiritual *Source*', i.e. God.[86] Coleridge is
wanting to produce – in opposition to Paley – a genuinely spiritual
ethics. He sees the spirit as the focal energy of the union of the will
and the reason: it is the *return* or *reflection* of the soul to God.
Coleridge believes adamantly that Christian ethics cannot be separated from a consideration about what God in his nature is, i.e. as
the transcendent source of the world, as communicating love, and as
the immanent *aiding Spirit* which brings all creation back to himself.
Platonic metaphysics and Trinitarian doctrine coincide in
Coleridge's meta-ethics.

The reference to 'acts, exercises, and disciplines of the mind,
will and affection' (*Aids*, p. 40) is related to the idea of the *ascent* of
the mind via introductory, prudential, moral and religious and
spiritual aphorisms (*Aids*, p. 38). Though Coleridge uses Kant's
language and agrees with Kant that the moral will is the centre of
the personality, Coleridge concentrates upon the mystical ideas of
the gradual and progressive *purification* of the finite will into
accordance with the divine will ('in our present state we have only
the Dawning of this inward Sun' (*Aids*, p. 98). Indeed, the
distinctive character of religious morality, for Coleridge, lies in the
attempt to achieve a fitness between the moral *agent* and the *goal*
of moral aspiration.[87] What is required is not just reflection in the
sense of *consideration* of the particular moral issue but a *transformation*. As the loosely-knit character is distracted and energies
are dissipated by manifold goods, the unified person finds the
supreme good in striving for its likeness. Yet, even here, it is not

---

[86] cf. Coleridge: 'Not the outward Deed, constructive, destructive or neutral; not the Deed as
a possible Object of the Senses; is the Object of Ethical Science' (*Aids*, p. 294); 'Reason (is
the Faculty) of Contemplation' (*Aids*, p. 223).
[87] Coleridge: '1. Every State, and consequently that which we have described as the State of
Religious Morality, which is not progressive, is dead or retrograde. 2. As a pledge of this
progression, or, at least, as the form in which the propulsive tendency shows itself, there are
certain Hopes, Aspirations, Yearnings, that, with more or less of consciousness, rise and stir
in the Heart of true Morality as naturally as the Sap in the full-formed Stem of a Rose flows
towards the Bud, within which the Flower is maturing' (*Aids*, p. 103).

at all clear that Coleridge's ethical Platonism is a repudiation of his adherence to Kant. All moral action, for Kant, has the goal of the realisation of the highest good, which means the concord of virtue and happiness A. E. Taylor notes: 'In fact, though Kant would have been horrified by so "fanatical" a phrase, he is at bottom quite agreed with "Dionysius" that "deification" (θέωσις) is the ultimate goal of the moral life.'[88]

Kant is worried about the enervating and debilitating effect of the belief in divine grace upon the moral agent;[89] however, Coleridge considers it a metaphysical mistake to think that the *aids* of the spirit are an alien influence:

It is sufficient, in short, to prove that some distinct and consistent meaning may be attached to the assertion of the learned and philosophic Apostle, that 'the Spirit beareth witness with our spirit' – *i.e.* with *the Will* as the Supernatural in Man and the Principle of our Personality – of that I mean, by which we are responsible Agents; *Persons*, and not merely living *Things*. (*Aids*, p. 77–8)

This is what Coleridge meant by calling Kant a miserable psychologist (*Notebooks* i. 1717) and praising the psychology of the Platonists (cf. *Notebooks* iii. 3935).[90] Kant is right to associate ethics with universalisation but is oddly inconsistent concerning the consequences of this ethics for the concept of the self.

The life of moral endeavour is characterised by twilight between these two realms.[91] The moral agent attempts to see more clearly into the good and this attempt to attain a clearer vision is akin to the life of *faith*:

Awakened by the cock-crow – (a sermon, calamity, a sick bed, or providential escape) the Christian pilgrim sets out in the morning twilight, while yet the truth (the νόμος τέλειος ὁ τῆς ἐλευθερίας) is below the horizon. Certain necessary *consequences* of his past life and his present undertaking will be *seen* by the refraction of its light: more will be apprehended and conjectured. The phantasms that had predominated during the long hours of darkness, are still busy. Though they no longer present themselves, as distinct Forms, yet they remain as formative Motions in the Pilgrim's soul, unconscious of its own activity and overmastered by its own workmanship. (*Aids*, pp. 35–6)

---

[88] A. E. Taylor, 'Theism' in *Encyclopaedia of Religion and Ethics*, vol. xii. p. 280.
[89] Kant, *Die Religion innerhalb der Grenzen der bloßen Vernunft*, § 296.
[90] Anya Taylor pointed out to me Coleridge's praise of the Platonists as psychologists.
[91] cf. *Aids*, p. 9, n. 8. The quotation of 'Unless ye believe ye shall not understand', Isaiah 7: 9, a favourite Augustine text.

Here we see Coleridge's connection between the law of freedom and the vision of God. Coleridge's reference to the light of reason is not a desperate and abrupt theological manoeuvre, but guided by an idea about the formative and perpetual feature of the genuinely moral life. Knowledge of the divine in the soul must be conveyed by indwelling Logos because 'WHAT PROCEEDS FROM A DIVINE IMPULSE, THAT THE GODLIKE ALONE CAN AWAKEN' (*F* i. p. 524); the old Platonic principle that 'like can only be known by like'. The growth of the moral consciousness, for Coleridge, is the *answer* to the questioning of the inner teacher – the logos – and in the process of this active response to the divine initiative in the spirit, the moral agent acquires the meaning of true freedom.

At precisely this juncture, ethics and philosophical theology are closely related. Aristotle thinks of God as the supreme being, as 'Thought thinking itself' who sustains the motions of the heavens. The sage, for Aristotle, may be able to enter into the realm of divine self-contemplation, but there can be no divine initiative. Christian theism has a rather different view of the relation of divine transcendence to human action. Here we find both the self-sufficiency of the divine and also the divine initiative; so that the human capacity for fellowship with God is at least in part bestowed by God. The ethical efforts of human beings must be genuine endeavours, but also reactions to actual communion with God, where the supreme good is experienced by his creatures. The moral life is a response to the *aids* of the divine:

> Whenever, therefore, the Man is determined (*i.e.* impelled and directed) to act in harmony of inter-communion must not something be attributed to this allpresent power as acting *in* the Will? and by what fitter names can we call this than the LAW, as empowering; THE WORD, as informing; and THE SPIRIT, as actuating? (*Aids*, p. 77)

Clearly, Coleridge is using the triad LAW, WORD, and SPIRIT to convey the doctrinal significance of the ethical life. We have seen that Coleridge takes over the concept of tri-unity from the Neoplatonic and Christian Platonic metaphysics as essentially the principle of the indwelling spirit: man-in-God and God-in-man; albeit not a crude pantheism. In the *Biographia* (*BL* i. p. 171). Coleridge talks of the first lesson of 'philosophical discipline' lying in the weaning of attention from mere degrees to differences in kind. In *Aids to Reflection* he speaks of prudence preparing and predisposing men to the sense and acknowledgement of a principle differing not merely in degree but in kind, from the faculties and instincts of the higher and more intelligent animals (the ant, the beaver, the elephant) and which principle is your proper humanity. (Aids, p. 50)

This principle is not immanent but *transcendent and can only be appropriated through faith*. Man has a *'higher gift'*, a 'living (that is, self subsisting) soul, a soul having life in itself. And man became a living soul. He did not merely *possess* it, he *became* it. It was his proper *being*, his truest *self*, *the* man *in* the man' (*Aids*, p. 15). Faith is opposed not to reason but to sight. It is simply 'fidelity to our own being' (*SW* ii. p. 834).

The *symbol* which Coleridge repeatedly uses is that of light. The first step to self-knowledge is to take pity on one's soul (*Aids*, p. 53); effectively to realise the extent of one's need. This recognition, for Coleridge, is the beginning of true enlightenment. How do we pass from the awareness of ignorance to *enlightenment*? Coleridge believes that divine initiative is the only possible answer: the true moralist sees the best human ethical action as the reflection to the divine which is the *effective* source of goodness. This meaning of reflection is more than is generally meant by it, yet it is, Coleridge insists, the meaning which a Christian ought to mean by it, because the indwelling light referred to in the aphorism is the *indwelling Logos* (*Aids*, p. 15).

Real moral effort begins with dissatisfaction with *the man*, and the fulfilment of the moral life is the discovery of real identity by the welding together and purifying of the diverse forces of the natural man into a coherent *simplified* moral agent. The answer to the question of what freedom might be, for Coleridge, is dependent upon the idea of God: if man is made in God's image, he must have a self-determining will. When the will is placed in accordance with reason, the spirit rises through which the will of God flows and activates the will of man, so that the finite will wills the things of God, and the understanding becomes illuminated as it has communion with the divine. Coleridge writes:

Last and highest, comes the *spiritual*, comprising all the truths, acts and duties that have an especial reference to the Timeless, the Permanent, the Eternal: to the sincere love of the True, as truth; of the Good *as* good: and of God as both in one. It comprehends the whole ascent from uprightness (morality, virtue, inward rectitude) to *godlikeness*, with all the acts, exercises, and disciplines of mind, will and affection, that are requisite or conducive to the great design of our redemption from the form of the evil one, and of our second creation or birth in the divine image. (*Aids*, p. 40)

This idea of the ethical life as the approximation of one's goal is expressed by means of imagery of mirroring. Righteousness is the 'perfect conformity and commensurateness with the immutable Idea of Equity, or perfect Rectitude. Hence the close connection between the words righteousness and *god*liness, *i.e.* godlikeness' (*Aids*, p. 274). Coleridge stresses the Platonic heritage of this idea: the ascent of the soul which 'seeks its *summit* in the imitation of the Divine nature' (*Aids*, p. 41).[92] The Cambridge Platonist Ralph Cudworth in his *The True Intellectual System of the Universe* writes: 'Virtue is defined to be, assimilation to the Deity.[93] It is Coleridge's aim to produce *aids to reflection* for the formation of a manly, that is *vir*tuous character.

Add to your faith *knowledge*, and to knowledge *manly energy:* for this is the proper rendering of ἀρετήν, and not virtue, at least in the present and ordinary acceptation of the word. (*Aids*, p. 18)

The manly character is Christ-like.[94] Coleridge speaks of DESIRE prevailing over the WILL (the *Man*hood, the *Vir*tus) against the command of the universal reason (*Aids*, p. 260). Cudworth writes:

Happinesse is nothing but that inward sweet delight, that will arise from the Harmonious agreement between our wills and Gods will. There is nothing contrary to God in the whole world nothing that fights against him but *Self will* . . . Now our onely way to recover God & happiness again, is not to soar up with our Understandings, but to destroy this *Self-will* of ours: and then we shall find our wings to grow again, our plumes fairly spread, and our selves raised aloft into the free Aire of perfect Liberty, which is perfect Happinesse.[95]

This is what Coleridge describes as the 'restoration of the Will to perfect Freedom' which is the '*end* and consummation of the redemptive Process . . . the entrance of the Soul into Glory, *i.e.* its

---

[92] Socrates thinks that the best method in divinity is to dwell on the (relative) proximity of the good man to God (Plato, *Theaetetus*, 176aff.); cf. Coleridge's idea of 'conformity with the *Idea* of the divine Giver' in *Aids*, p. 83.

[93] Cudworth, *True Intellectual System*, vol. i. p. 315.

[94] Paul, 1 Cor. 1: 24: 'Christus Dei virtus et Dei sapientia.' *Virtus* was the translation of the Greek δύναμις (a key term in Plotinus' metaphysics) and Marius Victorinus, Augustine's great philosophical mentor, used the term in his Christology. See Beierwaltes on Augustine's vision of Christ as *virtus* or divine self-explication, *Identität und Differenz*, p. 82.

[95] Ralph Cudworth, *A Sermon Preached before the Honourable House of Commons at Westminster, March 31 1647* (Cambridge: Daniel, 1647), pp. 19–20.

union with Christ' (*Aids*, p. 160). In a note (*Aids*, p. 37) Coleridge discusses Leighton's assertion that will is *voluntas* and not *arbitrium* and it 'is carried towards happiness not simply as will, but as nature'. The will is not really the mere capacity for decision, i.e. *arbitrium*, but is really the fundamental orientation of the soul. Coleridge remarks that this insight depends upon the exact meaning of the term *self*. Coleridge quotes Marinus, the biographer of the greatest of later Neoplatonists – Proclus – as his first motto, to this effect: 'So a soul, gathering itself together and collecting all things to itself, most easily and surely becomes blessed' (*Aids*, p. 4). The happiness of the soul depends upon this concentration upon the self, and the attainment of deeper selfhood than that of the unreflective man. The second motto is: 'All divine and human learning has three elements: knowledge, will and power, whose single principle is the mind, with reason for its eye, to which God brings the light' (*Aids*, p. 4). The two mottos suggest that the fulfilment of human life lies in the reorientation of the finite will into harmony with the divine will, and this reorientation is envisaged as a discovery of the genuine self as a *reflection* of the divine light. Thus the attainment of freedom through the combination of will and reason is experienced as grace: that is the overflowing goodness of the divine. Platonism denied that mankind has sufficient resources to live the good life without divine aid, and shared with Christianity the idea that the realisation of what might be called anachronistically 'personality' involves dependence upon God and other persons. The Stoics and Epicureans generally denied this tenet, but Coleridge is quite sincere in his advocacy of ancient heathen wisdom:

And here it will not be impertinent to observe, that what the eldest Greek Philosophy entitled *the Reason* (ΝΟΥΣ) and *Ideas*, the philosophic Apostle names *the Spirit* and *Truths spiritually* discerned: while to those who in the pride of Learning or in the over-weaning meanness of modern Metaphysics decry the doctrine of the Spirit in Man and its possible communion with the Holy Spirit, as *vulgar* enthusiasm; I submit the following Sentences from a Pagan Philosopher, a Nobleman and a Minister of State – 'Ita dico, Lucilî! SACER INTRA NOS SPIRITU SEDET, malorum bonorumque nostrorum observator et custos. Hic prout a nobis tractatus est, ita nos ipse tractat. BONUS VIR SINE DEO NEMO EST.' SENECA. (*Aids*, p. 146)

The quote from Seneca is part of Coleridge's appeal to the Christian Platonic tradition of interpretation of Γνῶθι σεαυτόν, 'Know Thyself!' The definition and proper character of man is derived from the indwelling divinity; it is 'to be taken from his Reason rather than from his Understanding' (*Aids*, p. 207).[96]

Often have I heard it said by advocates for the Socinian Scheme – True! we are all sinners; but even in the Old Testament God has promised Forgiveness on Repentance. One of the Fathers (I forget which) supplies the Retort – True! God has promised pardon on Penitence: but has he promised Penitence on Sin? – He that repenteth shall be forgiven: but where is it said He that sinneth shall repent? But Repentance, perhaps the Repentance required in Scripture, *the Passing into a new mind*, into a new and contrary Principle of Action, this METANOIA, is it in the Sinner's own power? at his own liking? (*Aids*, p. 132)

Coleridge lays weight upon the etymology of the Greek for repentance, 'μετάνοια in the compound of meta and nous, i.e. reason or spirit' (*Aids*, p, 132). Conversion or reflection of the soul can only be effected by the divine spirit. The philosophical or metaphysical issue is this: what is required for this reflection of the soul are *divine aids*, the idea which A. E. Taylor, pupil of T. H. Green, says, with justified exaggeration, 'has been, in substance, that of all the classical British moral philosophers from Cudworth to Green . . . We know our true good, which is no other than God Himself, by obscure, but none the less real and impressive, personal contacts with God.'[97] This is the philosophical problem of the source of the initiative for moral improvement. If the real task of the moral life is not just the rational expression of one's personality but the *reformation* of the person (which Kant, Plato, and serious religious experience seems to suggest), it is a genuinely philosophical question, and not simple piety, to ask where the source of this transformation might be located.[98] Coleridge thinks it is evident that the source of renewal cannot come from the personality which must be renewed. It must come from without: from God.

Hegel writes:

Meister Eckhart, a Dominican monk of the fourteenth century, says in the course of one of his sermons on the inner life, 'The eye with which God sees me is the eye with which I see him; my eye and his eye are one and the same.'[99]

Hegel uses the drastic imagery of the medieval Dominican Platonist

---

[96] cf. Coleridge, *Aids*, pp. 294 ff.
[97] A. E. Taylor, *Faith of a Moralist*, vol. i. pp. 238–9.
[98] Ibid., pp. 222 ff.
[99] Hegel, *Philosophy of Religion*, vol. i. p. 347.

to insist upon the point that the mind of God is not an object, an *ens* or a *Ding*, but an active *subject*. Reflection upon knowledge reveals a power working upon and within the finite mind: for Hegel, the absolute is not an object but the process by which reality comes to become aware of itself, and reason is the medium of this awareness. That is a stronger thesis than Coleridge would uphold; he could not accept such transparency of vision. Yet it is not alien in spirit. The great weakness of eighteenth-century theology, whether Paley or Jacobi, was its inability to do justice to the profoundly Christian notion of a transcendent God who is also immanent, and most profoundly present in the striving of the soul, a God who is not just the goal of the good life but its sustaining power.

AUTONOMY AND THE EUTHYPHRO DILEMMA

Paley's ethics points to a much deeper contention between Coleridge and the author of the celebrated *Principles of Moral and Political Philosophy*. The principle of utility, as Graham Cole notes, is 'not part of the definition of the good, but rather an epistemic criterion for discerning the will of God'.[100]

By virtue of the two principles, that God wills the happiness of his creatures, and that the will of God is the measure of right and wrong, we arrive at certain conclusions; which conclusions become rules; and we soon learn to pronounce actions right or wrong, according as they agree or disagree with our rules, without looking any farther: and when the habit is once established of stopping at the rules, we can go back and compare with these rules even the Divine conduct itself; and yet it may be true (only not observed by us at the time) that the rules themselves are deduced from the Divine will.[101]

This is what in contemporary terminology is known as a divine-command theory of ethics. Goodness is defined by God's will. The point of utility is not the definition of what is 'good' but to establish the nature of God's will.

The obvious problem with a divine-command theory is that it makes the deity arbitrary. For Coleridge, given his belief in the ideas, it means that the obligation of any divine command must ensue from that goodness which constitutes the divine nature, which in turn

---

[100] G. Cole, 'Discovering God's will: Paley's problem with special reference to "The Christian Sabbath"' in *Tyndale Bulletin* 39 (1988), p. 135.

[101] Paley, *Works*, vol. ii.p. 62.

entails that the awareness of obligation in a rational moral agent is founded upon the identity of that internal law and the law of the divine essence. Coleridge is quite adamant that he opposes not only Hobbesian materialism and determinism and a pseudo-Platonism which has no conception of man's fallenness (*Aids*, pp. 139–40), but a theology which reduces the deity to 'infinite Power, and thence deducing that Things are good and wise because they were created, and not created through Wisdom and Goodness' (*Aids.* p. 140). Coleridge notes: 'Against these Tenets I maintain, that a Will conceived separately from Intelligence is a Non-entity, and a mere Phantasm of Abstraction' (*Aids*, p. 141). For the Platonist, even God is 'constrained' by the moral law, and it is by participation in the archetypal realm of divine goodness that the agent can experience the law as an internal and not as a merely external compulsion (cf. *LS*, p. 186n.). Autonomy is internal determination.

Even John Stuart Mill was struck by the theological implications of Paley's voluntarism:

in the textbook adopted by the Church (in one of its universities) for instruction in moral philosophy, the reason for doing good is declared to be, that God is stronger than we are, and is able to damn us if we do not. This is no exaggeration of the sentiments of Paley, and hardly even of the crudity of his language.[102]

Kant's categorical imperative presents a vision of obligation not as brute power compelling with sanctions and rewards, but as the recognition and development of a deeper self; as the 'nisus of a nature eagerly seeking its appointed place in the Cosmos'.[103] Cudworth while discussing the biblical and Platonic idea of becoming 'partaker of the Divine nature', writes:

God is therefore God because he is the highest and most perfect Good: and Good is not therefore Good, because God out of an arbitary will of his, would have it so. Whatsoever God doth in the world, he doth it as it is suitable to the highest Goodnesse; the first Idea and fairest Copy of which is his own Essence. Vertue and Holinesse in creatures, as *Plato* well discourseth in his *Euthyphro*, are not *therefore Good, because God loveth them*, and will have them be accounted such; but rather *God therefore loveth them because they are in themselves simply good.*[104]

John Smith speaks of the righteousness of the gospel as transcending

[102] Mill and Bentham, *Utilitarianism*, p. 206.
[103] J. A. Stewart, *The Myths of Plato* (London: Centaur, 1960), p. 463.
[104] Cudworth, *Sermon*, p. 26.

the Jewish law because it is a '*true command over the inward man,* which it acts and informs; whereas the *Law* by its *menaces* and *punishments* could only *compell* men to an *External* observance of it in the *outward* man'.[105] It is the affinity and participation of the finite in the Divine mind, an 'Internal and God-like frame of Spirit which is necessary for a true conjunction and union of the Soul of Men with God'[106] which constitutes the ethical, not the obedience of man to God as an arbitary suzerain, like bondage of a serf to his master. This conviction finds expression in the doctrine that the persons of the Godhead are essential and eternal. If the Trinity were merely 'economic', i.e. facts about the the actions of God in relation to the history of his people, this salvation might reflect something extrinsic to God. He happens to have acted in relation to Adam and his successors in a particular manner, but this does not tell us about his essential nature. This insistence upon the essential or immanent Trinity of mutually giving and receiving persons is to postulate a Godhead whose inherent nature is self-giving love, quite apart from any contingent, historical facts about humanity.

We totally misunderstand the underlying controversy if we envisage it as a conflict between a secular utilitarianism and Coleridge's religious morality. Paley's ethics is just as religious as that of Coleridge, and in some respects, perhaps, more conventionally pious. As we have seen, the eschatological component of Christian ethics is much more prominent in Paley than in Coleridge. Furthermore, for Coleridge, Christian ethics is intuitive: obedience to the divine will as it is revealed to the moral agent through the indwelling spirit. The New Testament would seem to serve merely as a guide or criterion, for Coleridge, for spiritual discernment. For Paley, the scriptural ethical teaching plays a much more intrinsic role in his ethics: Scripture and the light of nature are the joint sources of our knowledge of God's will. He writes:

Now there are two methods of coming at the will of God on any point:
1. By his express declarations, when they are to be had, and which must be sought for in Scripture.
2. By what we discover of his designs and disposition from his works; or as we usually call it, the light of nature.[107]

[105] Smith, 'The difference between legal and evangelical righteousness' in his *Select Discourses,* p. 318.
[106] Ibid., p. 311.
[107] Paley, *Works,* vol. ii. pp. 50–1.

Hence Coleridge can afford much more latitude in his approach to Scripture than Paley; for Coleridge Scripture plays a regulative role in Christian ethics, for Paley a constitutive. This is one of the reasons why Paley's ethics is not really 'utilitarian' whereas Coleridge's ethics is thoroughly Platonic and Kantian. Coleridge can insist that the content of Christian ethics does not differ from the best secular morality: the forming of the human mind according to 'the DIVINE IMAGE' (*Aids*, p. 25). The difference is rather that Christianity provides a different motivation for the good life in its assertion of the Incarnation and redemptive work of Christ and the sanctification of the Spirit. The ancient philosophers tried to elevate the moral character by informing the mind. Christianity worked in the opposite direction: it gave the heart hope and thus restored the intellect by (here he uses Platonic language) presenting 'for its contemplation Objects so great and so bright as cannnot but enlarge the Organ, by which they are contemplated' (*Aids*, p. 191). It means, however, that Coleridge is, in a sense, much more liberal than Paley. This is certainly not a battle between a worldly Hanoverian and the arch-religious Romantic.

The real issue is one of metaphysical theology; whether we can know God's will or nature. Here there is some irony in the fact that Paley is perceived as a dry Augustan rationalist and Coleridge as the excitable Romantic advocate of the heart. In terms of ethics Paley takes a pragmatic-sceptical view of morality in which the divine will is revealed through scripture and human happiness, whereas Coleridge pursues the more rationalist position that morality is based upon the perception of the divine nature as goodness. The extent of Coleridge's 'essentialism' in contrast to Paley's rather pragmatic-empiricist epistemology should become evident in our discussion of the distraction between Reason and Understanding.

CHAPTER 4

God is truth: the faculty of reflection or human Understanding in relation to the divine Reason[1]

Ever since the creation of the world his invisible nature, namely, his eternal power and deity, has been clearly perceived in the things that have been made. (Romans 1: 20)

... it is no mere verbal bond which unites truth of revelation to truth of discovery.[2] (F. J. A.Hort)

It is still a *metaphysical faith* that underlies our faith in science – and we men of knowledge today, we godless men and anti-metaphysicians, we, too still derive *our* flame from the fire ignited by a faith millennia old, the Christian faith, which was also Plato's, that God is truth, that truth is *divine*.[3] (Nietzsche)

Hume, in his *Dialogues Concerning Natural Religion*, uses the figure of Simonides from Cicero's classic work on natural theology *De Natura Deorum* as a figure of caution and prudent reserve in the attempt to show that the postulation or assumption of a spiritual world as the basis of the material world is unwarranted.[4] Simonides' unwillingness to answer the question of the nature of God is taken by Hume as an instance of genuine philosophical caution. Coleridge employs the figure of Simonides for his own purposes:

I would disturb no man's faith in the great articles of the (falsely so called) Religion of Nature. But before the man rejects, and calls on other men to reject, the revelations of the Gospel and the Religion of all Christendom,

---

[1] 'Deus est veritas': cf. Augustine, *Confessions*, x. 24: 'I found God, who is Truth itself'; *Confessions*, vii. 10; 'And far off, I heard your voice saying I am the God who IS . . . I might more easily have doubted that I was alive than that Truth had being. For we catch sight of the Truth, as he is known through his creation.'
[2] F. J. A. Hort, *The Way, the Truth, the Life*, second edition, edited by B. F. Westcott (London: Macmillan, 1897), p. 75.
[3] Friedrich Nietzsche, *On the Genealogy of Morals*, translated by W. Kaufmann and R. J. Hollingdale (New York: A. A. Knopf and Random, 1969), p. 152.
[4] Hume, *Dialogues Concerning Natural Religion*, part iii, p. 51, in his *Principal Writings on Religion*, edited by J. C. A. Gaskin (Oxford: Clarendon, 1993).

I would have him place himself in the state and under all the privations of a Simonides, when in the fortieth day of meditation the sage and philosophic Poet abandoned the Problem in despair. (*Aids*, p. 239, cf. pp. 557 ff.)

Furthermore, Coleridge insists:

both Reason and Experience have convinced me, that in the greater number of our ALOGI, who feed on the husks of Christianity, the disbelief of the Trinity, the Divinity of Christ included, has its origin and support in the assumed self-evidence of this Natural Theology and their ignorance of the insurmountable difficulties which (on the same mode of reasoning) press upon the fundamental articles of their own Remnant of a Creed. (*Aids*, pp. 254–5)

Coleridge claims, as much as Hume, that a natural religion or a natural theology antecedent to revelation breaks down under philosophical criticism. As the best way of seeing this and preventing the 'pugnacious dogmatism or *partial* Reflection', Coleridge suggests perusal and study of Bayle's presentation of Simonides' difficulties or the treatise of Pomponatius (*Aids*, p. 241).

Coleridge believes that the English theologians in the eighteenth century had failed to expound the rich speculative heritage of the sixteenth- and seventeenth-century divines. The rather mechanical view of religion of Locke and Paley has little to do with the good news of Paul and John. Coleridge maintains as early as 1806:

I fear that the mode of defending Christianity, adopted by Grotius first; and latterly among many others, by Dr Paley, has increased the number of infidels; – never could it have been so great, if thinking men had been habitually led to look into their own souls, instead of always looking out, both of themselves, and of their nature. (*CL* ii. 1189)

Dr Paley is not attacked because of his rationalism but because he diverts Christianity away from its centre: the indwelling Logos. Paley's *Natural Theology*, as much as the deists', constitutes 'the utter rejection of all present and living communion with the universal Spirit' (*Aids*, p. 88). In order to experience this Logos, mankind must turn within. Coleridge maintains that the only way to hold together a vital religion and a reasonable apprehension of reality is the vision of the Logos as the pattern of the transcendent Godhead in the cosmos. Priestley writes:

We have seen what notions the Christian fathers entertained of the *second principle*, in what has been called the *Platonic Trinity*, viz. the divine *nous* or *logos*, which properly signifies the Divine *mind*, *reason*, or *wisdom;* that power by means of which God produced the visible world.[5]

Coleridge would agree with Priestley's analysis of the Platonic position: the *nous* or *logos* as the second person of the Trinity is the power by which God produced the visible world, and the only way of meeting the objections of the Pyrrhonian sceptics is to dismantle the division between natural and revealed religion. Coleridge wishes to press for the opinion of Plotinus, Augustine, Malebranche, or Berkeley that all knowledge is a species of revelation (cf. *BL* i. 285).

Coleridge's reflections in the passage in *Aids to Reflection* from p. 216 to p. 250 constitute the central part of his anti-empiricist argument. He wishes to show that the empiricist case rests upon an untenable view of experience which in fact resolves into a lifeless abstraction. This very perceptive attack upon the empiricist view of experience is combined with a high Platonic and transcendental view of knowledge as essentially revelation of 'an existing and self-subsisting reality' (*Aids*, p. 178): as theophany.

Plato presents nature as a system of sensuous symbols, an opaque divine language or a dim mirror, which discloses enigmatically its intelligible source. Coleridge's division between reason, understanding, and sense should be understood in connection with the Platonic thesis that all finite knowledge is a species of divine self disclosure. This coheres with the speculations in German Idealism about the nature of the absolute. When Coleridge says that reason is subjective revelation, revelation objective reason, (*CL* vi. 895) he is formulating a *speculative* view of revelation which developed in the wake of Kant's thought – especially under the influence of Lessing. In Coleridge's work *The Friend* the connection between revelation and being is evident:

Hast thou ever raised thy mind to the consideration of EXISTENCE, in and by itself, as the mere act of existing? . . . Is it not REVELATION . . . is it not GOD? (*F* i. 516)

The concept of revelation for the German Idealists was not propositional in the traditional sense of revelation in, say, Aquinas or for the Reformers. The orthodox concept of revelation as the communication of supernatural propositions had been severely attacked by the Enlightenment. The response of the Idealists was to propose a view of revelation as the revelation of God's being rather than the

---

[5] Priestley, *Theological and Miscellaneous Works*, vol. vi. pp. 204–5.

revelation of specific propositions. This is linked with the idea of reason as an objective principle, i.e. Logos or the self-revelation of God, and the Platonic view of knowledge as illumination from above and without the finite mind. The symbol of light expresses neatly the revelatory function of reason (cf. *Aids*, pp. 328; 469; 218).[6] Goethe, who played an important role in the rediscovery of Plotinus in German thought,[7] is reported to have said to Schopenhauer: 'What! Light is only present when you see it? No! it is rather *you* who would not be here if light itself did not see you.'[8] The idea is expressed succinctly by Plotinus when he argues that the discursive reasoning of the finite mind presupposes the illuminating reason-intellect: 'Sense perception is our messenger, but Intellect is our king'.[9]

The Idealists took over the idea of revelation as the *presupposition* of reason from the counter-Enlightenment thinkers like Hamann and Jacobi but maintaining the Enlightenment's concern for the *rational justification* of religion. The positivism of the Socinians and the semi-Socinians is the theological context of Coleridge's distinction between reason and understanding and it explains why Coleridge uses the term reason to mean both the realm of the ideas transcending the finite mind, and the ideas as immanent in human thought. When he writes of the practical or speculative reason Coleridge means the immanent reason. Reason *itself* is neither speculative nor practical; it consists of the thoughts of God in which the 'essences of all things co-exist in all their distinctions yet as one and indivisible' (*F* i. 516). Human beings have a limited capacity to contemplate the essence of reality. The understanding can only judge phenomena from which it can form generalisations. Yet by virtue of reason humanity can attain truths which are not sensory. These truths are occasioned by experience but are not objects of

---

[6] Eriugena is worth mentioning in this context. He saw the world as an indirect disclosure of God – as theophany. The self-disclosure of being is for Eriugena a profoundly religious revelation. Two articles by Werner Beierwaltes are very informative on the Neoplatonic background and presuppositions of this favourite of Coleridge: 'Negative affirmation: world as metaphor' in *Dionysius* 1 (1977), pp. 127–59 and 'The revaluation of John Scottus Eriugena in German Idealism' in *The Mind of Eriugena*, edited by J. O'Meara and L. Bieler (Dublin: Irish University Press, 1973).

[7] See Beierwaltes, *Platonismus und Idealismus*, pp. 93–100.

[8] Goethe, *Gespräche*, vol. ii. p. 245, cited by Hadot, *Plotinus*, p. 63 n. 25. On the Neoplatonic metaphysics of light see Beierwaltes, 'Plotins Metaphysik des Lichtes' in *Die Philosophie des Neuplatonismus*, edited by Clemens Zintzen (Darmstadt: Wissenschaftliche Gesellschaft, 1977), pp. 75–117.

[9] Plotinus, *Treatise* v. 3 (49) 3, 45–6.

experience; they are rather the very conditions which phenomenal appearances require in order to form a law-like intelligible structure. The basic principles of religion, ethics, physics, and mathematics are known a priori by virtue of the mind's inner light and based upon intuitive evidence.

Let us return to the repeated polemic in *Aids to Reflection* aimed at William Paley. We have argued for the position that Paley appears characteristically Socinian. We shall see that he presents a forensic approach to the question of the validity of Christianity in the sense that he emphasises miracles as *proofs* of revelation. Yet he also employs the argument 'to' design which shows his debt to rational natural theology. This is most famously the case in his work *Natural Theology*.

In crossing a heath, suppose I pitched my foot against a *stone*, and were asked how the stone came to be there: I might possibly answer, that for any thing I knew to the contrary, it had lain there for ever: nor would it perhaps be very easy to shew the absurdity of this answer. But suppose I had found a *watch* upon the ground, and it should be inquired how the watch happened to be in that place; I should hardly think of the answer which I had before given, that, for any thing I knew, the watch might have always been there. Yet why should not this answer serve for the watch as well as for the stone? . . . For this reason, and for no other, viz. that, when we come to inspect the watch, we perceive (what we could not discover in the stone) that its several parts are framed and put together for a purpose.[10]

Paley argues in *Natural Theology* that the beauties of biology lead one to infer rationally a designer; a thought which has an obvious precedent in Romans 1: 20 where St Paul states that God's 'invisible nature' has been 'clearly perceived' in the visible created realm: if we consider a watch we can see a relationship of instrument and goal; the component parts are so constructed that it keeps time. If we compare this with an eye we can also see evidence of contrivance, only at a much greater degree.

The marks of *design* are too strong to be gotten over. Design must have a designer. That designer must have been a person. That person is GOD.[11]

Coleridge swiftly rehearses the most sophisticated objections to Paley's *Natural Theology*; he remarks that the (so-called) demonstrations of a God either prove too little or too much (*Aids*, pp. 184–5). Here he seems to be thinking of Hume's Philo objection that the

---

[10] Paley, *Works*, vol. iii. p. 3.   [11] Paley, *Works*, vol. iii. p. 260.

analogy between the universe and human productions is too weak, because we cannot infer from an imperfect world to a perfect designer.[12] 'Too much' may be a reference to the argument of Cleanthes against Demea that if there must be a necessary being, this item could be the physical cosmos.[13] Coleridge further objects to the sleight of hand: in arguing from perceived purpose in the world, a designer is implictly presupposed (*Aids*, p. 185). Finally he makes the Kantian objection that the 'cosmological' argument or that from the 'order in nature' presupposes the Ontological[14] insofar as the necessary objectivity of the idea of God is assumed.

Coleridge's attacks upon Paley are often cited approvingly as an instance of Coleridge's refusal to follow Paley's arid and desiccated rationalism. Here, it has been suggested, is clearly Romantic frustration with the Age of Reason. Yet if one puts aside this cliché, the issue becomes rather more complex. Firstly, Paley's lucid exposition encourages such commentators to give very short shrift to his formulation of the design argument. This is to underestimate the force and influence of his argument;[15] often based on the premise that Hume's critique of natural theology is so devastating that Paley was foolish to rehearse precisely the arguments which Hume had exposed. Much depends, however, on how much force one attributes to Hume, and the plausibility of Philo's Epicurean suggestion that the appearance of order might be created through 'unguided matter' over time.[16] As we shall see, Coleridge rejects this idea as resolutely as Paley. He is just as convinced as Paley that nature reflects intelligence.

If we tend to sympathise with Coleridge on the issue of evidences this is perhaps largely through Darwin's influence; we have a theory which broadly explains the adaptation of organs to particular ends – the production of organs is now understood as the means by which an organism can adapt and survive within a particular environment. Not all organisms are successful in adapting to their environment, and that successful adaptation might appear as the benevolent contrivance of the designer is the result of the gradual extermination of the weaker species and the survival of the stronger species.

[12] Hume, *Principal Writings*, p. 69.   [13] Ibid., p. 92.

[14] Kant, *Critique of Pure Reason*, A603, B631.

[15] J. T. Baldwin, 'God and the world: William Paley's argument from perfection, a continuing influence' in *Harvard Theological Review* 85 (1992), pp. 109–20.

[16] Hume, *Principal Writings*, p. 86.

Coleridge's language of 'All things strive to ascend, and ascend in their striving'[17] (*Aids*, p. 118) sounds akin to evolutionary theory; yet 'evolutionary' theory is perhaps a misnomer inasmuch as it implies progression. If the adaptation required for survival is determined by random factors rather than guiding providence, it may involve a reduction of capacities and coarsening of the organism's sensibility. Coleridge is entirely out of sympathy with the conviction that species could 'evolve' by blind change, and would perceive the idea as a contradiction in terms.[18]

The teleological argument has lost much of its intuitive force, but it is one of the more attractive of the traditional arguments for theism. It is also of Platonic lineage. In the tenth book of his *Laws* Plato argues from the beauty and order of the cosmic motions to a mover which is a perfectly good soul; here we find effectively a combination of what Kant calls the cosmological and the teleological argument, and this argument is developed by Aristotle and Cicero.[19] Although both Hume and Kant criticise the design argument, they both treat the 'proof' with respect. Hume believes that a 'purpose, an intention, a design strikes everywhere the most careless, the most stupid thinker' and Kant sees this as the oldest, clearest, and most reasonable of the arguments for the existence of God (*Kritik der reinen Vernunft* A623/ B651). Without a plausible substitute in the form of evolutionary theory, and in the light of the compelling nature of the argument, it is difficult to understand Coleridge's hostility. Yet, although Coleridge does not present a demonstration for God's existence on the basis of 'evidence' of contrivance, he produces some very interesting Platonic-Kantian reflections about the fact that we are able to construct highly sophisticated theories about the universe and seem thereby to perceive a high degree of order. In this way he wishes to cast doubt upon Hume's Epicurean conviction that the cosmos is probably the result of random motion rather than guiding intelligence.

Hume, in his *Dialogues Concerning Natural Religion* (1779), gave grounds for scepticism concerning the metaphysical significance of the idea of divine workmanship. The whole of natural theology,

[17] There may be a hint of Plotinus: 'all things aspire to contemplation', *Ennead*, iii. 8 (30) 1.1.
[18] G. R. Potter, 'Coleridge and the idea of evolution' in *Proceedings of the Modern Languages Association* 40 (1925), pp. 379–97. For Coleridge's thought on 'nature' see T. H. Levere, *Poetry Realized in Nature: Samuel Taylor Coleridge and Early Nineteenth Century Science* (Cambridge University Press, 1971) and R. Modiano, *Coleridge and the Concept of Nature* (London: Macmillan, 1985).
[19] M. J. Charlesworth, *Philosophy of Religion: the Historic Approaches* (London: Macmillan, 1972).

Hume argues, rests upon the thought that the cause of order in the universe bears some, probably remote, analogy to the human mind. It may be natural for men to project their own values into the universe, but we have no reason for thinking these projections true. Consider the idea that a spider spun the world out of its web. This seems ridiculous to us because a spider is a small contemptible creature, but for a world inhabited exclusively by spiders, this would be a very natural belief. The centre of Hume's attack is the idea that it is irrational to deem *thought*, this 'little agitation of the brain', the model of the universe.[20] Coleridge's Idealism is based upon the idea that thought is not merely a 'little agitation of the brain' but the structural principle of the universe. He writes:

> One question would occur to every reflecting hearer. Pray would this THEOLOGICAL spider have the power of DOUBTING its perception and conclusion? If so, and if the spider be but a nickname for a rational Being . . . and . . . means no more than a serious sober man arguing in defence of his Maker, must there not be . . . some power, call IT, with Lord Bacon the 'LUMEN SICCUM'; OR 'the pure light', with LORD HERBERT; CALL IT 'REASON', or call it the Faith OF Reason (WITH KANT), must there not be some power that stands in human nature but in some participation of the eternal and universal by which man is enabled to question, nay to contradict, the irresistable impressions of his own senses, NAY the necessary deductions of his own understanding – to CHALLENGE and disqualify them, as partial and INCOMPETENT? (*PL*, p. 374)

Coleridge believes that the distinction between the understanding as the adaptive power of mankind and reason as the divine light or Logos provides the only possible response to Hume's theological spider; Paley's mistake lies in inferring from the facts of the human understanding to a designer God, while preserving an epistemology suprisingly close to Hume.[21] A deeper scrutiny of the nature of human knowledge reveals a much deeper and more effective answer to Hume's scepticism: the distinction between reason and understanding. Coburn quotes a note on the distinction between reason as 'Anthropomorph partaking of the Divine: the Understanding as Anthromorph, *partaken* of by inferior animals vide Huber on Bees: and *ditto on Ants*' (*PL*, p. 461). This is illuminated by the long passages in *Aids to Reflection* about animal instinct and the understanding.

---

[20] Hume, *Principal Writings*, p. 50.
[21] See N. Hitchin: 'Paley continued to accept a modified form of Hume's epistemological position', 'Probability and the Word of God', p. 403.

These are not absent-minded forays into abstruse scientific investigation of the age, but constitute the heart of Coleridge's argument in *Aids to Reflection*. Serious reflection upon human thought and behaviour will not, Coleridge thinks, lend weight to the Enlightenment criticism of a Trinitarian religion as an edifice of corruption and a vestige of superstition, and the commonplace Hanoverian dismissal of communion of the soul with the divine as 'enthusiasm'. Reflection on these matters, rather, will support the vision of God as not just the goal of human thought and endeavour but its initiator and sustainer. A theology of evidences for a designer is intellectually truncated; adequate evidence for religion must be adduced, Coleridge thinks, not from items in the natural world, but from the nature of the *spirit* as a reflection of the eternal Logos.

The doctrine of 'ideas' or 'forms' is usually perceived as the centre of Platonic philosophy. However, it is quite misleading to think of the 'ideas' in those terms dictated by Aristotle's famous 'third man' criticism or medieval disputes about universals and particulars. The traditional Platonist is often insouciant about questions of the classification of genera and species or inferences from specific items of perception to abstract terms. The abiding concern is the relation of the soul to God, and the significance of the 'theory of ideas' for Cudworth or Coleridge is as a doctrine about the communion of the finite mind with God.

The Christian (Neo-)Platonic doctrine is simply that sensible objects are reflections of the intelligible world which is the mind of God: 'a mind before the world, and senior to all things; no ectypal, but archetypal thing, which comprehended in it, as a kind of intellectual world, the paradigm or platform, according to which this sensible world was made'.[22] Cudworth, like most of the living Platonic tradition, has little interest in questions about abstract objects of knowledge; the 'ideas' are primarily the causal source of the objects of the phenomenal world. This 'causality' is not temporal, nor is it a relation between events, in the sense of Hume's or Kant's theory. It is a twofold nexus between a maker and the thing made; a relation of participation whereby the effect is conceived as an inferior likeness or reflection of its cause, and the effect or likeness is dependent upon its source.[23]

---

[22] Cudworth, *True Intellectual System*, vol. iii. p. 65.
[23] See Taylor, 'Theism' in *Religion and Ethics*, pp. 266 ff.

The central idea is that the physical world is transitory and ephemeral, and that dissatisfaction with the empirical realm drives the mind to look beyond the shadows of the cave. The world which is apprehended by the senses possesses no inherent independence, and it is not self-explanatory. Hume attempts to defuse the intuition that the world must be dependent upon a transcendent self-explanatory maker by arguing that though each part of nature may be dependent upon other parts, taken as a whole nature is self-explanatory. But this is an odd position. Our universe could have been very different if the same laws of nature were combined with somewhat different physical facts. The emergence of conscious life, for example, required certain laws and certain initial conditions. There are a large number of possible universes which lack the complexity required in order to produce conscious life. Is it not a reasonable question to ask why the universe contains sufficient nomological order and complexity to produce such intelligence?

Hume seems more plausible when he argues that this is not a reasonable question, and we should accept the world as brute fact. But science has been inspired by the desire to look beyond brute facts and perceive intelligible law-like structures. We naturally think of reality in terms of a scale of being: hallucinations; perceptual experiences; scientific laws; all represent ascending degrees of what counts as 'real'. Furthermore, since explanatory power and simplicity constitute evidence for ascertaining reality rather than appearance, it is a reasonable presumption that since we seek unified explanatory structures, there is a corresponding unity in reality. Theism conceives of the transcendent source of this unity as a perfect self explanatory being. The idea that the supreme being is both necessary and perfect is rooted in the intuitively plausible assocation of inferiority with dependence. A machine that is dependent upon little or very cheap fuel seems obviously better than an otherwise analogous machine which is dependent for sustenance upon far more resources. If we accept that the idea of a chain of being is a natural conception of reality, it is short step to conceiving it as the Platonist does, as a hierarchy of excellence in which superiority is marked by relative independence, and supreme reality by absolute freedom from external constraint or dependence.

One might suggest that such considerations are sterile abstractions, but for Coleridge they have profound religious significance.

He believes that the very consciousness of human finitude is the indication that this finitude has been transcended; if our human condition was just the Humean state of forming beliefs through instinct, habit, and custom – if we were entirely finite, we would not be aware of our finitude as such. The very fact that we consider the world as limited and dependent presupposes an intelligible world: the divine Logos. As much as Nietzsche, Coleridge thinks that the desire for truth beyond utility is closely bound to a sense of human weakness, and the inadequacy of merely human self-reliance. But, whereas Nietzsche thought this deplorable, Coleridge thought it the basis of the unity of religion and true philosophy. Knowledge, on his theory, is only possible inasmuch as phenomenal stimuli provoke the finite mind into conscious communion with the divine mind; a communion which is only possible because of a fundamental kinship of the finite and infinite mind. Hence epistemology involves theology.

THE FAITH OF SCIENCE

The difference between the ideas and the conceptions of the understanding, between reason and understanding is, for Coleridge, radical. The understanding is discursive whereas reason is fixed, the understanding appeals to another faculty whereas reason appeals to itself. Reason illuminates and regenerates the understanding. Coleridge's intent is anti-nominalist and anti-Socinian: he wishes to demonstrate that the human understanding differs from animal understanding or instinct precisely on account of the *illuminating* and *regenerating* effect of the divine reason. In short, Coleridge wishes to show that human knowledge worthy of the name is derived neither from sense nor from the operations of the finite mind but from God (cf. *F* i. 515–16). He is scathing about the bigotry of that 'faithless and loveless spirit of fear which plunged Galileo into a Prison' (*Aids*, p. 245) or even the idolatry which burnt Bruno at the stake (*Aids*, p. 400) for alleged atheism. Coleridge insists that the 'Mistakes of scientific men have never injured Christianity, while every new truth discovered by them has either added to its evidence, or prepared the mind for its reception' (*Aids*, p. 245).

Philosophers have traditionally attributed knowledge to three different sources: sensory experience, mind or God. This is to say that knowledge may be:

A read off from the world;
B read into the world;
C revealed from a transcendent source: ideas or God.[24]

'A' is unsatisfactory because in science often the conclusions extend far beyond the given data and the gap is difficult to straddle by empiricist means. The second possibility, 'B', explains how the gap between the data and the conclusions might be overcome, but this cannot explain our confidence in the employment of relatively simple laws in our theory construction. 'C' would explain how the observation of regularities can lead to the acceptance of laws: they depend upon a capacity to imagine intelligible structure. Coleridge expounds 'C', and this adherence to 'C' can be illuminated by considering his attitude to two of the great British empiricists, Hume and Bacon, on the issue of induction.

Hume sees himself as developing a programme which was inaugurated by Bacon 'and some late philosophers in *England*, who have begun to put the science of man on a new footing, and have engaged the attention, and excited the curiosity of the public'.[25] Hume states proudly that whatever the achievements of other nations, England has a supremacy in reason and philosophy through the Baconic philosophy.

Coleridge's reaction is a reflection upon the enormously high ratio of rational to empirical grounds for theoretical advances in the physical sciences like Newton's theory of gravitation. Coleridge sees the possibility of science as evidence of the mind's ability to imagine hidden forms of order and thereby to achieve results.[26] This is evidence of an affinity between mind and reality which cannot be explained in terms of the Humean constraints of custom, habit, and instinct. Such factors may help explain how an animal responds to its environment; but humanity differs from the animal kindom in its capacity to shape its own environment – paradigmatically through science. Here the evidence suggests that this shaping activity has theoretical origins: Galileo, Copernicus, and Kepler were all more or less influenced by Neoplatonism and the conviction that the real order of reality transcends the senses and is a mathematical harmony. Science should discover simple, elegant mathematical relations through which the many can be understood in terms of

[24] R. C. S. Walker, *Kant* (London: Routledge, 1978), p. 174.
[25] Hume, *Treatise*, xvii.
[26] Thomas Nagel, *The View from Nowhere* (Oxford University Press, 1986), pp. 82–6.

underlying unities. Copernicus did not simply 'observe' that the earth is a planet, but combined this observation with a particular theory, which itself was metaphysically inspired:[27] Coleridge is fond of the Platonic assumption that geometers copy the intelligible archetype of figures within their minds.[28] Their knowledge is essentially intuitive and, according to Platonic tradition, god-like – Plato was reported to claim that 'God is always doing geometry.'[29] Coleridge mentions Bacon in association with the Pythagorean Kepler (*Aids*, pp. 75, 243) or refers to the 'Genius of Kepler' which was 'expanded and organized in the soul of Newton' (*Aids*, p. 401), the Kepler who argued that the universe is a geometrical harmony for 'the Creator, who is the very source of geometry and, as Plato wrote, "practices eternal geometry," does not stray from his archetype'.[30] Long before Thomas Kuhn's *The Structure of Scientific Revolutions* Coleridge made the very interesting observation that epoch-forming revolutions have coincided with the 'rise and fall of metaphysical systems' (*LS*, p. 15). Coleridge, however, is not interested in the paradigm shifts of such epochs, but the fact that man can modify his environment through his theory building, through his imagination, and that an intelligent and ethically conscious creature who can make and mould his environment, rather than being made by it, can barely be explained as the product of nature. Once this irrefutable fact about the will, or man's spiritual nature, grounded in

---

[27] E. A. Burtt, *The Metaphysical Foundations of Modern Science* (New York: Doubleday, 1955), pp. 36–71 and A. Koestler, *The Sleepwalkers* (Harmondsworth: Penguin, 1968), pp. 201 ff. and 394 ff.

[28] Plato, *Euthydemus*, 290c and *Republic*, 527a, b.

[29] *Plutarch's Moralia*, translated by P. Clement and H. B. Hoffleit (Cambridge, Mass.: Harvard University Press, 1986), vol. ix. p. 119.

[30] J. Kepler, 'The harmonies of the world' in *Great Books of the Western World*, edited by M. J. Adler (Chicago: Encyclopaedia Britannica, 1992), vol. xv. p. 1017. Coleridge's use of the Pythagorean tetractys is a clear sign of his Platonism and his avowal of intuitive-geometrical vision as the paradigm of knowledge. In Plato's most Pythagorean dialogue *Timaeus* (31a, 32c) the demiurge forms the universe out of *four* elements. Pythagoras was the founder of the tetractys which, as Spitzer points out, 'was associated by legend with the Apollonian oracle at Delphi. Inasmuch as it explained the laws of heavenly and earthly music, the tetractys was the key to the laws of nature; inasmuch as it made possible the imitation of divine, it permitted man to approach divine perfection, hence its moral, religious, "cathartic" aspect.' Spitzer, *World Harmony*, p. 67. The passage concerning the Pythagorean tetractys (*Aids*, pp. 178–82) starts with a reference to the Delphic Oracle, 'the Scire teipsum', and argues from the nature of mind to logical, chemical and ultimate theological issues in the footnote about subject and object – notoriously a Coleridgean topic. The classic account of the geometrical mysticism in the Christian Platonic tradition is Mahnke, *Unendliche Sphäre*. For Coleridge's appropriation see Uehlein, *Manifestation des Selbstbewußtseins*, pp. 121–5.

the divine reason is established, the rest of nature, the various stages of the universe, the earth, and prehuman life, can be seen as part of a general purposiveness in the cosmos, which culminates in mankind.

The first mistake of empiricism, for Coleridge, is the sensualism which cannot accommodate the fact that our theories about reality are underdetermined by the senses. The dependence of the understanding as proximate or adaptive intelligence upon reason is evinced by the Newtonian as opposed to the Ptolemaic system (*Aids*, p. 236). Coleridge believes that inductive reasoning is quite untenable as the *bulwark* of empiricism. Induction (Latin *inductio*) is a rendering of Aristotle's ἐπαγωγή and is the process of reasoning from the observance of particular instances to a general law or principle. The arguing from the particular to the general reveals, Coleridge thinks, how the adaptive intelligence which mankind shares with the animal kingdom must be *illuminated* by transcendent reason. Francis Bacon (1561–1626) whom Coleridge calls 'the British Plato', writes that the goal of science is the discovery of forms – hidden essences: 'the form of a thing is the very thing itself, and the thing differs from the form no otherwise than as the apparent differs from the real'.[31] Furthermore, Bacon insists that 'the power of man cannot possibly be emancipated and freed from the common course of nature, and expanded and exalted to new efficients and new modes of operation, except by the revelation and the discovery of Forms of this kind'.[32] The thought that the forms are revealed and that this revelation is the condition of human knowledge determines Coleridge's unusual interpretation of Bacon. Indeed, induction for Coleridge is a central argument for his *Platonic* view of science and he even describes Lord Bacon as 'the great Restorer of the genuine Platonic Logic, viz Progress by Induction' (*Notebook* i. 457–8; see also *CL* v. 15). This picture of Bacon is rather counter-intuitive – not least because it flies in the face of Bacon's avowed hostility to Plato. Yet, notwithstanding this polemic, when Bacon contrasts the 'idols of the mind' and the 'ideas' of the divine he seems to be toying with the Platonic resonances of the words 'ideas' and 'idols'.[33]

[31] Bacon, *Works*, vol. iv. p. 137.
[32] Bacon, *New Organon* in his *Works*, vol. iv. p. 17.
[33] Stephen Clark puts it: 'The death of God is the death of scientific realism.' *God's World*, p. 216.

Perhaps rather more significantly, Bacon represents for Coleridge the shift from authority to experience. Scholasticism began with revealed truth and argued from general principles to particular tenets; those facts which did not fit in with revealed or general principles were rejected. Such a scholastic approach to knowledge uses deductive logic as its primary tool. Baconian science uses experience rather than logic as its foundation. The Cambridge Platonists rejected Protestant scholasticism and emphasised the Platonic theology in which a progressive dynamic revelation of the logos played a central role: 'every Art & science must come furnished with some praecognita, and theology not from meer Speculation which is usher'd in by syllogisms and Demonstrations; but that which springs forth from true Goodness'.[34] Cudworth's stepfather supported Bacon's *Instauratio Magna*, and the Platonists were a central element of the broadly Baconian climate of mid-seventeenth-century England:

Because of their great personal reputations, important academic positions, and the long lasting influence of their writings, the Platonists were one of the most important formative influences on English natural philosophy in the second half of the seventeenth century. Cambridge graduates ranging in stature from Newton and Ray to Power and Hall, were noticeably susceptible to Platonic philosophy.[35]

Coleridge's enthusiasm for Bacon is in harmony with his admiration for seventeenth-century England, and of course Immanuel Kant used a passage from Bacon's *Instauratio Magna* as his motto for the *Critique of Pure Reason*.[36] Coleridge's appeal to Bacon serves the rhetorically powerful end of employing the great hero of his opponents. Bacon was a hero for the French Enlightenment, and Coleridge's reclaiming him for Platonism is quite consciously provocative.[37]

Hume is one of those philosophers who saw themselves as pursuing the Baconian paradigm and developing the implications of

[34] Smith, *Discourses*, p. 1.

[35] Webster, *The Great Instauration: Science, Medicine and Reform 1626–1660* (London: Duckworth, 1973), p. 145. The Moravian philosopher-theologian John Amos Comenius is a good instance of a Platonic enthusiasm for natural science and the Royal Society. cf. Johann Amos Comenius, *Der Weg des Lichtes. Via Lucis*, edited by Uwe Voigt (Hamburg: Meiner, 1997). The text *Via Lucis* was consciously aimed at the English Parliament and presented to the Royal Society.

[36] Schelling, by way of contrast, speaks of 'the corruption of philosophy by Bacon'. See his *Ideas for a Philosophy of Nature*, p. 52.

[37] A. Quinton, *Francis Bacon* (Oxford University Press, 1980), pp. 79–80.

the new philosophy. On Hume's account our beliefs have little justification apart from the fact that we have formed them. We have, on Hume's theory, spread our beliefs on to the world under natural pressures, and we tend to see them as corresponding to a reality which is essentially independent of mind. Philosophical reflection, Hume thinks, leads us to see the gap between beliefs and reality as bridged by little more than instinct. What we unreflectively assume to be the uniformity of nature is in fact no more than the projection of these universal laws on to the world on the basis of a small sample. Hume's example of the sun rising is a classic instance.[38] This is an instance of the general problem of inferring a general principle from particular instances. We cannot prove any principle by criteria which assume the validity of the principle in question. Hume's solution was to appeal to custom and instinct in problems such as induction. But this had the rather paradoxical result that Hume – whose intent was to introduce experimental reasoning into the moral sciences – subverted the very principles of science.

The model of the mind as lamp cannot capture the epistemological requirement of objectivity: it gives an account of how we might form our beliefs but it leaves mysterious the fact of their truth.[39] The fact that the mind in science can perceive patterns far in excess of the limited observational material available to it suggests to Coleridge that Hume's lamp model of the mind is too weak. What is required is the mind as mirror – not the empiricist mirror which passively reflects nature, but the Platonic mirror in which the soul perceives precisely those truths not revealed by nature: knowledge does not come from the senses, the human mind, but from *God* – 'this knowledge being a true heavenly fire kindled from God's own Altar', in John Smith's phrase.[40]

The student must realise, claims Coleridge, that Hume's scepticism was not about the relation of cause and effect in nature: 'What Hume doubted was the *necessity* of the connection between A and

[38] D. Hume, *An Enquiry Concerning Human Understanding* in *Enquiries Concerning Human Understanding and Concerning the Principles of Morals*, third edition, edited by P. H. Niddich (Oxford: Clarendon, 1975), pp. 25–6.

[39] M. H. Abrams' celebrated account of the change from Augustan to Romantic modes of thought as the paradigm shift from the mirror to the lamp in *The Mirror and the Lamp* (New York and Oxford: Clarendon, 1953) is misleading for just this reason. Considered as philosophers Hume is the philosopher of the lamp (the projectionist) and Coleridge as the Platonic idealist, is the philosopher of the mirror.

[40] Smith, *Discourses*, p. 21.

any given B not included in A, as a necessity of reason and insight' (*Logic*, p. 191). For Coleridge, Hume's account makes science quite inexplicable. Knowledge cannot be explained as the instinct-induced projection of beliefs because this ignores the *volitional* element without which science would be barely intelligible. Coleridge is striking a raw nerve of empiricism. As Michael Ayers states with respect to John Locke: 'Paradoxically enough, empiricism is notoriously weak in its philosophy of experiment. If the rationality of our expectations and general beliefs derives entirely from past experience, why should we bother to be selective about the experiences we are about to have?'[41] Coleridge's argument is that facts cannot 'give birth to' principles. He claims:

unless you had a Principle of selection, why did you take notice of those particular Facts. You must have a Lantern in your hand to give light; otherwise all the materials in the world are useless, for you can neither find them, and if you could, you could not arrange them.

. . . Then what do you say to Bacon's Induction? This – that it is *not* what is now a days so called, but which is in fact *De*duction only. (*TT* i. 192)

The very fact that the understanding seeks laws of simplicity and elegance suggests a higher purposiveness which is entirely neglected by Hume's account. Reason, Coleridge wishes to argue, endows our thinking with the METHOD of the will (*F* i. 523) and this is the elevation of the spirit above the semblances of custom and senses to a world of spirit (*F* i. 524). Bacon's induction begins with the '*prudens quaestio*' (the forethoughtful query) which he affirms to be the prior half of the knowledge sought, '*dimidium scientiae*'. If we ask what gives birth to this *quaestio*, Coleridge avers that Bacon's answer is the *Lux Intellectus* – the influence of reason freed from the idols and freed from the passions and distortions of the human understanding, and in particular the inordinate pride which leads men to think that the forms of the reflective faculty constitute the measure of both nature and God.

Science means having a method or path towards the truth ('A PRINCIPLE OF UNITY WITH PROGRESSION', *F* i. 476), and the possibility of progression on this path presupposes the ability of the mind to ask questions and form theories which transcend radically the available sense data. Bacon's philosophy, for Coleridge, like that of Plato, exemplifies the art of method by awakening self-development. Just as the dialectic in Plato means the scrutiny and purging of

[41] M. Ayers, *Locke, Epistemology and Ontology* (London: Routledge, 1991), vol. ii. p. 159.

the mind's habitual errors, and the awakening of the germinal power of the soul to contemplate the ideas, this process is one of gradual and painstaking enlightenment. The mind must be purged of its natural attachments to a false reality and awakened to its kinship with the divine; a process of detachment and reorientation. From a different but logically related angle, it is of note that the twentieth-century expert on mysticism Baron von Hügel has referred to science as an 'instrument and channel of purification and detachment',[42] in particular in combating the natural egotism of religion itself which often fondly imagines that the universe is made for human ends.

Coleridge is convinced that the philosophy of Bacon is closer to the spirit of Platonic thought than the more fantastic Platonism of the Italian Renaissance 'enthusiasts' because his philosophy explicitly disavows crude empiricism. Bacon writes:

the true method of experience . . . first lights the candle, and then by means of the candle shows the way; commencing as it does with experience duly ordered and digested, and from it educing axioms against new experiments, even as it was not without order and method that the divine word operated upon the created mass.[43]

The image is Christian: the candle-light of experimental science is the attempt to pursue the intelligible Word, the light of the world, in creation. Bacon insists that the divine mind has graciously allowed us to follow in the pattern of his word: 'the divine wisdom and order must be our pattern'.[44]

A key factor is also the relation between theoretical and practical reason. The attempt to purify the mind is an ascetic endeavour – a discipline. The title of Bacon's work *Instauratio Magna* refers to the consecration of Solomon's temple. Bacon claims to be 'founding a holy temple' in his renewal of the human understanding. The association of renewal or regeneration with cleansing is important for Coleridge; Bacon writes of the need

to approach with humility and veneration, to unroll the volume of Creation, to linger and meditate therein, and with minds washed clean from opinions to study it in purity and integrity.[45]

---

[42] Baron Friedrich von Hügel, *The Mystical Element of Religion as studied in Saint Catherine of Genoa and her Friends*, second edition (London: Dent and Sons; New York: Dutton and Co., 1927), p. 380.

[43] Bacon, *Works*, vol. iv. p. 81.   [44] Ibid., vol. viii. p. 101.

[45] Ibid., vol. v. pp. 132–3.

Experimentation is rooted not so much in the brutal mastery of nature as in the humility of the human mind.[46] Method consists of grounding intellectual progress on sound principles, and this is a process of purification. Bacon often speaks of the spiritual nature of science and the *Instauratio* concludes with a prayer to God to protect the work which came from his goodness and returns to 'thy glory'.[47]

In a letter to Wordsworth Coleridge speaks of the necessity of a revolution in *disciplining* the human mind in order to recognise the difference in kind between the self-conscious rational mind and merely instinctive intelligence (*CL* iv. 575). Coleridge wishes to show that the scientific and practical progress of mankind has its roots in the self-subjection to the light of reason in which the 'Will of the individual, the *particular* will, has become a Will of Reason, the man is regenerate' (*Aids*, p. 217). Bacon uses the language of *renewal* quite explicitly: the great instauration which Bacon demands of science is a regeneration which is attained by *purifying* the mind from its idols. The antitheses between darkness and light, blindness and vision, sleep and wakefulness, are biblical (and Platonic) metaphors. The Christian imagery of awakening, illumination, and rebirth is quite central in Bacon's prose.

God hath framed the mind of man as a mirror or glass capable of the image of the universal world, and joyful to receive the impression thereof, as the eye joyeth to receive light; and not only delighted in beholding the variety of things and vicissitude of times, but raised also to find out and discern the ordinances and decrees which through all these changes are infallibly observed.[48]

The natural state of the human mind is not that of an 'equal and clear glass' wherein the beams of things should reflect according to their true incidence but an 'enchanted glass' which distorts the truth unless it is 'delivered and reduced'.[49] Bacon in the *Novum Organum* rejects the idea that the 'sense of the mind of man is the measure of things'.[50] Rather, the 'human Understanding is like a false mirror, which, receiving rays irregularly, distorts and discolours the nature

---

[46] Bacon, *Works*, vol. v. p. 132–3.   [47] Bacon, *Works*, vol. viii. p. 53.
[48] Bacon, *Works*, vol. iii. p. 265.   [49] Bacon, *Works*, vol. iii. p. 395.
[50] Consider Protagoras' famous sophistical (in both senses of the word) tenet 'πάντων χρημάτων μέτρον ἄνθρωπος', man is the measure of all things, and Plato's retort that, for us God is the measure of all things: 'Ὁ θεὸς ἡμῖν πάντων χρημάτων μέτρον.' Plato, *Laws*, 716c.

of things by mingling its own nature with it'.[51] Bacon thinks that this natural state of distortion must not be adjusted but *renewed*. This is great renewal, an INSTAURATIO MAGNA. Left to itself, the mind is full of errors: it must be purged and renewed.

Coleridge would have agreed with Nietzsche that the faith of science is essentially a metaphysical faith shared by Plato and Christianity, that God is truth.[52] It is the belief in its metaphysical value which gives the ascetic ideal its power. The metaphysical and ascetic ideal stand or fall together. Bacon reveals, Coleridge thinks (and Bacon, he avers, is akin to Plato here), that our knowledge – no less than the moral life – is based not upon a mere accommodation of facts but upon the *renewal* of the mind itself. Coleridge writes:

Most truly . . . does our immortal Verulam teach – that the human understanding, 'ipsa sua natura radios ex figura et sectione propria immutat': that our understanding not only reflects the objects *subjectively*, that is, substitutes for the inherent laws and properties of the objects the relations which the objects bear to its own particular constitution; but that in all its conscious presentations and reflexes, it is itself only a phaeno-menon of the inner sense, and requires the same corrections as the appearances transmitted by the outer senses. But that there is potentially, if not actually, in every rational being, a somewhat, call it what you will, the pure reason, spirit, lumen siccum . . . and that in this are to be found the indispensable conditions of all science. (*F* i. 490–1)

On the basis of such a passage one can see why Coleridge calls the understanding the faculty of reflection, because it reflects the rays of the *lumen siccum*, or *lumen intellectus*.

And it is not only the right but the possible nature of the human mind, to which it is capable of being restored . . . There is a sublime truth contained in his favourite phrase – Idola Intellectus. He tells us that the mind of man is an edifice not built with human hands, which needs only be purged of its idols and idolatrous services to become the temple of the true and living Light. (*F* i. 491)

Method in Bacon is the 'discipline' by which the human mind is purified from its idols and raised to the contemplation of ideas, based upon the deep and solemn conviction in the necessary role of this 'guiding light', in the aids, as it were, of the divine spirit, and the possibility of the purification and renewal of natural understanding:

that grand prerogative of our nature, A HUNGRING [*sic*] AND THIRSTING

---

[51] Bacon, *Works*, vol. iv. p. 54.
[52] F. Nietzsche, *On the Genealogy of Morals*, pp. 153 ff.

AFTER TRUTH, as the appropriate end of our intelligential, and its point of union with, our moral nature; but therefore after truth, that must be found within us before it can be *intelligibly* reflected back on the mind from without, and a religious regard to which is indispensable, both a guide and object to the just formation of the human BEING (*F* i. 495)

This is in the spirit of Augustine's claim: 'Where I found truth, there I found my God, who is the truth itself' (*Confessions* x. §24).[53] The guide and object for the just formation of the human being is the *lumen siccum*: if man stands poised between the sensible and intelligible realms, his true being lies *above* not *below*. If his natural state is darkened by idols, the capacity to turn from darkness to light has its basis in divine grace, in the guiding light of the divine spirit.

In his *Philosophical Lectures* Coleridge sees Bacon as proposing a meditation upon the laws which reason reveals to man; the scientist is awaiting the correspondence of laws to ideas (*PL*, p. 333). This concentration within 'our spirits' is an act of the will which mirrors the spiritual act or will which lies at the basis of nature: in order to arrive at truth the scientist must first go within himself and discover there the energy which informs the material universe. This is the true Baconic philosophy which sees nature as the mirror of the spirit. Hence knowledge is not a matter primarily of epistemological behaviour, developing mechanisms of good belief formation, but a relationship to a particular realm: the highest knowledge is an intuitive grasp of the world as a temple of the divine. Coleridge's spiritual pupil F. J. A. Hort wrote in his Hulsean Lectures:

Not in vain said the Lord that it is the pure in heart, they whose nature has been subdued from distraction into singleness, who shall see God; or, we may add, who shall see the steps of the ladder by which we may mount to God.

The stedfast and prescient pursuit of truth is therefore itself a moral and spiritual discipline.[54]

Hort expresses Coleridge's position with particular pertinence. Knowledge as the pursuit of wisdom is pre-eminently a spiritual discipline, and the highly selective use of Bacon is supposed to point to the extent to which the *renewed will* is involved in knowledge – in the perception of the ideas. This emphasis upon the will is part of Coleridge's Kantian polemic against naturalism. Coleridge defines

---

[53] It is possibly derived from Augustine. See *Aids*, p. 107 n. 1.
[54] Hort, *Way, Truth, Life*, p. 93.

the spiritual as being not physical, and not passive. Mind cannot be identified with physical objects since the realm of objects presupposes some knower. The natural realm considered by itself is a realm of the chain of cause and effect: 'The moment we assume an Origin in Nature, a true *Beginning*, an actual First – that moment we rise *above* Nature, and are compelled to assume a *supernatural* Power' (*Aids*, p. 270). It is because of our spiritual nature that it is possible to assume a vantage-point from which to contemplate the natural realm. This provides the reason for the self-refuting nature of naturalism: if 'all is Nature' (*Aids*, p. 159) there is no freedom of the will, and if there is no freedom, there is no means of establishing truth or falsehood. If mankind really were strictly determined by natural laws – part of an inexorable flux of events and with no means of, as it were, stepping outside – there could be no science.

Such rationalism has a more religious flavour than empiricism: it is the conviction of a natural affinity between the truths of nature and the human mind which both generates and sustains the gradual development of a more and more accurate view of reality; or what William James refers to as the belief that the 'inmost nature of reality' is congenial to and harmonizes with human powers[55] – an idea which has it roots in Plato's *Meno*. The capacity of the universe to generate organisms which are capable of understanding that universe suggests an affinity or communion between the mind of man and the divine mind. As Bacon writes: 'God hath framed the mind of man as a glass capable of reflecting the image of the universal world.'[56] It suggests that we are more 'at home' in the universe than Weber's idea of disenchantment of reality through secularisation suggests.[57] As Thomas Nagel observes, it is just as irrational to believe that God does not exist because one does not want a supreme being to exist as to believe that God does exist because one wishes this to be the case.[58] Clearly there are many secular intellectuals who find the idea of some cosmic authority to be quite appalling, quite apart from any rational considerations: even though they will often claim quite adamantly to be rationalists fighting irrationalism. This is what William James is concerned to

[55] W. James, *The Will to Believe* (New York: Dover, 1956), p. 86.
[56] Bacon, *Works*, vol. iii. p. 220.
[57] T. Nagel. *The Last Word* (Oxford University Press, 1997), p. 130.
[58] Nagel, *The Last Word*, p. 130.

emphasise in his idea of the 'will to believe'. He is arguing that it is a mistake to see theism alone as a 'choice', whereas other points of view are forced upon us by virtue of sense experience and rationality. Materialism, according to James, is the choice of the barest and most abstract world as the reality par excellence, and in this way materialism attempts to exclude certain facts which are particularly characteristic of mankind and its concerns. The 'unseen order', James argues, is not a purely impersonal order but a purposeful power of which the closest analogy for us is personality. Materialism is not a doctrine about the nature of composition of the universe but a claim that there is no real moral order and purpose in it and hence that we are, as it were, 'not at home' in the universe.[59]

REASON AND REFLECTION

Kant had pointed in the right direction, in the classically Platonic manner, by meeting the Epicurean and the Pyrrhonist through 'challenging the tribunal to which they appeal' (*Aids*, p. 241). The issue at stake is not whether the mind should be seen as active or passive but the status of the 'will' in knowledge. Hume denies that the will plays a central role in knowledge. Coleridge wishes to maintain that the *will*, properly understood, is the key to scientific knowledge. The mistake of empiricism is its *abstraction*. Mankind is not a detached observer but a practical agent, and the sceptical naturalism of sensualistic empiricism is an abstract construction modelled upon the natural sciences. Not only is empiricism unable to *explain* the nature of natural science, it is rooted in lifeless abstraction. Coleridge's counter-model aims to accommodate both the transcendent and the affective or volitional element in knowledge. He sees knowledge as rooted both

1. objectively in the experience of ideas as a theophany
and
2. subjectively in the affective nature and in the will.

Once knowledge itself is seen in these terms, Coleridge thinks it is possible to see why science properly understood is an ally of religion.[60]

---

[59] James, *The Will to Believe*, pp. 63–144.
[60] One might note that Coleridge claims that the writings of the mystics 'contributed to keep alive the *heart* in the *head*; gave me an indistinct, yet stirring and working presentment, that

The understanding isolated from the divine reason is the faculty of reflection (*Aids*, p. 223), and, in order to explain the abstraction, we only need to consider firstly the correct and secondly the perverted role of the understanding.

The Understanding is

1. the principle of proximate action;
2. the mode of thinking (cf. *Aids*, p. 413; *Notebooks* iv. 5210).

The understanding as 2 is the faculty which generalises what Coleridge calls the 'notices' of the senses. The understanding then, considered exclusively as an organ of human intelligence, is the faculty by which we reflect and generalise, that is to say *abstract*. The human understanding depends upon both sense and reason. If one considers the act of perception, the process of observation depends upon three acts which draw upon sensory materials: attention, abstraction, and generalisation. This is requisite for thought, but should be guided by the awareness that the human capacity for abstraction is distorting when detached from the human personal affective nature. Our perception of reality *as* the experience of a realm of meanings is not the projection of unscientific subjective feeling upon a scientifically describable objective reality – as if one could differentiate, as Hume does, between that which we spread on the world and that which *is*.[61] The perception of reality as a web of meanings is tied up to the fact that human experience of reality is primarily personal and affective and only secondarily – given scientific abstraction – non-personal and objective.

In *A Treatise of Human Nature* Hume argues that human adaptive intelligence is identical in kind, if not in degree with animal instinct. The common defect of traditional accounts of the mind is that they assume a 'subtility and refinement of thought' which exceeds not merely animals but children and the uneducated.[62] This clearly shows the falseness, for Hume, of such systems. In 'adapting means to ends' Hume argues, animals and children, men, and even philosophers are governed by the same maxims: experimental reasoning itself, which we possess in common with animals, which is

---

all the products of the *mere* normal *reflective* faculty partook of DEATH' (*BL*, i. 152). The debt to the mystics lay in their rich, albeit often raw, appeal to experience. cf. *Aids*, pp. 236 ff.

[61] A clear and forthright modern statement of Hume's view is Simon Blackburn, *Spreading the Word* (Oxford: Clarendon, 1984), esp. pp. 210 ff.

[62] Hume, *Treatise*, p. 177.

vital for the whole conduct of life, is a species of instinct or mechanical power, that acts in us without our knowledge. In short 'Nature, by an absolute and uncontroulable necessity has determin'd us to judge as well as to breathe and feel.'[63]

Proximate or adaptive intelligence as an adaptive power is evident throughout the animal kingdom: it is the capacity to adjust to the immediate environment. This proximate intelligence is particularly evident in bees and ants and Coleridge uses examples of how these insects solve particular problems; bees can work together to build supports for a comb and ants can solve architectural difficulties. This is humbler than human engineering, but, Coleridge insists, the difference is one of degree. As problem solvers, human beings show *more* ingenuity than animals. What is lacking in the animal kingdom is not the proximate or adaptive intelligence but the capacity to contemplate ultimate ends. Coleridge insists that instinct and understanding are not antitheses. The genuine antithesis is between animal instinct and the divine ideas. Coleridge's first example is that of the caterpillar's stomach. This vital power selects and adapts the appropriate means – the vegetable congesta – for the proximate end of the sustenance of the animal. Coleridge calls this vital power *life*. A higher species of adaptive power is that of the whole animal; the caterpillar as it seeks food or lays eggs. This is *instinct*. Thirdly, he considers the contemporary scientific evidence: Hüber's narration about bees and ants; an instance of not merely animal instinct but instinctive intelligence (*Aids*, pp. 219ff.).

These are three powers of the same kind; life, instinct, and instinctive intelligence. They share the same central character; the purposes are determined by the particular organisation of the animals. There is selection, Coleridge insists, but not choice, volition *but not will* (*Aids*, p. 247). The understanding is not instinct, but it does not differ from instinct on its own merits but merely as a result of the co-existence of a higher diverse power in the same subject. Understanding is thus *adaptive* power in the form of instinctive intelligence co-existing with *reason, free will, and self-consciousness*. Understanding does not differ in kind from instinct; it differs only inasmuch as it is irradiated by the divine reason – *lumen intellectus*.

[63] Ibid., p. 183.

The most obvious instance of contemplating ultimate ends is morality. Yet also evident is the contemplative element in natural science where reason is the source of not proximate ends but 'necessary and universal Principles' (*Aids*, p. 232) by virtue of which sensory information is affirmed or denied, or as the power by which universal and necessary conclusions can be inferred from particular and contingent appearances.

The point is that highly complex instinctual procedures such as those of bees and ants are quite unlike human intelligence; the latter is not just the response to a given environment but the capacity to form and re-form that very environment. This means that the possibilities open to mankind are, compared with those of animals, quite unlimited.

Coleridge sees empiricist philosophy as unduly abstract because it only sees reason in terms of the understanding or what the scholastics called *ratio*:

Notions of the Understanding that have been generalized from *Conceptions*; which conceptions, again, are themselves generalized from objects of sense. Neither the one or the other, therefore, have any force except in application to objects of Sense and within the sphere of sensible Experience. What but absurdity can follow, if you decide on Spirit by the laws of Matter? if you judge that which, if it be at all, must be *super*-sensual, by that faculty of your mind, the very definition of which is 'the faculty judging *according* to Sense?' (*Aids*, p. 269)

The issue is particularly pertinent for Coleridge: the unity and integrity of experience. Thought, and particularly disciplined thought, demands abstraction from the flux of experience and an emphasis upon particular items of experience and excludes others. This is correct as long as one is aware of the abstraction as *partial and as serving a particular purpose*. The scientific abstract intellect is, however, only a part of what John E. Smith has called the 'concrete human situation'. He writes:

The real situation for man, in short, the concrete, is the moral, religious, political situation; all else is abstraction in relation to that and cannot be allowed to stand by itself . . . To start with the abstractions of our most precise knowledge means that we shall be condemned to end with them as well and thus fail to reach the concrete. But if we start with the most important aspects of our experience and our life in the world we shall have a vantage point from which to view, criticize and evaluate the abstractions required by all knowledge . . . Royce was right when he argued that there is no pure intellect but that all thought and knowledge stand essentially related to the will.[64]

If philosophy has reality as its domain, value commands philosophical attention as much as sensual experience. Although natural science cannot produce a satisfactory account of ethics or religion, science itself cannot be sustained without an admiration for truth which is essentially ethical and religious. This is a point of enormous significance for *Aids to Reflection*. Coleridge dwells upon the ascetic and religious imagery in Bacon's philosophy of science in order to make the idealistic point that scientific endeavour presupposes transcendent values: the conviction that truth is attainable, demands self-sacrifice for its attainment and that its pursuit is a good *per se*. Reason is rather broader than Hume will admit: it is not just deductive and inductive but what A. E. Taylor calls 'an indefinite capacity of seeking and finding on all occasions the way of response which, in this situation, will be best adapted to the achieving of an ideal which we never envisage with perfect definiteness';[65] a pre-scientific capacity which becomes evident when we argue about what ought to be believed or done.

The law of the understanding and fancy is the means for the finite mind of arranging the sense data of experience into a phenomenal world. Mankind is continually tempted to identify the transcendentally ideal realm or the phenomenal realm with 'reality'. This, for Coleridge, is a form of fetishism; he compares the fetish of the 'imbruted African' with the 'soul debasing errors of the proud fact-hunting materialist' (*F* i. 518). 'Truth is self-restoration: . . . It is by the agency of indistinct conceptions, as the conterfeits of the Ideal and the Transcendent, that evil and vanity exercise their tyranny on the feelings of man' (*F* i. 36–7). The purpose of philosophy lies in the 'opening of the inner eye to the glorious vision of that existence which admits no question out of itself, acknowledges no predicate but the I AM IN THAT I AM'. The aim of philosophy is the contemplation of true reality as opposed to the abstractions of the finite mind.

Coleridge's negative agenda – the attack on the abstractions of empiricism – is linked to a positive account of the special value of intuitive knowledge. Real knowledge for Coleridge is a matter of

---

[64] John E. Smith, *America's Philosophical Vision* (University of Chicago Press, 1992), pp. 117–18.
[65] A. E. Taylor, *Does God Exist?* (London: Macmillan, 1966), p. 82.

seeing – whether at the perceptual level, such as the white of the wall, or the postulates of geometry:

knowledge of *spiritual* truth is of necessity immediate and *intuitive*: and the World or Natural Man possesses no higher intuitions than those of pure *Sense*, which are subjects of *Mathematical* Science. (*Aids*, p. 158)

It is important to consider that such an appeal is far from irrationalism. On the contrary, the capacity to provide proofs or discursive grounds for beliefs is on occasion a sign of inferior knowledge. The native speaker may be incapable of describing the grammatical rules of his language and yet 'know' his tongue far better than the assiduous non-native student who can expound all of the rules of the language and yet still makes mistakes in the use of idioms, etc.[66] Coleridge means that if you ask someone why they believe that syrup is sweet, that person must reply that they have experienced it so. This is immediate and incontrovertible knowing. And, similarly, in geometry we have immediate assurance of truth which is different in kind from the assurances of discursive ratiocination. The understanding

gives rise to Maxims or Rules which may become more and more *general*, but can never be raised into universal Verities, or beget a consciousness of absolute Certainty; though they may be sufficient to extinguish all doubt. (Putting Revelation out of view, take our first Progenitor in the 50th or 100th year of his existence. His experience would probably have freed him from all doubt, as the Sun sank in the Horizon that it would re-appear the next morning. But compare this state of Assurance with that which the same man would have had of the 37th Proposition of Euclid, supposing him like Pythagoras to have discovered the *Demonstration*.) (*Aids*, p. 235)

Coleridge's appeal is perhaps mystical, but it is not necessarily irrational. Knowledge at the perceptual and geometrical level is a sort of experience by which the knower *knows* without further demonstration.[67]

Coleridge wishes to maintain that reason 'goeth through all understanding, and remaining in itself regenerateth all powers' (*Aids*, p. 218). This is an 'influence from the *Glory of the Almighty*, this being one of the names of the Messiah, as Logos or co-eternal Filial word' (*Aids*, p. 219). Coleridge concludes this passage with a quotation from Heraclitus: 'To discourse rationally it behoves us to derive strength

---

[66] I owe this example to George Watson.
[67] cf. Plato's seventh letter; Plato, *Symposium*, 211; Plato, *Republic* 509ff. Aristotle, *Metaphysics*, 1072b f; Plotinus, *Treatise*, iii. 8 (30), 4; Coleridge, *BL* i. 240.

from that which is common to all men: for all human understandings are nourished by one DIVINE WORD' (*Aids*, p. 219). Reason is *in* the understanding in the sense that reason informs and is translucent in the understanding but is not thereby dissipated. Coleridge maintains that reason remains in itself while it 'regenerateth all powers'. The model is that of the transcendent Godhead which eternally *is* self-contained and yet overflows: the Filial co-eternal Word, a God who is immanently self sufficient and yet sustaining the world.

This is far removed from the fideism of F. H. Jacobi. Jacobi envisages God in the typical Enlightenment manner as extra mundane: as a quasi spatially transcendent object outside the world which he mistakenly took for the orthodox Christian concept.[68] Coleridge emphasises both God's immanence on the basis of his infinity and God's incomprehensibility. As infinite, God must be thought of as *in* all as the ground of all. Yet this is compatible with the conviction of the 'one-sided dependence' in the relation between God and world.[69] 'God is a Circle, the centre of which is every where and the circumference nowhere' (*Aids*, p. 233).

An analogy with Nicholas of Cusa serves a number of points. Firstly, he is the source of talk of God as the 'absolute', and has often been cited as an important precursor of the German Idealists; most notably by Werner Schulz and Hans Blumenberg.[70] Secondly, the Platonists Cusa and Coleridge use *mathematical* models for the Trinity ('O be assured, my dear Sons! that Pythagoras, Plato and Speusippus, had abundant reason for excluding from philosophy and theology not merely practical those who were ignorant of mathematics' (*Marg* i. 615.) Nicholas of Cusa thinks of the Father as *unitas*, the Son as *aequalitas absoluta*, and the Spirit as the *connexio*[71] – a tradition which goes back to the school of Chartres and the mathematical model of the tri-une God as $1 \times 1 \times 1 = 1$. Nicholas of Cusa's thought is that God is '*idem*' 'the same' and as such prior to any distinction between identity and difference. As absolute identity, he is paradoxically 'non-aliud'; the 'not other':

[68] cf. Josef Piper, *Die Wahrheit der Dinge* (Munich: Alber, 1948), pp. 48–50.
[69] The phrase is from W. R. Inge, *God and the Astronomers* (London: Longman, 1934), p. 223.
[70] Walter Schulz, *Der Gott der Neuzeitlichen Metaphysik* (Pfullingen: Neske,1957), pp. 11–30; H. Blumenberg, *Die Legitimität der Neuzeit*, second edition (Frankurt: Suhrkamp, 1988), pp. 558–638; Jasper Hopkins, *Nicholas of Cusa's Dialectical Mysticism*, second edition (Minneapolis: Arthur Banning, 1988), pp. 51–93; Beierwaltes, *Identität und Differenz*, p. 174 n. 114.
[71] See Beierwaltes, *Denken des Einen*, pp. 368–84.

Yea, this is the test and character of a truth so affirmed, that in its own proper form it is *inconceivable*. For *to conceive* is a function of the Understanding, which can be exercised only on subjects subordinate thereto. And yet to the forms of the Understanding all truth must be reduced, that is to be fixed as an object of reflection, and to be rendered *expressible*. And here we have a second test and sign of a truth so affirmed, that it can come forth out of the moulds of the Understanding only in the disguise of two contradictory conceptions, each of which is partially true, and the conjunction of both conceptions becomes the representative or *expression* (= the exponent) of a truth *beyond* conception and inexpressible. (*Aids*, p. 233)

This distinction between reason and understanding means that God cannot serve as an explanation. Paley's appeal to a divine craftsman and his artefact analogies is open to the objection raised by Hume, Russell, or Flew: how can an appeal to God *explain* anything? Explanation presupposes a web of laws, and therefore cannot be applied outside the universe. Furthermore, even if the brute fact of the universe is mysterious, appeal to an infinite, omniscient being will increase and not reduce the mystery. In short, these objections amount to doubt whether anything could possibly explain everything in any intelligible manner. Coleridge can concede these objections by Hume and his twentieth-century followers because he thinks both Paley and Hume argue as if God were an empirical hypothesis. However, the idea that the world is 'created' means simply that 'nature' is incomplete and dependent upon a transcendent absolute source. That means that the causal connections of phenomenal experience and scientific investigation cannot exhaustively classify and explain reality. God is not another, albeit ultimate, explanatory item, but the source of that intelligibility which is presupposed at the level of the understanding. Coleridge can reply to the sceptic who claims that an appeal to an ineffable deity is incomprehensible, that the capacity of the mind to understand its environment is no less incomprehensible. However, the conviction that the facts of the world suggest a purposive intelligence does not mean, for Coleridge, that we can penetrate this purpose. Coleridge's rational theology does not entail the Hegelian thought that the absolute becomes rationally transparent. This is quite coherent: one assumes that other rational agents have specific purposes, but these can remain opaque or inscrutable.

NOTIONAL SPECULATION

Coleridge wished to argue against the approach of Paley which appeals to the world as a set of facts which point to a designer God, whose sovereign will serves as the explanation for the appearance of order and design in the world. God is not, for Coleridge, an explanatory item, a mysterious supernatural agent who can be seen as the ultimate mover and framer of the physical universe, but the intelligible ground and archetype of the sensible realm. The doctrine of the Logos militates against this view of a supernatural demiurge, who produced the world as good but might presumably have produced a rather different world; perhaps a rather bad world. If the principle of creation, the Logos, is of *one substance* with the Father and not his arbitary product, divine creation is inevitably good: the divine will is not indeterminate. The Logos reflects the very substance of the Father. But equally Coleridge wishes to argue against the Humean view that the universe is a gigantic coincidence which human beings just happen to have the capacity to understand.

We have seen that Coleridge envisages being as truth itself on the Platonic model. It is within the context of the idea of reason as a divine theophany that we should attempt to understand Coleridge's remarks about mere notional speculation. He is not attacking speculative theology as such, but a theology which is not adequately aware of the limits of finite reflection. This becomes evident when one scrutinises pages 304 and 305 of *Aids*. Coleridge insists that he first attempted to show (pp. 134–43) that 'there *is* a Spiritual Principle in Man' and this was followed by an attempt to distinguish between religious truths and the deductions of a speculative science in order to prove that the former are 'not only equally rational with the latter, but that they alone appeal to Reason in the fulness and living reality of the Power' (*Aids* p. 304). The expression 'the fulness and living reality of the Power' indicates that Coleridge is thinking of reason as an objective power in which mankind can participate. There are several passages on pages 161–206 which suggest that Coleridge is presenting an *essentially* ethical religion; that is, the assertion that religious beliefs are *reducible* to ethical beliefs. This thought would be supported by his recommendation to translate theological terms into their moral equivalents (*Aids*, p. 74). Yet this is wholly incompatible with the general structure of Coleridge's argument, which rests upon the transition from religious morality to spiritual religion (*Aids*, p. 304). The reason for the confusion rests in the similarity between the British deists who interpreted historical Christianity as *exclusively* the expression of an undogmatic, timeless ethics[72] and the German thinkers like Lessing and Kant who *interpreted* the meaning of the dogmas of the Christian faith using moral categories: a related but essentially quite distinct endeavour. Coleridge quotes and expands upon Bishop Burnet's assertion that

Religion is designed to improve the nature and faculties of Man . . . to the rendering us capable of a more perfect state, entitled the kingdom of God, to which the present Life is *probationary* . . . every Part of Religion is to be judged by its relation to this main end . . . since the Christian scheme is Religion in its most perfect and effective Form, a revealed Religion, and therefore in a *special* sense proceeding from that Being who made us and knows what we are, of course therefore adapted to the needs and capabilities of Human Nature; nothing can be a part of this holy faith that is not duly proportioned to this end. (*Aids*, pp. 188–9)

Coleridge remarks that in council and synod the 'divine Humanities of the Gospel gave way to speculative systems, and Religion became a Science of Shadows under the name of Theology' (*Aids*, p. 192). Such remarks sound akin to Kierkegaard, Dostoevsky, or Karl Barth in anathematising 'natural theology' and we are arguing that Coleridge should be understood as an idealist; just the kind of thinker rejected by Kierkegaard or Barth. If he is saying that ethics should determine religious truths, he seems to be following a very different track: towards deism. How should we interpret such utterances?

When Coleridge speaks of the 'divine Humanities', he is using the dogmatic language of the councils and synods. Furthermore, when Coleridge speaks of the Doctors forgetting that the '*Heart*, the *Moral* Nature, was the beginning and the end, and that Truth, Knowledge, and Insight were comprehended in its expansion' (*Aids*, p. 192) one must bear in mind what Coleridge means by the *moral* nature of man and its relation to eternity. This is bound inextricably to the Mystery of 'the birth into a new and spiritual life' (*Aids*, p. 204) which is part of the ascent from uprightness to *godlikeness*. (*Aids*, p. 40) and 'the entrance of the Soul into Glory, *i.e.* its union with Christ' (*Aids*,

[72] Deism was attractive after the English civil war and the religious controversies of the eighteenth century. The Deists thought that Christianity should stand the test of reason; this remains a standard challenge of the Enlightenment. With Deism one first has the idea of Christianity as a religion alongside other religions, particularly Judaism, which the deists tend to see as a legalistic religion.

p. 160). Hence when Coleridge insists that the law of conscience and not the canons of discursive reason should decide in cases of doctrines such as election, this does not mean that the *human* sense of moral propriety should be the canon of the essence of Christianity. That would be exactly deism, or in a modified form, Socinianism.

Coleridge is following the Cambridge Platonists in his invective against mere speculation. It is quite typical of the Cambridge Platonists to attack systematic and doctrinal theology and to appeal to the living spirit of religion. John Smith is relentless in his criticism of the 'thin and aiery knowledge' of 'meer speculation', 'Jejune and barren speculations'.[73] Coleridge, we have seen, is writing in the mystical tradition when he argues against the application of the understanding in theological matters: philosophy, he believes adamantly, has a spiritual function in stripping away false expectations. In a notebook entry Coleridge jots down a revealing thought about

The great moral importance of negative Knowledge and Belief in Religion. In this way only can the process of unsensualizing the Soul and purifying the temple of the mind from Idols in order to prepare for the Epiphany of the Ideas *Notebooks* iv. 5215)

The *stripping away* of the categories of the understanding is the mystic preparation for the *epiphany* of the divine reason. The last words of Plotinus' treatise on self-knowledge are the command: 'ἄφελε πάντα': 'Take away everything!' Plotinus writes:

and this is the soul's true end, to touch that light and see by its self, not by another light, but by the light which is also its means of seeing. It must see that light by which it is enlightened: for we do not see the sun by another light than its own. How can this happen? Take away everything![74]

Coleridge uses the image of seeing the sun by means of its own light, and speaks of Bacon's use of 'fantastical and mystical phrases' such as the lucific vision, that is, the light-making vision, as an image of 'Reason in contradiction from the Understanding' (*Aids*, p. 215). The soul's end is to see that light by which it is enlightened:

This *seeing* light, this *enlightening* eye, is Reflection. It is more, indeed, than is ordinarily meant by that word; but it is what a *Christian* ought to mean by it, and to know too, whence it first came, and still continues to come – of

[73] Smith, *Discourses*, pp. 4–8. See Jones, *Spiritual Reformers*.
[74] Plotinus, *Treatise* v. 3 (49) 17, 39.

what light even this light is *but* a reflection. This, too, is THOUGHT. (*Aids*, pp. 15–16)

Reflection ordinarily means the discursive understanding, but Coleridge avers that a Christian should also be aware that discursive mind *reflects* the light of eternal reason: the Logos.[75] He refers to John Smith's observation that when we 'reflect' on reason, this is a light 'which we enjoy, but the Source of which is not in ourselves' (*Aids*, p. 253); and we can contrast this construal of 'reflection' with the observation of Hume's Philo that the 'ancient PLATONISTS were the most religious and devout of all the pagan philosophers' and yet Plotinus thought 'intellect or understanding is not to be ascribed to the Deity' and that the best consists not of the usual religious acts of worship but of a 'certain mysterious self-annihilation or total extinction of our faculties'. Hume notes that this apophatic theology is rather extreme, but he thinks that representing the deity as 'so intelligible and comprehensible, and so similar to the human mind, we are guilty of the grossest and most narrow partiality, and make ourselves the model of the universe'.[76] Coleridge insists:

Man alone was created in the image of God: a position groundless and inexplicable, if the reason in man do not differ from the understanding. For this the inferior animals, (many at least) possess *in degree*: and assuredly the divine image or idea is not a thing of degrees. (*LS*, p. 19)

The Platonist is primarily interested in living the good life, in becoming 'like God', and is convinced that this requires strenuous effort and discipline: the 'manly' character. The main objection and aversion to determinism, Neo-Epicureanism, ultra-Calvinism or divine-command theories, lies in their capacity to subvert the will through abstract metaphysical assumptions and inferences. Coleridge wishes to maintain that life is inherently valuable, and goodness worth pursuing, and that these tenets are self-verifying. The doctrine of reflection which Coleridge shares with the Cam-

---

[75] cf. W. Wordsworth, *The Prelude*, i. 404–5: 'thy soul received / The light reflected, as a light bestowed' or Ezra Pound on Eriugena's Platonic light mysticism:

sunt lumina, said the Oirishman to King Carolus, 'OMNIA,
all things that are are lights'
and they dug him out of the sepultre
soi disantly looking for Manichaeans.

(Ezra Pound, Canto LXXIV. Quoted by Beierwaltes in *Platonismus und Idealismus*, p. 188. cf. *Platonism and the English Imagination*, edited by A. Baldwin and S. Hutton (Cambridge University Press, 1994) and Beierwaltes, 'Plotins Metaphysik', pp. 75–115. *Principal Writings*)

[76] Hume, *Principal Writings*, p. 58.

bridge Platonists is that the reflection of the soul upon itself reveals the immutable verities which are simultaneously the principles of human action and knowledge and the ideas of God. Yet these are not speculative principles but principles of what William James calls the 'passional nature'; or, in Coleridge's terms, 'Derivatives from the practical, moral and spiritual Nature and Being of Man' (*Aids*, p. 188). William James' resounding words: 'Be not afraid of life. Believe that life *is* worth living, and your belief will help create the fact' is congruent with Coleridge if seen as the corollary of the Jamesian tenet, 'The inmost nature of the reality is congenial to *powers* which you possess.'[77]

Reason for Coleridge is precisely related to the highest goals of humanity which transcend the merely sensual, and yet is not abstract but the very 'Plenitude of reality' (*Aids*, p. 401). Coleridge contrasts the abstract 'generalising' function of the understanding with 'the Power' of *intuitive* knowledge ('Reason is that highest sense, in which the speculative is united with the practical' (*Aids*, p. 217 n. 5). The conclusion of *Aids to Reflection* is an outright philosophical attack upon the abstraction of the scientific intellect. The enemy of a spiritual religion, Coleridge believes, is the abstraction of science which excludes the essential difference between an organ and a machine by 'abstracting from corporeal substance all its *positive* properties' (*Aids*, p. 399). Though this was a useful '*Fiction of Science*'[78]

Des Cartes propounded it as *truth of fact*: and instead of a World *created* and filled with productive forces by the Almighty Fiat, left a lifeless Machine whirled about by the dust of its own Grinding: as if Death could come from the living Fountain of Life; Nothingness and Phantom from the Plenitude of Reality! the Absoluteness of Creative Will! (*Aids*, p. 400-1)

The translucence of the invisible energy in the organic realm does not constitute 'fancies, conjectures, or even hypotheses but facts; to deny them which is impossible, not to reflect on which is ignominious' (*Aids*, p. 398). This means the outward material realm, though not unreal, is symbolic of the inward, the spiritual and the personal, and directed against the abstractions of an empiricism which sees *reality* as consisting of atoms, and persons as determined by pleasure and pain.

Finally, Coleridge is concerned to avoid the degradation of the idea that the cosmos reflects intelligence into the ludicrous idea that

---

[77] James, *The Will to Believe*, pp. 62 and 86.
[78] Schelling uses the idea of 'Fictions of Science'. See his *Ideas for a Philosophy of Nature*, p. 78

it is made for specifically human convenience. Coleridge's philosophising may belong to that of the tender-minded (James), he may be convinced of the mind's loving affinity or communion with the hidden structures of the universe, but his view of religion is less than consoling. It is predicated upon the rejection of the conviction that human and divine purposes coincide, and that mankind is the singular object of divine providence. In fact, one might say that the rejection of this phantasy is one of the signal differences between religion and superstition. Coleridge refers to Isaiah 55: 8–9 enthusiastically: 'My Ways are not as your Ways, nor my Thoughts as your Thoughts' (*Aids*, p. 190).

Hume's Philo expresses vividly and eloquently the classical moral objection to theism; that the world cannot be the product of a good God, since the universe as a whole presents 'nothing but the idea of a blind nature, impregnated by a great vivifying principle, and pouring forth from her lap, without discernment or parental care, her maimed and abortive children'.[79]

Coleridge follows Kant in looking primarily at the inward law rather than any outward facts, and what this inward law reveals to the mind which is conscious of it as conscience. If we are aware of a binding moral law as human beings, this entails that humanity is not subject to merely natural forces. Furthermore, the rhetorical image of nature as profligate and the work of a careless craftsman seems to presuppose that human happiness is the main end of creation; but this is an assumption which Coleridge rejects. If we accept the sovereign value of goodness, this must be the aspiration of rational conscious persons, and this goal requires genuinely free agents. If struggle and conflict are the fuel and discipline of the attainment of goodness, there is certainly no knock-down inference from the 'facts' of the world to atheism or agnosticism. Freedom, Coleridge insists, is a matter of degrees. The rational agent who has attained some focus and unity in his or her character, so that first-order decisions are determined not by whim, but by deeper principles or commitments or interests, cannot be expected to forge the requisite focus and unity without genuine suffering and loss. A properly free agent is not moulded by successful adaption to the environment; it is not just that this would mean automatism, but it is difficult to see how freedom in this Platonic-Kantian sense is intelligible without real suffering.

[79] Hume, *Principal Writings on Religion*, p. 113.

5

The great instauration: reflection as the renewal of the soul[1]

... unless one is born anew, he cannot see the kingdom of God. (John 3: 3)

We should finally be clear that Christianity is not something external so that we are called Christians because we confess this or that doctrine . . . or do this good thing or avoid that bad thing. All these things can be just as much means or the fruits of Christianity if these are heartfelt. These are not the essence of Christianity: the essence consists of the rebirth.

(P. J. Spener, 1695)[2]

... if a man would be a student of divinity let him learn and practise his baptism. (William Perkins[3])

Coleridge is concerned to isolate a particular genesis of the Deism and Unitarianism of the eighteenth century. His insistence that the moral life requires divine aids, a communion with the divine spirit, leads him to trace a genealogy of Deism which sees the root of the problem exemplified in the Arminian Cambridge divine Jeremy Taylor. His understandable revulsion from the asperity of the Augustinian-Calvinistic emphasis upon human depravity and need, and his fear that this would subvert all attempts to preach and attain true holiness, led Taylor to assert a degree of human ethical sufficiency which seemed to subvert Christian stress upon human need for grace. Perhaps ironically, Coleridge employs arguments

---

[1] See the title of Francis Bacon's work, *Instauratio Magna*, published in 1620.

[2] Wir müssen allemal wissen, unser Christenthum bestehe in nichts Äußerlichem, dab wir eben Christen heißen, zu dieser oder jener Lehr uns bekennen, . . . äußerlich ein und ander Gutes tun und das Böse lassen. Denn alle diese Dinge können wohl so Mittel also Früchte des *Christentum* sein, wenn dieses in dem Herzen ist. Sie sind das aber rechte *Wesen davon* nicht, sondern das stehet in der Wiedergeburt. P. J. Spener, *Der Evangelische Glaubens-Trost* (Frankfurt am Main: Zummer, 1710), quoted by R. Schäfer in his article 'Das Wesen des Christenthums' in *Historisches Wörterbuch der Philosophie*, edited by J. Ritter (Darmstadt: Wissenschaftliche Buchgesellschaft, 1971-), vol. i. pp. 1008-16. The quotation from Spener is on p. 1012.

[3] Quoted by K. Stevenson, *The Mystery of Baptism in the Anglican Tradition* (Norwich: Canterbury, 1998), p. 155.

from the philosophy of autonomy, of Kant, to sustain his moderate Augustinianism against Taylor's Arminianism. Taylor was inclined to use arguments culled from the Dutch Arminian jurists, especially Hugo Grotius. Hence Coleridge is inclined to dismiss this moralising semi-Pelagianism as Grotianism, and sometimes speaks (disparagingly) of the Grotio-Payleian scheme in this context. The backdrop of this theological discussion in *Aids* is metaphysical. Both the Arminian and the Socianian schemes tend to reduce or render otiose the idea of communion with the divine spirit, and this tendency Coleridge is determined to counter. Coleridge's pitting the Prussian philosopher against the Caroline divine, Kant against Taylor, is both ingenious and instructive; and shows how Coleridge in his commentary could address metaphysical problems with particular power.

I more than fear, the prevailing taste for Books of Natural Theology, Physico-Theology, Demonstrations of God from Nature, Evidences of Christianity, &c. &c. *Evidences* of Christianity! I am weary of the Word. Make a man feel the *want* of it; rouse him if you can, to the self-knowledge of his need of it, and you may safely trust it to its own Evidence. (*Aids*, pp. 405–6)

This passage has been much misunderstood. Firstly, evidences of Christianity are not just those of physico-theology or the evidences or proofs of natural religion. 'Evidences' are also evidences of *revelation*. Contrary to the common assumption the issue is not simply that of *natural* theology but of the nature of *revealed* theology. Furthermore, I think we can show that the real issue in the polemic against Paley is Coleridge's defence of the indwelling logos. Paley represents a mildly Socinian or Antitrinitarian theology that, Coleridge believes, has significantly and banefully influenced the Church of England.

Mark Pattison in his memorable essay in *Essays and Reviews* of 1860, 'Tendencies of religious thought in England 1688–1750' observes of the term 'rationalism':

It is often taken to mean a system opposed to revealed religion, and imported into this country from Germany at the beginning of the present century . . . Rationalism was not an anti-Christian sect outside the Church making war against religion. It was a habit of thought ruling all minds, under the conditions of which all alike tried to make good the particular opinions they might happen to cherish. The Churchman differed from the Socinian, and the Socinian from the Deist, as to the number of articles in his creed; but all alike consented to test their belief by the rational evidence for it . . . The title of Locke's treatise *The Reasonableness of Christianity* may be said to have been the solitary thesis of Christian theology in England for a great part of a century.

If we are to put chronological limits to this system of religious opinion in England, we might, for the sake of a convenient landmark, say that it came in with the Revolution of 1688, and began to decline in vigour with the reaction against the Reform movement about 1830. Locke's *Reasonableness of Christianity* would thus open, and the commencement of the Tracts for the Times mark the fall of Rationalism . . . For it was not merely that Rationalism then intruded as a heresy, or obtained a footing of toleration within the Church, but the rationalizing method possessed itself absolutely of the whole field of theology. With some trifling exceptions, the whole of religious literature was drawn into the endeavour to 'prove the truth' of Christianity.[4]

In the definitive Socinian compendium called the 'Rakow Catechism' (1609) the Christian religion is defined as one that is 'the divinely revealed path to eternal life' (*via patefacta divinitus vitam aeternam consequendi*).[5] The sole source of this path is the New Testament. Harnack, in an almost Coleridgean invective, writes of Socinianism:

The Christian religion is the theology of the New Testament. Here we find the basis of that positivism with which Faustus shaped his work. A positivism, indeed, which is frustrating if one considers what religion really is. All knowledge of God, for Faustus, is delivered from above [*von Aussen her gewirkt* – effected from without] and is contained in a single book given for once and all. Christ is not the revelation in the book; rather 'in the book God has revealed Himself, His will and the path to salvation'.[6]

The other main principle of Socinianism apart from its biblical 'positivism' was its rather narrow rationalism. Far removed from Augustinian anthropology with its picture of mankind wandering and wallowing in sinful estrangement from God, waiting for grace, man is a rational though finite creature who can perceive rationally

[4] Mark Pattison, 'Tendencies of religious thought in England, 1688–1750', in *Essays and Reviews*, tenth edition (London: Longman, Green, Longman and Roberts, 1862), pp. 310 11.
[5] Benrath, 'Humanisten und Antitrinitarier' in *Handbuch der Dogmen*, vol. iii. p. 67ff.
[6] 'Die Christliche religion ist Theologie des Neuen Testamentes. Hierin liegt der positive Charakter begründet, den Faustus seiner Schöpfung zu geben verstanden hat, freilich eine Positivität, die unerfreulich ist, sobald man daran denkt, was die Religion ist. Alles Wissen des Göttlichen ist von Aussen her gewirkt und liegt lediglich beschlossen in dem einmal gegebenen Buche. Nicht Christus ist die Offenbarung in dem Buche, sondern "in dem Buche hat Gott sich selbst, seinen Willen und den Weg zum heil offenbar gemacht"' (p. 5). A. von Harnack, *Dogmengeschichte*, fourth edition (Tübingen: Mohr, 1990), vol. iii. p. 785.

the God-given true path to salvation. Socinian theology was severely critical of traditional dogmas. Faustus Socinus accepted the Virgin Birth, physical resurrection of Christ, and the exaltation to the right hand of God, but the orthodox Christological doctrine of two natures is rejected as contrary to sound reason (*ratio sana*). Jesus Christ is divine because he is a prophet of a new covenant, and Communion and baptism express this new covenant. The doctrines of predestination and prevenient grace are rejected; God and man are both viewed as free and the notion of a redemptive sacrifice is rejected.[7] Nevertheless Faustus Socinus is expressly tolerant of other churches.[8] Harnack describes this as 'supernatural rationalism'.[9] That is to say that the apologetic strategy for Christianity within Socinianism consists of a rationalism buttressed by supernaturalism. Miracles and a fairly narrowly construed 'reason' provide the means of justification for Christian belief.

Within the theological development of Socinianism the rational and ethical element became increasingly dominant. Johan Völkel (d. 1618) in his work *De vera religione* (1630) used arguments of natural theology. The point of Christianity, he believes, is a rational life. Andreas Wissowatius (1608–78) in *Religio rationalis* (1685) envisages the Christian religion as above reason (*supra rationem*) but not against reason (*contra rationem*) and he lays great weight upon miracles (cf. Coleridge, *LS*, p. 177).[10] Later Socinianism came to be associated with the name of the Dutch theologian Jacobus Arminius (1560–1609), who argued that the object of theology was not God's actual nature but man's service of the divine. 'Arminianism' came to be used as a blanket term of abuse for those theologians who emphasised ethics and were averse to disputing dogmatic subtleties of the Trinity, Incarnation, or predestination (cf. *Aids*, pp. 163; 164; 276; 305; 307; 311).[11]

The title of Locke's work *The Reasonableness of Christianity, as Delivered in the Scriptures* (1695) suggests a Socinian project. Socinian theology, especially since Wissowatius, combined a scriptural positivism with a strong rationalism. The *reasonableness* of Christianity as *delivered* by Scriptures expresses this seemingly odd mixture of positivism, i.e. acceptance of the brute fact of revelation, and a

---

[7] Ibid., vol. iii. p. 779.   [8] Ibid., vol. iii. p. 784   [9] Ibid., vol. iii. p. 785
[10] Benrath, 'Humanisten und Antitrinitarier' in *Handbuch der Dogmen*, vol. iii. pp. 69 ff.
[11] H. Trevor-Roper, *Catholics, Anglicans and Puritans, Seventeenth Century Essays* (London: Secker and Warburg, 1987), pp. 166–230.

rationalism that insists upon the essential reasonableness of the central Christian tenets. The exact nature of Locke's theology is a particularly contentious affair, revolving around rather minute debates about phases in Locke's development or particular documents, or about how 'Socinianism' should be defined. There is, however, much evidence that suggests that Locke's theology was in substance evidently influenced by later Socinian theology.[12] Revelation is seen in an empirical manner: God reveals himself in particular acts. These facts are not incompatible with reason because 'rational' means effectively moral. However counter-intuitive this equation may seem to the modern mind, the rationality of moral behaviour is for Locke guaranteed by the Christian message of heavenly rewards. The promise of eternal life is the foundation and cement of genuine morality.[13]

In *The Great Debate on Miracles* R. M. Burns has argued that Locke belonged to a school of 'liberal Anglicans' or 'moderate evidentialists' who presented a liberal and scientifically aware apology for the Christian faith which revolved around the concept of the miracle. Locke was certainly not a deist. A deist maintains the propriety of believing in a God as the author of nature or as moral governor, but denies revelation. Revelation, however, plays a central role in Locke's theology, because revelation is seen as a necessary supplement to natural theology. The revelation of the divine commands in Jesus Christ was practically a necessary supplement to natural reason: 'Though the works of nature, in every part of them, sufficiently evidence of a Deity; yet the world made so little use of their reason, that they saw him not, where, even by the impressions of himself, he was easy to be found.'[14] Locke sees the task of the Evangelists in providing sufficient evidence of a deity: 'Their great

---

[12] John Marshall, *John Locke, Resistance, Religion and Responsibility* (Cambridge University Press, 1996), pp. 384–451. Alan P. F. Sell defends Locke's position in his book *John Locke and the Eighteenth Century Divines* (Cardiff: University of Wales Press, 1987), pp. 185–267. esp. pp. 214–15. W. M. Spellman, *John Locke and the Problem of Human Depravity* (Oxford: Clarendon, 1988) places Locke among the moderate latitudinarian divines of the late seventeenth century. Of particular interest is M. Wiles, *Archetypal Heresy*, pp. 70 ff.

[13] 'The view of heaven and hell will cast a slight upon the short pleasures and pains of this present state, and give attractions and encouragements to virtue, which reason and interest, and the care of ourselves, cannot but allow and prefer. Upon this foundation, and upon this only morality stands firm, and may deny all competition. This makes it more than a name; a substantial good, worth all our aims and endeavours; and thus the Gospel of Jesus Christ has delivered it to us.' John Locke, *The Reasonableness of Christianity as delivered in the Scriptures* in *The Works*, eleventh edition, 10 vols. (London: Tegg, 1823), vol. vii. pp. 150–1.

[14] Ibid., vol. vii. p. 135.

business was to be witnesses to Jesus, of his life, death and resurrection, and ascension which put together, were undeniable proofs of his being the Messiah.'[15] Hence Locke presents revelation as a necessary supplement to the inadequacy of human reason. The fact that this revelation occurred in Jesus of Nazareth is *proven* by his life, death, resurrection, and ascension. In particular the miraculous events of Jesus' life and the central miracle of the resurrection constituted 'undeniable proofs' of his divine mission:

The evidence of our Saviour's mission from heaven is so great, in the multitude of miracles he did before all sorts of people, that what he delivered cannot but be received as the oracles of God, and unquestionable verity. For the miracles he did were so ordered by the divine providence and wisdom, that they never were, nor could be denied by any of the enemies or opposers of Christianity.[16]

Locke's Christology is (classically Socinian) 'from below'. It attempts to establish the status of Jesus as the Christ by adducing evidence for the claim that Jesus is able to 'show his commission from heaven, that he comes with authority from God, to deliver his will and commands to the world'.[17] In particular Locke's emphasis upon the prophetical office of Christ suggests Socinian influence.

One might object at this point: was not the emphasis upon miracles simply a conventional part of the Christian apologetic armoury? Is not Locke's strategy quite orthodox? The answer is that miracles were generally, in fact, not of signal importance in traditional Christian apologetics. As L. E. Elliot-Binns remarks, Jesus is presented in the gospels as wary of them (Matt. 4: 5 f.; Luke 4: 9ff.) and St Paul is equally cautious (1 Cor. 1: 22ff.).[18] He also points out that Alexandrine Christianity did not place much emphasis upon miracles as apologetic weapons.

Socinianism was humanist and nominalist, even Antiochene,[19] in its temper and was inclined to see Trinitarian dogma as a root of division. Locke was convinced of the 'little satisfaction and consistency that is to be found in most of the systems of divinity'[20] and decided instead to concentrate upon 'the sole reading of Scripture

---

[15] Ibid., vol. vii. p. 98   [16] Ibid., vol. vii. p. 135.   [17] Ibid., vol. vii. p. 142.

[18] L. E. Elliot-Binns, *English Thought 1860–1900: the Theological Aspect* (London: Longman, Green, and Co., 1956), p. 55.

[19] cf. Harnack, *Dogmengeschichte* (Tübingen: Mohr-Siebeck, 1904), vol. iii. p. 785. Faustus has affinities with the Antioch school of theologians. On these Fathers see Kelley, *Early Christian Doctrines* (London: Adam and Charles Black, 1977), pp. 301 ff.

[20] Locke, *Works*, preface to vol. vii.

(to which they all appeal) for the understanding of the Christian religion'. 'Reasonable' also means the rejection of 'vain philosophy and foolish metaphysics'.[21] The emphasis upon the fundamentals of faith and the attack upon the distortions of clerical intellectuals, in Locke's theology, were typically Socinian.

Hence, paradoxically, the most fervent advocates of miracles at the turn of the eighteenth century were not conservatives fighting a rearguard battle against deists, but progressive liberal 'Anglicans' with Socinian sympathies. Locke writes:

> To one who is once persuaded that Jesus Christ was sent by God to be a King, and a Saviour of those who do believe in him; all his commands become principles; there needs no other proof for the truth of what he says, but that he said it. And then there needs no more, but to read the inspired books, to be instructed: all the duties of morality lie there clear, and plain, and easy to be understood . . . The credit and authority our Saviour and the apostles had over the minds of men, by the miracles they did, tempted them not to mix (as we find in that of all the sects and philosophers, and other religions) any conceits, any wrong rules, anything tending to their own by-interest, or that of a party in their morality.[22]

R. M. Burns writes of the 'non traditional spirit of this theological outlook' that meant that 'a number of its adherents – such as Newton or Clarke – tended increasingly towards an Arian Christology because of rationalistic difficulties with Trinitarianism; but they expressed no such scruples concerning belief in miracles'.[23] One should rather say that precisely because of their difficulties with Trinitarianism they laid weight upon the miracles. Hume remarks that 'Newton, Locke, Clarke, &c. being *Arians* or *Socinians*, were very sincere in the creed they professed.'[24]

Coleridge's reluctance to appeal to miracles as brute facts is based upon an opposition to the supernatural rationalism of 'the Orthodox *de more Grotii*, who improve the *letter* of Arminius with the *spirit* of Socinus' (*Aids*, p. 338) – men who will doubtless deem Coleridge guilty of 'irrational and Supersitious Mysticism' (ibid.). The Socinianism or semi-Socinianism of Paley is a *religio dimidiata* where the 'paramount object of Christ's Mission and Miracles, is to supply the missing Half by a clear discovery of a future state; and (since "*he*

---

[21] Ibid., p. 8.   [22] Ibid., pp. 146–7.

[23] Robert Michael Burns, *The Great Debate on Miracles, from Joseph Glanville to David Hume* (Lewisburg: Bucknell, 1981), p. 268.

[24] Hume, *Principal Writings*, p. 190.

alone discovers who proves") by proving the truth of the doctrine, now for the first time declared with the requisite authority, by the requisite, appropriate, and alone satisfactory *evidences' (Aids,* p. 357). By way of contrast, the religion of Paul, Coleridge believes, is the belief in Christ not as a teacher, but as a cosmic power, the agent in creation and the source of spiritual life: 'I believe Moses, I believe Paul; but I believe *in* Christ' (*Aids,* p. 359).

What does this believing *in* Christ mean? Paley argued that the Pauline language of dying and rising in Christ was an expedient to convey the great change required of heathen conversion in the earliest Christian era, but that this language of regeneration means 'nothing' in 'the present circumstances of Christianity'.[25] It is precisely this language of dying to live, rebirth in Christ, which Paley thinks meaningless in the contemporary circumstances of Christianity, that Coleridge perceives as the very essence of the Christian religion. Coleridge is deeply Pauline in his theology of redemption. Effectively, he concentrates upon St Paul's Christ mysticism and relegates the *forensic* language used by Paul to a figurative status. Paul, the 'learned Apostle' (*Aids,* p. 320) uses four *metaphors* for the illustration of the consequences of Christ's redemption: sin offerings, atonement, ransom from slavery, satisfaction of a creditor's claim; here the 'number and the variety' (*Aids,* p. 321) of the words suggest that they are metaphors. But when Paul is using the symbol of rebirth, he is in agreement with John the Evangelist who writes 'κατὰ πνεῦμα, i.e. according to the *Spirit,* the inner and substantial truth of the Christian Creed' (*Aids,* p. 322). The essence of the Christian religion is renewal of the soul: 'a re-*generation*, a *birth*, a spiritual seed impregnated and evolved, the germinal principle of a higher and enduring Life, of a *spiritual* Life' (*Aids,* p. 322) which is the mystical principle of communion with the divine spirit. Here is the privilege of adoption: Paul's priestly-cum-legal talk of sin offering, atonement, ransom, and satisfaction of a debt are mere illustrations of the consequences of the redemptive act (*Aids,* p. 320). This idea of Christianity as rebirth links Coleridge to the Cambridge Platonists, Kant, and, even, Hegel and Schelling.

Most theories of salvation in western theology have been determined by Anselm (1033–1109). His theory is forensic: that of penal

---

[25] Paley's sermon 'Caution in the use and application of scriptural language' in his *Works*, vol. iv. pp. 267–9.

substitution. Anselm's theory remained dominant throughout the Middle Ages and was largely accepted by the Reformers. The attack upon the idea of satisfaction after the Reformation arose largely from the Socinians.

Coleridge objects to the doctrine of penal substitution whereby the Son satisfies the wrath of the Father:

Are Debt, Satisfaction, Payment in full, Creditors *Rights* &c. nomina *propria*, by which the very nature of Redemption and its occasion is expressed? or are they, with several others, figures of speech for the purpose of illustrating the nature and extent of the consequences and effects of the redemptive Act . . .? (*Aids*, p. 327)

The agent and cause of redemption is the co-eternal Word, the act is a mystery, the effect is being born anew 'in the *spirit* to Christ, the consequence is the sanctification from sin' (*Aids*, p. 332). Coleridge hints that the oddness of the theory of forensic transaction between the persons of the Trinity rests upon a misunderstanding of the nature of the Trinity.

he gave himself for us that we might live in him and and he in us. There is but one robe of Righteousness, even the Spiritual Body, formed by the assimilative power of faith for whoever cateth the flesh of the Son of Man drinketh his blood. Did Christ come from Heaven, did the Son of God leave the Glory which he had with his Father before the World began, only to *show* us a way of life, to *teach* truths, to *tell* us of a resurrection? Or saith he not, I *am* the way, I *am* the truth, I *am* the Resurrection and the Life. (*Aids*, p. 316)

This is, once again, anti-Socinian. Coleridge emphasises participation (assimilation) in the eternal Word – 'he gave himself for us that we might live in him and he in us' – rather than the Socinian theology of the man Jesus as the unique prophet whose mission is proved by evidences. The Socinians attacked the seeming injustice of the doctrine of atonement. They regarded the idea that a sinless man should bear the burden of the sins of others as ridiculous. For Socinianism Jesus was only a man – even if he had a special relationship to God; the unity of divine and human nature seems contradiction for the Socinians. Either God is just and he must punish the *offenders* not a *substitute* or, conversely, God is merciful and forgives mankind without demanding satisfaction. Furthermore, the Socinians attacked the idea that God's justice demands satisfaction as presupposition for the forgiveness of sins. Forgiveness and satisfaction, they argued, are mutually exclusive, and if God has the power to forgive what should stop God from doing just that! Furthermore, Jesus can hardly be said to fulfil the requirements of justice, since, if eternal death is the punishment and he arose on the third day, he cannot have fulfilled this requirement.

Coleridge fulminates against 'Grotianism', another strand in the rather eclectic theology of latitudinarian eighteenth-century divines such as Paley, whose work served as a vehicle of the dissemination of ideas of continental writers such as Grotius or Pufendorf.[26] Grotius' *Defensio Fidei Catholicae de Satisfactione Christi* (1617) was thoroughly Arminian. Grotius insisted that it is enough to maintain Christ taught forgiveness: his death was a vicarious punishment. The essence of atonement for Grotius is not a payment of an exact debt or substitution but remission on account of forensic satisfaction – he developed an administrative and juridical theory of atonement.[27] Coleridge regards the use of models of sovereignty and administration as utterly inadequate for a spiritual conception of divine forgiveness. First of all, the analogy between sin and crime is manifestly insufficient. Remorse is perhaps more likely to be found amongst law-abiding citizens than amongst criminals; and – even if Grotius was right to point to the weakness of the idea of sin as debt – at least Anselm's theory explained the *necessity* of incarnation. This is the point of Coleridge's example of Edmund Angelini, a man offering himself as satisfaction for the misdeeds of Mr Fauntleroy. Mr Angelini argued that if Christ died as an atonement for the sins of the guilty, he too should be allowed to. Coleridge notes that it is contrary to justice that an innocent person should be sacrificed but 'a person ALTOGETHER innocent – Aye! that is a different question!' (*Aids*, p. 331).

In *The Friend* Coleridge is quite adamant: he objects to the attempt to

make the mysteries of faith what the world calls *rational* by theories of original sin and redemption borrowed analogically from the imperfection of human law-courts and the coarse contrivances of state expedience.

Among the numerous examples with which I might enforce this warning, I refer, not without reluctance, to the most eloquent, and one of the most learned of our divines; a rigorist, indeed concerning the authority of the Church, but Latitudinarian in the articles of its faith; who stretched the latter almost to the advanced posts of Socinianism, and strained the former

---

[26] Paley, *Works*, vol. ii. p. 5.
[27] *Encyclopedia of Religion and Ethics*, ed. Hastings, vol. vi. pp. 441–2.

to a hazardous conformity with the assumptions of the Roman hierarchy. (*F* i. 433)

Coleridge is speaking of Jeremy Taylor. Taylor, for Coleridge, is an instance of the failure of the established church to erect a sound doctrinal edifice. In his attempt to criticise the Augustinian-Anselmian view of sin and redemption, Taylor falls into a semi-Socinianism. Coleridge agrees with Taylor that the Anselmian view is inadequate, but he believes that the resolution of the problem requires a thoroughgoing revision of the metaphysics of atonement and consideration of the nature of symbols and metaphors.

In the face of the forensic Socinian, Grotian, theology of the Locke–Paley school, with its emphasis upon 'facts' of miracles, and dislike of dogmas, Coleridge found a spiritual interpretation of Christianity in its doctrinal form in Lessing and the Idealists. The *essence* of Christianity for the idealists rests in an interpretation of the central doctrines of the Christian religion rather than in ethics buttressed by miracles. Coleridge wrote of Lessing:

before the time of Grotius's de Veritate Christiana no *stress* was lay'd upon the judicial law-cant kind of evidence for Christianity which had been so much in Fashion/ and Lessing very sensibly considers Grotius as the greatest Enemy that Xtianity ever had. (*CL* ii 861)

Lessing wrote a short commentary as the editor of the Reimarus Fragments, where he claimed that the 'inner truth' of Christianity, which is sufficient for believers, is prior to all written proofs. Thus faith is guaranteed by God quite apart from the reliability of the biblical documents.

Coleridge remarks:

Yet Lessing himself could not held [sic] the Harmonists more cheap than I do, or have been more jealous of the historic Exegesis, or in short a more sturdy Anti-Grotian-hodiernâ linguâ, Anti-Paleyian. (*Marg.* iii. 666)[28]

Coleridge's highly positive attitude to Lessing is perhaps surprising given Lessing's modern reputation as a severe critic of the historical reliability of Scripture. Coleridge's view of Lessing as an anti-Grotian anti-Paleyian is rooted in the German Idealist appropriation of a contemplative and spiritual vision of Christianity as opposed to the rationalistic supernaturalism in the Socinians. Henry Chadwick observes: 'It has not perhaps been sufficiently recognized how much

---

[28] cf. Coleridge: 'The Grotio-Paleyian Scheme of Christian Evidence', *Marg.* iii. p. 763.

the ideas of *The Education of the Human Race* go back to Lessing's reading of the early Church Fathers, especially the Christian Plato-nists of Alexandria, Clement and Origen'.[29] And this extends well into the circle of philosophers influenced by Lessing: Kant and the Idealists. A. E. Taylor observes that the vision of the divine purpose within Kant's moral theology as the formation of persons 'fit to enjoy a happiness which is yet to come . . . chimes in with the Athanasian conception of the purpose of the Incarnation, "He became man that we might become divine" '.[30]

There is a strong link between the Greek patristic soteriology and the theology of German Idealism. Christ, for the Greek Fathers, is the second Adam who realises the real vocation of man. Daniélou writes of Clement of Alexandria that ' "Justification" in Clement's writing is synonymous with likeness to God, perfection and posses-sion of the Holy Spirit.'[31] Christ's function is to enable mankind to partake of the divine life. For Irenaeus Christ recapitulates the Fall and thereby makes a new life possible: a new relationship without sin (cf. *Aids*, p. 385). Athanasius sees Jesus both as a particular human being *and* the image of mankind: his resurrection and eternal life are construed as effecting the deification of mankind. German idealist theology, though largely ambiguous on the nature of Christology, shares with the Greek Church Fathers a generally pneumatological or spiritual view of atonement as the reconciliation of mankind with the infinite, and the re-attainment of lost unity.[32] Given that the German idealists used the Neoplatonic model of salvation as the triadic movement of μονή, πρόοδος, ἐπιστροφή, it was natural that their philosophy of religion should recall that of the Alexandrian divines.

The idealist view of the Christian religion is dominated by the notion of the cosmic Christ in the gospel of John and the epistles of Paul. The idea of the 'Gotteskindschaft' (Divine sonship) forms the central idea of their theology.[33] Hegel's *Lectures on the Philosophy of Religion* and Schelling's *Freiheitschrift* develop a systematic account of reality centred around this topic. The core of this

[29] G. E. Lessing, *Theological Writings*, translated by Henry Chadwick (London: Adam and Charles Black, 1956), p. 40.
[30] A. E. Taylor, *Does God Exist?*, p. 19.
[31] J. Daniélou, *Gospel Message and Hellenistic Culture* (London: Westminster, 1980), vol. ii. p. 412.
[32] The classic account is F. C. Baur, *Die Christliche Gnosis, oder die Christliche Religionsphilosophie in ihrer Geschichtlichen Entwicklung* (Tübingen: Osiander, 1835).
[33] Reardon, *Religion in the Age of Romanticism*, pp. 59–116.

theology is a speculative doctrine of the Trinity as relational unity, a speculative view of the Fall and a cosmic Christology. Horst Fuhrmans writes:

If the basic point of German Idealism was the idea that all being and history is prevailed by Spirit and the Logos; if for Hegel history is born of the prevailing of the Idea which is basically a process, an ascent towards the increasingly essential in which the accidental is removed and put away, this basic insight was deepened by Schelling . . . the prevailing and all determining Logos is none other than Christ, who did not come down from heaven in the incarnation, but rather rose from the bowels of terrestrial being up to the incarnation in order to escort fallen being and redeeming it leads it to salvation.[34]

The model is not a Stoic-Spinozistic pantheism but the Neoplatonic model of the reflection or return of the many to the One: the *exitus* and *reditus*. It was Hegel's mature conviction that God's nature is to restore his alienated creation and this restoration is attained through the transformation of death: through God assuming and transforming that which is alien to him. Atonement is the divine abrogation and sublimation of alienated creation. The roots of this conception are evident in Schelling's philosophical theology. Schelling wrote in 1804: 'The great goal of the universe and its history is nothing other than the complete reconciliation and reintegration with the Absolute.'[35]

Coleridge shares resolutely the interests of the German Idealists in his philosophy of religion. On 12 January 1818 Coleridge wrote of '*Christian* Philosophers, in whose minds there are but four main classes of Truth God The living tri-une God. The alienation from God and the reconciliation to him in the Word & through the Spirit' (*CL* iv. 809). This is the Neoplatonic-idealistic view of the tri-une salvation through the *reditus* of finite being to its divine source. The presence of God in the soul, in the depths of human personality, the

---

[34] 'Wenn es das Grundlegende des deutschen Idealismus war, alles Seiende und alle Geschichte zu fassen als durchwaltet vom Geist und geprägt vom Logos, wenn für Hegel Geschichte geboren wird aus dem Walten de Idee, die darum von Grund auf Prozeß ist, Aufstieg ins immer Gültigere, darin alles Zufällige abgetan und abgedrängt wird, so hat das Schelling damals vertieft, als er einsah . . . der im Sein und in der Geschichte waltende und alles formende Logos ist niemand anders als Christus, der bei seiner Menschwerdung nicht vom Himmel herniederstieg, der vielmehr emporstieg zur Inkarnation aus den Gründen des Weltseins, in denen er seit dem Sündenfall geweilt hat, um dem Gefallenen Sein das Geleit zu geben und es erlösend wieder ins Heile zu führen.' Fuhrman's introduction in Schelling, *Über das Wesen*, pp. 31–2.

[35] Schelling, 'Die große Absicht des Universum und seiner Geschichte ist keine andere als die vollendete Versöhnung und Wiederauflösung in die Absolutheit.' *Philosophie und Religion* in *Schriften von 1801–1804*, p. 629.

immanence of the eternal in the temporal; the apprehension of the divine, Coleridge believes, is a faculty which all possess as the condition of spiritual *renewal*: redemption is primarily spiritual at-one-ment rather than substitutionary satisfaction (*LS*, p. 55). Deification rather than satisfaction is at the centre of Coleridge's speculative theology: 'an assimilation to the Principle of Life, even to him who is *the* Life' (*Aids*, p. 323).[36] Atonement is at-one-ment in the sense of the regeneration and reflection of the soul to God (*LS*, p. 55). Deification is not a characteristically western concept, and is a sign of Greek patristic influence.[37] It suggests Coleridge's debt to both seventeenth-century English Platonists and the Lessing–German Idealistic tradition.

The Greek patristic view of atonement was that Christ is our *representative* not our substitute, and that the effect of his work extends to humanity and creation. The classic formulation is in the father of Trinitarian orthodoxy, Athanasius: Christ became man that we might become divine;[38] by taking our nature he effected a change in human nature.[39] Coleridge's vision of the Christian religion is inextricably linked to his conception of human moral need. This 'spiritual' view of the essence of Christianity is largely rooted in a Christian Platonic interpretation of St Paul. As the American voluntaristic Idealist Josiah Royce writes:

Christianity has never appeared simply as the religion taught by the Master. It has always been an interpretation of the Master and of his religion in the light of some doctrine concerning his mission, and also concerning God, man, and man's salvation, – a doctrine which, even in its simplest expressions, has always gone beyond what the Master himself is traditionally reported to have taught while he lived.[40]

---

[36] Torrance notes: 'Union with Christ probably had a more important place in Leighton's theology than that given to it in the thought of any other Scottish theologian.' *Scottish Theology: from John Knox to John McLeod Campbell* (Edinburgh: T. &T. Clark, 1996), p. 174.

[37] G. Bonner, 'Augustine's conception of deification' in *Journal of Theological Studies*, 37 (1986), pp. 369–86. N. Lossky, *Launcelot Andrewes, the Preacher* (1555–1626): *The Origins of the Mystical Theology of the Church of England*, translated by A. Louth (Oxford: Clarendon, 1991), pp. 249–71.

[38] Αὐτὸς γὰρ ἐνηνθρώπησεν, ἵνα ἡμεῖς θεοποιηθῶμεν. Athanasius, *De Incarnatione*, § 53, 2 in *Sur l'Incarnation du verbe*, edited by Charles Kannengiesser (Paris: Editions du Cerf, 1973), p. 458.

[39] The source of this idea in Patristic literature was Clement of Alexandria, one of the favourites of the Cambridge Platonists. For Clement's use of the language of divinisation, see B. McGinn, *Foundations of Mysticism*, p. 107.

[40] J. Royce, *The Problem of Christianity*, with a new introduction by J. E. Smith (University of Chicago Press, 1968), p. 66.

For Royce, like Coleridge and the German Idealists, Paul is the essential expression of the Christian faith. 'Paul's idea of salvation from original sin through grace, and through loving union with the Spirit of the Master, is inseparable from his special opinions regarding the Church as the body of Christ, and regarding the supernatural existence of the risen Christ as the Spirit of the Church.'[41]

It was natural that Idealism saw a vital connection between the doctrine of the Trinity and the spiritual nature of man as close-knit ideas. The kinship of the divine and human spirit is a basic Idealist tenet and the central Trinitarian texts in the New Testament are those relating to Christ as a cosmic principle and instrument in creation and the indwelling of the spirit of Christ in the soul of the believer. St Paul writes:

For we have received, not the spirit of the world, but the spirit which is of God; that we might know the things that are freely given to us of God . . . But the natural man receiveth not the things of the spirit of God: for they are foolishness unto him: neither can he know them, because they are spiritually discerned. 1 Cor. 2. 12, 14 (*Aids*, p. 146 n. 3; cf. p. 77)

Yet it would be false to associate Coleridge with a facile idealistic optimism. It is striking how many contemporary images of guilt, terror, and horror are derived from 'Romantic Agony': from Mary Shelley's *Frankenstein* to Coleridge's Mariner. This is in part the rejection of the unduly mechanistic anthropology of the Enlightenment. Bentham is an extreme instance:

Nature has placed mankind under the governance of two sovereign masters, *pain* and *pleasure*. It is for them alone to point out what we ought to, as well as determine what we shall do. On the one hand the standard of right and wrong, on the other the chain of causes and effects, are fastened to their throne.[42]

Coleridge attacks this mechanistic anthropology at two points. Firstly, he denies that mankind is an inherently selfish creature. This presupposes a woefully inadequate psychology; in fact human beings have instincts, loyalties, and ideals which extend far beyond private pleasures. Yet also there is a capacity for self-inflicted pain which is quite inscrutable, but very much a part of the human psyche. Iris Murdoch observes that 'modern psychology has provided us with what might be called a doctrine of original sin . . . [Freud] presents

---

[41] Ibid., p. 146.
[42] Bentham in Mill and Bentham, *Utilitarianism*, p. 65.

us with . . . a realistic and detailed picture of the fallen man'. She
notes that he 'takes a throughly pessimistic view of human nature
. . . introspection reveals only the deep tissue of ambivalent motive,
and fantasy is a stronger force than reason'; although she also
observes that 'partially similar views have been expressed before in
philosophy, as far back as Plato'.[43]

ROBERT LEIGHTON AND DYING TO SELF

Coleridge refers to Leighton 'who perhaps of all our learned Protestant Theologians best deserves the title of a spiritual Divine' (*Aids*, p.
155). Coleridge discovered Leighton during his spiritual crisis of
1813–14. The failure of his marriage and the final collapse of the
ambiguous and ultimately disconcerting relationships with Sara
Hutchinson and Wordsworth led to a breakdown. In this period of
grave illness, Coleridge discovered Leighton. The composition of *Aids
to Reflection* was a not a time in which Coleridge could enjoy and reflect
the security of Highgate as refuge for the troubled sage. Rather, it
mirrors a period when Hartley Coleridge's loss of a fellowship at the
most distinguished Oxford college caused his father not merely
paternal anguish, but agonising self-doubt about his own life.

At the period of his discovery of Leighton Coleridge writes: 'O I
have had a new world opened to me, in the infinity of my own Spirit'
(*CL* iii. 463–4) and 'O how I have felt the impossibility of any real
good will not born anew from the Word and the Spirit' (*CL* iii. 463).
What is the link between infinity and rebirth? Nature is a process of
development until the point of death of the organism. Spirit, by way
of contrast, is a process of repeated dying to itself. The life of the
spirit is determined by a law of the renunciation of the superficial
ego with its isolated interests and desires and the identification and
realisation of the individual with a greater unit than the selfish ego.
The natural limit of an organism in death is an *external* fact. The
spiritual 'dying to live' is an *internal* process which manifests infinity.
This dying of the old self is the quickening of the new life, or being
'born anew'. Coleridge writes of 'the principle, which pervades all
Leighton's Writings – his sublime View, I mean, of Religion and
Morality as the means of reforming the human Soul in the Divine
Image (*Idea*)' (*Aids*, p. 534) and one can imagine how for Coleridge in

---

[43] Iris Murdoch, 'On "God" and "good"', p. 341.

his depression this essentially mystical doctrine in Leighton seemed far from morbid but the deepest possible optimism. The life of a Christian seemed the exchange of a living death for a dying life: 'the union betwixt them and their Redeemer . . . not simply by his *power* . . . but *they by his life as their life*' (*Aids*, p. 304). John Beer notes that 'they by . . . life' in this sentence is an insertion of Coleridge's. Instead of the Socinian emphasis upon the resurrection as proof and guarantee of Christ's message, here we find the cross and resurrection as the pattern of the spirit. The divine suffering is not an isolated event but a revelation of ultimate reality: 'the lamb of God, slain from the foundation of the World' (*Aids*, p. 309). Christianity is the affirmation that suffering is not an unpleasant by-product of an otherwise splendid world, but part of the divine fabric.

And yet Coleridge was *finding* his earliest convictions. In an early note in the 1790s he remarked:

Brutal Life – in which we pursue mere corporeal pleasures & interests –

Human Life – in which for the sake of our own Happiness . . . & Glory we pursue studies and objects adapted to our intellectual faculties.

Divine Life – when we die to the creatures & to self and become deiform by following the eternal Laws of order from the pure Love of Order & God. (*Notebooks* i. §256, p. 258)

Charles Lamb, in desperation because of a family tragedy in 1796, wrote to Coleridge in the hope of consolation.[44] Coleridge replied that mankind cannot achieve any degree of heavenly bliss without imitating Christ and Lamb should see himself as a sharer of earthly miseries in order that he might become a partaker of the divine nature. The imitation of Christ, argues Coleridge, means to endure agonies and still to say 'Thy will be done' (*CL* i. 143, p. 238). The notions of partaking in the divine nature and life as a *peregrinatio animae* are very much rooted in the Christian Platonic tradition and in Anglicanism.[45] Evidently puzzled, Lamb replied 'What more than this do those men say, who are for exalting the man Christ Jesus into the second person of an unknown Trinity, – men, whom you or I scruple not to call idolaters?' But it is the idea of the *reformation* of the human will according to the pattern of the Incarnate Word and the

---

[44] His sister killed their mother in a fit of insanity.

[45] R. Hooker, 'Whence is it (saith St Augustine) that some be holier than others, but because God doth dwell in some more plentifully than in some others', in his *Ecclesiastical Polity*, v. 56, 10 in *Works*. For the concept of participation see A. M. Allchin, *Participation in God: a Forgotten Strand in Anglican Tradition* (London: Darton, Longman, and Todd, 1988).

renewed spirit that is central to Robert Leighton's mystical thought which Coleridge dwells upon in *Aids to Reflection*.

God, for Leighton, is not a feudal lord demanding his rights and exacting strict justice or payment of a debt, but a father who offers sonship through death to sin and rebirth in the image of Christ. Although human life in the universe is and should be a 'state of warfare' (*Aids*, p. 31) because the physical world is 'evermore at variance with the Divine Form' (*Aids*, p. 26), a circumstance that exerts its own grim discipline, God's own nature is personal love.

Our condition is universally exposed to fears and troubles . . . Thus men seek safety in the greatness, or multitude, or supposed faithfulness of friends . . . But wiser men, perceiving the unsafety and vanity of these and all external things, have cast about for some higher course. They see a necessity of withdrawing a man from externals, which do nothing but mock and deceive those most who trust most to them . . . So then, though it is well done, to call off a man from outward things, as moving sands, that he build not on them, yet, this is not enough; for his own spirit is as unsettled a piece as in all the world, and must have some higher strength than its own, to fortify and fix it. (*Aids*, p. 120)

God, for Leighton, is the fortifying and fixing force of human life: the 'beginner and sustainer of the Divine life of grace within us' (*Aids*, p. 101). Those who hear the Word receive 'spiritual life and strength'. In this way

God communicates happiness to those who believe, and works that believing into happiness, alters the whole frame of the soul, and makes a new creation, as it begets it again to the inheritance of glory. (*Aids*, p. 102)

Despite the strong emphasis in Leighton upon sin and divine grace, there is also something of a humanism in his theology: 'Now, in this is the excellency of Man, that he is made capable of a communion with his Maker, and, because capable of it, is unsatisfied without it: the soul being cut out (so to speak) to that largeness, cannot be filled with less' (*Aids*, p. 128). (Whichcote writes: 'There is a Capacity in Man's Soul, *larger* than can be Answered by anything of his Own, or any Fellow-Creature.'[46]) Leighton has a vital and ethical view of salvation (religion as the seed of a deiform nature); not as something *alien* to man. His conviction is that salvation is the realisation of the divine purpose: the unfolding of the divine potential in man – 'we

---

[46] Whichcote, *Moral and Religious Aphorisms* , § 847.

truly *are*, only as far as God is with us, so neither can we truly *possess* (*i.e.* enjoy) our Being or any real Good, but by living in the sense of his holy presence' (*Aids*, p. 92). This perfect development is the product of a transformation 'in Christ' the universal archetypal man of Pauline and Alexandrine Platonism: the Logos. This is the key to *life*: 'Religion doth not destroy the life of nature but adds to it a life more excellent' (*Aids*, pp. 95–6). The soul has a natural hunger, a *desidirium naturale*, for spiritual life and the overwhelming conscious-ness of God in the soul is an élan vital.[47] Such is Coleridge's meaning when he exclaims: 'Christianity is not a Theory, or a Speculation; but a *Life*' (*Aids*, p. 202).[48]

Coleridge writes:

It will suffice to satisfy a reflecting mind, that even at the porch and threshold of Revealed Truth there is a great and worthy sense in which we may believe the Apostle's assurance, that not only doth 'the Spirit aid our infirmities;' that is, *act on* the Will by a predisposing influence *from without*, as it were, though in a spiritual manner, and without suspending or destroying its freedom . . . but that in regenerate souls it may act *in* the will; that uniting and becoming one with our will and spirit, it may 'make intercession for us,' nay, in this intimate union taking upon itself the form of our infirmities, may intercede for us . . . (*Aids*, p. 78)

Salvation is a living relationship with a personal God whose eternal nature is love; it is not simply the satisfaction of justice or the escape from debt. The emphasis is upon the 'redemption of our personal being' (*Aids*, p. 299); the renewal of the will which is the 'Principle of our Personality' (*Aids*, p. 77).

William James famously argued in his classic work *Varieties of Religious Experience* that the most profound form of religious belief, that which James calls the 'twice-born' type, is the product of bitter disappointment and sadness. This is the conviction in the goodness of life which develops in an environment of adversity, melancholy, and virtual despair; 'healthy-mindedness is inadequate as a philo-sophical doctrine, because the evil facts which it refuses positively to account for are a genuine portion of reality; and they may after all be the best key to our life's significance, and possibly the only

---

[47] See Torrance, *Scottish Theology*, pp. 157–79.

[48] It is noteworthy that the French existentialist philosopher Gabriel Marcel wrote on Coleridge and Schelling after listening to Bergson. Bergson lectured on Plotinus at the Collège de France (1897–9) and on Berkeley's *Siris* in 1907–8 during Marcel's study in Paris. I owe this point to Lewis Owens. The dynamism and vitalism of the mystics fed into twentieth-century existentialism.

openers of our eyes to the deepest levels of truth'.[49] This sense of alienation from God is in fact the prelude to renunciation and conversion. Christianity, James notes, is – like Buddhism – essentially a religion 'of deliverance': 'man must die to an unreal life before he can be born into the real life'.[50] James' justly famous depiction of this 'second birth' concentrates upon St Augustine.[51] Strikingly, James observes that 'for this extremity of pessimism to be reached, something more is needed than observation of life and reflection upon death. The individual must in his own person become the prey of a pathological melancholy':[52] Coleridge discovered Leighton in a period of severe depression. Leighton exemplifies the Platonic-Pauline mystical principle that renunciation as the path to personal self-realisation is the overriding truth of the spiritual life.

One point at which Coleridge differs radically from Kant is on the topic of experience. Coleridge's theology of a 'living communion with the Universal Spirit' (*Aids*, p. 88) is emphatically experiential, and he polemicises against the eighteenth-century Anglican attack upon claims of 'an immediate consciousness, a sensible Experience, of the Spirit in and during its operation on the soul' (*Aids*, p. 83). The predecessors of Paley had prepared the ground for an externalist view of Christianity by ridiculing the idea of the immediate experience of the Divine: 'pilloried by Butler, sent to Bedlam by Swift, and (on their re-appearance in public) *gibbeted* by Warburton' (ibid.). It is odd that in his assertion of an experiential account of the Christian religion Coleridge should appeal to Kant, for whom God is not an object of possible experience.

And yet the thrust of Kant's philosophy of religion, its radically interior nature, the insistence that the idea of God resists the analysis of the scientific intellect, and is bound to the moral aspiration and confidence in providential order – all of these ideas are structurally compatible with Coleridge's avowal of the experiential knowledge of the divine; and, in particular, Kant's analysis of the 'radical evil' in the human will; of what William James calls the 'divided self'.

ORIGINAL SIN

A life of Wickedness is a life of Lies; and an Evil Being or the Being of Evil, the last and darkest mystery. (*Aids*, p. 92)

---

[49] W. James, *The Varieties of Religious Experience* (Harmondsworth: Penguin, 1982), p. 163.
[50] Ibid., p. 165.   [51] Ibid., pp. 166ff.   [52] Ibid., p. 145.

The dogma of original sin was subjected to considerable attack by prominent Enlightenment thinkers. The story of a minor transgression by a primordial couple in a paradisal garden resulting in the severest punishment of all mankind barely coheres with theological tenets of the divine benevolence and wisdom, and it was easy for Diderot, d'Holbach, and Helvétius to subject the doctrine as a historical explanation of empirical data to ridicule.

Yet it is an enormously powerful symbol of the perceived human condition, of a sense of estrangement and alienation which is inextricably linked to human nature. Kolakowski observes that if the story had been understood as an *explanation* of the misery of human history, Adam and Eve would have been objects of hatred, and yet their depiction in art and folklore has been overwhelmingly benevolent and understanding; as if their temptation is very familiar to us.[53] The symbolic expression of such facts of human experience is not absurd, and poets, artists, and pyschologists dwell on this topic in a very imaginative and powerful manner; not least Coleridge in the sombre and chaotic imaginative world of *The Rime of the Ancient Mariner*, where the theme of the pilgrimage, sin, and wilful evil, and recognition of that evil is so prominent and powerful.[54] The doctrine of original sin is a point at which Christianity is particularly susceptible to powerful and damaging criticism. Yet it is also a doctrine which exerts a particular fascination: the sense of the indelibility of guilt, and human self-discontent find powerful expression in the symbol of the Fall. It is a mark of Coleridge's ingenuity as a theologian that he is able to harness this powerful symbol, while carefully avoiding the most vulnerable aspects of the dogma.

Coleridge provides a *philosophical interpretation* of the doctrine as a symbol of the human condition: 'the fact of a moral corruption connatural with the human race. In the assertion of ORIGINAL SIN the Greek Mythology rose and set' (*Aids*, p. 285). It is a 'Fact acknowledged in all Ages, and recognised, but not originating, in the Christian Scriptures' (*Aids*, p. 287). Coleridge's interpretation revolves around the Kantian concept of causality. It seems, prima facie, odd to speak of the philosophical interpretation of the ecclesiastical doctrine. Yet the philosophical rehabilitation of the dogma of sin has its roots in Kant and Schelling and became

---

[53] Kolakowski, *Religion*, p. 51.
[54] J. A. Stewart, 'The Augustinian "cause of action" in Coleridge's *Rime of The Ancient Mariner*' in *Harvard Theological Review* 60 (1967), pp. 177–211.

influential in twentieth-century existentialism through Kierkegaard's concept of anxiety. That which seemed monstrous to the Enlightenment, the doctrine of biologically inherited sin, is transformed by Kant, Schelling, and Kierkegaard into a description of the inherent structure of humanity's habitual moral condition.[55] Coleridge belongs to this tradition of refashioning the dogma.

One might argue that the concept of sin is a symptom of the neurotic guilt-ridden mentality of Christian theology. Yet Coleridge would deny this. He insists that it is proper consideration of ethics which drives theology to consider evil and sin with due seriousness. Goethe said of Kant, who astonished his contemporaries by asserting a version of the doctrine of sin: he 'had criminally smeared his philosopher's cloak with the shameful stain of radical evil . . . so that Christian too might yet be enticed to kiss its hem'.[56]

Rousseau, who did more to wake Kant from his dogmatic slumbers than Hume, presents an image of an originally good human nature which is corrupted by society; he points to the human environment – especially the educational and civic organisations. These require reorganisation on the premises of man as inherently good, but who requires the right community in which to develop this goodness. For utilitarians, who see happiness as the good and morality as essentially prudential, and instrumental, that is as a means to the end of happiness, moral badness is primarily a pedagogical problem. For the utilitarian the state of mind of an agent is subordinate to the effects of particular acts.

Kant, by contrast, sees the good will as the unconditional good, and thus the quality of that will is the most significant fact about the moral life. Guilt, as Adams observes, is generated by the anti-utilitarian principle of the good will as the sole unconditional good.[57] And, unlike Rousseau, Kant blames the individual will rather than human society: humanity is accountable for the propensity to evil. Moral evil is the subordination of moral duty to sensuous inclination or self-love and radical evil is the freely willed choice of an evil ground of maxim-making that results in this subordination of

---

55 S. Kierkegaard, *The Concept of Anxiety: a Simple Psychologically Orientating Deliberation on the Dogmatic Issue of Hereditary Sin*, translated by R. Thomte with A. B. Anderson (Princeton University Press, 1980) and M. Heidegger, *Sein und Zeit* § 39 (Tübingen: Niemeyer, 1993).

56 Michalson, *Fallen Freedom*, p. 17.

57 R. M. Adams, 'Introduction' in Kant, *Religion within the Boundaries of Mere Reason and Other Writings*, edited by A. Wood, and G. di Giovanni (Cambridge University Press, 1998), pp. xi ff.

the moral incentive to the sensuous, which means that moral evil is not a privation – perhaps based on ignorance – but a positive and inscrutable reality in the process of maxim-making. There is a battle in human nature between the 'original predisposition to good' and a 'natural propensity to evil'. In the depiction of this conflict Kant claims that evil is innate, but humanity is not deprived of freedom by virtue of the fact that we are radically evil. This would mean that we would have no moral consciousness. The idea of the good will is inherently religious because it breaches no qualification or limitation, and as such one can barely hope to find it instantiated in the empirical realm. The aspiration to absolute goodness must be a fact about the agent's inward disposition not simply the conformity to external norms.

We call an Individual a *bad* Man, not because an action is contrary to the Law, but because it has led us to conclude from it some *Principle* opposed to the Law, some private Maxim or By-law in the Will contrary to the universal Law of right Reason in the Conscience, as the *Ground* of the action. But this evil Principle again must be grounded in some other Principle which has been made determinant of the Will by the Will's own self-determination. For if not, it must have its ground in some necessity of Nature, in some instinct or propensity imposed, not acquired, another's work not our own. (*Aids*, p. 286)

Here Coleridge is giving expression to the basic Kantian tenet that the source of evil does not lie in any external object determining the will through inclination or in any natural impulse; it rests in a rule made by the will for the use of its freedom, that is in a *maxim*. A maxim is a subjective determination of the will, and its relation to the moral law determines the moral quality of the maxim. The formulation of the categorical imperative is: 'Act as if the maxim of your action were to become through your will a universal law of nature.'[58] This is not a rule-based but a maxim-based imperative. There is some debate about Kant's exact meaning, but a maxim is a guiding principle which is more flexible than a rigid rule and yet intelligible rather than whimsical or mechanical. The idea is that an agent faced by varied circumstances cannot simply follow rules and yet ethical behaviour must have a rational structure. For example, a considerate and generous man with a young family to support will have quite different responsibilities from those of an equally generous and

[58] H. J. Paton, *The Moral Law*, p. 84.

considerate bachelor; it would be odd to expect the former to donate large sums to charity, whereas it a may be a duty for the latter. Yet we may perceive a similar character through the application of the same maxims to different circumstances, even if the concrete norms of external action differ radically. The use of maxims provides Kant's ethics with the means to avoid either a narrow and dogmatic ethics of specific rules of behaviour or a relativistic irrationalism.

Further, a maxim is always subjectively valid even when it is not universally valid (i.e. does not conform to the categorical imperative). This is because even when we are not morally good we are still far from being simply creatures of whim or naive spontaneity; our rational nature involves our use of principles, whether these be good or bad.

We have no choice in our predisposition to good, since 'the ground-work of *Personal* Being is a capacity of acknowledging the Moral Law (the Law of the Spirit, the Law of Freedom, the Divine Will)' (*Aids*, p. 286); a predisposition to personality which involves the capacity for respect for the moral law – this constitutes our potential to be rational human beings. But we do have a choice in our propensities to evil, and hence are culpable. Although our sensuous nature is morally neutral, there is a moral dimension which arises from the sensuous condition. One cannot eliminate sexual instincts, but one can gain a measure of control and discipline over these instincts – we exercise some responsibility over and hence account-ability for our sensuousness. But Kant actually believes that all rational beings succumb to the propensity to evil, even if he does not really argue for it – apart from through tales of depravity.[59]

One might argue that Kant is faced with two conflicting narratives or paradigms – the Enlightenment adherence to autonomy and the inherited Christian story of the Fall and salvation. Kant seems to veer uneasily between the two. His failure to resolve this antinomy is a sign of both the incoherence and the profundity of his thought.[60] Or perhaps it is because his conception of autonomy ultimately generates an essentially religious ethics, one where the agent cannot entirely grasp what is required for the radical restructuring of the personality in accordance with the supreme good. A popular misconception of Kant's autonomy is based on the assumption that

---

[59] Kant, *Religion*, p. 56.
[60] This is the position of Michalson in *Fallen Freedom*.

Kant's views on the subject are stated exhaustively in the *Moral Law*. But that book is just a *Groundwork for a Metaphysics of Morals*, and Kant's further reflections, especially those in his *Religion* show how seriously any metaphysics of practical reason and freedom has to deal with the fact of 'the crooked timber of humanity' and its need for assistance; or, put in other terms, that Kant's reflections upon the demands of the moral life lead him into an ancient debate about nature and grace. That Coleridge is capable of drawing Kant into a theological controversy is not a sign of his exegetical carelessness and misunderstanding of the Prussian philosopher, but of the Englishman's profound insight into the deeper layer of Kant's thought. R. M. Adams notes of the anti-utilitarian emphasis upon the unconditional quality of the good will in Kant:

> It is one of the points at which his thought about good and evil in human nature is deeply attuned to the dynamics of the Lutheran piety in which he was reared. That was a piety in which the absolute perfection of the divine ideal brings into strong relief, by contrast, the universality, subtlety, and depth of evil in human motivation, which in turn gives rise to a powerful need for salvation.[61]

Coleridge applies his Kantian analysis to a critique of one of his favourite writers: Jeremy Taylor. This contemporary of the Cambridge Platonists shared many of their interests and inclinations; and his is a particularly magnificent instance of the baroque prose which Coleridge admired so fervently – 'this most eloquent of Divines' (*Aids*, p. 257). Hence Jeremy Taylor is no 'straw man' nor a butt of sheer theological polemic; he serves to show what 'no impartial person can deny': that the doctrines of the Church of England in the sixteenth century were determined by a strong view of grace and these were replaced by an Arminianism, which Coleridge regarded as Grotianism or semi-Socinianism (*Aids*, p. 161, Comment).[62] Jeremy Taylor is taken as an instance of Arminianism which culminates in the semi-Socinianism of William Paley. Coleridge detects a gradual slide from a fully dogmatic Trinitarian Christian theology via Arminianism to a barely disguised Unitarianism within the folds of the established Church of England.[63]

---

[61] Kant, *Religion*, p. xv.

[62] cf. Alan P. F. Sell, *The Great Debate: Calvinism, Arminianism, and Salvation* (Grand Rapids, Mich.: Bake Book House, 1982), p. 26.

[63] For the influence of Jeremy Taylor's view of sin upon Locke, see Spellman, *Locke and Human Depravity*, pp.97–103.

In his discussion of original sin Coleridge selects aphorisms from the 'ablest and most formidable antagonist of this doctrine', the semi-Pelagian Anglican bishop Jeremy Taylor (1613–67) chaplain to Charles I and from 1658 onwards Bishop of Down and Connor.[64] Jeremy Tayor, best known for his devotional writings, became embroiled in a controversy about his tract *Unum Necessarium* concerning Taylor's Arminianism and alleged Pelagianism.[65] Taylor argues that the result of Adam's Fall was a deprivation of many of the advantages of prelapsarian life, but it did not lead to the utter depravity of mankind. Adam was made 'naked of his supernatural endowments', sentenced to death, and 'fell under the evils of a sickly body, and a passionate, ignorant and uninstructed soul'.

His sin left him to his *Nature*: and by Nature, whoever was to be born at all, was to be born a child, and to do before he could understand, and be bred under laws to which he was always bound, but which could not always be exacted; and he was to choose when he could not reason, and had passions most strong when he had his understanding most weak. (*Aids*, pp. 265–6)

Adam's plight is that of being deprived of supernatural aids, and having to make do with a nature which, though not depraved, has a most uneasy relationship between its powers and its duties: 'it is hard for a man to live up to the rule of his own Reason and Conscience' (*Aids*, p. 266). Worse still, the difficulties encountered by the individual human nature are made almost intolerable by social life. The problem of trying to accommodate and co-ordinate diverse individual interests means that 'every man dashes against another, and one relation requires what another denies' (*Aids*, p. 266).

Coleridge's first specific criticism is that although Taylor admits

---

[64] On Jeremy Taylor's life and thought see J. Tulloch, *Rational Theology and Christian Philosophy* (Hildesheim: Olms, 1966), vol. i. pp. 344–410; P. Elmen, 'Jeremy Taylor and the Fall of man' in *Modern Language Quarterly* 14 (1952), pp. 139–48; T. G. Steffan, 'Jeremy Taylor's criticism of abstract speculation' in *Studies in English* 20 (1940), pp. 96–108; R. F. Brinkley, 'Coleridge's criticism of Jeremy Taylor' in *Huntington Library Quarterly* 13 (1950), pp. 313–23.

[65] Pelagius believes that man is a sinner but this does not mean that he has no freedom of will. Grace is that which helps enable the realisation of freedom: grace is an *adjutorium Dei*. For Augustine the sinner does have not the freedom of Adam, i.e. the freedom to choose good or bad, but only freedom to choose bad. True freedom, however, is identical with the good will, which, on account of and after the Fall, can only be achieved through grace. Augustine's difference from Pelagius is that grace is necessary not just for the knowledge but for *will*: it precedes human will (*gratia praeveniens*) against opposition (*gratia operans*) and co-operates with the human will (*gratia cooperans*) and helps to bind mankind to the good (*gratia perseverans*). There is a Pelagian tendency in Socinianism and the biblical critic Semler (1725–91). A lively and sympathetic modern discussion of Pelagius is B. R. Rees, *Pelagius: a Reluctant Heretic* (Woodbridge: Boydell, 1991).

the universality of original sin he cannot explain why sin should be 'original'. Taylor's view of sin amounts to a belief in a 'quantum' of sufferings. Taylor deals with sin as if it were something external to, and different from, the will. Firstly, he has not made clear the difference between evil and sin: 'A Sin is an Evil which has its ground or origin in the Agent, and not in the compulsion of Circumstances' (*Aids*, p. 266). Evil is thus the wider-ranging concept: it may be related to circumstances outside the agent and not within the originant will of the agent. *Original* sin means, in a typical instance of Coleridge's linguistic ingenuity, evil which *originates* in the will. For Coleridge the statement that 'Adam's sin left him to his Nature' is metaphysically incoherent.

The Power which we call Nature, may be thus defined: A Power subject to the Law of Continuity, (*Lex Continui. In Naturâ non datur Saltus*) which law the human understanding, by a necessity arising out of its own constitution, can *conceive* only under the form of Cause and Effect. That this *form* (or law) of Cause and Effect is (relatively to the World *without*, or to Things as they subsist independently of our perceptions) only a form or mode of *thinking*; that is a law inherent in the Understanding itself. (*Aids*, p. 267)

This is a Kantian view of the mind representing nature, the sum of possible experience, as a closed and determined causal domain. As observers of nature, we must do this. But this is not an adequate description of reality; the philosopher must also consider the noumenal realm, the location of the free rational will. Here Coleridge makes the (rather Berkeleyian) point that causation is a projection of the human experience of will on to outward experience, and that 'every appearance of origination in *Nature* is but a shadow of our casting. It is reflection of our own *Will* or Spirit' (*Aids*, p. 268).

Coleridge is arguing that the way in which we think compels us to accept that all events in time have *causes which are also events in time*. Yet the act portrayed dramatically in the story of Genesis 3 must resist, Coleridge avers, any *causal* explanation. The story of the Fall narrates events in a temporal sequence, but the point of the story is the nature of man as a noumenal timeless being. Sin must be prior to man's conceptual organisation of experience.[66] On this Kantian foundation, Coleridge argues that Taylor has confused *original* with *hereditary* sin. Taylor thinks of original sin as an event in time which

---

[66] Robert F. Brown, 'The transcendental fall in Kant and Schelling' in *Idealistic Studies* 14 (1984), pp. 49–66 and N. P. Williams, *The Ideas of the Fall and Original Sin*, The Bampton Lectures 1924 (London: Longmans, Green and Co., 1927), pp. 497 ff.

had a causal influence upon all subsequent events in time, whereas Coleridge thinks that the account in Genesis clearly relates to a 'pretemporal' event.[67] For Kant, mankind is, as a species (*Gattungs-wesen*) evil insofar as he prefers selfish inclination to the moral law. This inclination (*Hang zum Bösen*) can only be moral guilt if it is the result of human choice. Kant refers to a choice before time: an intelligible and pre-temporal deed is the basic sin which underlies all particular sins – a transcendental fall which is the reason for radical evil and original sin.[68] The tension between the postulate of freedom and the awareness of the radical evil inclination of man is resolved metaphysically rather than historically; or at least the attempt is made. A. E. Taylor notes that

The famous Kantian mythus of the 'ante-temporal' intelligible act of choice which fixes our status as sheep or goats once and for all is no more than a confession that no explanation is forthcoming. At bottom Kant is merely reverting to the Augustinian nightmare of the *massa perditionis*, though he tries to 'save the face' of his Deity by pretending that it is we who 'reprobate' ourselves for all eternity.[69]

Coleridge's replacement of the theory of hereditary-biological trans-mission of guilt with the Kantian-Schellingian idea of a pre-temporal fall is at best obscure.

Although Jeremy Taylor rejects the traditional doctrine of heredi-tary sin, he does not see that his own account suffers from a kindred weakness in his confusion of original sin with external calamity. This calamity being common to all men, it is supposed to arise from their common nature. Jeremy Taylor is horrified by the thought that this calamity should be a reason for God to inflict everlasting torment upon mankind; he asserts that as a penalty for his crime Adam lost all his 'super natural aids and graces' and thereby obedience to God became incomparably difficult in comparison to the prelapsarian state where mankind was endowed with rectitude and supernatural grace proportionate to the required obedience. Yet however exacting Adam's postlapsarian task of obedience may have been, it was not – Jeremy Taylor thought – impossible, even though he admits that no man has ever achieved this theoretical rectitude. Coleridge thinks

---

[67] For a critique of Coleridge's view see F. R. Tennant, *The Sources of the Doctrines of the Fall and Original Sin* (Cambridge University Press, 1903), p. 59.

[68] Kant, *Religion innerhalb der Grenzen der bloßen Vernunft*, § 39 n. in his *Werke*, or in recent English translation, *Religion*.

[69] Taylor, *Faith of a Moralist*, vol. i. pp. 217–18.

that Taylor's argument is flawed: its sophistry lies in asserting for the whole that which is only valid for the part. Any person can snap a horsehair: this does not mean that the same person can break a horse's tail; one might be able to walk two or three paces without being able to walk for two or three leagues. Perfect rectitude may be possible for a short span of a person's life but impossible for a lifetime (cf. *Aids*, p. 277).

The main problem with Jeremy Taylor's account is his concept of equity, and the conviction that by rejecting the notion of human depravity he can defend divine justice. God's punishment in the average case is just the same as in Adam's case: the just response to a freely chosen failure. Yet true equity, Coleridge thinks, seems to dictate just the opposite.

> Surely, that the supplementary Aids, the super-natural Graces correspondent to a Law above Nature, should be increased in proportion to the diminished strength of the Agents, and the increased resistance to be overcome by them! But no! . . . (Adam's) descendants were despoiled or left destitute of these Aids and Graces, while the obligation to perfect obedience was continued. (*Aids*, p. 278)

Hence Taylor's semi-Pelagian scheme is vitiated by its manifold injustice; just like the orthodox Augustinian doctrine of a *massa perditionis*. A landowner is given the right to proceed legally against trespassers upon his property, but this does not mean that it is morally correct for the landowner to proceed criminally; on the contrary, one can imagine cases where the landowner's conscience should forbid the execution of his legal right. Similarly, it is quite specious to attempt to justify divine punishment when God is exacting punishment for failure of a standard of obedience which is practically impossible (*Aids*, p. 278).

Jeremy Taylor's concern for 'holy living' and obedience to the new divine covenant in Christ seemed Pelagian, it seemed to deny the need for divine grace and mercy, and his theology was vigorously criticised as anti-Augustinian, an issue which perhaps cost him an English bishopric.[70] Taylor asserts that conscious and deliberate sin precludes divine forgiveness.[71] This was a doctrine which Coleridge thought was 'calculated to drive men to despair'. Coleridge's objection to Arminianism – and it was Taylor who opened his eyes to this

[70] H. Trevor Hughes, *The Piety of Jeremy Taylor* (London: Macmillan, 1960), pp. 31–5.
[71] C. F. Allison, *The Rise of Moralism* (London: SPCK, 1966), pp. 82–95.

– was that it was in substance quite as cruel as Calvinism, while appearing far more humane. Calvinism contained an element of truth in its emphasis upon ineluctable divine graciousness, but distorted this truth into a false and cruel total system by trying to expound a mystery in a relentlessly logical mode. Coleridge's own views were 'equidistant' from both Arminianism and Calvinism (*F* i. 434) but he regarded Calvinism to be 'a lamb in wolf's skin', and Arminianism as the reverse (ibid.). Taylor's theology, in Coleridge's opinion, was effectively just as rigorous and harsh at the pastoral level as Calvinism, but without possessing the grain of truth of Calvinism: 'In short, Socinianism is just as inevitable deduction from Taylor's scheme as Deism or Atheism is from Socinianism' (*NED* i. 248).

Coleridge's discussion of sin is preceded by his distinction between Reason and Understanding, spirit and nature, and the significance of mankind's position between these two realms. Sin, for Coleridge, is the state of being illuminated by reason but not acknowledging the *lumen intellectus*: the light of reason. All mankind employs the light of reason in their thought and action, but only a few acknowledge it. The human understanding has no independent existence for Coleridge – it depends upon reason or sense for its materials: it is sensory instinct *and* divine reason.

Sin is traditionally thought of in various and sometimes conflicting ways as rooted in sensuality, pride, and self-will.[72] The view that sin is based upon sensuality is sometimes thought to be Platonic, but Augustine dismisses the idea that the 'bad behaviour of the soul is due to the influence of the flesh'.[73] Sensuality as the explanation of sin would be too materialistic or Gnostic-Manichean to suit the Platonists – sensuality is a component of sin, but sin per se must have a spiritual motor. Pride seems a much better candidate, and is clearly seen as the distinctive characteristic of sin; but the Christian Platonists tend to see pride as the culmination rather than the root of sin.[74] The origin of sin is self-will. Plato states clearly that

the cause of each and every crime we commit is precisely this excessive love of ourselves, a love which blinds us to the faults of the beloved and makes

[72] cf. W. R. Inge, *Personal Idealism and Mysticism* (London: Longmans, Green, and Co., 1907), pp. 154–86.
[73] Augustine, *City of God*, xiv. 3; p. 550.
[74] In Genesis 3 Satan explicitly appeals to the pride of Eve, and Jesus is presented in the New Testament as humble, cf. Phil. 2: 6.

us bad judges of goodness and beauty and justice, because we believe we should honour our own ego rather than the truth.[75]

Sin, for Coleridge, is the opposition of the finite *will* to the Infinite will; this is the standard Christian Platonist or mystical view;[76] a point he makes by playing with the word 'original'. He writes that 'Original Sin, is a Pleonasm, the epithet not adding to the thought, but only enforcing it. For if it be Sin, it must be *original*: and a State or Act, that has not its origin in the will, may be calamity, deformity, desease, or mischief; but a *Sin* it cannot be' (*Aids*, pp. 270–1).[77] Kant defines evil in terms of sensuous incentives gaining the upper hand in the formation of maxims. Sensuousness is given, we cannot be blamed for it. But we exercise freedom over the ways in which the sensuous incentives affect us. The self legislating capacity which is at the basis of Kant 's theory of freedom is the capacity to control and re-order what is given naturally to human beings. This is a struggle for all rational agents, and one which is enevitably lost. Moral evil is the inscrutable and free process by which one sort of incentive overrides another. Moral evil is an unaccountable quality of the free will.

The Understanding which is the faculty of 'means to proximate ends' is a sophistic principle when it is not allied to reason, it becomes the 'Advocate of the Passions and the Appetites', appetite rather than of Reason (*Aids*, p. 259ff.). Thus the Genesis story of Adam being tempted by Eve is a symbol of the seduction of the rational will by desire – of the perversion of the understanding. Coleridge insists that a symbol is the *translucence* of the eternal through and in the temporal, and the myth of the Fall is the symbolic expression of mankind's 'natural' state.[78] It expresses the human experience of sin as it reveals itself in time and is an object of consciousness, but the fact which the symbol symbolises is not historical but a mystery revealing itself in history.[79]

---

[75] Plato, *Laws*, 732a, translated by T. J. Saunders (London: Heinemann, 1970), p. 196.

[76] cf. W. R. Inge, *Christian Mysticism* (London: Methuen, 1899), p. 185.

[77] Kant does not use the German theological term for hereditary sin 'Erbsünde', but uses the Latin term *peccatum originarium* which does not bear the connotation of heredity. See introduction by Allen Wood and George di Giovanni in Kant, *Religion*, p. xii.

[78] Coleridge's view of the Genesis account of Eden as a symbolic description of the origin of sin and the nature of freedom is fiercely criticised by Tennant in his *Fall and Original Sin*, p. 80. Elaine Pagels' account of the patristic exegesis of the Genesis paradise story, *Adam, Eve, and the Serpent* (Harmondsworth: Penguin, 1990) shows how it inspired much speculation about the nature of freedom.

[79] cf. Davidson, *Coleridge's Career*, pp. 218ff.

Coleridge wishes to reconstruct what we might call the Augustinian spiritual metaphysics of man's state as the *experimentum suae medietatis* – as the experiment of his own middle position between nature and spirit – without resorting to that 'monstrous fiction of hereditary sin' which Coleridge sees as an unacceptable exposition of the dogma of original sin.[80] This is 'the perversion of the Article of Original Sin by Augustine, and the frightful conclusions which this *durus pater infantum* drew from the Article thus perverted' (*Aids*, p. 373).

In a discussion concerning the disproportion between moral worth and worldly goods which forces the mind upon that which distinguishes man from beast, or the diversity between the injunctions of the mind and the will, and the unsatisfactory nature of the sensual realm, Coleridge remarks that contemplative natures are led from such consideration to reflections concerning the 'riddle of man' (*Aids*, p. 348–50). Coleridge writes approvingly of the 'single remark of St Augustine, that there neither are nor can be but three essential differences of Being, viz the Absolute, the Rational Finite, and the Finite irrational; i.e. God, Man, and Brute' (*CCS*, p. 169). Man's situation is that of the middle point between the finite and the infinite. He can turn – and this is his natural state – to the sensual realm or he can participate through the aids of the spirit in the realm of the spirit.

Coleridge's conviction is that the imperfect human understanding can be 'effectively exerted only in *subordination* to, and in a dependent *alliance* with, the means and aids supplied by the all-perfect and supreme Reason' (*Aids*, p. 141):

Whenever by self-subjection to this universal Light, the Will of the Individual, the *particular* Will, has become a Will of Reason, the man is regenerate: and Reason is then the *Spirit* of the regenerated man, whereby the Person is capable of a quickening inter-communion with the Divine Spirit. (*Aids*, p. 217)

Here we find the nerve of Coleridge's philosophy and his spirituality. The spirit is an 'Energy not a Soul' (*Aids*, p. 152 n. 6) and it is an energy of renewal: 'The imitation of and participation in the Divine means a "soul renewed"' (*Aids*, p. 127), the forming 'anew of the Divine Image in the soul' (*Aids*, p. 26), the 'second creation or birth in the divine image' (*Aids*, p. 40). Coleridge describes this as:

[80] cf. R. Berlinger, *Augustins dialogische Metaphysik* (Frankfurt: Klostermann, 1961), pp. 196 ff.

'the finite will reduced to harmony with, and in subordination to, the reason, as a ray from that true light which is both reason and will, universal reason, and will absolute' (*Aids*, p. 42). The property of spirit 'is to improve, enliven, actuate some other thing, not to constitute a thing in its own name' (*Aids*, p. 152) or 'quickening inter-communion with the Divine Spirit' (*Aids*, p. 217) which is assimilation to the incarnate Word (*Aids*, p. 385). Coleridge depicts the trans-formation of the soul through participation in the divine light of Reason.

Traditional Augustinian theology attempts to give a *causal* expla-nation of the Fall in terms of mankind's pride or finitude which is a biologically inherited depravity for the children of Adam.[81] Coleridge rejects such a move as an illegitimate application of the causal category to the realm of the ideas. In Coleridge's Kantian modification of the doctrine of original sin man's fallenness and consequent estrangement from the good is simply not a question susceptible of explanation; we can only conceive of *'nature'* as a chain of cause and effect. Through the will, that is, through the moral being, mankind exerts a qualitatively different power: an originating power (*Aids,* pp. 267ff.). In nature there is no origin but a chain of cause and effect. If we allow that the evil is supposed to imply the impossibility of referring to a time, time is alien to it. This is the 'precise import' of the Scriptural doctrine of *original* sin.

We can see that Coleridge accepts, to a limited extent, the Socinian-Enlightenment criticism of the traditional account. Coleridge makes it clear that he does not take the story of the Fall to be an historical event: he takes Adam to mean the human race, and considers Adam's Fall to express the universal condition of mankind. Coleridge notes that Paul uses the phrase the 'old man' synony-mously with Adam (*Aids*, p. 290). Hence sin is not the inherited product of the act of Adam – a biologically transmitted deficiency – but a *structural* deficiency in mankind.[82] It must originate in the human spiritual nature through the structural tensions between the wants of an animal and a divine spirit.

---

[81] cf. Kelly, *Early Christian Doctrines*, p. 361. Much more polemical is K. Flasch, *Logik des Schreckens* (Mainz: Dieterich'sche Verlagsbuchhandlung, 1990).

[82] Kierkegaard also rejects the idea of inherited sin. Kierkegaard maintains the universality of sin, but *as* the free repetition of Adam's act. He discusses the idea of sin with the concept of anxiety. cf. M. Theunissen, *Der Begriff Verzweiflung* (Frankfurt am Main: Anton Hain, 1993), pp. 13–42.

Coleridge also treats the story of Genesis as a *myth*, and he compares it with the story of Prometheus and Cupid and Psyche. Coleridge claims that original sin was an acknowledged mystery to the Greeks (*Aids*, p. 284). Hence the idea of sin is not a specifically Christian doctrine: it is quite unfair to attack Christianity, he claims, with arguments which apply to any religion. The doctrine of sin is a conviction which Christianity shares with every religion and every philosophy which accepts the existence of a responsible will. The doctrine of redemption from sin gives the believer grounds for belief in the divinity of the Redeemer rooted in the 'economy' of his soul (*Aids*, p. 188).

Coleridge's distinction between 'regret' and 'remorse' is based upon the difference between evil in circumstances (things that *stand around* us (*Aids*, p. 26)) and sin which is an evil which has its ground or origin 'in the Agent' (*Aids*, p. 266).

Now the LAW – (that is, the Knowledge of the Law –) in the conscience working remorse detects and exposes this imposture: and compells the ACT (i.e. the Agent, the Sinner considered abstractly in reference to this his Sin) to know and confess its abiding *present*ness. In the very pang of Remorse the guilty person *finds* and is made to *feel*, that the ACT is present in its abiding Principle and as one with its Principle . . . the regenerate Will, which the Apostle aptly and significantly calls the *New Man*, is by Grace and not by the Law. Does not our ordinary Experience confirm this, and bear witness to the truth of ST Paul's doctrine? REMORSE may suffice to *torment*, but Remorse without Hope never yet *reformed*, a Sinner. Remorse is no *Purgatory Angel*. Now there is no true Hope but in and thro' Christ. (*Aids*, p. 471)

Coleridge's point in stating that remorse is no *Purgatory Angel* is that the self-knowledge of one's need, the shameful knowledge of remorse, is not enough to renew the soul. More is required than simply a response to the environment or the merely human realm. The sense of guilt or shame towards God demands some power which is not within the finite agent's resources. The answer to this problem is to see the divine not merely as the goal and ideal of the moral life but as the empowering energy of the attempt to become like God. Kant uses the idea of 'divine assistance' for practical purposes as an object of rational hope, a supplement to the inadequacy of merely human aspiration; yet strictly guarding against superstition or a debilitating complacency that it is God's responsibility: it is not essential to know what aids God provides, 'but it is essential to know *what a human being has to do himself* in order to become worthy of this assistance'.[83] John Oman pertinently observed that 'under the new names Rationalism and Romanticism, we recognise the old antagonisms of free-will and predestination which at one era bore the names Pelagianism and Augustinianism, and, at another, Arminianism and Calvinism'.[84]

Nor is this idea of the bondage and renewal of the soul a theological appendage to Coleridge's philosophy. One might support Coleridge's reflections on a philosophical idea of sin with the observation that both Plato and Kant were inclined to see mankind as essentially flawed and the genuinely moral life as a *renewal* rather than as the *expression* of the natural man. Plato distinguishes, in effect, between a dying-to-life and living-in-death in the contrast between the philosopher who in the *Phaedo* (66c–68b) practises death through the progressive purification of the soul from inferior and base attachments and the lover of body (68c). The Christian mystics, in as much as they knew Plato, interpreted him so. And in Kant's *Religion within the Boundaries of Mere Reason* Coleridge could find the Pauline 'new man'.[85]

BAPTISM AND SPIRITUAL RENEWAL

Coleridge returns in *Aids to Reflection* to Leighton during the discussion of baptism. Leighton, who is commenting on John the Baptist, dwells on the connection between baptism and preaching 'the word unfolding the Sacrament, and the Sacrament unfolding the Word' (*Aids*, pp. 359ff.). This is the ceremony of the new life; without the divine illumination the most luminous truths are shrouded in obscurity: 'Noonday is as midnight to a blind man' (*Aids*, p. 361).

the Word unfolding the Sacrament, and the Sacrament sealing the Word . . . the Word is a Light and the Sacraments have in them of the same Light illuminating them. This (sacrament) of Baptism, the ancients do particularly express by *Light*. (*Aids*, p. 360–1)

Why did Coleridge choose the doctrine of baptism to conclude his discussion of the renewed life? This is perhaps because the birth to a new life is the decisive idea of *Aids to Reflection*, and this renewal is

---

[83] Kant, *Religion*, p. 72.
[84] J. Oman, *Grace and Personality* (Cambridge University Press, 1919), p. 16.
[85] Kant, *Religion*, p. 68.

symbolised in the life of the church with the sacrament of baptism. The baptism symbolises the dawning of light which effects the beginning of the vision glorious: the participation in the life of Trinity:

this actuation of the 'I AM,' (εἰμὶ ἐν μέσῳ αὐτῶν) . . . the spiritual Christ, one and the same in all the faithful, is the originating and perfective focal unity. Even as the physical life *is* in each limb and organ of the body. 'all in every part;' but is *manifested* as life, by being one in all and thus making all *one*: even so with Christ, our Spiritual Life! (*CCS*, p. 120)

Here we see the combination of the language of Exodus 3: 14 of the great I AM with the expression 'I am in the midst of them' of Matthew 18: 20 to express the immanent reality of God in the moral life. The idealist interest in the spiritual community (in Hegel the *Kultus*, or Royce's the 'Beloved Community') which is constituted and sustained by the Spirit is linked to the Christian Platonic exegesis of the great I AM of Exodus 3: 14.[86] In a passage discussing Socinianism Coleridge writes:

For be assured, never yet did there exist a full faith in the divine WORD . . . which did not expand the intellect while it purified the heart . . . that living Principle, at once the Giver and the Gift! of that anointing Faith which in endless evolution 'teaches us of all things, and is truth!' For all things are but parts and forms of its progressive manifestation, and every new knowledge but a new organ of sense and insight into this one all-inclusive Verity. . . (*LS*, pp. 175, 177)

Aids to Reflection ends with a tribute to the Church of England as '*most* Apostolic Church; that its doctrines and ceremonies contain nothing dangerous to Righteousness or Salvation; and that the imperfections in its Liturgy are spots indeed, but spots on the sun, which impede neither its Light nor its Heat, so as to prevent the good seed from growing in a good soil and producing fruits of Redemption' (*Aids*, p. 381). John Beer notes that 'the employment of small type at this point' may have merely been the 'printer's device to conserve space' (*Aids*, p. lxxxvii). In his book *Coleridge's Poetic Intelligence*, John Beer recounts Leigh Hunt's puzzlement and exasperation concerning Coleridge's theological predilections: 'What makes Coleridge talk in that way about heavenly grace, and the holy church, and that sort of thing?' Lamb said: 'Ah! there's a

---

[86] On the point of an idealist interpretation of St Paul see Royce, *Problem of Christianity*, pp. 251 ff.

great deal of fun in Coleridge.'[87] At the point at which the sage of Highgate *seems* to present an antiquated, flaccid, and dreary ecclesiastical Romanticism, one discovers a very potent and imaginative vision of the nature of human culture. The Romantics were often inclined to employ religious terms and idioms in an aesthetic mode without any deep commitment to traditional religious tenets: Romantic museums and theatres have the appearance of temples, and poets are commonly presented as priests.[88] However, Coleridge's reflections on culture, church, and state are perfectly genuine; it is not an ironic mask. Indeed, these reflections play a vital part in Coleridge's counter-offensive against the dominant theological tenets of the eighteenth century.

[87] J. Beer, *Coleridge's Poetic Intelligence*, p. 287.
[88] J. Rohls, ' "Sinn und Geschmack für das Unendliche" Aspekte romantische Kunstreligion' in *Neue Zeitschrift für systematische Theologie und Religionsphilosophie* 27/1 (1985), pp. 1–24.

6

The vision of God: reflection culture, and the seed of a deiform nature

In him we live and move and have our being. (Acts 17: 28)

My great aim and object is to assert the *Superhuman* in order to diffuse more widely the faith in the *Supernatural* (*CCS*, p. 44)

I value and love his philosophy mainly because it has led me to this discovery, and to the practical conclusion, that those who are called to the work of teaching must cultivate and exercise their understandings, in order that they may discriminate between what is factitious and accidental, or belongs to artificial habits of thought, and that which is fixed and eternal, which belongs to man as man, and which God will open the eyes of every humble man to perceive. (F. D. Maurice)[1]

William Paley argues upon the basis of Scripture and reason, confident that both agree and compliment each other. Signally lacking is any appeal to church or tradition.[2] Coleridge's counter-principle is: 'CHRISTIANITY WITHOUT A CHURCH EXERCISING SPIRITUAL AUTHORITY IS VANITY AND DISSOLUTION' (*Aids*, p. 298) and he believes that the idea of 'Original Sin' will be taught as part of the 'Science of Ethics, as taught by the clerisy, that is, the "permanent learned Class"' (*Aids*, p. 295). Such utterances appear to be reactionary, and yet behind the rather Burkean exterior lies a quite radical (and perhaps eccentric view) of a group of educators, an organised body dedicated to the cultivation of society.

HUME, GIBBON, AND THE BASIS OF 'ENLIGHTENMENT'

At the end of *Aids to Reflection* Coleridge quotes Paley's apparently Socinian account of the Christian religion.

---

[1] F. D. Maurice, *Kingdom of Christ*, 2 vols., edited by A. R. Vidler (London: SCM, 1958), vol. ii. p. 355.

[2] cf. G. Cole, 'Paley and the myth of "Classical Anglicanism"' in *The Reformed Theological Review*, 54 (1995), pp, 3, 97–109.

'Had Jesus Christ delivered no other declaration than the following – The hour is coming, in which all that are in the grave shall hear his voice, and shall come forth: they that have done good, unto the resurrection of life, and they that have done evil, unto the resurrection of damnation, – he had pronounced a message of inestimable importance, and well worthy of that splendid apparatus of prophecy and miracles with which his mission was introduced and attested . . . He alone discovers, who proves; and no man can prove this point, but the teacher who testifies by miracles that his doctrine comes from God. (*Aids*, p. 411)

William Paley was the most distinguished defender of Christian theism against the scepticism of the enlightened historians. Hume's attack upon 'miracles' and Gibbon's monumental *Decline and Fall of the Roman Empire* fired a powerful reaction against the enlightened historians, and Paley's counter-attack was widely admired. Further, if we look at the passage which Coleridge is quoting, we can see that Paley is attacking the *irony and breezy humour* of Gibbon's critique of Christianity and his description of its rise as the triumph of barbarism. Paley describes Gibbon as the writer who 'has contrived to weave in his narration one continued sneer upon the cause of Christianity and upon the writings and characters of its ancient patrons . . . Who can refute a *sneer*?' Gibbon attacked Christianity and 'Neither let it be observed, is the crime or danger less, because impure ideas are exhibited under a veil, in covert and chastised language.'[3]

The passage which Coleridge quotes from Paley in *Aids to Reflection* is *Paley's attack upon Gibbon.*[4] The 'proofs' or 'evidences' at stake are not merely those of the natural world; Coleridge is not attacking primarily the arguments from or to design: Paley's 'watch' as it were. Coleridge is attacking Paley's argument for the 'evidences' or 'proofs' of Christianity as a religion which are culled from *the history of Christianity.*

Hume uses examples culled from the practices and traditions of the Roman Church, but this is not his target. Rome was a byword for superstition in the eighteenth century and such examples would be rhetorically effective. His real target is rational theology: either of a deistic or a Socinian nature. In part I of his *Dialogues concerning Natural Religion* Hume explains that for the Church Fathers, the Schoolmen and the Reformers 'nothing was more usual, among all religious teachers, than declamations against reason'[5] and it was

---

[3] Paley, *Moral and Political Philosophy*, pp. 278–9.
[4] G. Cole, ' "Who can refute a Sneer?" Paley on Gibbon' in *Tyndale Bulletin* 49: 1 (1998), pp. 57–70.
[5] Hume, *Principal Writings* pt. i. p. 13.

'Locke [who] seems to have been the first Christian, who ventured openly to assert that *faith* was nothing but a species of *reason*'.

The book titles of the deists: John Toland's *Christianity not Mysterious* (1696), that is, a rational Christianity, or Matthew Tindal's *Christianity as Old as the Creation or the Gospel a Republication of the Religion of Nature* (1730) reveal how Locke's theories were developed by his deist followers. The secure basis of Christianity is its reasonableness, which is derived from the ethical core of Jesus' teaching. The Socinian element in Locke's teaching – the proof of the divine role of Jesus through his miracles–provided the background of a long debate which was petering out at the time when Hume published his famous essay on miracles in 1748.

... we may conclude, that the *Christian religion* not only was at first attended by miracles, but even at this day cannot be believed by a reasonable person without one. Mere reason is insufficient to convince us of its veracity; and whoever is moved by *faith* to assent to it, is conscious of a continued miracle in his own person, which subverts all the principles of his understanding, and gives him a determination to believe what is most contrary to custom and experience.[6]

Hume's irony is prudent and reserved. Though clearly an opponent of metaphysical theism and the Christian religion, he eschews the strident anticlericalism of the radical French Enlightenment. Gibbon wrote with evident antipathy of the 'intolerant zeal' of those who 'laughed at the scepticism of Hume, preached the tenets of Atheism with the bigotry of dogmatists, and damned all believers with ridicule and contempt'.[7] Gibbon's history was deeply influenced by the irony and scepticism of Hume.[8] Hume's attack upon Christian theology was not dogmatic; it was based upon the attempt to show that the central tenets of Christian theology are either otiose, incoherent, or morally dubious. His target was not traditional orthodoxy but the Socinian Grotian-influenced eighteenth-century rational theology.

Hume attempts to show in his ethics that morality is perfectly intelligible without reference to a metaphysical theism. In chapter

[6] Hume, *Enquiries Concerning Human Understanding and Concerning the Principles of Morals*, third edition, edited by P. H. Niddich (Oxford: Clarendon, 1975), x, pt. ii. p. 131.
[7] Gibbon, *Memoirs of My Life*, edited by G. A. Bonnard (London: Nelson, 1966), p. 136.
[8] M. Andreas Weber, *David Hume und Edward Gibbon* (Frankfurt am Main: Hain, 1990), pp. 80 ff. and Louis Kampf, 'Gibbon and Hume' in *English Literature and British Philosophy: A Collection of Essays edited with an Introduction by S. P. Rosenbaum* (University of Chicago Press, 1971), pp. 109–18.

XI of the *Enquiry*, 'Of a Particular Providence and of a Future State', he develops the ethical consequences of his criticism of theism: since mankind is not entitled to infer any divine attributes it is impossible to infer from metaphysics any moral values from theism. This idea forms the theoretical basis of Hume's empirical historical observations in his *Natural History of Religion*. The title of a 'natural' history is instructive. Hume wishes to *explain* religious beliefs simply with recourse to natural phenomena and with recourse to his central tenet that only affections can move the will. Primitive mankind was bewildered and terrified and impressed by natural happenings and disasters which he ascribed to warring gods, and thought that he might be able to placate these gods by bribery and flattery; in such an irrational manner religious cults developed and flourished.

Hume's *Natural History of Religion* considers the origin, development, and influence of religion. The origin of religion is clearly non-rational and serves to satisfy feeling and affection: citing evidence of the irrationality of the origins of religion against the deistic tenet that the primitive and pristine religion among men is monotheistic, Hume insists that the belief in many gods is the earliest form of religion. As religion develops, it tends to sway between monotheism and polytheism. Finally, Hume denies that monotheism is morally superior to polytheism because polytheism is naturally more tolerant and is not so inclined to the brutal persecution perpetrated by theists in the conviction that they are serving the only God.

Gibbon's *Decline and Fall of the Roman Empire* reveals Hume's influence not just in the humanism which condemns bigotry and commends tolerance, but also Hume's emphasis upon the irrational elements in the establishment of a religion and the ambiguous if not pernicious effect of religion upon morality. Gibbon wished to ridicule the supernatural account of Christian origins. In the notorious chapter XV of the *Decline and Fall* Gibbon discusses the historical development of Christianity as a religion. He states his intent to deal with natural rather than with divine causes; the former are 'secondary' as opposed to 'primary', i.e. divine, causes. He writes: 'The theologian may indulge in the pleasing task of describing religion as she descended from heaven, arrayed in her native purity. A more melancholy task is imposed to the historian.'[9] The irony requires the reader's recognition of the imputedly inflated

---

[9] Gibbon, *Decline and Fall of the Roman Empire*, vol. i. p. 446.

ambitions of theology. The mock modesty of the enlightened historian is clear as Gibbon designates the rise of *Christianity as the Triumph of Barbarism:* it is evident that Gibbon does not have a high opinion of the 'pleasing task' of theology. Gibbon illustrates the particular intolerance of Christianity: whatever attention Christian devotion has lavished upon saints and martyrs, he argues, Christians have inflicted far greater severities upon infidels than they suffered at the hands of the latter. Gibbon is insistent that the dubious morality of the religious attitude of Christians is starkly reflected in the empirical history of the rise and the establishment of the Christian religion as the product of a social need, the result of a constellation of social and political factors. But it was *not* a triumph of reason.

Gibbon is particularly scathing about Platonism and he 'regarded the whole Trinitarian controversy as perhaps the most egregious example of that catastrophic infection of Christianity by neo-Platonism from which was engendered the purulence of theological dispute, the Catholic or Nicene doctrine of the Trinity'[10] perplexed by the 'metaphysical subtleties' of patristic theology: he calls the circumincession of the Trinity the 'darkest corner of the whole theological abyss'.[11] After the extinction of paganism the Christians became embroiled in absurd speculations about the Godhead and, employing Pétan, Cudworth, and Mosheim, Gibbon traces a direct line from the attempt of Plato to 'explore the mysterious nature of the deity' in terms of a 'threefold modification' up to the doctrinal formulations of the councils of the Christian church.[12] Much of the power of Gibbon's analysis rested upon the affinity between his analysis of the corruption of Christianity through Platonism, and that of radical dissenting Protestants such as Priestley. Possibly Paley was provoked to a response in part because of the appearance of common ground between Gibbon's presentation of Christianity and some of his own tenets.

Coleridge remarked: 'Gibbon's style is detestable; but his style is not the worst thing about him . . . Gibbon was a man of immense reading, but he had no philosophy' (*TT,* i. 418). Coleridge's remark is unfair; both with regard to the animadversion concerning Gibbon's

---

[10] David Womersley, introduction to Edward Gibbon, *Decline and Fall of the Roman Empire*, vol. i. p. lx.
[11] Gibbon, *Decline and Fall of the Roman Empire*, vol. i. p. 783. cf. Coleridge, *Notebooks* iii. 3813–16.
[12] Gibbon, *Decline and Fall of the Roman Empire*, vol. i. p. 771.

magnificent style, and because Gibbon was plainly influenced by his friend Hume and had eloquently expressed the ideals of the radical Enlightenment in his dislike of metaphysics as a pillar of 'priest-craft'.[13]

With the breakdown of the Roman Empire the church was the guardian and transmitter of culture and it was only at the Enlightenment that this position was challenged and that the church was seen as a bulwark of barbarism by Voltaire and Gibbon. Coleridge's view of the national church as a 'blessed accident, a providential boon, a grace of God, a mighty and faithful friend' or Christianity as 'an aid or instrument, which no State or Realm could have produced out of its elements . . . most awfully, a GOD-SEND!' (*CCS*, p. 55) is directly opposed to Gibbon's view of Christianity as the triumph of barbarism. Christianity is the integral part of a process of education and cultivation 'planned and conducted by unerring Providence' (*F* i. 506). It is the evolving Logos which is the root of genuine freedom mediated through the church which 'reflects the light of heaven from its shaft' (*CCS*, p. 55).

Coleridge thinks that a Paleyian defence of Christianity is intellectually worthless. Against those who wish to cast doubt upon the central tenets of Christian doctrine Coleridge wishes to produce an apology which uses *evidence of the spirit* rather than that of *miracles*. This evidence of the spirit goes to the heart of human life. Hume and Gibbon assume the existence of a quality of human culture (e.g. Augustan Rome or Enlightened France) by which they judge the Christian religion as barbarous and uncultured. Coleridge argues for the *providential necessity of religion in the formation of humane culture*. An essential part of his argument rests upon the distinction between culture and civilisation.[14] *Civilisation* is a 'mixed good'; it may be just the sign of the 'hectic of disease and not the bloom of health' (*CCS*, pp. 42–3). Civilisation means the material and impersonal conditions of the social fabric: a highly civilised nation is one where these material conditions have reached a certain level of complexity. *Culture*, on the contrary, is based upon that which is spiritual and personal.

It is the State itself in its intensest federal union; yet at the same moment the Guardian and Representative of all personal Individuality. For the Church is the Shrine of Morality: and in Morality alone the Citizen asserts

---

[13] Shelby T. McCloy, *Gibbon's Antagonism to Christianity* (London: Williams and Norgate, 1933).

[14] R. Geuss, 'Kultur, Bildung, Geist' in *Morality, Culture and History: Essays on German Philosophy* (Cambridge University Press, 1999), pp. 29–50.

and reclaims his personal independence, his *integrity* . . . Morality *as* Morality, has no existence for *a People*. (*Aids*, p. 292)

One can compare this with the important passage in which Coleridge argues for 'One universal Presence, a One present to all and in all', as the presupposition of 'the great Community of *Persons*' (*Aids*, p. 77). The role of the clerisy lies in the educing of that divine potential, of the supernatural in mankind which, as Coleridge argues throughout *Aids*, is the presupposition and goal of human freedom and personality. Culture is based upon that which constitutes mankind as distinct from the animal kingdom: our capacity to participate in the divine. From this perspective Jerusalem is the fulfilment of the promise of Athens and not its repudiation.

Coleridge produces a counter-argument against Hume and Gibbon at a much more sophisticated level than Paley. He proposes that 'in all ages, individuals, who have directed their meditations and their studies to the nobler characters of our nature, to the cultivation of those powers and instincts which constitute the man, at least separate him from the animal, and distinguish the nobler from the animal part of his own being, will be led by the *supernatural* in themselves to the contemplation of a power which is likewise super-*human*; that science, and especially moral science, will lead to religion, and remain blended with it' (cf. *CCS*, p. 44). In any civilisation there must be a group whose task it is to educe and cultivate this divine element, personality, in mankind. He calls this group the 'clerisy' and he means a body of learned men who, though they do not necessarily possess a sacerdotal role, nevertheless serve to awaken the divine potential in the population.

A Learned Order . . . First, those who are employed in adding to the existing Sum of Power and Knowledge. Second . . . those whose office it is to diffuse through the community at large the practical Results of Science. Third, the Formers and Instructors of the Second – in Schools, Halls and Universities, or through the medium of the Press. (*Aids*, p. 295)

As such they, the 'clerisy', belong to the church in the broadest sense, whereas the clergy constitute the church *stricto sensu*. Whereas a civilisation is concerned with the conditions of the outward life, culture is concerned with the educing of the personality: that is, with the renewal of the spiritual self in the light of the ideas of reason. Coleridge sees evidence of this activity in the work of the concrete church in Britain where truths which Plato found difficult have been diffused to the humblest homes through the existence of a national church *(CCS*, p. 75). J. S. Mill noted the strikingly radical idea in Coleridge that the justification of the established status of the Church of England lies not in worship or religious rites but in the education and cultivation of the whole nation![15]

There is an instructive contrast between Coleridge and Paley in their respective social thought. 'Pigeon Paley' was quite contemptuous towards the national social élite: in a parable on private property he describes a group of pigeons gathering grains which they put into a heap for 'one, and that the weakest, perhaps worst, pigeon of the flock', who is able to squander the grains at his pleasure. If one other pigeon attempts to take a grain from the heap, the others will turn upon this pigeon and kill it: 'if you should see this, you would see nothing more than what is every day practised and established among men'.[16] Yet, despite this ridicule and cynicism, Paley is deeply conservative. He staunchly defends these privileges and inequalities, with their roots in avarice and cruelty, for the sake of their utility. Reform, he believes, will make matters worse, not better. Coleridge's approach is the exact opposite, despite his apparent later conservatism, which inspired and provoked such bitter rebuke by radicals such as Hazlitt. We find in the *Lay Sermons* a pungent critique of social injustice. To those who claim, in the spirit of laissez-faire economics, that 'Things are always *finding*, their level', Coleridge replies: 'But Persons are not *Things* – but Man does not find his level. Neither in body nor in soul does the Man find his level!' *(LS*, p. 206). Coleridge helped Robert Peel's extension of the 1802 Factory Act in 1819 for the regulation of child labour in the cotton mills.[17]

Furthermore, he develops a theory of society as constituted by a balance between the landed aristocracy (as the principle of permanence) and the mercantile-industrial power (the principle of progression). During the debates prior to the Reform Act in 1832 such a theory seems like a romantic Toryism. Yet, on closer inspection, his theory is more liberal than it might otherwise appear: both these 'interests' of permanence and progression are ultimately subject to the third principle: the 'nationality' *(CCS*, pp. 32ff.). This is a principle of a property in trust for the nation, from which the

---

[15] Mill in Mill and Bentham, *Utilitarianism*, p. 208.
[16] Paley, *Works*, vol. ii. p. 74.
[17] Holmes, *Coleridge, Darker Reflections*, pp. 474ff.

educators of the nation can be sustained; these constitute the 'national church' and cultivate that humanity which is presupposed in true citizenship. Those to whom society owes most are not the squires or the captains of industry, but the educators. The 'clerisy' (not the clergy, but clearly cognate) conserves and fosters the most valuable assets of the nation. In some respects, what seems to be a defence of aristocracy and the established church constitutes an implicit, yet severe, critique of the inadequacies of the de facto institutions. Certainly Mill was astute in observing that Coleridge's reflections upon society showed 'a better Liberal than Liberals themselves; while he is the natural means of rescuing from oblivion truths which Tories have forgotten, and which the prevailing schools of Liberalism never knew'.[18] Coleridge's vision of church and state is closer to Plato's *Republic* than Burke's *Reflections* (cf. *LS*, p. 62).

The driving issue in Plato's epistemology is education (a fact which is perhaps not obvious in the modern context where theories of education play a peripheral role in the syllabus), but, faced with the challenge of the Sophists peddling their 'knowledge' or 'wisdom', Plato presents a theory of 'knowing' which is definitely not an instrument to gain wealth or success, but a description of the formation of a character, and a political state, which can love and imitate the good for its own sake (cf. *SW* I pp. 659f).

Hume envisages education as 'an artificial and not a natural cause . . . built almost on the same foundation of custom and repetition as our reasonings from causes and effects'.[19] But for Coleridge the mind is not a mechanism which automatically responds to stimulus, and education is not a mode of cause and effect, impinging upon the mind from without. Rather it is the discipline and cultivation of *latent* powers. The prerequisite of genuine cultivation of the mind is not observation but reflection. This means drawing upon the spiritual immaterial resources at hand – the inherited world of language, and the traditions and ideals expressed in a particular culture over time – in the history of a people. Minds are not inert instruments, but have to be nurtured, formed, and re-formed.

Coleridge's idea of the national church should be understood in the light of his reflections about education and culture. Such a national church, which can sustain the clerisy, is a providential boon,

---

[18] Mill in Mill and Bentham, *Utilitarianism*, p. 225.
[19] Hume, *Treatise of Human Nature*, p. 117

but it should not be confused with the invisible church. This, the highest sense of the word church, cannot be identified with any nation or interest but with the realm of the ideas: the 'true and only contra-position of the Christian Church is to the world. Her paramount aim and object, is indeed *another* world, not a world *to come* exclusively, but likewise *another world that now is*' (*CCS*, p. 117). The purpose of the church is to encourage the people of a land to regard the world of the senses as 'signs, instruments, and mementos' of its connection with this other world. The church is not a state-institute but the state in its most intense 'federal union', and the guardian of personal being and morality (*Aids*, p. 292). By means of an interesting twist of argument against Hume and Gibbon, the church becomes for Coleridge the source and sustainer of humane culture rather than its barbarous opponent: 'a permanent Learned Class, having authority and possessing the respect and confidence of the country ' (*Aids*, p. 295).

The 'potential divinity' in every man – τῷ Θεῷ οἰκείῳ (i.e. to the indwelling God) – 'is the ground and condition of his *civil* existence' (*CCS*, p. 52) and this is cultivated by the clerisy. The idea of the indwelling spirit is the centre of Coleridge's political philosophy. The function of the church, invisible or visible, is not to provide a refuge from the miseries of this world, an opiate for the masses, but to 'rouse and emancipate the soul' from its debasing slavery to the senses and to awaken it to the true criteria of reality, i.e 'Permanence, Power, Will manifested in Act and Truth operating as Life' (*Aids*, p. 407). The church should make every man aware that the realm of phenomenal experience provides only a very partial and inadequate picture of reality, and that the materials of phenomenal experience are the stuff from which a life according to the image of the divine may be educed. This struggle to realise the image of the divine in the world is a participation in 'the other world which now is'. Coleridge insists upon the historic enlightening function of the church: 'The diffusion of light and knowledge' through England, 'by the exertions of the Bishops and clergy, by Episcopalians and Puritans, from Edward VI. to the Restoration, was as wonderful as it is praiseworthy, and may be justly placed among the most remarkable facts of history' (*Aids*, p19). Coleridge further refers to the highly *civilized*, though fearfully *uncultivated*, inhabitants of ancient India who are capable of hideous self-mutilation but 'all this is so much less *difficult*, demands so much less exertion of will than to *reflect*' (*Aids*, pp. 22–3). In the original notebook entry this reads 'than to think, and to become by a habit of action what we thinking know to be our IDEA' (*Aids*, p. 23 n. 6). This 'IDEA' is the divine form (or idea) which is at variance with the world (*Aids*, p. 26), 'the Divine image, into which the worldly human is to be transformed' (*Aids*, p. 28).

What the Apostles were in an extraordinary way befitting the first annunciation of a Religion for all Mankind, this all Teachers of Moral Truth, who aim to prepare for its reception by calling the attention of men to the Law in their own hearts, may, without presumption, consider themselves to be, under ordinary gifts and circumstances; namely, Ambassadors for the Greatest of Kings, and upon no mean employment, the great Treaty of Peace and Reconcilement betwixt him and Mankind. (*Aids*, p. 69)

This cultivating role of the church is threatened by the Socinianism and ultra-Socinianism which 'have even dipt under the garden-fence of the Church' (*Aids*, p. 344) and detract from the 'honor of the Incarnate Word by disparaging the light of the Word, that was in the beginning, and which lighteth *every* man . . . ' (*Aids*, p. 345).

At the centre of 'culture' Coleridge sees a community of scholars and teachers who are dedicated to wisdom rather than curiosity: a 'permanent Learned Class' (*Aids*, p. 295). It is the 'habitual unreflectingness' which is the reason for the malaise of the age, the fact that the principles of thought of the clergy and the gentry are grounded in a false philosophy: a Socinian empiricism. The gentry and the clerisy were substituting 'Locke for Logic and Paley for Morality' (*CL*, p. 138).[20] *Aids to Reflection* is addressed to those in the process of developing a manly character: 'it was *especially* designed for the studious young at the close of their education or on their first entrance into the duties of manhood and rights of self-government . . . *first* . . . to the members of our two Universities: *secondly* (but only in respect of this mental precedency *second*) to all alike of whatever name, who have dedicated their future lives to the cultivation of their Race as Pastors, Preachers, Missionaries, or Instructors of Youth' (*Aids*, p. 6). From 1822 to 1827 Coleridge was running classes for young men between the ages of nineteen and twenty-five. *Aids to*

---

[20] cf. 'A nation that substitutes Locke for Logic, and paley for Morality, and both this and that for Polity, Philosophy and Theology cannot but be slaves. But if this be with the Gentry, Clerisy, & the learned in all liberal professions, it is so with the Nation – or a Revolution is at hand.' *CCS*, p. 46. Augustine: 'nos sumus tempora: quales sumus, talia sunt tempora' in his *Sermo* lxxx. 8 in *Sancti Aurelii Augustini Opera*, ed. Migne, 38, p. 498.

Reflection itself developed out of a teaching – one might even say a seminar context.[21]

This cultivation is the key to genuine freedom. Educing of the divine image is not mere training. Coleridge maintains that *training* is the skilful adaptation of mankind to his environment whereas *educating* is the educing of that by virtue of which mankind transcends its environment. Thus education provides the possibility of a genuine freedom: not merely the absence of certain constraints, but the power to shape and unify one's life through communion with the divine spirit (*Aids*, p. 78). This idea should not lead to fanaticism because the working of the spirit may be inferred but not perceived (*Aids*, p. 79). 'In Scripture the term spirit, as a power or property seated in the human soul, never stands singly, but is always *specified* by a genitive case following . . . It is the "Spirit of Meekness" (a meek Spirit), or 'the Spirit of Chastity,' and the like. The moral Result, the specific Form and Character in which the Spirit *manifests* its presence, is the only sure pledge and token of its presence' (*Aids*, pp. 72–3). The supernatural can be known through its practical effects in human culture rather than by reference to immediate esoteric experiences or by reference to miracles. The individual finds freedom in the very concrete entanglements and obligations of friendship, work, family, church, and state rather than in ecstatic separation from these – the plight that Aristotle saw as fit only for a beast or a God. Stephen R. L. Clark writes in a beautiful and deeply Christological aphorism: 'Justice, civilisation, is not the bargain of godless brigands that modern moralists have suggested: it is the service of the divine in human and defenceless form.'[22]

Coleridge believes that freedom is the fruit of that vision of the Good which must be awakened and formed within society by that class of educators, the 'clerisy', because otherwise a materially and commercially vibrant society will produce a swarm of people trained for proximate goals, but not a society of responsible persons. Of course Coleridge does not envisage a society of philosophers, and he is bitterly critical of those reform movements in education which he thought would end in plebification rather than leading to illumination (*CCS*, p. 69). Coleridge's idea is that the clerisy provides the foundation of civil order by eliciting the divine; by cultivating a

---

[21] Holmes, *Coleridge, Darker Reflections*, p. 524
[22] Stephen R. L. Clark, *Civil Peace and Sacred Order* (Oxford: Clarendon, 1989), p. 109.

genuinely humane society. As we have noted, here is the Rous-
seauian-Kantian distinction between civilisation and culture. Kant
writes: 'We are cultivated to a great extent through art and science;
we are civilised to the point of excess in all sorts of social arts and
proprieties. But it would be an error to think we are moral: here is
much that is lacking.'[23] The idea of the moral aspect or component
in culture as opposed to civilisation is quite clear in Kant. Etymologically civilisation denotes an urban as opposed to an agrarian
society. The word 'culture', with its etymological association of
organic cultivation (e.g. *agri cultura* or *hortorum cultura*), was quite a
natural metaphor in the Renaissance for the process of παιδεία
which was rooted in the Greeks of the classical city state and
emulated by the imperial Romans.[24]

Coleridge rejects adamantly the Rousseauian distinction between
nature and culture: a cultured life is mankind's nature. Indeed, a life
of mere nature is unnatural for men because of man's access to
reason, 'the best and holiest gift of heaven and the bond of union
with the giver' (*F* i. p. 190). The brutal man is no more 'natural' than
cultured humanity any more than the incontinent or the violent are
truer to their bodily functions than those healthy and sane. An
amusing anecdote about an exchange with his old friend Thewell
does much to illustrate Coleridge's ideas on this issue:

Thewell thought it unfair to influence a child's mind by inculcating any
opinions before it should come to years of discretion and able to choose for
itself. I showed him my garden and told him it was my botanical garden.
'How so?' said he – 'it is covered with nothing but weeds.' 'Oh' I replied –
that is only because it has not yet come to its age of discretion and choice.
The weeds, you see, have taken the liberty to grow, and I thought it unfair
in me to prejudice the soil towards roses or strawberries. (*TT* i. 181)

The Enlightened attempt to discover demonstrable principles
which are self-evidently the basis of knowledge or society is quite
hopeless. Coleridge believes that '*bottoming* on fixed principles' (*F* i.

---

[23] 'Wir sind im hohen Grade durch Kunst und Wissenschaft cultiviert. Wir sind civilisiert bis
zum Überlästigen – zu allerlei gesellschaftlicher Artigkeit und Anständigkeit. Aber uns
schon für moralisiert zu halten, daran fehlt noch sehr viel. Denn die Idee der Moralität
gehört noch zur Cultur; der Gebrauch dieser Idee aber, welcher nur auf das Sittenähnliche
in der Ehrliebe und der äußeren Anständigkeit hinausläuft, macht bloße die Civilisierung
aus.' Kant, *Idee zu einer allgemeinen Geschichte in weltbürgerlicher Absicht* (Berlin: de Gruyter,
1968), vol. viii, p. 26.
[24] cf. Whichcote, *The Works of the Learned Benjamin Whichcote* (Aberdeen: Alexancer Thomson,
1751), vol. ii. p. 50: 'the remedy of culture and education'.

326) means recognising the rights and obligations which are part of a historical tradition *and* seeing in these contingent traditions and pre-civil human networks the embodiment of an eternal (hence 'fixed' principles) spiritual force of which mankind is the custodian. Reflection is not rejected by the appeal to tradition. Culture is the product of reflection upon the concrete conditions of human life as the realisation of the eternal in time, and as such it is rooted in contemplation of the divine. Theology is not the arcane study of antiquated and irrelevant texts and rites, and abstruse and futile disputations despised and ridiculed by the 'Enlightened', but 'the root and trunk of the knowledges that civilized man' (*CCS*, p. 47). Theology always claimed rightful precedence amongst the clerisy since

under the name of Theology, or Divinity, were contained the interpretation of languages; the conservation and tradition of past events; the momentous epochs, and revolutions of the race and nation; the continuation of the records; logic, ethics, and the determination of ethical science, in application to the rights and duties of men in all their various relations, social and civil; and lastly, the ground-knowledge, the prima scientia as it was named, – PHILOSOPHY, or the doctrine and discipline of *ideas*. (*CCS*, pp. 46–7)

Coleridge's invective against the 'Anglo-Gallic' antipathy to metaphysics among his contemporaries and his critique of the overbalance of the commercial spirit in England reflect his conviction that philosophy is part of the broader culture: 'A true philosophy in the learned class is essential to a true religious feeling in all classes' (*F* i. 447) if the nation is to avoid becoming 'perilously over-civilized, and most pitiably uncultivated' (*F* i. 500). Observing that the author of the Hebrews does not oppose faith to *reason* but rather to *sight*, Coleridge, who famously defines faith as 'fidelity to our Being' (*SW* ii. p. 834) envisages the genuine education of man as the cultivation of the 'inward man' through faith in the invisible, whereas civilisation is the product of a concentration upon 'outward and sensible things'. Furthermore culture is inherently ascetic: a pilgrimage (*F* i. 500–1).

COLERIDGE'S PHILOSOPHICAL MYSTICISM

Coleridge refers ironically to those members of the church 'Orthodox *de more Grotii*, who improve the *letter* of Arminius with the *spirit* of Socinus', 'who have sufficient data to bring me in guilty of irrational and Superstitious Mysticism' (*Aids*, p. 338). The centre of *Aids to Reflection* is the distinction between reason and understanding, between discursive reasoning and that rational apprehension expressed by the Greek word νοῦς or the scholastic term *intellectus*. The centrality of this issue for Coleridge shows him to be within the parameters of German Idealism. The thrust of Coleridge's philosophy is Idealistic-cum-Platonic: the *prima scientia* is PHILOSOPHY as 'the doctrine and discipline of ideas' (*CCS*, p. 47). Coleridge's distinction between reason and understanding is based upon the Greek belief in the *communion* between the human soul and the Logos as the locus of the ideas: the central tenet of philosophical mysticism. But in Coleridge we find little of the ecstatic rapture, swooning, dark night and personality commonly associated with 'mysticism'. It could be argued that the irrationalist overtones of the word 'mysticism' are so strong that it is a mistake to use the term in the context of Coleridge's thinking. We shall use the concept for two reasons. Firstly, Coleridge's emphasis upon the affective component in knowledge is typical of the philosophical mystical tradition. Secondly, Coleridge himself points to the term when he begins his conclusion by stating that he expects that his work will be dismissed as visionary raving or transcendental trash. Coleridge says that he does not wish to consider verbal abuse but there is one criticism which will be that of gifted and moderate minds. This is the charge that Coleridge has been indulging in mysticism, the main ideas of which are taken from William Law after he 'had lost his senses in brooding over the visions of a delirious German cobbler, Jacob Boehme' (*Aids*, p. 384).

Coleridge distances himself from both Law and Boehme. Boehme is a representative of an esoteric mystical movement in German thought called the spiritualists (*Spiritualisten*). Writers like Boehme perpetuated the traditions of the German mystics in German Protestantism and he was a great influence upon the English mystical divine William Law (1686–1761) (cf. *Aids*, p. 384).[25] The emphasis upon the will, the contrast between the natural and the spiritual, the birth of Christ within the soul, and the rejection of penal atonement are all to be found in Law as well as in Coleridge. Law's is also a deeply spiritual and ethical view of religion whereby the real faith consists in suffering, dying, and rising, with Christ.

[25] W. R. Inge, *Studies in English Mystics*, The Saint Margaret's lectures 1905 (London: John Murray, 1906), pp. 124–72.

What Coleridge calls 'assimilation by faith', that is the *unio mystica*, is at the centre of his mystical theology.

Much of the text of *Aids to Reflection* is devoted to the issue of 'enthusiasm'. The leaders of this are called by Rufus Jones the 'Spiritual Reformers'. Boehme is the most famous instance of thinkers who were influenced by medieval German mysticism, Renaissance Humanism, and the teaching of the Reformation. Characteristic for all these was a rejection of the forensic view of atonement in Luther, an emphasis upon God as love, taking up justification into sanctification, and an emphasis upon the inner Word. It was a strongly personal religion: 'the redemption of our personal Being, and the re-union of the Human with the Divine, by and through the Divine Humanity of the Incarnate Word' (*Aids*, p. 299). Redemption is not a legal transaction or the exacting of precise conditions of justice but the renewal of 'our personal Being'. Rufus Jones notes of the seventeenth-century mystics: 'Here is the genuine beginning in modern times of what has come to be the deepest note of present day Christianity, *the appreciation of personality as the highest thing in earth or heaven*, and the initiation of a movement to find the vital sources and resources for the inner kindling of the spirit, and for raising the whole personal life to higher functions and to higher powers.'[26]

Coleridge was concerned that the excesses of the spiritualists had led to an outright rejection of the idea of 'Spiritual Presence and Agency' (*Aids*, p. 83) by orthodox Church of England men and he fears that as the 'Compiler of the Aids to Reflection, and Commenter on a Scotch Bishop's platonico-calvinistic commentary' he will be ridiculed on the model of Swift, Warburton and Samuel Butler. Coleridge's concern is itself quite revealing. Rufus Jones included the Cambridge Platonists Benjamin Whichcote and John Smith in his book *Spiritual Reformers in the Sixteenth and Seventeenth Century*. In many of their concerns, interests, sources, and ideas, the Cambridge Platonists and William Law had much in common with continental Reformers such as Hans Denck, Sebastian Franck, Valentine Weigel, and Jacob Boehme. Coleridge is particularly anxious about the challenge that he is a 'mystic' or a 'spiritualist' because both are close to the truth. Leighton in particular, as we shall see, is a writer imbued in the mystical and spiritualist traditions of the radical Reformation.

---

[26] Jones, *Spiritual Reformers*, p. xlix.

At the end of *Aids to Reflection* Coleridge presents a dialogue between 'Antinous' and 'Nous'. There is little doubt that Coleridge identifies his own thought with Nous: the defender of reason and a spiritual philosophy and hence the proponent of a genuine mysticism. (The names of the dialogue partners recall Berkeley's *Three Dialogues* between Hylas and Philonous.) 'Antinous' asks what 'Nous' means by 'mysticism'. 'Mysticism' in its pejorative sense means the confusion of abnormal interior states of mind with a privileged perception of reality (*Aids*, p. 389). Such is the opposite of true mysticism as the attainment of increasing objectivity. A bad mysticism can be divided into two sorts: a fanatical mystic is one who attempts to impose his vision on the rest of society, and an enthusiastical mystic is one whose mysticism may be regrettable but can co-exist with excellent qualities. The fanatical mystic is a menace to society, the enthusiastical mystic is, on the contrary, harmless. 'Nous' goes further to employ a parable. Two pilgrims are in the wilderness and they alight upon an oasis. The first is an uneducated enthusiast like Jacob Boehme. While resting by the oasis his fancy modifies his perception of reality and his 'dreams transfer their forms to real objects; and these lend a substance and "outness" to his dreams'. He attempts to describe the vision using the language of Scripture (*Aids*, p. 392). This delirious and uncritical mind is Boehme. The second pilgrim has an equal predilection for visions but has the advantages of fortune and education: he also invests the scene with the hue of his equally excitable mind and he interprets 'the moonlight and the shadows as the peculiar genius and sensibility of the individual's own spirit'. He is a refined enthusiast: like Fénelon. The native of this area who visits the spot will recognise in the latter's tale a 'dream of the truth', and even in the former account there is 'Truth mingled with the Dream' (*Aids*, pp. 390ff.).

What does Coleridge intend in the dialogue and the parable? He is clearly trying to bring some definition and focus to the concept of 'mysticism'. He is trying to make the distinction which the German can make between *Mystik* and *Mystizismus*; that is, between a disciplined speculative form of thought aimed at the vision of God and self-indulgent visionary enthusiasm. Coleridge wants to disassociate himself from such unphilosophical, or rather undisciplined, mystics.

Having analysed mysticism in the pejorative sense of the word, Coleridge goes on to explain why the term 'mysticism' is used as a term of reproach against his own writing. The explanation lies in the prevalence of materialism. Although the confessed materialist like Joseph Priestley is rare, the tacit intellectual temper of the age is materialist. Although many regard themselves as Christians and distinguish the soul from the body and the mind from matter, 'reality' tends to be identified almost exclusively with material reality. The word 'real' is taken to be a synonym for 'tangible'. When one considers the meaning of the word 'mind' it will be thought of in terms of negatives: as non solid or invisible (*Aids*, pp. 394ff.). Coleridge regarded this as a product of the temper and style of the philosophy which had come to dominate English thought since Locke.

In order to appreciate the point of the discussion we should turn to the appendix to *On the Constitution of the Church and State* where Coleridge presents a dialogue between Demosius of Toutocosmos and Mystes the Allocosmite. The former is literally 'this worldly', the latter 'a Denizen of another world'. Coleridge goes on to define the name MYSTES for the hero of the dialogue:

MYSTES, from the Greek μύω – one who *muses* with closed lips, as meditating on *Ideas* which may indeed be suggested and awakened, but cannot, like the images of sense and conceptions of the understanding, be adequately *expressed* by words. (*CCS*, p. 165)

In the same book Coleridge defines PHILOSOPHY as the 'doctrine and discipline of ideas' (*CCS*, p. 47). The philosophical mysticism of Plato and Plotinus is a contemplative discipline. Coleridge insists that the Platonic dialectic consists in the ascent of the mind by means of the gradual emancipation of the mind from the despotism of the senses and the passions, and the development of the capacity for the perception of intelligible reality. The disciplining and raising of the mind to penetrate '*spiritual realities that can only be spiritually discerned*' (*CCS*, p. 47) is a complex *reflective* process, and Coleridge's appeals to strenuous thought are recurrent throughout *Aids to Reflection* (cf. *Aids*, p. 541). Coleridge's 'mysticism' is not just philosophic (the same could be said of Jacobi) but almost rationalistic:

Where a person mistakes the anomalous misgrowths of his own individuality for ideas, or truths of universal reason, he may, without impropriety, be called a *Mystic*, in the abusive sense of the term; though pseudo mystic, or phantast, would be a more proper designation. Heraclitus, Plato, Bacon, Leibniz, were Mystics, in the primary sense of the term: Iamblicus, and his successors, Phantasts. (*CCS*, p. 165)

Coleridge clearly wishes to identify the tenor of his thought with the sort of rigorous but profound thought characteristic of the great philosophers like Plato and Bacon. This is a reflective mysticism, according to which reality is strictly unfathomable for the unassisted mind, and philosophy depends upon the attempt to avoid self delusion and to follow the tracks of the ideas. The ascent of the mind to the ideas is a task of purification and has a strongly religious component. It has little in common with esoteric forms of religion and superstition; a point which the parable of the distorted vision of the enthusiastic pilgrims should make clear. An accurate vision of the ideas, albeit through a glass darkly, requires a discipline of mind and soul which the esoteric visionary like Boehme usually lacks.

The genuine mystic in Coleridge's dialogue in *On the Constitution of the Church and State* (1830) is called an Allocosmite (pp. 165, 174, 184) because his convictions are determined by the belief in 'another world which now is' (*CCS*, p. 117). His position is distinguished from that of the 'toutocosmite' (*CCS*, pp. 165, 174, 184) who believes solely in *this world*, i.e. the realm of the senses, and the heterocosmite who believes in a world *radically other* than this world.

The position of the mystic, the allocosmite, is the philosophical position delineated and defended throughout *Aids to Reflection*. As opposed to Hume's conviction that man is simply an intelligent land mammal or Priestley's conviction that man's religious vocation is dependent upon the miraculous intervention of a *deus ex machina* upon a purely material world, Coleridge wishes to defend the view of Augustine that man is more than natural and that man's vocation is best understood as a pilgrimage from the sensual to the intelligible *inaugurated* by the Incarnation and *aided by the Spirit*. This pilgrimage is characterised not so much by a flight to a radically other realm, as by the painstaking disclosure of the inteligible as the basis of the phenomenal: the physical world becomes 'translucent of the invisible energy' to the pilgrim who seeks this other world 'which now is'.

Christian theologians such as Clement of Alexandria spoke of the 'mysteries' of Christianity, Christ as a teacher of mysteries.[27] John Smith, the most eloquent of the Cambridge Platonists, wrote: 'There

---

[27] cf. Daniélou, *Gospel Message and Hellenistic Culture*, p. 341 and Henry Chadwick, *Early Christian Thought and the Classical Tradition: Studies in Justin, Clement and Origen* (Oxford: Clarendon, 1992), p. 57.

are hidden Mysteries in Divine Truth, wrapt up one within another, which cannot be discerned but only by divine "Epoptists."[28] This is probably a reference to Clement of Alexandria, who writes of the ἐποπτικὴ θεωρία or contemplative vision as the goal of the mysteries.[29]

It is nevertheless misleading to call Coleridge a mystic outright because of the almost entire lack of an apophatic or Dionysian mysticism in his thought. One of Plotinus' favourite texts is Plato's assertion in the *Republic* 509b that the good is 'beyond being'. The absolute transcendence of the One is the basis of the mystical *via negativa*, which is mitigated in Plotinus by the role of νοῦς, i.e. that which the Christian Platonists tend to call the λόγος and which Coleridge calls 'Reason'. Alongside the Platonist's avowal of the transcendence of the One, is the stress upon the influence and transparency of the rich realm of the divine mind νοῦς – the basis of the *via affirmativa*. We have seen how Coleridge, like the seventeenth-century Platonists, believes that the one vital ramification of the Christian teaching, that the Logos is consubstantial with the Father – and not created – means that God cannot be thought of as a wilful or arbitrary demiurge, but is at one with that creative pattern which is the source of the cosmos, and which is reflected in the beauty and order of nature, human culture, and society.

What conclusions should we draw from this discussion? Coleridge is aware that he is 'gossiped about, as devoted to metaphysics, and worse than all to a system incomparably nearer to the visionary flights of Plato, and even to the jargon of the mystics, than to the established tenets of Locke' (*BL* ii. 240). The source of his philosophy in Neoplatonism and Spiritual Reformers indicates his adherence to a speculative or philosophical mysticism with Platonic roots. This is the basis of the manifest centrality of the appeal to religious experience which undergirds *Aids to Reflection*: 'Make a man feel the *want* of it; rouse him, if you can, to the self-knowledge of his *need* of it' (*Aids*, p. 406). Uppermost in Coleridge's mind is the Platonist-mystical conviction that theoretical knowledge of God is inextricably linked to spiritual progress: 'as much as *we are, we know*' (*Aids*, p. 30); accurate vision presupposes the purification of character, and the purging of the soul is the prerequisite of the vision divine.

---

28 Smith, *Discourses*, p. 8.
29 Clement of Alexandria, *Clemens Alexandrinus*, edited by O. Stählin (Berlin: Akademie, 1985), vol. ii. p. 370.

7

Epilogue
The candle of the Lord and Coleridge's legacy

COLERIDGE AND ANGLO-SAXON VICTORIAN IDEALISM

I pity the man who can see the connection of his own ideas. Still more do I pity him, the connection of whose ideas any other person can see. Sir, the great evil is, that there is too much commonplace light in our moral and political literature; and light is an enemy to mystery, and mystery is a great friend to enthusiasm. Now the enthusiasm for abstract truth is an exceedingly fine thing, as long as the truth, which is the object of the enthusiasm, is so completely abstract as to be altogether out of the reach of human faculties; and, in that sense, I have myself an enthusiasm for truth, but in no other, for the pleasure of metaphysical investigation lies in the means, not in the end; and if the end could be found, the pleasure of the means would cease. The mind, to be kept in health, must be kept in exercise. The proper exercise of the mind is elaborate reasoning. Analytical reasoning is a base and mechanical process, which takes to pieces and examines, bit by bit, the rude material of knowledge, and extracts therefrom a few hard and obstinate things called facts, every thing in the shape of which I cordially hate. But synthetical reasoning, setting up as its goal some unattainable abstraction, like an imaginary quantity in algebra, and commencing its course with taking for granted some two assertions which cannot be proved, from the union of these two assumed truths produces a third assumption, and so on in infinite series, to the unspeakable benefit of the human intellect. The beauty of this process is, that at every step it strikes out in two branches, in a compound ratio of ramification, so that you are perfectly sure of losing your way, and keeping your mind in perfect health, by the perpetual exercise of an interminable quest; and for these reasons I have christened my eldest son Emanuel Kant Flosky.

Nightmare Abbey (Penguin: Harmondswoth, 1986) p. 67

Thomas Love Peacock's biting satire of Coleridge as Mr Flosky is, in fact, extremely perceptive. The ἄσκησις or training of body and mind; the speculative Pythagorean-Platonic geometry; the mystical 'enthusiasm' for 'mystery'; and the emphatic identification with

Kant's thought; and, most significantly, the attempt to defend metaphysics against the fetishism of materialism: these elements constitute the distinctive characteristics of Coleridge's very original version of the Christian Platonist legacy which he had inherited from Cudworth and Berkeley and which he shared with Schelling.

Yet is not Coleridge's Platonic idealism quixotic? Is it not redolent of Romantic wistfulness for antiquated institutions and impractical values when Coleridge insists upon the church as an enlightening force? Arthur Hugh Clough, although admiring Coleridge's 'great perceptive and analytic power', inclined to see him as a 'man who has so great a lack of all reality and actuality' (*Aids*, p. cxliii). We have argued, however, that Coleridge is a redoubtable opponent of philosophical abstraction. Further. Coleridge exerted considerable influence upon late nineteenth-century philosophical idealism, which was a supremely practical philosophy.[1]

J. S. Mill divided the Victorians into Benthamites and Coleridgeans. If Sidgwick belonged to the former, T. H. Green belonged to the latter – not by virtue of any detailed study of Coleridge's work, but by virtue of the intellectual climate which Coleridge, aided by Carlyle, created in England. Mill was a close friend of Carlyle, but it is clear that Mill regarded Coleridge as the more significant mind. The main basis of Coleridge's philosophical influence upon the Victorians is *Aids to Reflection*. I wish to offer some suggestions as to why this book can be seen as one of the major sources of Anglo-American idealism.

The disciples of Coleridge were concentrated for a time at Trinity College, Cambridge,[2] but it is Jowett's Balliol which nurtured British Idealism as a philosophical force.[3] Philosophers like T. H. Green in Oxford combined, in a quite Coleridgean manner, Platonism with high German Idealism and a deep sense of the spiritual power and relevance of Christianity for the modern mind. Green (1836–82) was a pupil at Rugby, which had been formed by the Coleridgean Thomas Arnold (1795–1842), and then the pupil of Benjamin Jowett. John Beer gives us a concise account of Coleridge's influence upon Oxford via the Rugby–Balliol connection in his Editor's Introduction (*Aids*, pp. cxxxviiff.).

---

[1] cf. *Philosophy, Politics and Citizenship: the Life and Thought of the British Idealists*, edited by A. Vincent and R. Plant (Oxford: Blackwell, 1984).

[2] Sanders, *Coleridge and the Broad Church Movement*, pp. 123ff.

[3] P. Hinchliff, *Benjamin Jowett and the Christian Religion* (Oxford: Clarendon, 1987).

Oxford Idealism has often been described as Hegelianism but this is hard to substantiate. Hegel's speculative logic and his terminology are often disregarded by the British 'Hegelians'. T. H. Green quotes Kant more often than Hegel and was interested in the late theistic idealism of Lotze. The basic themes of T. H. Green's thought are Coleridgean: he attacks both the empiricist view of mind and the utilitarian view of ethics. In place of these, he produces an ethics of self-realisation and the idea of God as 'one spiritual self-conscious being of which all that is real is the activity and expression . . . we are related to this spiritual being, not merely as parts of the world which is its expression, but as partakers in some inchoate measure of the self-consciousness through which it at once constitutes itself and distinguishes itself from the world'.[4]

The emphatic vision of the practical and social fruits of philosophy which permeates the more typical British Idealists such as T. H. Green, John Caird, or John Muirhead had strong roots in the conviction that the world is a realisation of a spiritual principle. 'The world is an evolving sacrament of the spirit', and 'freedom means dying to live' are the two great principles of British Idealism. These two momentous principles were stated in *Aids to Reflection* and became the back-bone of the Germano-Coleridgean party; effective even amongst thinkers who were rather suspicious of the finer points of the philosophy of S. T. Coleridge.

Idealistic thought tends to combine philosophy and theology, and Balliol was the source of much idealistic theology.[5] In particular, Gore, Scott Holland, and Illingworth are examples of a striking combination of philosophical idealism and an incarnational theology. Although avowed High-Churchmen, they owed, in many respects, more to the Platonic-Alexandrine spirit of Coleridge, Maurice, and Westcott than to Keble or Newman. W. R. Inge once wrote:

Coleridge may be said to have revived the theology of the Cambridge Platonists and William Law, and this meant that English theology was to become more Greek and less Latin. The Incarnation instead of the Atonement now became the central doctrine of Christianity. Thus was initiated a line of thought really in accordance with the genius of the

---

[4] Green, *Works*, vol. iii. p. 143.
[5] A. M. Ramsey, *From Gore to Temple, The Development of Anglican Theology between 'Lux Mundi' and the Second World War*, The Hale Memorial Lectures of Seabury-Western Theological Seminary (London: Longman, 1960.)

nation, which in spite of the common sense, empiricism and practicality which it had become the fashion to attribute to our countrymen, has always been idealistic, and disposed to welcome the religious philosophy which comes down through St Paul, St John and the Greek Fathers from the tradition of the School of Plato. This religious philosophy belongs mainly to the second half of the century, and its influence spread from Oxford after the University had recovered itself from the ecclesiastical fever of the forties.[6]

The great biblical scholars Westcott, Lightfoot, and Hort all owed at least inspiration to Coleridge and his enthusiasm for St John. (Hort was very deeply indebted to Coleridge (cf. *Aids*, p. cxlii).) In a discussion of English reactions to radical Hegelian biblical criticism, Robert Morgan writes of the 'generally platonist and sacramental outlook' of Anglicanism which meant that the Incarnation rather than the Resurrection became the 'testing-ground of traditional Christianity' in the late nineteenth century.[7] This outlook owed much to Coleridge. Coleridge's emphasis upon the native link between idealism and Christianity, a tradition derived from Spenser, Everard Digby, Thomas Jackson, the Cambridge Platonists, and other theologians of the seventeenh century, encouraged a respect for traditional Christianity together with an awareness of historical and critical considerations and a willingness to reflect upon the philosophical problems tracing Christianity. It forged a particular English response to the debate about the 'Hellenisation of Christianity' which has raged from Pétau to Harnack. Hort's adamant assertion that 'Plato and St Athanasius must stand or fall together'[8] is a reaffirmation of Cudworth and Coleridge.

Yet we cannot confidently speak of the Anglo-Saxon Platonism running from the Cambridge Platonists through Coleridge up to the late nineteenth century without reflection upon Coleridge's achievement. Coleridge shared their combination of philosophical prowess and spiritual sensitivity, but they were relatively isolated figures, and William Law was hostile to philosophy. Berkeley is perhaps closer to Coleridge than William Law. Berkeley's theory of the phenomenal world as a divine visual language is deeply Platonic, but Berkeley is too original a mind to be seen as continuing the philosophy of

[6] W. R. Inge, *Protestantism* (London: Benn, 1930), pp. 109–10.
[7] R. C. Morgan, 'Non Angli sed angeli' in *New Studies in Theology*, edited by S. Sykes and D. Holmes (London: Duckworth, 1980), pp. 1–29. But see the remarks of G. Cole, 'Paley and the myth of Classical Anglicanism', pp. 3, 97–100.
[8] 'Coleridge', p. 340.

religion of the Cambridge Platonists. Coleridge's achievement was to harness German Idealism as an invigorating force against the debilitating effects of empiricism and utilitarianism. He did not wish to translate Schelling into English, but to show that the intuitions of the greatest British poets and theologians, and some of England's philosophers, could be buttressed and developed with aids from German philosophy.

It is clear from the evidence of John Beer's introduction that Coleridge's direct influence at Oxford decreased towards the end of the nineteenth century, just at the time when Green and Caird were in their ascendency. Yet his thought, and particularly *Aids to Reflection* prepared the ground in the mid century for the ascendancy of the *soi-disant* Hegelianism of Green, Nettleship, F. H. Bradley, John Caird, Muirhead, and Henry Jones. G. D. Boyle wrote in 1895:

the influence of Coleridge is not what it used to be when I first knew Oxford as an undergraduate, when tutors were in the habit of recommending *The Friend* and *Aids to Reflection* to such of their pupils as were reading for honours. (*Aids*, p. cxxx–cxxxix)

Mark Pattison admitted his debt to the 'strong infusion of Coleridgean metaphysics' and noted critically in his 'Tendencies of religious thought in England, 1688–1750' that Coleridge had reintroduced rationalism in English religious thought. This, of course, was the high Platonic 'rationalism' of the Cambridge Platonism rather than the rationalism of Locke and Paley. Hort wrote:

The prodigious changes which have taken place in the last forty years render much of the *Aids to Reflection* very perplexing to those who forget the time when it was written. Because the Warburtonian doctrine, that all language respecting direct spiritual influences is purely metaphorical, is scarcely intelligible to us now, we must not forget that in the first quarter of the century it was almost an axiom of orthodoxy, and its denial associated with fanatical Methodism.[9]

It was Coleridge's purpose to renew belief in the spirit without falling into enthusiasm. Victorians forgot, Hort avers, how this spirit of freedom arose. In a sense it was Coleridge's success which led to his relative obscurity in the late Victorian and Edwardian periods which were so strongly influenced by his ideas and ideals. Many of the principles for which he fought, such as the rejection of utilitarianism, or a spiritual view of religion, became the standard fare of

[9] Hort, 'Coleridge', in *Cambridge Essays*, vol. ii. p. 346.

the British Idealists. In 1890 *almost all* English-speaking philosophers were idealists. A satisfactory history of idealism in this period has not been written, but Coleridge plays a seminal role in the development of the movement.

COLERIDGE AND TWENTIETH CENTURY RELIGIOUS THOUGHT

On account of his influence upon the Victorians, one might consider that Coleridge's philosophy is too arcane and antiquated for contemporary religious thought. However, it has been observed that Coleridge's thought has a deep affinity with that of the great Danish philosopher of religion and Christian apologist Søren Kierkegaard. The 'Try It!' approach to Christian apologetics – Coleridge's emphasis upon the will and the emotions in religious epistemology – is perceived as a forerunner of Kierkegaard's view of faith as a venture, and perhaps even of the theology of Karl Barth. Coleridge's outbursts against the arid rationalism of Paley, and evidences and proofs of Hanoverian England, can be seen to parallel the fulminations of Kierkegaard against the complacency of Danish Hegelian theology, or even Karl Barth, as pastor of Safenwil against the liberalism of his German teachers. However, the surface affinity deceives.

The central tenet of Karl Barth's *Epistle to the Romans* is that 'God is in heaven and man is on earth', a tenet which he explicitly derives from Kierkegaard's infinite qualitative distinction between God and man. We have argued that Coleridge's religious philosophy is based on the opposing tenet of the reciprocal immanence of human and divine: that God is 'in' man and man is 'in' God. Such is the significance of Coleridge's repeated avowal of the Delphic injunction 'Know Thyself!'

Kierkegaard sets up the Idealistic-Coleridgean type of theology as his explicit target in the third chapter of his *Philosophical Fragments*, which he (through the pseudonym of Johannes Climacus) identifies as the Socratic view that a human being has access to knowledge of the divine through self-knowledge. Kierkegaard playfully quotes Plato's *Phaedrus* where Socrates explicitly refers to the demand of the 'Delphic inscription' to investigate myself.[10] The *Philosophical Fragments* confronts this Delphic exhortation to self-knowledge with its

---

[10] S. Kierkegaard, *Philosophical Fragments*, translated by D. Swenson, revised by H. Hong (Princeton University Press, 1967), pp. 48–9.

implication that religious truth is 'within' the believer and in which the Socratic teacher is merely the 'occasion' of knowledge, with the Christian vision of salvation as the confrontation with the paradox of the Incarnation; not as the occasion of truth – as in the case of Socrates – but the very 'condition' of truth delivered from without. Kierkegaard is attacking Hegel and Lessing through the figure of Socrates, a theological tradition which he rightly identifies as Platonically inspired.

Another example of the stark contrast between Coleridge and Kierkegaard is to be found in *Fear and Trembling*. Here Kierkegaard takes up the Old Testament story of Abraham and Isaac, and the attempt of Abraham to offer his son as a sacrifice. Kierkegaard (through the pseudonym of Johannes de Silentio) uses the bizarre narrative to illustrate his principle of the 'teleological suspension of the ethical' where an 'absolute duty toward God' conflicts drastically with ethical intuitions. Kierkegaard employs the tale to reinforce his tenet that the individual as particular is 'higher than the universal',[11] the unique individual may be summoned in 'fear and trembling' to act in a manner which clearly infringes a universal law. How very different is Coleridge's conviction that faith cannot conflict with reason, and his fear of an arbitrary divine-command theory of ethics. Instead of the ascent from prudence to morality to religion in Coleridge, Kierkegaard presents an abrupt break between the ethical and the religious.

The tenor of *Fear and Trembling* and the doctrine of 'teleological suspension of the ethical' points to a further contrast with Coleridge. Kierkegaard views 'Christendom' as 'apostasy from Christianity'[12] and the Christian life as almost impossible to attain. Coleridge takes the opposing view that western Christendom and particularly Protestant culture has absorbed Christian ideals, however imperfectly, into its actual structures. Hence the deliberate ambiguity of the term 'clerisy'. At this point we can sense Coleridge's debt to the Christian humanism of the Cambridge Platonists who, though opposed to any 'all creature-magnifying self sufficiency'[13] saw Christianity, in Tulloch's fine phrase,

---

[11] S. Kierkegaard, *Fear and Trembling and The Sickness unto Death* translated by. W. Lowrie (Princeton University Press, 1968), p. 91.

[12] Kierkegaard, *The Last Years: Journals 1853–1855*, edited by R. G. Smith (London: Collins, 1965), p. 238.

[13] Quoted by B. F. Westcott, *Religious Thought in the West* (London: Macmillan, 1891), p. 368.

as 'an education and consecration of all his (i.e.. man's) higher activities'.[14]

Coleridge presents an egregious contrast with Kierkegaard. Modern Christian thought is determined by its relation to the criticisms of traditional Christian theology which arose during the Enlightenment and the question as to the 'reasonableness of Christianity'. It is possible to isolate three responses to the challenge. The first is that of Kierkegaard and Karl Barth: here we find the response that Christianity is not, cannot be, and should not be 'reasonable'. Christianity is by its nature a scandal and an offence to the intellect, a paradox. The second reply consists of accepting entirely the critique by the cultured despisers and reinterpreting Christianity within the parameters of an entirely modifed metaphysics and belief system. An example of such a total acceptance of the radical Enlightenment critique would be Feuerbach or D. F. Strauss. The third response would be to accept the validity of the epistemological, moral, and metaphysical objections, but to deny that 'cultured despisers' employ an adequate conception of rationality. Coleridge replies to critics of Christianity not by appealing to paradox, nor by divesting Christian beliefs of their content, but by claiming that the despisers of Christianity judge its tenets exclusively through the instrument of the understanding and not through reason. As John Stuart Mill observes: 'He thus goes quite as far as the Unitarians in making man's reason and moral feelings a test of revelation; but differs *toto coelo* from them in their rejection of its mysteries, which he regards as the highest philosophic truths'.[15]

Coleridge often jokes about the term 'Enlightenment' (e.g. *CCS*, pp. 14, 17). The word 'Enlightenment' has its roots in the mystical tradition. Plato in the seventh letter (341c–d) writes of a sudden insight into the nature of the good and this is the result of disciplined striving. The biblical doctrine of the *imago Dei* is used to develop this thought concerning the divine illumination of the human mind by the Christian mystics: the ideas of *imago Dei*, divine revelation, and participation in the divine light, in Christian theology are replaced by the period of the Anglo-Gallic Enlightenment with an emphasis upon the emancipation of the human mind: illumination is seen as increasing the task of mankind rather than divine grace. Kant

---

[14] J. Tulloch, *Rational Theology and Christian Philosophy* (Hildesheim: Olms, 1966), vol. ii. p. 115.
[15] Mill and Bentham, *Utilitarianism*, p. 222.

defined the Enlightenment as the 'emancipation from mankind's self-inflicted immaturity': '*Ausgang des Menschen aus seiner selbst verschuldeten Unmündigkeit*'.[16] Coleridge shares the characteristically enlightened emphasis upon *emancipation*, but differs radically in his view of its source and nature.

Yet, like Hegel, Coleridge shared many of the ideals and concerns of the Enlightenment. It was quite impossible for Coleridge to reject the 'inquiring spirit' of philosophical reflection and historical critical scholarship on the basis of ecclesiastical authority and tradition. For all his conservatism, Coleridge accepts many of the Enlightenment criticisms of Christianity. He rejects the 'monstrous fiction' of hereditary (biologically transmitted) sin, theories of penal substitution, and other juridicial theories of atonement; he accepts and welcomes biblical criticism; he insists that God cannot be thought of in categories of empirical experience as a unique object. In all these respects Coleridge is a product of the Enlightenment. This is the classical Idealist position: to accept the strength of the Enlightened critique *and yet* to criticise the narrow and abstract concept of rationality of the enlightened thinkers. *Reason* is the determining concept in *Aids to Reflection*.

Hence in contrast to Kierkegaard and the 'meta-critique' of the German counter-Enlightenment, Coleridge believes that Christianity must be subject to philosophical scrutiny. However, in contrast to the radical Hegelians, Coleridge does not see the primary task of philosophy as the radical critique and destruction of the claims of historical and dogmatic Christianity. He tries to avoid the Scylla and Charybdis of the theological positivism which demands immunity from rational criticism and the speculative radicalism which reduces religion to the forlorn and childlike expression of metaphysical notions.

Coleridge is not liberal in the sense that he has a minimal sense of human frailty and the need for divine 'aids.' His sustained critique of Arminianism and the centrality of his analysis of the failings of Jeremy Taylor's semi-Pelagianism should suffice to dispel such errors. Nevertheless, in terms of his general apologetic strategy Coleridge should be seen as a part of a liberal theological tradition which has its roots in the Cambridge Platonists, but also includes Paley. For all his rhetorical invective against Paley, and notwith-

---

[16] Kant, *Werke*, vol. viii. p. 35.

standing the profound metaphysical disagreements with Paley, Coleridge remains within that apologetic tradition of Christianity which employs 'natural theology'. Coleridge shares much more with Paley than he admits: the stress upon the practical dimension of the Christian faith, and a latitudinarian temper; and most significantly the robust faith which is reflected in a great nineteenth-century Cambridge divine, Brooke Foss Westcott, when he quotes with approval from the founding figure of the Cambridge Platonists, Benjamin Whichcote, whose statue can be seen on the Cambridge University Divinity School building,[17] the following words: 'there is nothing true in divinity which is false in philosophy, or the contrary'.[18]

The dominance of Barthianism throughout the twentieth century provided a singularly hostile climate for 'natural' or apologetic philosophical theology. The titles of this dominant Barthian tendency vary somewhat: 'post-liberal', 'radical orthodoxy', 'confessional', etc., but the result is the same. Theology should be seen as *Church Dogmatics*. Narrative is a key term of those contemporary theologians like Hans Frei, George Lindbeck, or Stanley Hauerwas who propound reason within the bounds of religion and attempt to inure Christianity from critique by its cultured despisers. Conservative post-modern theology has combined the antifoundationalism of French post-structuralism with a Barthian positivism: the postmodern attack on foundations seems to justify the ultimately Barthian refusal to engage in dialogue with the cultured despisers of religion. Gerard Loughlin writes:

Long before it was fashionable to be non-foundational, Hans Frei (1922–1988) had learnt from Karl Barth (1886–1968) that Christian faith rests not upon universal human reason or human self-consciousness, but is sustained through and as commitment to a story.[19]

---

[17] G. Rupp, The Cambridge centenary: the Selwyn Divinity School (1879–1979)' in *The Historical Journal* 14 2 (1981), pp. 417–28.

[18] B. F. Westcott, *Religious Thought in the West*, p. 394. cf. the passage from Eriugena, 'veram esse philosophiam veram religionem, conversimque veram religionem esse veram philosophiam', quoted in n. 45. Eriugena's *de Divisione Naturae* was edited by the Cambridge professor of Greek Thomas Gale (1635/6–1702) in 1681, of whom Cudworth speaks as 'my learned friend Mr Gale' (*True Intellectual System of the Universe*, vol. i. p. 539). It can hardly be a coincidence that this early medieval Christian Neoplatonist was rediscovered by a contemporary of Henry More and Ralph Cudworth. Eriugena was, furthermore, a favourite of Coleridge, a 'wonderful man'. *PL*, p. 270.

[19] Gerald Loughlin, *Telling God's Story: Bible, Church and Narrative Theology* (Cambridge University Press, 1996), p. 33.

Post-modern theologians present Christianity as a 'narrative', along-side other 'narratives'. Yet the immunity which Kierkegaard or Barth and their 'post-modern' successors achieve is purchased at a great cost, and it is particularly open to those reductionistic genetic objections which have proliferated since the nineteenth century, which reject the Christian religion as a consoling illusion. Coleridge, like Cudworth and Paley, or Temple and Raven, represents a tradition of defending religious beliefs against the cultured despisers without retreating into splendid theological isolation.

Attacking rationality may fend off the cultured despisers of religion but it removes one of the important sources of religious belief: reason as the 'candle of the Lord'. Enlightenment is, after all, a Platonic metaphor, and the Enlightenment ideal of discernment has clear roots in the spiritual and intellectual ideals of the Christian west.[20] Whichcote's famous description of reason as the 'candle of the Lord' is a luminous instance of the continuity between the Hellenic–Christian legacy and the Enlightenment; just as the term 'renaissance', or 'renovatio' literally resonates with the deeply Christian components of the origins of modernity.[21]

> You will see Coleridge – he who sits obscure
> In the exceeding lustre and the pure
> Intense irradiation of a mind,
> Which, with its own internal lightning blind,
> Flags wearily through darkness and despair –
> A cloud-encircled meteor of the air,
> A hooded eagle among blinking owls.[22]

Coleridge was a defender of the mystery of reason as opposed to what he regarded as the unreflective sensualism of his age. Panajotis Kondylis sees the philosophy of the Enlightenment as the rejection of the Platonic–Aristotelian rationalism of classical, medieval, and early modern philosophy and the rehabilitation of the *sensual*. Rather than envisaging man as an essentially rational or spiritual creature,

---

[20] Plato, *Seventh Letter*, 341c–d; cf. W. Beierwaltes, 'Erleuchtung', in *Historisches Wörterbuch der Philosophie*, ed. J. Ritter vol. ii. pp. 712–17.

[21] cf. J. Tulloch, *Rational Theology and Christian Philosophy* (Edinburgh: William Blackwood, 1872), vol. ii. p. 99. There is some truth, I suggest, in the old contrast between a conservative Oxford of Laudians, Jacobites, and Tractarians, and the liberal Cambridge of Platonists, latitudinarians, and the Broad Church men. cf. J. Gascoigne, *Cambridge in the Age of Enlightenment* (Cambridge University Press, 1989).

[22] Shelley, quoted in Holmes *Coleridge, Darker Reflections*, p. 455.

endowed with the 'candle of the Lord', in the Enlightenment mankind emerges as a bundle of habits, shaped by a particular environment and customs.[23] In a similar vein Edward Craig has presented the Enlightenment as a shift of attention from the 'mind of God' to the 'works of man'.[24] If this is justified – and there is more than enough evidence to show that Hume, for example, can be seen in just this way, we must see Coleridge as the advocate of an older rationalism. Coleridge saw the 'philosophy' of his age as a 'hunger bitten and idea-less philosophy' (*LS*, p. 30); he saw himself as rousing the soul to an awareness of forgotten truths: those of an older rationalism which was founded upon the Delphic injunction of self-knowledge.

The dominating figure amongst the religious sceptics was, of course, David Hume. Hume, like Coleridge, thinks that 'Know Thyself!' is the centre of philosophy. *A Treatise of Human Nature* famously constitutes the attempt to bring the experimental method into philosophy. He uses the word 'reflection' as a synonym for reason: reflection leads to puzzles, Hume thinks, because our reason or reflection is simply not able to fathom the hidden structure of the universe. He thinks that mankind is imperfectly adapted to the emotional rigours of his environment and seeks consolation in a metaphysics which yields security that the universe corresponds to the most deeply felt human values. Traditional metaphysics provides a cosmic consolation and a comforting illusion on a higher plane than the kind which the masses seek in superstitious religion. Only a hardy few will be able to face the fact that human beings are simply rather more complex than other animals but different in degree, not in kind. This is a rejection of the Platonic–Aristotelian–Cartesian conviction that mankind's distinctive essence is divine and rational. Although Hume was loath to identify himself with the strident naturalism of the radical wing of the French Enlightenment, he clearly felt no compelling reason to believe that human values are reflected in the structure of things: there may perhaps be reason for accepting some limited purposiveness in the universe, but far too little to support traditional metaphysics or anything like philosophical theism, or the Platonic–Aristotelian–Cartesian conviction that mankind's distinc-

[23] P. Kondylis, *Die Aufklärung im Rahmen des neuzeitlichen Rationalismus* (Stuttgart: Klett-Cotta, 1981).

[24] E. Craig, *The Mind of God and the Works of Man* (Oxford: Clarendon, 1987).

tive essence is divine and rational. As David Stove, in his bad-tempered but perceptive essay 'Idealism: A Victorian Horror Story', notes:

That idealism *is* a child of religion, needs no argument: it is obvious . . . *All* idealists are engaged, above everything else, in satisfying the religious demand for the universe to be reassuring or consoling, or at the very least, *kindred*.[25]

Coleridge believes that the intellectual, moral and aesthetic desires of humanity are not mysterious by-products of all-too-profligate nature but reflect the difference in kind between man and beast. Hume's brilliant and ironic transposition of the ancient adage '*Nil admirari*' (Don't wonder) contrasts vividly with Coleridge's belief that philosophy is rooted in wonder (*Aids*, pp. 236ff.) and his equally strong conviction that the equilibrium of 'Enlightened' mitigated scepticism will in fact debilitate and enervate those energies which inspire science and society as well as religion. Coleridge believes that the moral and volitional reaction of humanity to its environment is far deeper than the merely logical.[26] Our knowledge of God may well be mysterious, but no less so than the fact of our knowledge of ethical and scientific truths. Yet in order to appreciate this miracle of the affinity and kinship of the mind with the unseen world, it is necessary to pursue the spirit of the Delphic Oracle in the light of Plato, Aristotle, and Augustine: that self-knowledge does not reveal a bundle of impressions, but a mirror of the spirit.

The post-Enlightenment legacy of the 'death of God' has seemed to be inexorable for the past two centuries, allowing only for either of two responses. For those wishing to escape its grip, modernity is something to be overcome by means of a return to pre-modernity in one form or other. For those resigned to, or rejoicing in, its grip, any return to the Christian Platonic philosophical tradition in particular has seemed neither possible nor desirable.

Coleridge opens up a way for us to rethink our relation to the Enlightenment legacy. For Coleridge was in critical and creative negotiation with the principles and consequences of the Enlightenment. But that negotiation demanded of him a rethinking of the

---

[25] D. Stove, *The Plato Cult and other Philosophical Follies* (Oxford: Blackwell, 1991), p. 87.
[26] Compare Coleridge's idea of faith as 'fidelity to our being' with the remarks of William James, *The Will to Believe* (New York: Dover, 1956), pp. 111–44.

Christian Platonic tradition, principally through his wrestling with
Kant and contemporary German Idealism. Hort was right to
insist that Coleridge was 'a mind which expressed itself most
naturally in the form of commentary. Surely here is a striking
outward mark of his function as an interpreter of the old to the
new.[27]

It is this seemingly simultaneous – and even contradictory –
'forward-looking' and 'backward-looking' character of his thinking
that has made it so difficult to understand his relation to German
Idealism in particular, and his contribution to the philosophy of
religion in general. But he offers to us a way to rethink our own
relation to the Enlightenment legacy. It is precisely that which has
obscured Coleridge to us in the past that makes his thought so
fruitful for the future.

Of course, Coleridge had aims in philosophy which have become
singularly unfashionable and his penchant for idealist a priori arm-
chair speculations is not always endearing. His ability to combine
talk of pentads and triads with an episcopal air gives much of his
thought a pompous and vaguely preposterous feel, if not the
impression of opium-induced haze. Yet Coleridge shared fundamental speculative ambitions with Plato, Aristotle, Plotinus, and
Hegel, and his real flashes of insight do manage to transform that
initial impression of haze and deliberate obscurity which has
irritated Carlyle and numerous other critics. His was an affectionate
seeking after truth (*BL* i. 142) and an infectious relish for metaphysics. At his best, Coleridge radiates a translucent intellectual energy
and clarity which is unsurpassed by any religious philosopher in the
English nineteenth century. *Aids to Reflection* is doubtless a rambling
and highly digressive collection of marginalia on Robert Leighton
and ideas about the philosophical basis of morality and religion. But
it also constitutes an *Ideenparadies* which stamped Coleridge's deepest
convictions on the minds of eminent Victorians, and beyond. It is
only fair to recognise that the sage of Highgate was a successor of
Berkeley and predecessor of T. H. Green, a part of an Idealist
tradition in British thought whose provenance lies in the Florentine
Renaissance and passes through late antiquity to Plato. It is a
substantial part of our intellectual heritage; even if the fashions of
the twentieth century, like those of the eighteenth century, tended to

---

[27] Hort, 'Coleridge' p. 350.

militate against or were frankly hostile to Platonism. Coleridge would not be happy with such an argument for Platonism from culture and tradition. He thought that Platonic Idealism is true. And, of course, he could be right.

Bibliography

PRIMARY SOURCES

Aristotle, *Metaphysics*, translated and edited by W. D. Ross, Oxford: Clarendon, 1924.

Athanasius, *De Incarnatione* in *Sur l'Incarnation du verbe*, edited by Charles Kannengiesser, Paris: Editions du Cerf, 1973.

Augustine, *Aurelii Augustini Opera*, Corpus Christianorum, Series Latina, Turnhout: 1953– .

Sancti Aurellii Augustini, Patrologiae Cursus Completus, Series Latina, 12 vols., edited by J.-P. Migne, Paris: Migne, 1861–3.

Against Julian, translated by M. A. Schumacher, Washington: Catholic University of America Press, 1981.

Against the Academics, translated by J. J. O'Meara, Westminster Md.: Newman Press; London: Longman Green and Co., 1950.

City of God, translated by H. Bettenson, Harmondsworth: Penguin, 1984.

Confessions, translated by R. S. Pine-Coffin, Harmondsworth: Penguin, 1961.

Logik des Schreckens, De diversis quaestionibus ad Simplicianum 12, ed. K. Flasch, Mainz: Dieterich'sche Verlagsbuchhandlung, 1990.

On Free Choice of the Will, translated by Thomas Williams, Cambridge University Press, 1993.

On Genesis, translated by R. J. Teske SJ, Washington: Catholic University of America Press, 1991.

On the Psalms, translated by Dame S. Hebgin and Dame F. Corrigan, Westminster Md.: Newman Press; London: Longmans, Green, and Co., 1950.

The Enchiridion on Faith, Hope, and Love, translated by J. F. Shaw, Washington: Catholic University of America Press: 1991.

The Trinity, translated by E. Hill, New York: New City Press, 1996.

Bacon, F., *The Works of Francis Bacon*, edited by James Spedding, R. L. Ellis, and D. D. Heath, 14 vols., London: Longman and Co, 1857–74.

Balthasar, H. V. von, *Eine Theologische Asthetic*, Einsiedeln: Johannes Verlag, 1961.

Baxter R., *The Mischiefs of Self-Ignorance*, London: Tyton, 1662.
The Reasons of the Christian Religion, London: Tyton, 1667.
The Saints' Everlasting Rest, London: Tyton and Boulter, 1677.
Berkeley, Bishop George, *The Works of George Berkeley, Bishop of Cloyne*, 9 vols., edited by A. A. Luce and T. E. Jessop, London: Thomas Nelson and Sons, 1967.
Bosanquet, B., *The Principle of Individuality and Value*, London: Macmillan, 1912.
Brucker, Jakob, *Historia Critica Philosophiae*, Mertz and Meyer: Augustae Vindelicorum, 1723.
Bull, Bishop George, *Defensio Fidei Nicaenae* in vols. i. and ii. of *Bishop Bull's Works on the Trinity*, 3 vols., Oxford: Parker, 1852.
Burnet, G., *History of His Own Time*, 2 vols., vol. i. edited by G. Burnet Jr. and vol. ii. edited by Sir T. Burnet, London: Ward, 1724.
The History of the Reformation of the Church of England, 3 vols., London: Chiswell, 1681.
Butler, J., *Fifteen Sermons Preached at The Rolls Chapel*, London: Macmillan, 1913.
Chomsky, Noam, *Cartesian Linguistics*, London: Harper and Row, 1966.
Clement of Alexandria, *Clemens Alexandrinus*, edited by O. Stählin, Berlin: Akademie, 1985.
Comenius, Johann Amos, *Der Weg des Lichtes. Via Lucis*, edited by Uwe Voigt, Hamburg: Meiner, 1997.
Creuzer, Friedrich, *Symbolik und Mythologie der alten Völker, besonders der Griechen*, Leipzig und Darmstadt: Carl Wilhelm Leske, 1822.
Cudworth, Ralph, *A Sermon Preached before the Honourable House of Commons, at Westminster, March 31 1647*, Cambridge: Daniel, 1647.
A Treatise Concerning Eternal and Immutable Morality, with A Treatise of Free Will, edited by Sarah Hutton, Cambridge University Press: 1996.
The True Intellectual System of the Universe, 3 vols., edited by Harrison, London: Tegg, 1845.
Eriugena, John Scot, *Periphyseon* translated by I. P. Sheldon-Williams, Dublin: Dublin Institute for Advanced Studies, 1976– .
Eusebius Pamphilii, *Praeparatio Evangelica:, La Préparation Evangélique*, edited by E. Desplaces, Paris: Editions du Cerf, 1987.
Gibbon, E., *Memoirs of My Life*, edited by G. A. Bonnard, London: Nelson, 1966.
The History of the Decline and Fall of the Roman Empire, 3 vols., edited by David Womersley, Harmondsworth: Penguin, 1994.
Goethe, W., *Gespräche mit Eckermann, in den letzen Jahren seines Lebens*, edited by Ludwig Geiger, Leipzig: Insel, 1902.
Green, T. H., *Collected Works*, edited by R. L. Nettleship, 3 vols., London: Longman and Co., 1885 8.
Hamann, Johann Georg, *Schriften zur Sprache*, edited by J. Simon, Frankfurt: Suhrkamp, 1967.

Hartley, D., *Observations on Man, his Frame, his Duty, and his Expectations*, 2 vols., London: 1749, reprinted Hildesheim: Olms, 1967.

Hazlitt, W., *Complete Works*, 21 vols., edited by P. P. Howe, London and Toronto: Dent and Sons, 1930–4.

Hegel, G. W. F., *Enzyklopädie der Philosophischen Wissenschaft*, Hamburg: Meiner, 1975.

Lectures on the Philosophy of Religion, edited by P. C. Hodgson, 3 vols., Berkeley: University of California Press, 1984.

Phenomenology of Spirit, translated by A. V. Miller, sixth edition, Oxford: Clarendon, 1952.

Sämtliche Werke, edited by H. Glockner, 26 vols., Stuttgart: Fromann Holzboog, 1968.

Vorlesungen über die Philosophie der Religion, edited by G. Lasson, Hamburg: Meiner, 1966.

Werke, 20 vols., Frankfurt am Main: Suhrkamp, 1970.

Heidegger, M., *Sein und Zeit*, Tübingen: Niemeyer, 1993.

Herder, J. G., *Sämtliche Werke*, edited by B. Suphan, Hildesheim: Olms, 1967.

Hooker, R., *The Works*, 3 vols., edited by W. Speed Hill, Cambridge, Mass.: Harvard University Press and Belknap, 1977– .

Hort, F. J. A., 'Coleridge', in *Cambridge Essays, contributed by members of the University*, 4 vols., Cambridge University Press, 1856, pp. 292–351.

The Way, the Truth, the Life, second edition, edited by B. F. Westcott, London: Macmillan, 1897.

Hügel, Baron Friedrich von, *The Mystical Element of Religion as Studied in Saint Catherine of Genoa and her Friends*, second edition, London: Dent and Sons; New York: Dutton and Co., 1927.

Hume, D., *Enquiries Concerning Human Understanding and Concerning the Principles of Morals*, third edition, edited by P. H. Nidditch, Oxford: Clarendon, 1975.

Letters, edited by J. Y. T. Grieg, 2 vols., Oxford: Clarendon, 1932.

Principal Writings on Religion including Dialogues Concerning Natural Religion and The Natural History of Religion, edited by J. C. A. Gaskin, Oxford: Clarendon, 1993.

Treatise of Human Nature, second edition, edited by P. H. Nidditch and L. A. Selby-Bigge, Oxford: Clarendon, 1978.

Inge, W. R., *Christian Mysticism*, London: Methuen, 1899.

Faith and Knowledge, Edinburgh: T. and T. Clark, 1904.

God and the Astronomers, London: Longman, 1934.

More Lay Thoughts of a Dean, London: Putnam, 1932.

Outspoken Essays, London: Longmans, Green, and Co., 1919.

Personal Idealism and Mysticism, London: Longmans, Green, and Co., 1907.

The Philosophy of Plotinus, 2 vols., London: Longmans, Green, and Co., 1918.

Studies in English Mystics, London: John Murray, 1906.

The Platonic Tradition in English Religious Thought, London: Longmans, Green and Co., 1926.

Jackson, T. H., *A Treatise of the Divine Essence and Attributes*, 2 vols., London: Clarke, 1628.

Jacobi, Friedrich Heinrich, 'Über die Lehre des Spinoza in Briefen an den Herrn Moses Mendelssohn' in *Die Hauptschriften zum Pantheismusstreit*, edited by Heinrich Scholz, Berlin: Renther and Reichard, 1916, pp. 45–281.

Werke, Leipzig: Fleischer, 1812–25.

Kant, I., *Critique of Pure Reason*, translated by N. Kemp-Smith, London: Macmillan, 1982.

Prolegomena to any Future Metaphysics, edited by Beryl Logan, London: Routledge, 1996.

The Moral Law, translated by H. Paton, London: Hutchinson, 1981.

Werke, Akademie Textausgabe, Berlin: de Gruyter, 1968.

Religion within the Boundaries of Mere Reason and other Writings, edited by A. Wood and G. di Giovanni, Cambridge University Press, 1998.

Kepler, J., 'The harmonies of the world' in *Great Books of the Western World*, edited by M. J. Adler, Chicago: Encyclopaedia Britannica, xv (1992), pp. 1009–85.

Kierkegaard, S., *Fear and Trembling and The Sickness unto Death*, translated by W. Lowrie, Princeton University Press, 1968.

Philosophical Fragments, translated by D. Swenson, revised by H. Hong, Princeton University Press, 1967.

The Concept of Anxiety: A Simple Psychologically Orientating Deliberation on the Dogmatic Issue of Hereditary Sin, translated by R. Thomte with A. B. Anderson, Princeton and Guildford: Princeton University Press, 1980.

The Last Years: Journals 1853–1855, edited by R. G. Smith, London: Collins, 1965.

Lamb, C., *Essays of Elia*, Cambridge University Press, 1949.

Law, W., *Selected Mystical Writings, with Twenty-four Studies in the Mystical Theology of William Law and Jacob Boehme*, edited by S. Hobhouse, London: Daniel and Co., 1940.

Leighton, Robert, *Bibliotheca Leightoniana*, edited by W. J. Cowper, Dunblane: 1917.

The Whole Works, with a Life of the Author by J. N. Pearson, 2 vols., London: Henry Bohn, 1849.

Lessing, G. E., *Werke*, 3 vols., edited by H. G. Göpfert, Munich: Hanser, 1982.

Gesammelte Werke, edited by Paul Rilla, Berlin: Aufbau Verlag, 1968.

Die Erziehung des Menschengeschlechts, Bern; reprinted in Berlin: P. Lang, 1780.

Lessing's Theological Writings, translated and introduced by Henry Chadwick, London: Adam and Charles Black, 1956.

Lewis, C. S., *An Experiment in Criticism*, Cambridge University Press, 1961.

Locke, John, *An Essay Concerning Human Understanding*, Oxford: Clarendon, 1975.

The Works, eleventh edition, 10 vols., London: Tegg, 1823.

Marsh, J., 'Preliminary Essay to *Aids to Reflection*', reprinted in John Beer's edition, London: Routledge; Princeton University Press, 1993, pp. 491–529.

Maurice, F. D., *Kingdom of Christ*, 2 vols., edited by A. R. Vidler, London: SCM, 1958.

Moral and Metaphysical Philosophy, London: Macmillan, 1882.

Maurice, Frederick (ed.), *The Life of Frederick Denison Maurice*, London: Macmillan, 1884.

Mill, John Stuart and Jeremy Bentham, *Utilitarianism and Other Essays*, edited by A. Ryan, London: Penguin, 1979.

Moltmann, J., (ed.) *Anfänge der dialektischen Theologie*, 2 vols., Munich: Kaiser, 1985.

More, H., *The Philosophical Poems of Henry More, comprising 'Psychozoia' and Minor Poems*, edited by G. Bullough, University of Manchester Press, 1931.

The Philosophical Writings of Henry More, edited by Flora Isabel Mackinnon, New York: Oxford University Press, 1925.

Morgan, Caesar, *An Investigation of the Trinity of Plato and of Philo Judaeus, and of the Effects which an Attachment to their Writings had upon the Principles and Reasonings of the Fathers of the Christian Church*, Cambridge University Press, 1853.

Newman, Cardinal J. H., *Apologia Pro Vita Sua*, edited by M. J. Svalig, Oxford: Clarendon, 1967.

Nicholas of Cusa, *On Learned Ignorance*, edited by Jasper Hopkins, Minneapolis: Arthur Banning, 1981.

Dialectical Mysticism, second edition, Minneapolis: Arthur Banning 1988.

Nietzsche, F., *On the Genealogy of Morals*, translated by W. Kaufmann and R. J. Hollingdale, New York: A. A. Knopf and Random, 1969.

Sämtliche Werke, 15 vols., edited by G. Colli and M. Montinari, Berlin: de Gruyter, 1980.

The Twilight of the Idols, translated by R. J. Hollingdale, London: Penguin, 1968.

Nye, S., *Considerations on the Explications of the Doctrine of the Trinity by Dr Wallis, Dr Sherlock, Dr S-th [sic], Dr Cudworth and Mr Hooker; and also of the Account Given by Those who Say, the Trinity is an Unconceivable and Inexplicable Mystery*, London: Aylmer, 1693.

Oman, J., *Grace and Personality*, Cambridge University Press, 1919.

Paley, William, *The Works*, 4 vols., edited by R. Lynam, London: Dove, 1827.

Pannenberg, W., *Metaphysik und Gottesgedanke*, Göttingen: Vandenhoeck and Ruprecht, 1988.

Systematische Theologie, Göttingen: Vandenhoeck and Ruprecht, 1988.

'Christentum und Platonismus. Die kritische Platonrezeption Augustins in ihrer Bedeutung für das gegenwärtige christliche Denken' in *Zeitschrift für Kirchengeschichte* 96 (1985), pp. 147–61.

Pater, W., 'Coleridge' in *Strangeness and Beauty: an Anthology of Aesthetic Criticism, 1840–1910*, edited by E. Warner and E. Hough, 2 vols., Cambridge, 1983, vol. ii: 'Pater to Arthur Symons', pp. 45–54.

Pattison, Mark, 'Tendencies of religious thought in England, 1688–1750' in *Essays and Reviews*, London: Longman, Green, Longman and Roberts, 1862, pp. 306–98.

Peacock, T. Love, *Nightmare Abbey / Crotchet Castle*, edited by R. Wright, Harmondsworth: Penguin, 1969.

Pétau, Denis, *Theologicorum Dogmatum*, Paris: Cramoisy, 1644.

Plato, *The Dialogues of Plato*, translated by B. Jowett, fourth edition, Oxford University Press, 1953.

Gorgias, Harmondsworth: Penguin, 1988.

Laws, translated by T. J. Saunders, London: Heinemann, 1970.

Opera, 5 vols., edited by J. Burnet, Oxford: Clarendon, 1900–7.

Plutarch, *Moralia*, translated by P. Clement and H. B. Hoffleit, Cambridge, Mass.: Harvard University Press, 1986.

Plotinus, translated and edited by A. H. Armstrong, Cambridge, Mass.: Harvard University Press, 1966–88.

Priestley, J., *Theological and Miscellaneous Works*, edited by John Towill Rutt, London, 1817–31.

Proclus Diadochus, *Commentary on the First Alcibiades of Plato*, a translation and commentary by William O'Neill, The Hague: M. Nijhoff, 1965.

The Elements of Theology, revised and edited by E. R. Dodds, Oxford: Clarendon, 1933.

Pseudo-Dionysius, *The Complete Works*, translated by Colm Luibheid, London: SPCK, 1987.

Quincey, T. de, *Recollections of the Lakes and the Lake Poets*, edited by David Wright, Harmondsworth: Penguin, 1985.

Robinson, H. C., *Diary, Reminiscences, and Correspondence of Henry Crabb Robinson*, third edition, edited by T. Sadler, 2 vols., London: Macmillan, 1872.

Royce, J., *The Problem of Christianity*, with a new introduction by J. E. Smith, London and Chicago: University of Chicago Press, 1968.

Ryle, G., *The Concept of Mind*, Harmondsworth: Penguin, 1980.

Sallustius (the Neoplatonist), *Concerning the Gods and the Universe*, edited with prolegomena and translation by A. D. Nock, Cambridge University Press, 1926.

Schelling, F. W. J. von, *Ausgewählte Schriften*, 6 vols., edited by M. Frank, Frankfurt: Suhrkamp, 1985.

Ausgewählte Werke, Nachdruck der Ausgabe Stuttgart 1856–1861, Darmstadt: Wissenschaftliche Buchgesellschaft, 1966.

Ausgewälte Werke. Schriften von 1806–1813, Darmstadt: Wissenschaftliche Buchgesellschaft, 1988.

Bruno, or, On the Natural and the Divine Principle of Things, edited and translated by Michael G. Vater, Albany: State University of New York Press, 1984.

Ideas for a Philosophy of Nature, as an Introduction to the Study of that Science, translated by E. E. Harris and P. Heath, Cambridge University Press, 1988.

Materialien zu Schellings Philosophischen Anfängen, edited by M. Frank, Frankfurt: Suhrkamp, 1975.

'Philosophie und Religion' in *Schriften von 1801–1804*, Stuttgart: 1859–60, reprinted Darmstadt: Wissenschaftliche Buchgesellschaft, 1988.

Philosophische Untersuchungen über das Wesen der menschlichen Freiheit und die damit zusammenhängenden Gegenstände edited by Horst Fuhurmans, Stuttgart: Reclam, 1983.

Sämtliche Werke. I Abteilung, 10 vols., *II Abteilung*, 4 vols., edited by K. F. A. Schelling, Stuttgart and Augsburg: Cotta, 1856–61.

System der Weltalter. Münchener Vorlesung 1827/28, edited by S. Peetz from lecture notes by Ernst von Lasaulx, Frankfurt am Main: Klostermann, 1990.

Texte zur Philosophie der Kunst, edited with introduction by Werner Beierwaltes, Stuttgart: Reclam, 1982.

Werke. Historisch-kritische Ausgabe, im Auftrag der Schelling-Kommission der Bayerischen Akademie der Wissenschaften, edited by H. M. Baumgartner, H. Krings, and H. Zeltner, 4 vols., Stuttgart and Bad Cannstatt: Fromann Holzboog, 1976.

Schlegel, F., *Kritische-Friedrich-Schlegel Ausgabe*, 35 vols., edited by H. Eichner, Paderborn: Schöningh, 1967– .

Schleiermacher, F. D. E., *Der christliche Glaube nach den Grundsätzen der evangelischen Kirche*, edited by M. Redeker, Berlin: de Gruyter, 1884.

Kritische Gesamtausgabe, edited by Hans-Joachim Birkner et al., Berlin: de Guyter, 1980.

Über die Philosophie Platons, ed. P. M. Steiner, Hamburg: Meiner, 1996.

'Einleitung', reprinted in *Das Platon Bild*, edited by Konrad Kaiser, Hildesheim: Olms, 1969.

Scholz, H. (ed.), *Die Hauptschriften zum Pantheismusstreit. Zwischen Jacobi und Mendelssohn*, Berlin: Kantgesellschaft, 1916.

Schopenhauer, A., *Werke*, 10 vols., Zürcher Ausgabe, Zürich: Diogenes, 1977.

Silesius, Angelus, *Cherubischer Wandersmann*, Zürich: Manesse, 1989.

Smith, John, *Select Discourses*, London: W. Morden, 1660; reprinted New York: Garland, 1978.

Spinoza, B. *Ethics*, translated by A. Boyle, London: Dent, 1986.

Stanley, T., *The History of Philosophy*, London: Thomas Bassett, Dorman, Newman, and Thomas Cockerill, 1687.

Taylor, Bishop Jeremy, *The Whole Works of The Right Reverend Jeremy Taylor, DD*, edited by R. Heber, 15 vols., London: Ogle, Duncan, and Co., 1822.

Tillich, Paul, *Gesammelte Werke*, 14 vols., Stuttgart: Evangelisches Verlags-werk, 1959–74.

The Construction of the History of Religion in Schelling's Positive Philosophy: its Presuppositions and Principles, translated and edited by Victor Nuovo, Lewisburg: Bucknell, 1974.

The Theology of Culture, New York: Oxford University Press, 1959.

Troeltsch, E., *Die Bedeutung des Protestantismus für die Entstehung der modernen Welt*, Munich: Oldenbourg, 1928.

Tulloch, J., *Rational Theology and Christian Philosophy*, Hildesheim: Olms, 1966.

Westcott, B. F., *Religious Thought in the West*, London: Macmillan, 1891.

Whichcote, B., *Moral and Religious Aphorisms*, London: Elkin Mathews, and Marrot, 1930.

The Works of the Learned Benjamin Whichcote, Aberdeen: Alexander Thomson, 1751.

SECONDARY SOURCES

Aarsleff, H., *From Locke to Saussure*, Minneapolis: University of Minnesota Press, 1982.

The Study of Language in England, 1780–1860, Princeton University Press, 1967.

(ed.), *The Cambridge Companion to Locke*, Cambridge University Press, 1994.

Abrams, M. H., *The Mirror and the Lamp*, New York and Oxford: Clarendon, 1953.

Addinall, P., *Philosophy and Biblical Interpretation*, Cambridge University Press, 1991.

Allchin, A. M., *Participation in God: A Forgotten Strand in Anglican Tradition*, London: Darton, Longman, and Todd, 1988.

Allen, Michael J. B., 'Marsilio Ficino on Plato, the neoplatonists and the Christian doctrine of the Trinity' in *Renaissance Quarterly* 37 (1984), pp. 555–84.

Allison, H. E., *Lessing and the Enlightenment*, Ann Arbor: Michigan University Press, 1966.

Ameriks, K., 'Kant on the good will' in *Grundlegung zur Metaphysik der Sitten. Ein kooperativer Kommentar*, edited by O. Höffe, Frankfurt: Klostermann, 1993, pp. 45–65.

Andia, Ysabel de, 'παθὼν τὰ θεῖα' in *Platonism in Late Antiquity*, edited by S. Gersh and C. Kannengiesser, University of Notre Dame Press, 1992, pp. 239–58.

Annas, Julia, 'Self-knowledge in early Plato' in *Platonic Investigations*, edited by Dominic O'Meara, Washington: Catholic University of America, 1985.

Antognazza, Maria Rosa, 'Die Rolle der Trinitäts und Menschwerdungs-diskussion für die Enstehung von Leibniz "Denken"' in *Studia Leibnitiana* 1 (1994), pp. 56–75.

Armstrong, A. Hilary, *Christian Faith and Greek Philosophy*, London: Darton, Longman, and Todd, 1960.

'Platonism' in *Prospects for Metaphysics: Essays of Metaphysical Exploration*, edited by Ian Ramsey, London: George Allen, 1961.

'Plotinus' in *The Cambridge History of Later Greek and Early Medieval Philosophy*, edited by Armstrong, Cambridge University Press: 1967, pp. 195–271.

'The divine enhancement of earthly beauties: the Hellenic and Platonic tradition' in *Eranos* 53 (1984), pp. 49–81.

Assmann, J., *Moses the Egyptian: The Memory of Egypt in Western Monotheism*, Cambridge, Mass.: Harvard University Press, 1997.

Atherton, J. P., 'The Neoplatonic "One" and the Trinitarian "APXH"' in *The Significance of Neoplatonism*, edited by R. Baine Harris, Norfolk, Va.: Old Dominion University Press, 1976, pp. 173–85.

Ayers, M., *Locke, Epistemology and Ontology*, London: Routledge, 1991.

'Substance, reality, and the great, dead philosophers' in *American Philosophical Quarterly* 7 (1970), pp. 38–49.

Baldwin A. and S. Hutton (eds.), *Platonism and the English Imagination*, Cambridge University Press, 1994.

Baldwin, J. T., 'God and the world: Willam Paley's argument from perfection, a continuing influence' in *Harvard Theological Review* 85 (1992), pp. 109–20.

Barfield, O., *What Coleridge Thought*, London: Oxford University Press, 1971.

Barker, Sir Ernest, *Britain and the British People*, London: Oxford University Press, 1942.

Barth, J. R., *Coleridge and Christian Doctrine*, Cambridge, Mass.: Harvard University Press, 1969.

The Symbolic Imagination, Princeton University Press, 1977.

'Coleridge and the Church of England' in *The Coleridge Connection: Essays for Thomas McFarland*, edited by R. Gravil and M. Lefebure, London: Macmillan, 1990, pp. 291–307.

Beer, J., *Coleridge's Poetic Intelligence*, Basingstoke and London: Macmillan, 1977.

'Coleridge's religious thought: the search for a medium' in *The Interpretation of Belief: Coleridge, Schleiermacher and Romanticism*, edited by D. Jasper, London: Macmillan, 1986, pp. 41–65.

Coleridge the Visionary, Basingstoke and London: Macmillan, 1959.

Behler, E., *Studien zur Romantik und zur idealistischen Philosophie*, Paderborn: Schöningh, 1988.

Unendliche Perfektibilität. Europäische Romantik und Französische Revolution, Paderborn: Schöningh, 1989.

Beierwaltes, Werner, *Denken des Einen*, Frankfurt: Klostermann, 1985.

Identität und Differenz, Frankfurt: Klostermann, 1985.

Platonismus und Idealismus, Frankfurt: Klostermann, 1972.

Plotin. Über Ewigkeit und Zeit. Enneade III 7, Frankfurt: Klostermann, 1981.

Proklos Grundzüge seiner Metaphysik, Frankfurt: Klostermann, 1979.
Selbsterkenntnis und Erfahrung der Einheit. Plotins Enneade V 3, Frankfurt:
    Klostermann, 1991.
'Augustins Interpretation von "Sapientia" 11, 21' in *Revue des Etudes
    Augustiniennes* 15 (1969), pp. 51–61.
Das Problem des absoluten Selbstbewußtseins bei Johannes Scotus
    Eriugena' in *Platonismus in der Philosophie des Mittelalters*, edited by
    Beierwaltes, Darmstadt: Wissenschaftliche Buchgesellschaft, 1969,
    pp. 484–516.
'Deus est Veritas. Zur Rezeption des griechischen Wahrheitsbegriffes in
    der frühchristlichen Theologie' in 'Pietas. Festschrift für Bernhard
    Kötting' in *Jahrbuch für Antike und Christentum*, supplementary vol. viii
    (1980), edited by E. Dassman and K. Suso, pp. 15–29.
'Negati Affirmatio. Welt als Metapher. Zur Grundlegung einer mitte-
    lalterlichen Ästhetik durch Johannes Scotus Eriugena' in *Philoso-
    phischen Jahrbuch* 83 (1976), pp. 237–65. The English translation,
    'Negative affirmation: world as metaphor' is in *Dionysius* 1 (1977), pp.
    127–59.
'Plotins Metaphysik des Lichtes' in *Die Philosophie des Neuplatonismus*,
    edited by Clemens Zintzen, Darmstadt: Wissenschaftliche Gesell-
    schaft, 1977, pp. 75–117.
'Regio Beatitudinis. Zu Augustins Begriff des glücklichen Lebens' in
    *Sitzungsberichte der Heidelberger Akademie der Wissenschaften, Philosophisch-
    historische Klasse* 6 (1981). *Regio beatitudinis: Augustine's concept of happiness*,
    translated into English by Bernard Barsky, Villanova: Augustinian
    Institute, 1981.
'Subjektivität, Schöpfertüm, Freiheit' in *Der Übergang zur Neuzeit und die
    Wirkung in der Tradition*, Veröffentlichung der Joachim Jungius Gesell-
    schaft, Göttingen: Vandenhoeck, 1978, pp. 15–31.
'The Revaluation of John Scottus Eriugena in German Idealism' in *The
    Mind of Eriugena*, edited by J. O'Meara and L. Bieler, Dublin:
    University of Ireland, 1973.
'Visio Facialis Sehen ins Angesicht. Zur Coincidenz des endlichen und
    unendlichen Blicks bei Cusanus' in *Sitzungsbericht der Bayerischen Aka-
    demie der Wissenschaften*, Munich: Beck, 1988.
Beiser, F. C., *The Fate of Reason*, Cambridge, Mass.: Harvard University
    Press, 1987.
Benrath, G. A., 'Der Antitrinitarismus' and 'Humanisten und Antitrini-
    tarier', *Handbuch der Dogmen und Theologiegeschichte*, vol. iii. Göttingen:
    Vandenhoeck, 1984, pp. (1984), 49–66.
Benz, E., *Les Sources mystiques de la philosophie romanticque*, Paris: Wissenschaf-
    tliche Buchgesellschaft, 1968. The English translation by B. R.
    Reynolds and E. M. Paul is *The Mystical Sources of German Romantic
    Philosophy*, Allison Park, Penn.: Pittsburgh Theological Monographs,
    1983.

Marius Victorinus und die Entwicklung der Abendländischen Willensmetaphysik, Stuttgart: Kohlhammer, 1932.

Berlinger, R., *Augustins dialogische Metaphysik*, Frankfurt: Klostermann, 1962.

Bieman, E., *Plato Baptized*, University of Toronto Press, 1988.

Bigg, C., *The Christian Platonists of Alexandria*, Oxford: Clarendon, 1886.

Blackburn, S. *Spreading the Word*, Oxford: Clarendon, 1984.

Blumenberg, H. *Die Legitimität der Neuzeit*, second edition, Frankfurt: Suhrkamp, 1988.

Bond, H. L., *The Literary Art of Edward Gibbon*, Oxford: Clarendon, 1960.

Bonhoeffer, T., 'Die Wurzeln des Begriffs Theologie' in *Archiv für Begriffsgeschichte* 34 (1991), pp. 7–26.

Bonner, G., 'Augustine's conception of deification' in *Journal of Theological Studies* 37 (1986), pp. 369–86.

Booth, E., 'Saint Augustine's "de Trinitate" and Aristotelean and Neoplatonist Noetic' in *Studia Patristica* xvi/2, edited by E. A. Livingstone, Berlin: Akademic Verlag, 1985.

'Saint Augustine's "notita sui" related to Aristotle and the early Neoplatonists', *Augustiniana* 27 (1977), pp. 70–132 and 364–401; 29 (1979), pp. 97–124.

'Τò ὑπερεῖναι of pseudo-Dionysius and Schelling' in *Studia Patristica* edited by E. A. Livingstone, Leuven: Peeters, 1989, vol. xxiii. pp. 215–25.

Boulger, J., *Coleridge as Religious Thinker*, New Haven: Yale University Press, 1961.

Braun, L., *Geschichte der Philosophiegeschichte*, Darmstadt: Wissenschaftliche Buchgesellschaft, 1990.

Bretvold, L., *The Brave New World of the Enlightenment*, Ann Arbor: Michigan University Press, 1961.

Brinkley, R. F., 'Coleridge's criticism of Jeremy Taylor' in *Huntington Library Quarterly* 13 (1950), pp. 313–23.

Brisson, Luc, *Einführung in die Philosophie des Mythos I. Antike, Mittelalter und Renaissance*, Darmstadt: Wissenschaftliche Buchgesellschaft, 1996.

Broicher, C., 'Anglikanische Kirche und deutsche Philosophie' in *Preussische Jahrbücher* 142 (1910), pp. 205–33 and 457–98.

Brown, Robert F., *Schelling's Treatise on 'The Deities of Samothrace'*, Missoula, Mont.: American Academy of Religion Studies in Religion, 1974.

The Later Philosophy of Schelling: the Influence of Boehme on the Works of 1809–1815, Lewisburg: Bucknell, 1977.

'The transcendental fall in Kant and Schelling' in *Idealistic Studies* 14 (1984), pp. 49–66.

Brüggen, M., 'Jacobi und Schelling' in *Philosophisches Jahrbuch* 75 (1967–8), pp. 419–29.

Bubner, R., *Innovationen des Idealismus*, Göttingen: Vandenhoeck and Ruprecht, 1995.

Buchheim, T., *Eins von Allem. Die Selbstbescheidung des Idealismus in Schellings Spätphilosophie*, Hamburg: Meiner, 1992.

Burns, Robert Michael, *The Great Debate on Miracles, from Joseph Glanville to David Hume*, Lewisburg: Bucknell, 1981.

Burnyeat, M., 'Idealism and Greek philosophy: what Descartes saw and Berkeley missed' in *Idealism Past and Present*, edited by G. Vesey, Cambridge University Press, 1982, pp. 19–50.

Burtt, E. A., *The Metaphysical Foundations of Modern Science*, New York: Doubleday, 1955.

Caird, E., *Hegel*, Edinburgh and London: William Blackwell and Sons, 1909.

Calleo, D. P., *Coleridge and the Idea of the Modern State*, New Haven: Yale University Press, 1966.

Carré, M. H., *Phases of Thought in England*, Oxford: Clarendon, 1949.

Chadwick, Henry, *Early Christian Thought and the Classical Tradition: Studies in Justin, Clement and Origen*, Oxford: Clarendon, 1992.

Chadwick, Owen, *From Bossuet to Newman*, second edition, Cambridge University Press, 1987.

Chambers, E. K., *Samuel Taylor Coleridge: a Biographical Study*, Oxford: Clarendon, 1938.

Charlesworth, M. J., *Philosophy of Religion: the Historic Approaches*, London: Macmillan, 1972.

Christ, K., *Jacobi und Mendelssohn. Eine Analyse des Spinozastreits*, Würzburg: Königshausen und Neumann, 1988.

Clark, Jonathan C. D., *English Society 1688–1832: Ideology, Social Structure and Political Practice during the Ancien Régime*, Cambridge University Press, 1986.

Clark, Mary, *Augustine: Philosopher of Freedom*, New York: Desclée, 1958.

Clark, Stephen R. L., *A Parliament of Souls*, Oxford: Clarendon, 1990.

    Civil Peace and Sacred Order, Oxford: Clarendon, 1989.

    From Athens to Jerusalem: the Love of Wisdom and the Love of God, Oxford: Clarendon, 1984.

    God's World and the Great Awakening, Oxford: Clarendon, 1991.

    The Mysteries of Religion: an Introduction to Philosophy through Religion, Oxford: Blackwell, 1986.

    'Abstraction, possession, incarnation' in *Being and Truth: Essays in Honour of John Macquarrie*, edited by A. Kee and E. T. Long, London: SCM, 1986, pp. 293–317.

    'Waking-up: a neglected model for the afterlife' in *Inquiry* 26 (1983), pp. 209–30.

    'God's law and morality' in *Philosophical Quarterly* 32 (1982), pp. 339–47.

Clarke, M. L., *Paley, Evidences for the Man*, London: SPCK, 1974.

Clayton, J. W., 'Coleridge and the logos: the Trinitarian unity of consciousness and culture' in *The Journal of Religion* 70 (1990), pp. 213–40.

Coburn, Kathleen, *The Self-Conscious Imagination*, London: Oxford University Press, 1974.

Cole, G., 'Discovering God's will: Paley's problem with special reference to "The Christian Sabbath"' in *Tyndale Bulletin* 39 (1988), pp. 125–39.

'A note on Paley and his school – was Sir Leslie Stephen mistaken?' in *Tyndale Bulletin* 38 (1987), pp. 151–6.

'Paley and the myth of "Classical Anglicanism"' in *The Reformed Theological Review* 54 (1995), pp. 3, 97–109.

'Theological utilitarianism and the eclipse of the theistic sanction' in *Tyndale Bulletin* 42/2 (1991), pp. 226–44.

'"Who can refute a sneer?" Paley on Gibbon' in *Tyndale Bulletin* 49/1 (1998), pp. 57–70.

'Ethics and eschatology – Paley's system reconsidered' in *The Reformed Theological Review* 47/2 (1988), pp. 33–43.

Colish, M., *The Mirror of Language*, New Haven: Yale University Press, 1968.

Colley, L., *Britons: Forging the Nation, 1701–1837*, New Haven: Yale University Press, 1992.

Coreth, E., *Trinitätsdenken in neuzeitlicher Philosophie*, 2 vols., Salzburg: Pustet, 1986.

Coulter, J. A., *The Literary Microcosm: Theories of Interpretation of the Later Neoplatonists*, Leiden: Brill, 1976.

Craig, E., *The Mind of God and the Works of Man*, Oxford: Clarendon, 1987.

Craven, J. B., *The Esoteric Studies of Leighton*, Selkirk: Scottish Chronicle Press, 1918.

Curtius, Robert, *Europäische Literatur und Lateinisches Mittelalter*, Bern: Francke, 1954.

Daniélou, J., *Gospel Message and Hellenistic Culture*, London: Westminster, 1980.

Darwall, S., *The British Moralists and the Internal 'Ought' 1640–1740*, Cambridge University Press, 1995.

Davidson, Graham, *Coleridge's Career*, Basingstoke: Macmillan, 1990.

Deane, S., *The French Revolution and Enlightenment in England, 1789–1832*, Cambridge, Mass. and London: Harvard University Press, 1988.

Deck, John N., *Nature, Contemplation and the One: a Study in the Philosophy of Plotinus*, University of Toronto Press, 1967.

Dihle, A., *The Theory of Will in Classical Antiquity*, Sather Classical Lectures 48, Berkeley and London: University of California Press, 1982.

Dillistone, F. W., *Christian Understanding of the Atonement*, London: SCM, 1968.

Dockrill, D. W., 'The authority of the Fathers in the great Trinitarian debates of the sixteen-nineties' in *Studia Patristica*, edited by E. A. Livingstone, vol. xviii. 4, Leuven: Peeters, 1990, pp. 335–47.

'The heritage of patristic Platonism in seventeenth-century English philosophical theology' in *The Cambridge Platonists in Philosophical Context: Politics, Metaphysics and Religion*, edited by G. A. J. Rogers, J. M. Vienne, and Y. C. Zarka, Dordrecht: Kluwer, 1997, pp. 55–77.

Dodds, E.R., R. Schwyzer, et al., *Les Sources de Plotin*, Geneva: Vandœuvres, 1957.

Dörrie, H., 'Was ist spätantiker Platonismus?' in *Theologische Rundschau* 36 (1971), pp. 285–302.

Dowell, G., *Enjoying the World: the Rediscovery of Thomas Traherne*, London: Mowbray, 1990.

Duchrow, U., *Sprachverständnis und Biblisches Hören bei Augustin*, Tübingen: Mohr-Siebeck, 1965.

Edwards, M. J., 'Being, life and mind, a brief enquiry' in *Syllecta Classica* 8 (1997), pp. 191–205.

Elliot-Binns, L. E., *English Thought, 1860–1900: the Theological Aspect*, London: Longman, Green, and Co., 1956.

Elmen, P., 'Jeremy Taylor and the Fall of man' in *Modern Language Quarterly* 14 (1952), pp. 139–48.

Engell, James, *The Creative Imagination: Enlightenment to Romanticism*, Cambridge, Mass. and London: Harvard University Press, 1981.

Eräsmetsä, E., *A Study of the Word 'Sentimentalism' and of other Linguistic Characteristics of Eighteenth-Century Sentimentalism in England*, Helsinki Press, 1951.

Esposito, J. L., *Schelling's Idealism and Philosophy of Nature*, Lewisburg: Bucknell, 1977.

Fackenheim, E. L., 'Schelling's philosophy of literary arts' in *The Philosophical Quarterly* 4 (1954), pp. 310–26.

Farrer, A., *The Glass of Vision*, The 1948 Bampton Lectures, Glasgow: Dacre, 1948.

Festugière, A. J., 'L'ordre de lecture des dialogues de Platon au Vème et VIème siècle' in *Museum Helveticum* 26 (1969), pp. 281–96.

Flasch, K., *Augustinus*, Stuttgart: Reclam, 1980.

Ford, S. H., 'Perichoresis and interpenetration: Samuel Taylor Coleridge's Trinitarian conception of unity' in *Theology* 89 (1986), pp. 20–40.

Foster, M. B., '"We" in modern philosophy' in *Faith and Logic*, edited by B. Mitchell, London: George Allen and Unwin, 1957, pp. 194–220.

Frank, M., *Unendliche Annährung. Die Anfänge der philosophischen Frühromantik*, Frankfurt: Suhrkamp, 1997.

Franz, M., *Schellings Tübinger Platon-Studien*, Göttingen: Vandenhoeck, 1996.

Freier, H., *Die Rückkehr der Götter. von der Aesthetischen Überschreitung der Wissensgrenze zur Mythologie der Moderne. Eine Untersuchung zur systematischen Rolle der Kunst in der Philosophie Kants und Schellings*, Stuttgart: Reclam, 1976.

Fruman, N., *The Damaged Archangel*, London: George Allen and Unwin, 1972.

Fuhrmans, H., *Schellings Philosophie der Weltalter. Schellings Philosophie in den Jahren 1806–1821. Zum problem des Schellingschen Theismus*, Düsseldorf: Schwann, 1954.

'Der Gottesbegriff in der Schellingschen positiven Philosophie' in *Schelling-Studien*, edited by A. M. Koktanek, Munich: Oldenbourg, 1965, pp. 9–47.

'*Einleitung*', F. J. W. Schelling, *Uber das Wesen der Menschlichen Freiheit*, Stuttgart: Reclam, 1983, pp. 3–38.

'Schelling im Tübinger Stift' in *Materialien zu Schellings Philosophischen Anfängen*, Frankfurt: Suhrkamp, 1975, pp. 53–87.

Fulford, T., *Coleridge's Figurative Language*, Basingstoke: Macmillan, 1991.

Gaiser, K., *Das Platon Bild*, Hildesheim: Olms, 1969.

Galloway, A., *The Cosmic Christ*, London: Nisbet, 1951.

Gascoigne, J. A., *Cambridge in the Age of the Enlightenment*, Cambridge University Press, 1989.

Gleason, John B., *John Colet*, Berkeley and London: University of California Press, 1989.

Goodman, R. B., *American Philosophy and the Romantic Tradition*, Cambridge University Press: 1990.

Grafton, A., *Defenders of the Text: the Traditions of Scholarship in an Age of Science*, Cambridge, Mass.: Harvard University Press, 1991.

Griffin, R., 'Reflection in Locke and Coleridge', unpublished paper.

Gulyga, A., *Schelling. Leben und Werk*, Stuttgart: Deutsche Verlags-Anstalt, 1989.

Gysi, L., *Platonism and Cartesianism in the Philosophy of Ralph Cudworth*, Berne: Lang, 1962.

Hadot, P., *Exercices spirituels et philosophie antique*, Paris: Etudes Augustiniennes, 1987.

Plotinus, or The Simplicity of Vision, revised and augmented second edition, translated by M. Chase with an introduction by A. I. Davidson, Chicago and London: University of Chicago Press, 1993.

Porphrye et Victorinus, Paris: Etudes Augustiniennes, 1980.

'Etre, vie et pensée chez Plotin et avant Plotin' in *Les Sources de Plotin*, Geneva: Vandœuvres, 1960, pp. 105–41.

'Zur Idee der Naturgeheimnisse' in *Akademie der Wissenschaften und der Literatur, Mainz, Abhandlungen der Geistes und Sozialwissenschaften Klasse, Jahrgang*, vol. viii, Wiesbaden: 1982.

Hall, R., 'New words and antedatings from Cudworth's "Treatise of Freewill"' in *Notes and Queries* 7 (1960), pp. 428–9.

Hammacher, K., *Die Philosophie Friedrich Heinrich Jacobis*, Munich: Fink, 1969.

Hankey, W., *God in Himself*, Oxford: Clarendon, 1987.

'Augustinian immediacy and Dionysian mediation in John Colet, Edmund Spenser, Richard Hooker and the Cardinal de Bérulle' in *Augustinus in der Neuzeit: Colloque de la Herzog August Bibliothek de Wolfenbüttel 14–17 octobre 1996*, edited by K. Flasch and D. de Courcelles (1998), pp. 125–60.

'From metaphysics to history, from Exodus to Neoplatonism, from scholasticism to pluralism: the fate of Gilsonian Thomism in English-speaking North America' in *Dionysius* 16 (1998), pp. 157–88.

'Mens' in *Saint Augustine through the Ages: an Encyclopedia*, edited by A. Fitzgerald, Grand Rapids, Mich.: Eerdmans (forthcoming).

Harding, A. J., *Coleridge and the Idea of Love*, Cambridge University Press, 1974.

Coleridge and the Inspired Word, Kingston and Montreal: McGill, Queen's University Press, 1985.

Hardy, D., 'Coleridge on the Trinity' in *Anglican Theological Review* 69 (1987), pp. 5–15.

Harnack, Adolf von, *Lehrbuch der Dogmengeschichte*, Tübingen: Mohr-Siebeck, 1904.

Harries, K., 'The infinite sphere: comments on the history of a metaphor' in *Journal of the History of Philosophy* 13 (1975), pp. 5–15.

Harris, I., *The Mind of John Locke: a Study of Political Theory in its Intellectual Setting*, Cambridge and New York: Cambridge University Press, 1994.

Harrison, J. and P. Laslett, *The Library of John Locke*, Oxford: Clarendon, 1965.

Harrison, P., *'Religion' and the Religions in the English Enlightenment*, Cambridge University Press, 1990.

Hasler, L. (ed.), *Schelling. Seine Bedeutung für eine Philosophie der Natur und der Geschichte*, Stuttgart and Bad Cannstatt: Frommann-Holzboog, 1981.

Haven, R., 'Coleridge, Hartley and the mystics' in *Journal of the History of Ideas* 20 (1959), pp. 477–9.

Hedley, R. D., 'Coleridge's intellectual intuition, the vision of God, and the walled garden of Kubla Khan' in *Journal of the History of Ideas* 59/1 (1998), pp. 115–34.

'Pantheism, Trinitarian theism and the idea of unity: reflections on the Christian concept of God' in *Religious Studies* 32 (1996), pp. 61–77.

'Was Schleiermacher a Christian Platonist?', *Dionysius* 17 (1999), pp. 149–67.

Hedwig, K., *Sphaera Lucis. Studien zur Intelligibilität des Seienden im Kontext der mittelalterlichen Lichtspekulation*, Münster: Aschendorff, 1980.

Henrich, Dieter, *Selbstverhältnisse. Gedanken und Auslegungen zu den Grundlagen der Klassischen Deutschen Philosophie*, Stuttgart: Reclam, 1982.

Henry, Paul, 'The Adversus Arium of Marius Victorinus' in *Journal of Theological Studies* 1 (1950), pp. 42–55.

Hillerdal, G., *Reason and Revelation in Richard Hooker*, Lund: Håkan Ohlssons Press, 1962.

Hitchin, N., 'Probability and the Word of God: William Paley's Anglican method and the defence of the Scriptures' in *Anglican Theological Review* 72/3 (1997), pp. 392–407.

Hodgson, P. C., *The Formation of Historical Theology: a Study of Ferdinand Christian Baur*, New York: Harper Row, 1966.

Holland, R. F., *Against Empiricism: on Education, Epistemology and Value*, Oxford: Blackwell, 1980.

Holmes, R., *Coleridge, Darker Reflections*, London: HarperCollins, 1998.

Coleridge, Early Visions, London: Hodder and Stoughton, 1989.

Holte, R., 'Glück' in *Reallexicon für Antike und Christentum* 11 (1979), pp. 264–8.

Holz, H., *Die Idee der Philosophie bei Schelling*, Munich: Alber, 1977.

Hopkins, Jasper, *Nicholas of Cusa's Dialectical Mysticism*, second edition, Minneapolis: Arthur Banning, 1988.

Horn, C., *Augustinus*, Munich: Beck, 1995.

Horstmann, Rolf-Peter, *Die Grenzen der Vernunft. Eine Untersuchung zu Zielen und Motiven des deutschen Idealismus*, Frankfurt am Main: Anton Hain, 1991.

Horton, H., *David Friedrich Strauss and his Theology*, Cambridge University Press, 1973.

Hunt, J., *Religious Thought in England from the Reformation to the End of the Last Century*, Edinburgh: Strahan and Co., 1873.

Religious Thought in England in the Nineteenth Century, London: Gibblings, 1896.

Hutton, Sarah, 'Thomas Jackson, Oxford Platonist, and William Twisse, Aristotelian' in *Journal of the History of Ideas* 39 (1978), pp. 521–34.

Jaeger, W., *Die Theologie der frühen griechischen Denker*, Stuttgart: Kolhammer, 1953.

James, W., *The Will to Believe*, New York: Dover, 1956.

Jane, S., 'Ficino and the Platonism of the English Renaissance' in *Comparative Literature* 4 (1952), pp. 214–38.

Jaspers, D., *Coleridge as Poet and Religious Thinker*, London: Macmillan, 1985.

Jenkyns, R., *The Victorians and Ancient Greece*, Oxford: Blackwell, 1981.

Jolley, Nicholas, 'Leibniz on Locke and Socinianism' in *Journal of the History of Ideas* 39 (1978), pp. 233–50.

Jones, Rufus, *The Spiritual Reformers in the Sixteenth and Seventeenth Centuries*, London: Macmillan, 1914.

Kallich, M., *The Association of Ideas*, The Hague: Mouton, 1970.

Kampf, L., 'Gibbon and Hume' in *English Literature and British Philosophy, A Collection of Essays*, edited with an introduction by S. P. Rosenbaum, University of Chicago Press, 1971, pp. 109–18.

Kelly, J. N. D., *Early Christian Doctrines*, fifth edition, London: Adam and Charles Black, 1977.

Kessler, E., *Coleridge's Metaphors of Being*, Princeton University Press, 1979.

Kiblanski, R., *The Continuity of the Platonic Tradition during the Middle Ages*, London: Warburg, 1939.

Kirk, K. E., *The Vision of God*, Cambridge: James Clarke and Co., 1991.

Knight, Frida, *University Rebel: the Life of William Frend, 1757–1841*, London: Gollancz, 1971.

Knittermeyer, H., *Schelling und die romantische Schule*, Munich: Reinhardt, 1929.

Knox, Bishop E. A., *Robert Leighton, Archbishop of Glasgow: a Study of his Life, Times and Writings*, London: James Clarke, 1930.

Kobusch, Theo, *Sein und Sprache. Historische Grundlegung einer Ontologie der Sprache*, Leiden: Brill, 1987.

Koestler, A., *The Sleepwalkers*, Harmondsworth: Penguin, 1968.

Kolakowski, L., *Metaphysical Horror*, Oxford: Blackwell, 1988.
  Religion, Glasgow: Fontana, 1982.
Kondylis, P., *Die Aufklärung im Rahmen des neuzeitlichen Rationalismus*, Stuttgart: Klett-Cotta, 1981.
Konersmann, R., *Spiegel und Bild*, Würzburg: Königshausen und Neumann, 1988.
Krämer, H. K., *Der Ursprung der Geistesmetaphysik*, Amsterdam: P. Schippers, 1967.
Kremer, K., 'Selbsterkenntnis als Gotteserkenntnis nach Plotin' in *International Studies in Philosophy* 13 (1981), pp. 41–68.
Kristeller, P. O., *Renaissance Thought and its Sources*, edited by M. Mooney, New York and Guildford: Columbia University Press, 1979.
  'Stoic and Neoplatonic sources of Spinoza's *Ethics*' in *History of European Ideas* 1 (1984), pp. 1–15.
Knox, E. A., *Robert Leighton, Archbishop of Glasgow: A Study of his Life, Times and Writings*, London: James Clarke and Co., 1930.
Kroll, R. W. F., *The Material World: Literate Culture in the Restoration and Early Eighteenth Century*, Baltimore and London: Johns Hopkins University Press, 1991.
Lash, N., *Easter in Ordinary, Reflection on Human Experience and the Knowledge of God*, London: SCM, 1988.
Lauth R., *Die Entstehung von Schellings Identitätsphilosophie in der Ausseinandersetzung mit Fichtes Wissenschaftslehre*, Freiburg: Karl Alber, 1975.
  Transcendentale Entwicklungslinien, Hamburg: Meiner, 1989.
Le Mahieu, D. L., *The Mind of William Paley: a Philosopher and His Age*, Lincoln, Neb.: University of Nebraska Press, 1976.
Leisegang, H., 'Die Erkenntnis Gottes im Spiegel der Seele und der Natur', *Zeitschrift für philosphische Forschung* 4 (1949–50), pp. 161–83.
Lennon, T. M., *The Battle of the Gods and Giants: the Legacies of Descartes and Gassendi, 1655–1715*, Princeton University Press, 1993.
Levere, T. H., *Poetry Realized in Nature: Samuel Taylor Coleridge and Early Nineteenth-Century Science*, Cambridge University Press, 1981.
Lichtenstein, A., *Henry More: the Rational Theology of a Cambridge Platonist*, Cambridge, Mass.: Harvard University Press, 1962.
Loades, A., 'Coleridge as a theologian: some comments on his reading of Kant' in *Journal of Theological Studies* 29 (1978), pp. 410–26.
Lockridge, L. S., *Coleridge the Moralist*, Ithaca, NY: Cornell University Press, 1977.
Lossky, N., *Launcelot Andrewes, the Preacher (1555–1626): the Origins of the Mystical Theology of the Church of England*, translated by A. Louth, Oxford: Clarendon, 1991.
Loughlin, G., *Telling God's Story: Bible, Church and Narrative Theology*, Cambridge University Press, 1996.
Louth, A., *The Origins of the Christian Mystical Tradition*, Oxford: Clarendon, 1981.

Lucas, J. R., *The Freedom of the Will*, Oxford: Clarendon, 1970.
The Principles of Politics, Oxford: Clarendon, 1985.
'The soul' in *Faith and Logic*, edited by B. Mitchell, London: George Allen and Unwin, 1968, pp. 132–48.
Mackie, J., *The Miracle of Theism*, Oxford: Clarendon, 1977.
McAdoo, H. R., *The Spirit of Anglicanism: a Survey of Anglican Theological Method in the Seventeenth Century*, London: Adam and Charles Black, 1965.
McCloy, S. T., *Gibbon's Antagonism to Christianity*, London: Williams and Norgate, 1933.
McFarland, T., *Coleridge and the Pantheist Tradition*, Oxford: Clarendon, 1969.
Romanticism and the Forms of Ruin: Wordsworth, Coleridge and Modalities of Fragmentation, Princeton University Press, 1981.
McGinn, B., *The Foundations of Mysticism*, London: SCM, 1992.
McKusik, J. C., *Coleridge's Philosophy of Language*, New Haven: Yale University Press, 1986.
McLachlan, H. J., *Socinianism in Seventeenth Century England*, Oxford: Clarendon, 1951.
Mahnke, Dietrich, 'Die Rationalisierung der Mystik bei Leibniz und Kant' in *Blätter für Deutsche Philosophie* 13 (1939), pp. 1–73.
Unendliche Sphäre und Allmittelpunkt. Beiträge zur Genealogie der Mathematischen Mystik, Halle: Max Niemeyer, 1937.
Manchester, P., 'The Noetic triad in Plotinus, Marius Victorinus and Augustine' in *Neoplatonism and Gnosticism*, edited by J. Bergman and R. T. Wallis, Albany: State University of New York Press, 1992, pp. 207–22.
Marcel, G., *Coleridge et Schelling*, Paris: Aubier-Montaigne, 1971.
Markus, R. A., 'Marius Victorinus and Augustine' in *The Cambridge History of Later Greek and Early Medieval Philosophy*, edited by A. H. Armstrong, Cambridge University Press, 1967, pp. 331–419.
Marshall, John, *John Locke: Resistance, Religion and Responsibility*, Cambridge University Press, 1996.
Martz, L., *The Paradise Within: Studies in Vaughan, Traherne and Milton*, New Haven: Yale University Press, 1964.
Maxsein, A., *Philosophia Cordis*, Salzburg: Müller, 1966.
Mehta, V. R., 'The origins of English Idealism in relation to Oxford' in *Journal of the History of Ideas* 13 (1975), pp. 177–87.
Meijering, E. P., *Orthodoxy and Platonism in Athanasius: Synthesis or Antithesis?*, Leiden: Brill, 1974.
Mellor, A. K., *English Romantic Irony*, Cambridge, Mass. and London: Harvard University Press, 1980.
Mennemeier, F. N., 'Fragment und Ironie beim jungen F. Schlegel' in *Poetica* 2 (1968), pp. 348–70.
Merlan, Philip, *Monopsychism, Mysticism, Metaconsciousness*, The Hague: Nijhoff, 1963.
Michalson, Gordon E., Jr., *Fallen Freedom: Kant on Radical Evil and Moral Regeneration*, Cambridge University Press, 1990.

Lessing's 'Ugly Ditch': a Study of Theology and History, University Park, Penn., and London: Pennsylvania State University Press, 1985.

Model, A., *Metaphysik und reflektierende Urteilskraft bei Kant. Untersuchungen zur Transformierung des Leibnizschen Monaden Begriffs in der 'Kritik der Urteilskraft',* Frankfurt am Main: Hain, 1987.

Modiano, Raimonda, *Coleridge and the Concept of Nature,* London: Macmillan, 1985.

Molland, E., 'Clement of Alexandria and the origin of Greek philosophy' in *Symbolae Osloenses* (1936), pp. 57–85.

Moran, D., *The Philosophy of John Scottus Eriugena,* Cambridge University Press, 1989.

Morgan, R. C., 'Non Angli sed angeli' in *New Studies in Theology,* edited by S. Sykes and D. Holmes, London: Duckworth, 1980, pp. 1–29.

Muirhead, John H., *Coleridge as Philosopher,* London: Macmillan, 1930.

The Platonic Tradition in Anglo-Saxon Philosophy, London: Macmillan, 1931.

Müller, C. W., *Gleiches zu Gleichem. Ein Prinzip frühgriechischen Denkens Klassisch-Philologische Studien,* Wiesbaden: Harrassowitz, 1965.

Munz, P., *The Place of Hooker in the History of Thought,* London: Routledge, 1952.

Murdoch, Iris, 'On "God" and "good"' and 'The idea of perfection' in *Existentialists and Mystics: Writings on Philosophy and Literature,* edited by P. Conradi, London: Chatto and Windus, 1997.

Murray, K. M. E., *Caught in the Web of Words: James A. H. Murray and the 'Oxford English Dictionary',* with a preface by R. W. Burchfield, New Haven and London: Yale University Press, 1995.

Murray, R., *The Cosmic Covenant,* London: Sheed and Ward, 1992.

Nagel, T., *The Last Word,* New York: Oxford University Press, 1997.

The View from Nowhere, New York: Oxford University Press, 1986.

Nahm, M. C., *Genius and Creativity: an Essay in the History of Ideas,* New York: Harper and Row, 1956.

'The theological background of the theory of the artist as creator' in *Journal of the History of Ideas* 8 (1947), pp. 363–72.

Negele, M., *Grade der Freiheit. Versuch einer Interpretation von G. W. F. Hegels 'Phänomenologie des Geistes',* Würzburg: Königshausen and Neumann, 1991.

Neumann, G., *Der Aphorismus. Ideenparadiese Aphoristik bei Lichtenberg, Novalis, Friedrich Schlegel und Goethe,* Munich: Fink, 1976.

Der Aphorismus. zur Geschichte, zu den Formen und Möglichkeiten einer literarischen Gattung, Darmstadt: Wissenschaftliche Buchgesellschaft, 1976.

Neuschäfer, Bernhard, *Origenes als Philologe,* Basel: Reinhardt, 1987.

Newsome, D., *Godliness and Good Learning,* London: Murray, 1961.

Two Classes of Men: Platonism and English Romantic Thought, London: Murray, 1974.

Nock, A. D., *Conversion,* Oxford: Clarendon, 1933.

Nuttall, G. F. and O. Chadwick (eds.), *From Uniformity to Unity, 1662–1962*, London: SPCK, 1962.

O'Daly, G. J. P., *Plotinus' Philosophy of the Self*, Shannon: Irish University Press, 1973.

O'Donohue, J., *Person als Vermittlung. Die Dialektik von Individualität und Allgemeinheit in 'Hegels Phänomenologie des Geistes'*, Mainz: Grünewald, 1993.

O'Neill, Onora, *Constructions of Reason: Explorations of Kant's Practical Philosophy*, Cambridge University Press, 1989.

Oosthout, H., *Modes of Knowledge and the Transcendental: An Introduction to Plotinus Ennead V3. (49) with a Commentary and Translation*, Amsterdam: Grüner, 1991.

Orsini, G. N., *Coleridge and German Idealism*, Carbondale: Southern Illinois Press, 1969.

Pagels, Elaine, *Adam, Eve and the Serpent*, Harmondsworth: Penguin, 1990.

Parnell, P. E., 'The Sentimental Mask' in *Periodical of the Modern Languages Association* 78 (1963), pp. 529–35.

Paton, H. J., *The Categorical Imperative: A Study in Kant's Moral Philosophy*, third edition, London: Hutchinson, 1958.

Peetz, Siegbert, *Die Freiheit im Wissen. Eine Untersuchung zu Schellings Konzept der Rationalität*, Frankfurt: Klostermann, 1995.

'Schelling' in *Literaturlexikon: Autoren und Werke deutscher Sprache*, edited by W. Killy, Gütersloh: Bertelsmann Lexikon Verlag, vol. x (1991), pp. 185–90.

Perkins, M. A., *Coleridge's Philosophy: the Logos as Unifying Principle*, Oxford: Clarendon Press, 1994.

Pfeiffer, Rudolph, *Geschichte der Klassichen Philologie von den Anfängen bis zum Ende des Hellenismus*, Munich: Beck, 1978.

Pieper, J., *Die Wahrheit der Dinge*, Munich: Alber, 1948.

Pippin, Robert B., *Hegel's Idealism: The Satisfactions of Self-Consciousness*, Cambridge University Press, 1989.

Plant, R., and A. Vincent, *Philosophy, Politics and Citizenship: the Life and Thought of the British Idealists*, Oxford: Blackwell, 1984.

Prickett, S., *Coleridge and Wordsworth, the Poetry of Growth*, Cambridge University Press, 1970.

Romanticism and Religion: the Tradition of Coleridge in the Victorian Church, Cambridge University Press, 1970.

Putallaz, F.-X., *Le Sens de la réflexion chez Thomas d'Aquin*, with a preface by R. Imbach, Paris: Vrin, 1991.

Pym, D., *The Religious Thought of Samuel Taylor Coleridge*, New York: Barnes and Noble, 1978.

Quinton, A., *Francis Bacon*, Oxford University Press, 1980.

Ramsey, A. M., *From Gore to Temple: the Development of Anglican Theology between Lux Mundi and the Second World War, 1889–1939*, London: Longman, 1960.

Reardon, Bernard M. G., *Religion in the Age of Romanticism: Studies in Early Nineteenth-Century Thought*, Cambridge University Press, 1985.
   Religious Thought in the Victorian Age: a Survey from Coleridge to Gore, London: Longman, 1980.
Rees, B. R., *Pelagius: a Reluctant Heretic*, Woodbridge: Boydell, 1991.
Reuter, P., *Kants Theorie der Reflexionsbegriffe*, Würzburg: Königshausen und Neumann, 1989.
Ricken, F., 'Nikaia als Krisis des altkirchlichen Platonismus' in *Theologie und Philosophie* 44 (1969), pp. 312–41.
Riedweg, Christoph, *Pseudo-Justin (Markell von Ankyra?) Ad Graecos De Vera Religione (bisher 'Cohortatio ad Graecos')*, 2 vols., Basel: Reinhardt, 1994.
Rist, John M., *Augustine: Ancient Thought Baptized*, Cambridge University Press, 1994.
   'Plotinus and moral obligation' in *The Significance of Neoplatonism*, edited by R. Baine Harris, Norfolk, Va.: Old Dominion University Press, 1976, pp. 217–33.
Ritter, Adolf Martin, 'Dogma und Lehre in der Alten Kirche' in *Handbuch der Dogmen und Theologieschichte*, vol. i., Göttingen: Vandenhoeck, 1982.
Robbins, P., *The British Hegelians, 1875–1925*, New York: Garland, 1982.
Robin, L., *La Théorie platonicienne des idées et des nombres d'après Aristote. Etude historique et critique*, Paris: 1908, repr. Hildesheim: Olms, 1963.
Roche, W. J., 'Measure, number and weight in Saint Augustine', *The New Scholasticism* 15 (1941), pp. 350–76.
Rohls, J., *Geschichte der Ethik*, second edition, Tübingen: Mohr-Siebeck, 1999.
   Protestantische Theologie der Neuzeit, 2 vols., Tübingen: Mohr-Siebeck, 1997–8.
   ' "Sinn und Geschmack für das Unendliche" Aspekte romantische Kunstreligion' in *Neue Zeitschrift für Systematische Theologie und Religionsphilosophie* 27/1 (1985), pp. 1–24.
Roi, O. du, *L'intelligence de la Foi en la Trinité selon Saint Augustine*, Paris: Etudes Augustiniennes, 1966.
Ross, G. M., 'Leibniz und Renaissance Neoplatonism' in *Leibniz et la Renaissance: colloque du Centre national de la recherche scientifique (Paris), du Centre d'études supérieures de la Renaissance (Tours) et de la G. W. Leibniz-Gesellschaft (Hannover)*, edited by A. Heinekamp, Wiesbaden: Steiner, 1983.
Rowell, G. (ed.), *The English Religious Tradition and the Genius of Anglicanism*, with a foreword by Archbishop George Carey, Wantage: Ikon, 1992.
Rule, P. C., 'Coleridge's reputation as a religious thinker, 1816–1972' in *Harvard Theological Review* 67 (1974), pp. 289–320.
Sanders, C. R., *Coleridge and the Broad Church Movement*, Durham, NC: Duke University Press, 1942.
Sandkaulen-Bock, Birgit, *Ausgang vom Unbedingten: über den Anfang in der Philosophie Schellings*, Göttingen: Vandenhoeck and Ruprecht, 1990.

Schmidt-Biggemann, Wilhelm, *Philosophia Perennis. Historische Umrisse abendändischer Spritualität in Antike, Mittelalter und Früher Neuzeit*, Frankfurt: Suhrkamp, 1998.

Scholz, G., 'Schleiermacher und die Platonische Ideenlehre' in *Internationaler Schleiermacher Kongress*, edited by Kurt-Victor Selge, (1985), pp. 848–71.

Schönberger, R., 'Secundum rationem esse. zur Ontologisierung der Ethik bei Meister Eckhart' in ΟΙΚΕΙΩΣΙΣ *Festschrift für Robert Spaemann*, edited by R. Löw, Weinheim: Acta Humaniovum, 1987, pp. 252–72.

Schrickx, W., 'Coleridge and the Cambridge Platonists' in *Review of English Literature* 7 (1966), pp. 71–91.

Schultze, H., *Lessings Toleranzbegriff*, Göttingen: Vandenhoeck, 1969.

'Lessings Ausseinandersetzung mit Theologen und Deisten um "innere Wahrheit"' in *Lessing in heutiger Sicht*, edited by E. P. Harris and R. E. Schade, Bremen: Jaconi, 1977, pp. 181–2.

Schulz, Walter, *Der Gott der Neuzeitlichen Metaphysik*, Pfullingen: Neske, 1957.

Die Vollendung des deutschen Idealismus in der Spätphilosophie Schellings, Stuttgart: Kohlammer, 1955.

Schwyzer, H. R., 'Die zweifache Sicht in der Philosophie Plotins' in *Museum Helveticum* 1 (1944), pp. 87–99.

Sell, Alan P. F., *John Locke and the Eighteenth-Century Divines*, Cardiff: University of Wales Press, 1997.

Philosophical Idealism and Christian Belief, New York: Croom Helm, 1995.

The Great Debate: Calvinism, Arminianism, and Salvation, Grand Rapids, Mich.: Bake Book House, 1982.

The Philosophy of Religion, 1875–1980, New York: Croom Helm, 1988.

Shaffer, Elinor S., *Kubla Khan and the Fall of Jerusalem: the Mythological School in Biblical Criticism and Secular Literature, 1770–1880*, Cambridge University Press, 1975.

'Iago's malignity motivated: Coleridge's unpublished "opus magnum"' in *Shakespeare Quarterly* 19 (1968), pp. 195–203.

'Metaphysics of culture: Kant and Coleridge's *Aids to Reflection*' in *Journal of the History of Ideas* 31 (1970), pp. 199–218.

Siebeck, H., 'Über die Entstehung der Termini natura naturans und natura naturata' in *Archiv für die Geschichte der Philosophie* 3 (1890), pp. 370–8.

Simonutti, Luisa, 'Reason and toleration' in *Henry More, 1614–1687: Tercentenary Studies*, edited by Sarah Hutton with a biography and bibliography by R. Crocker, Dordrecht and Boston: Kluwer, 1990.

Smith, John E., *America's Philosophical Vision*, University of Chicago Press, 1992.

Smith, Jonathan Z., *Drudgery Divine: on the Comparison of Early Christianities and the Religions of Late Antiquity*, University of London Press, 1990.

Smith, Nigel, *Perfection Proclaimed: Language and Literature in English Radical Religion 1640–1660*, Oxford: Clarendon, 1989.

Sorley, W. R., *A History of English Philosophy*, Cambridge University Press, 1920.

Spaemann, R., ' "Freiheit" (in der neuzeitlichen Philosophie)' in *Historische Wörterbuch der Philosophie*, vol. ii., edited by J. Ritter, Basel: 1972, pp. 1088–98.

Spellman, W. M., *John Locke and the Problem of Human Depravity*, Oxford: Clarendon, 1988.

Spitzer, Leo, *Classical and Christian Ideas of World Harmony*, Baltimore: Johns Hopkins University Press, 1963.

Staborinski, Jean, *Jean-Jacques Rousseau: la transparence et l'obstacle*, Paris: Editions Gallimard, 1971.

Stead, G. C., 'The concept of mind and the concept of God in the Christian Fathers' in *The Making of Orthodoxy*, edited by R. Williams, Cambridge University Press, 1989, pp. 39–54.

Steffan, T. G., 'Jeremy Taylor's criticism of abstract speculation' in *Studies in English* 20 (1940), pp. 96–108.

Stevenson, K., *The Mystery of Baptism in the Anglican Tradition*, Norwich: Canterbury Press, 1998.

Stewart, J. A., *The Myths of Plato*, London: Centaur, 1960.

Stove, D., *The Plato Cult*, Oxford: Blackwell, 1991.

Stroud, B., *Hume*, London: Routledge, 1977.

Stuart, J. A., 'The Augustinian "cause of action" in Coleridge's *Rime of the Ancient Mariner*, in *Harvard Theological Review* 60 (1967), pp. 177–211.

Sullivan, Roger J., *Immanuel Kant's Moral Theory*, Cambridge University Press, 1989.

Swiatecka, M. Jadwiga, *The Idea of the Symbol: Some Nineteenth-Century Comparisons with Coleridge*, Cambridge University Press, 1980.

Szczucki, L. et al. (eds.), *Socinianism and its Role in the Culture of the Sixteenth to the Seventeenth Centuries*, Warsaw and Lodz: Polish Academy of Sciences Institutes of Philosophy and Sociology, 1983.

Taylor, A., *Coleridge's Defense of the Human*, Columbus: Ohio University Press, 1986.

Taylor, A. E., *Does God Exist?*, London: Macmillan, 1966.

Philosophical Studies, London: Macmillan, 1934.

The Faith of a Moralist, London: Macmillan, 1930.

Taylor, M., *The Soul in Paraphrase: George Herbert's Poetics*, The Hague: Mouton, 1974.

Temple, W., *Christus Victor*, London: Macmillan, 1930.

Mens Creatrix, London: Macmillan, 1923.

Tennant, F. R., *The Sources of the Doctrines of the Fall and Original Sin*, Cambridge University Press, 1903.

The Origin and Propagation of Sin, Cambridge University Press, 1908.

Theunissen, M., *Der Begriff Verzweiflung*, Frankfurt am Main: Anton Hain, 1993.

Thiel, U., 'Cudworth and seventeenth-century theories of consciousness' in *The Uses of Antiquity*, edited by S. Gaukroger, Dordrecht: Kluwer, 1991, pp. 79–99.

Tilliette, Xavier, *Schelling: une philosophie en devenir*, 2 vols., vol. i., *Le système vivant, 1794–1821*, vol. ii., *La dernière philosophie, 1821–1854*, Paris: Vrin, 1970.

'Vision plotinienne et intuition schellingienne: deux modèles de mystique intellectuelle' in *Gregorianum* 60 (1979), pp. 703–24.

Timm, Hermann, *Die heilige Revolution*, Frankfurt: Syndikat, 1978.

Gott und die Freiheit. Studien zur Religionsphilosophie der Goethezeit, Frankfurt: Klostermann, 1974.

Toews, J. E., *Hegelianism: the Path Toward Dialectical Humanism, 1805–1841*, Cambridge University Press, 1980.

Torrance, T. F., *Scottish Theology: from John Knox to John McLeod Campbell*, Edinburgh: T. and T. Clark, 1996.

Tränkle, H., 'ΓΝΩΘΙ ΣΕΑΥΤΟΝ zu Ursprung und Deutungsgeschichte des delphischen Spruchs', in *Würzburger Jahrbücher für die Altertumswissenschaft Neue Folge* 2 (1985), pp. 19–31.

Trevor-Roper, H., *Catholics, Anglicans and Puritans, Seventeenth-Century Essays*, London: Secker and Warburg, 1987.

Uehlein, F. A., *Die Manifestation des Selbstbewußtseins im konkreten 'Ich bin'*, Hamburg: Meiner, 1982.

Vater, Michael G., 'The human mind as idea' in *Diotima* 8 (1980), pp. 134–43.

'Schelling's "Neoplatonic system-notion"' in *The Significance of Neoplatonism*, edited by B. Harris, Norfolk, Va.: Old Dominion University Press, 1976, pp. 275–99.

Vickers, Brian, *Francis Bacon and Renaissance Prose*, Cambridge University Press, 1968.

Vogel, Cornelia J. de, 'Platonism and Christianity: a mere antagonism or a profound common ground?' in *Vigiliae Christianae* 39 (1985), pp. 1–62.

Wagner, Falk, *Der Gedanke der Persönlichkeit Gottes bei Fichte und Hegel*, Gütersloh: Bertelsmann, 1971.

Walker, R. C. S., '*Achtung* in the Grundlegung' in *Grundlegung zur Metaphysik der Sitten. Ein kooperativer Kommentar*, edited by O. Höffe, Frankfurt: Klostermann, 1993, pp. 97–116.

'The rational imperative: Kant against Hume' in *Proceedings of the British Academy* 74 (1988), pp. 113–33.

Ward, W. R., 'Anglicanism and assimilation, or mysticism and mayhem in the eighteenth century' in *Faith and Faction*, London: Epworth, 1993.

Watson, G., 'St Augustine and the inner word: the philosophical background' in *Irish Theological Quarterly* 54 (1988), pp. 81–92.

Watson, George, *Writing a Thesis*, Harlow: Addison, Wesley, and Longman, 1987.

Webb, C. C. J., *A Study of Religious Thought in England from 1850*, Oxford: Clarendon, 1933.

Studies in the History of Natural Theology, Oxford: Clarendon, 1915.

Webber, J., *The Eloquent 'I'*, Madison and London: University of Wisconsin Press, 1968.

Weber, M. A., *David Hume und Edward Gibbon*, Frankfurt am Main: Anton Main, 1990.

Webster, C., *The Great Instauration: Science, Medicine and Reform 1626–1660*, London: Duckworth, 1973.

Wellek, R., *A History of Modern Criticism 1750–1950*, New Haven: Yale University Press, 1955.

Immanuel Kant in England 1793–1838, Princeton University Press, 1931.

Wells, G. A., 'Man and future: an elucidation of Coleridge's rejection of Herder's thought', *Journal of English and Germanic Philology* 51 (1952), pp. 314–25.

Werkmeister, L., 'The early Coleridge: his "rage for metaphysics" ', *Harvard Theological Review* 54 (1961), pp. 99–123.

Wheeler, K., *Sources, Processes and Methods in Coleridge's 'Biographia Literaria'*, Cambridge University Press, 1980.

White, A., *Schelling: an Introduction to the System of Freedom*, New Haven and London: Yale University Press, 1983.

Wiggers, R., 'Zum großen Alcibiades 132d-133c' in *Philologische Wochenschrift* 25 (1932), pp. 700–3.

Wilbur, E. M., *A History of Unitarianism in Transylvania, England and America*, Cambridge, Mass.: Harvard University Press, 1952.

Wiles, M., *Archetypal Heresy: The Rise and Fall of British Arianism*, Oxford: Clarendon, 1996.

Wilkins, E. G., *The Delphic Maxims in Literature*, New York: Garland, 1979.

Willey, Basil, *Samuel Taylor Coleridge*, London: Chatto and Windus, 1972.

The Eighteenth Century Background: Studies on the Idea of Nature in the Thought of the Period, London: Chatto and Windus, 1940.

Williams, G. H., *The Radical Reformation*, Cambridge, Mass.: Harvard University Press, 1962.

Williams, N. P., *The Ideas of the Fall and Original Sin*, London: Longmans, Green, and Co., 1927.

Wolfson, H. A., *The Philosophy of Spinoza: Unfolding the Latent Processes of his Reasoning*, 2 vols., Cambridge, Mass.: Harvard University Press, 1962.

Wood, A. W., *Hegel's Ethical Thought*, Cambridge University Press, 1990.

Yolton, J. W., *A Locke Dictionary*, Oxford: Blackwell, 1993.

Thinking Matter: Materialism in Eighteenth-century Britain, Minneapolis: University of Minnesota Press, 1983.

Zehnpfenning, B., *Reflexion und Metareflexion bei Platon und Fichte*, Munich: Alber, 1987.

Zimmermann, A., *Der Begriff der Representatio im Mittelalter. Stellvertretung, Symbol, Zeichen, Bild*, Berlin: de Gruyter, 1971.

MANUSCRIPT SOURCE

S. T. Coleridge, 'On the Divine Ideas', microfilm 357 in Cambridge University Library, from the manuscript in the Henry E. Huntington Library, San Marino, California.

REFERENCE SOURCES

Bibiotheca Trinitariorum, edited by E. Shadel, Munich: Saur, 1984–8.
British Moralists, edited by L. A. Selby-Bigge, Oxford: Clarendon, 1897, 2 vols.
Cambridge History of Later Greek and Early Medieval Philosophy, edited by A. H. Amstrong, Cambridge University Press, 1967.
Cambridge History of the Bible, edited by S. L. Greenslade, Cambridge University Press, 1963, vol. iii.: *The West from the Reformation to the Present Day.'*
Dictionary of Christian Theology, edited by A. Richardson, London: SCM, 1981.
Dictionary of National Biography, edited by L. Stephen, London: Smith, Elder, and Co., 1885– .
Encyclopaedia of Philosophy, 8 vols., edited by P. Edwards, New York: Macmillan, 1967.
Encyclopedia of Religion and Ethics, 13 vols., edited by J. Hastings, Edinburgh: T. and T. Clark, 1908–26. (See esp. vol. xii, pp. 261–87, 'Theism'.)
Greek Lexicon, compiled by H. G. Liddell and R. Scott, ninth edition, Oxford: Clarendon, 1968.
Handbuch der Dogmen und Theologiegeschichte, edited by Carl Andresen, Adolf Martin Ritter, Klaus Wessel, Ekkehard Mühlenberg, and Martin Anton Schmidt, Göttingen: Vandenhoeck and Ruprecht, 1988.
Historisches Wörterbuch der Philosophie, edited by J. Ritter, Darmstadt: Wissenschaftliche Buchgesellschaft, 1971 –.
A New Dictionary of Christian Theology, edited by A. Richardson and J. Bowden, London: SCM, 1983.
Nineteenth-Century Religious Thought in the West, 3 vols., edited by J. P. Clayton, S. Katz, and N. Smart, Cambridge University Press, 1988.
Oxford Dictionary of the Christian Church, edited by F. L. Cross, Oxford: Clarendon, 1957–74.
Reallexicon für Antike und Christentum, edited by T. Klauser, Stuttgart: Hiersemann, 1950 – .
Trinitas: A Theological Dictionary of the Holy Trinity, Michael O'Carroll, Collegeville, Minn.: Liturgical Press, 1987.

Index

328